TOLSTOY'S ART AND THOUGHT, 1847–1880

TOLSTOY'S ART AND THOUGHT, 1847–1880

Donna Tussing Orwin

PRINCETON UNIVERSITY PRESS PRINCETON, NEW JERSEY

Copyright © 1993 by Princeton University Press
Published by Princeton University Press, 41 William Street,
Princeton, New Jersey 08540
In the United Kingdom: Princeton University Press,
Chichester, West Sussex

Library of Congress Cataloging-in-Publication Data

Orwin, Donna Tussing, 1947–
Tolstoy's art and thought, 1847–1880 / Donna Tussing Orwin.
p.   cm.
Includes bibliographical references and index.
ISBN 0-691-06991-3
1. Tolstoy, Leo, graf, 1828–1910—Criticism and
interpretation.   2. Tolstoy, Leo, graf, 1828–1910—Philosophy.
3. Philosophy in literature.   I. Title.
PG3415.P5078   1993
891.73'3—dc20   92-37860

This book has been composed in Adobe Palatino

Princeton University Press books are printed
on acid-free paper and meet the guidelines
for permanence and durability of the Committee
on Production Guidelines for Book Longevity
of the Council on Library Resources

Printed in the United States of America

10 9 8 7 6 5 4 3 2 1

To my parents

Contents

Acknowledgments _____

THIS BOOK draws extensively on the tradition of Tolstoy scholarship from his day to our own. My frequent references to other scholars within the text and in footnotes is meant to reflect my indebtedness to that tradition and my sense of being part of an ongoing discussion about the great writer.

My approach to the study of Tolstoy owes a great deal to my teachers, whom I would like to take this opportunity to thank. George Gibian was my first teacher of Tolstoy. With Patricia Carden I learned how to analyze a text, and I have subsequently learned from her own writings on Tolstoy. Antonia Glasse, by her example and her teaching, taught me to love scholarship. Allan Bloom introduced me to the study of philosophy and also taught me to neglect neither the real nor the ideal in human nature. In graduate courses I took with Donald Fanger I learned the value of literary history, and of placing myself clearly within the tradition of literary scholarship. Kiril Taranovsky taught me to look to Russian poetry in order to understand Russian prose. Kathryn Feuer inspired me with her personal generosity and her humane, intelligent approach to the study of Tolstoy.

I have also benefited greatly over the years from conversations about this project with friends and colleagues. Kathleen Parthé has encouraged my work on Tolstoy over the years. Leslie O'Bell, Ralph Lindheim, James Morrison, Gary Saul Morson, Werner Dannhauser, Arthur Melzer, and Anna Lisa Crone have read and commented on all or parts of the manuscript. Caryl Emerson and Richard Gustafson read the manuscript for Princeton University Press and offered helpful suggestions. I am grateful to the National Endowment of the Humanities for fellowship support of this project in 1988–1989, and to the Centre for Russian and East European Studies at the University of Toronto for its continuing support. The editors at Princeton University Press, and especially Rita Bernhard, my copy editor, have been most helpful. My husband, Clifford Orwin, has been my main support in this as in all my endeavors.

Note on Documentation _____

REFERENCES to *The Cossacks*, *War and Peace*, and *Anna Karenina* are by part and/or chapter and, like citations from the Jubilee edition of Tolstoy's works,* are included in the text. Textual references to the Jubilee edition are cited throughout with volume numbers and page numbers only. *War and Peace* I treat as fifteen parts divided into chapters. In other words, I ignore the further complication in the Russian original of the division into four or six books (depending on the edition used). All other citations are in footnotes, with two exceptions. When a work is cited more than once consecutively, the first citation is in a footnote with subsequent ones cited as ibid. and in the text; if a citation consists of a page number only, it is included in the text. All translations from the Russian, unless otherwise noted, are my own or modified versions of Aylmer Maude's translations of Tolstoy.

* *Polnoe sobranie sochinenii*. 90 vols. Moscow: Gosudarstvennoe izdatel'stvo "khudozhestvennaia literatura," 1928–1958.

TOLSTOY'S ART AND THOUGHT, 1847–1880

No form of idealism is harmful, so long as there is sensuousness. If you hold firmly to the earth, it stretches out the soul.

(Diary; 18 December 1856)

The Decline of art is the truest sign of the decline of civilization. When there are ideals, then works of art are produced in the name of these ideals; when there are none, as is true with us, there are no works of art! There's play with words, play with sounds, play with images.

(9 February 1908; reported by Gusev in *L. N. Tolstoi v vospominaniiakh sovremennikov,* 2:219)

Introduction

THIS BOOK is an attempt to reconstruct the ideas that led Tolstoy to write the masterpieces of his youth and middle age. Its three parts roughly coincide with the first three decades of Tolstoy's creative life. In the first, on the 1850s, I try to reconstruct what Tolstoy's initial vision might have been. The second part, on the 1860s, consists mainly of an analysis of *The Cossacks* and *War and Peace*, which are the fruits of Tolstoy's early humanism. The final section of the book deals with the disintegration of this initial vision under personal, philosophical, and historical pressures. I treat *Anna Karenina* as a product of Tolstoy's emerging new understanding, and I compare it to *War and Peace*.

I adhere to three general assumptions about Tolstoy, each of them familiar in some form to scholars. The first goes back to perhaps the most important essay on Tolstoy ever written, Apollon Grigor'ev's *The Early Works of Count L. N. Tolstoy* [*Rannie proizvedeniia gr. L. N. Tolstogo*], published in 1862. In it Grigor'ev argued that Tolstoy was a writer in search of an idea that would rescue him from the nihilism—Grigor'ev uses this word—generated by his own analytical powers. Grigor'ev thereby introduced the idea of Tolstoy as a divided man, who exposed the false idols of others yet longed to replace them with true gods who could withstand his analysis. In a variation on this theme, the populist N. K. Mikhailovsky declared outright that Tolstoy's thoughts, and hence his writings, were a confusing mixture of right- and left-wing ideas.[1] After Tolstoy's well-publicized religious conversion and his turn away from literature in the early 1880s, his contradictions seemed even more glaring. The Nietzschean writer and critic D. S. Merezhkovsky explored them in *Tolstoi as Man and Artist* (1902). Neither Merezhkovsky, nor Maxim Gorky (in his memoirs of Tolstoy, first published in 1919), thought much of Tolstoy's religious theories. Merezhkovsky called him the "Seer of the Flesh," implying that Tolstoy understood the body, but not the soul.

The formalist critic Boris Eikhenbaum introduced a new twist to this persistent theme of Tolstoy's divided nature. In his first book about Tolstoy, entitled *The Young Tolstoy* [*Molodoi Tolstoi*], Eikhenbaum, reacting against earlier critics who in his opinion wrote biography and not criticism, concentrated on Tolstoyan texts and their literary relation to earlier texts.[2] In *The Young Tolstoy* he wrote about the interrelationship of detail and generalization in Tolstoy's writing, with the latter giving form to the substance of the former (30–31). In reality, in Eikhenbaum's opinion as formulated in the later *Lev Tolstoy*, Tolstoy was a cynic, a nihilist.[3] Eikhenbaum thus borrowed Grigor'ev's idea, but, in the modern spirit, saw Tolstoyan nihilism as fundamental to his character and inescapable.[4]

Isaiah Berlin, in his famous essay *The Hedgehog and the Fox* (1953), made a similar point but gave it a broader, psychological and philosophical interpretation. Berlin, too, saw both details, or particularities, and generalizations in Tolstoy's work. As a political liberal, however, Berlin had a different view of Tolstoyan nihilism than Grigor'ev did, or even Eikhenbaum. For Berlin, it could be the positive basis of a pluralistic society in which individuals—details—would be fully appreciated and protected. In Berlin's striking metaphor, Tolstoy was a fox (someone who understood detail) who wanted to be a hedgehog (a systematizer):

> If we may recall once again our division of artists into foxes and hedgehogs: Tolstoy perceived reality in its multiplicity, as a collection of separate entities round and into which he saw with a clarity and penetration scarcely ever equalled, but he believed only in one vast, unitary whole. (39)

All of the critical writings on Tolstoy that I have mentioned have been extremely influential in their own time and continue to be read today. For personal and intellectual historical reasons, the critics see the dichotomy in Tolstoy and his writings in different ways. All agree that a dichotomy exists, and for all of them except Mikhailovsky it consists in contradictions between details that Tolstoy knows from observation and the way he makes sense of these details. It is no surprise, then, to see that two recently published and very different American books on Tolstoy, Richard Gustafson's *Leo Tolstoy: Resident and Stranger; A Study in Fiction and Theology* (1986) and Gary Saul Morson's *Hidden in Plain View: Narrative and Creative Potentials in 'War and Peace'* (1987), both again present Tolstoy as a divided man. In Gustafson's view, Tolstoy was a hedgehog who had to overcome his foxlike doubts in order to achieve happiness and to write his books; while for Morson, who is more in the Berlin camp, Tolstoy was a fox who took on systemizers in order to defend an attractive pluralism.

Where there is smoke, there must be fire. An idea that has been around for so long and has been defended by so many intelligent critics must have real substance to it. In fact, in the works I have cited, there is an important bit of evidence to show that Tolstoy himself saw his work in these terms. Eikhenbaum adopted the terms *minuteness* [*melochnost'*] and *generalization* [*generalizaciia*] from Tolstoy's own musings about his writing in his diary. Eikhenbaum built his theories about Tolstoy with the help of ideas that he borrowed from the subject himself. I have tried to do the same. My first task, therefore, has been to return to Tolstoy and to his time to try to understand what the dichotomy between "details" and "generalizations" might have meant to him. I take the view that both were in fact necessary to him, and I try to show why.

I have been inspired by Eikhenbaum's criticism, but I have set out to do both more and less than he did. My aim is to present Tolstoy's work as he may have understood it himself. Thus, my first chapter is on the opposition of analysis and synthesis, which was the defining, or structuring literary concept of the 1850s, when Tolstoy began his writing career. I show how contemporary critics, men whom Tolstoy knew personally and respected, understood his work in this way, and how Tolstoy's style and thought developed, in part, in response to them. Like Apollon Grigor'ev, whose article I discuss in chapter 1 and elsewhere, I see Tolstoy as an analyst in search of a synthesis, a realist in search of ideals.

On one level, Tolstoy was extremely consistent in his analysis of human nature and the human condition; on the other, he was inconsistent to the point of self-transformation. His understanding of the details of human psychology did not change much from his earliest years. What did change was his metaphysics. His repeated denigration of metaphysics as such has discouraged investigation of his own metaphysical beliefs, and yet he himself admitted more than once that he could not write or live without *scaffolding* [*podmostki*]:[5] this was composed of fundamental beliefs which, however foolish they may have come to seem to him subsequently, provided support for the details of human psychology that he understood so well.

In my opinion the primary reason for Tolstoy's upside-down approach to metaphysics is a trait that supplies the second unifying theme of this book, namely, his extreme individualism.[6] Tolstoy began with the fact of his own individual being and moved outward from it to encounter nature and human society. The purpose of his first work, his autobiographical trilogy, as he explained it in drafts, was to reveal "my particular personality" [*moiu osobennuiu lichnost'*] to the reader.[7] One of the main tasks of my book will be to explain how the young man who set out to defend and illuminate the "particular personality" came to reject that personality in the later part of his life. In my view, Tolstoy's positive and expansive defense of the individual reached a peak in *War and Peace*. *Anna Karenina*, while still defending the possibility of individual happiness, can only do so by radically changing the definition of an individual.[8]

Tolstoy began all his deliberations from the point of view of the individual self, and he limited his conclusions to what that self could use and understand. He believed only in things that he could confirm himself, with his senses, his reason, or his feelings. Conversely, he did not easily reject the validity of anything, no matter how strange or perverse, that he thought and felt. In the words of the critic and memoirist Pavel Annenkov, who was a close friend of Tolstoy in the 1850s, "he searched for explanations of all the phenomena of life and all questions of conscience in himself alone, not knowing and not desiring to know either aesthetic or philosophical explanations, supposing that they had been thought up on purpose by people in order to flatter themselves or others."[9] If, as Eikhenbaum so brilliantly argued, memory is the starting point of art for Tolstoy (ibid., 1:150–51), it is because in memory he could gather all of himself together and create a kind of whole organized around himself.

As the best critics of the 1850s already observed, Tolstoy's psychological analysis came first, and was the stronger for preceding any attempt to make sense of it.[10] It accepted the priority of self-love and self-interest. But Tolstoy was never satisfied with himself for long. He possessed a ruthless and a shameless honesty about himself (and a love of confession), which is one source of his greatness as a writer. His very self-love extended to a desire for standards of universal justice and love, so that he could be truly happy, and truly lovable and good, both to himself and others. His self-love required substantiation from independent sources; thence arose the need for absolutes that alone could make justice and especially goodness for the individual possible. These absolutes reintroduced the necessity of some kind of synthesizing metaphysics into Tolstoy's thought. Thus, the philosopher Nikolai Strakhov already in 1869, in the first of his three articles on *War and Peace*, observed that Tolstoy was a realist whose constant theme was true human dignity, which he sought in everyone, from the humblest soldier to Napoleon.[11]

Tolstoy's individualism meant that he was certain, perhaps even overly certain, of the universal validity of his personal experience. But his analysis always rested on firmer ground than the synthesis that he applied to it. The synthesis was more convincing for being anchored in recognizable human experience, but was always questionable in Tolstoy's own mind because it was not liable to direct proof. The analysis, on the other hand, was made enormously richer because it took into account that element of human nature—the need for dignity—from which arises the need for a synthesis. The tensions between the results of self-analysis and the longing for the kind of beliefs that analysis undermined caused those conditions of crisis and disillusionment which Eikhenbaum recognized as typical of Tolstoy.[12] Again and again, analysis would destroy beliefs necessary for life and art, and then hope, Phoenix-like, would rise from the ashes to form new dreams.

Tolstoy's individualism left him narrow but deep. He did not believe in history, for instance, until he could transform it into something that every individual undergoes and can understand. There is even evidence, in the form of a quotation from 1860, that all of history as portrayed in *War and Peace* can be understood as beginning from one individual "such as I am":

> In history the fundamental unit [*chastnost'*] and the one closest to us is the human being, such as I am. From several such units only with time does the student derive an understanding of the nation and state. And how many such units, comprising a unit of one state, are necessary before the student can understand the movement of nations and states.[13]

Not surprisingly, given this starting point, Tolstoy defended the individual against history in *War and Peace* and even judged historical events "as facts corresponding or not corresponding to its, the individual's, ideals."[14] To history he juxtaposed nature, which was present in embryo form in every individual even if not fully realized in each. He found his master in the great philosopher of nature, Jean-Jacques Rousseau, and with Rousseau's help he came to understand the role of nature in human life in all its labyrinthine complexity. No writer can surpass Tolstoy as a poet of the relation of man and nature.

By the same token, however, Tolstoy's individualism made it impossible for him to believe in any human endeavor in which all the participants were not full and equal partners. In his later life he rejected both church and state for a doctrine of religious and political anarchy. At the same time, he attacked the courts because by his lights no person had the right to judge and condemn another; he particularly attacked the rule of law as unjust because it was detached from the mandates of individual conscience.[15] In his psychology Tolstoy rejected as illegitimate those personality traits that make human beings political. Politics is bad because it threatens the independence of the individual. Even when, in the exceptional case of Prince Andrei in *War and Peace*, Tolstoy accepted the political man as natural, he portrayed him as someone whose education transforms him by teaching him that he cannot and should not try to govern others.

It may be that this trait, like the other ones I have mentioned, had its origin in personal characteristics that are difficult to discuss. The fact is, however, that the young Tolstoy was one of a number of what I am calling "individualists" who cropped up in Russia in the 1850s. Hence the interest in Turgenev and even N. G. Chernyshevsky, as well as Tolstoy, in memoirs and autobiography.[16] Chernyshevsky and his followers, different as they were from Tolstoy in other ways, believed "in the individual and his creative powers."[17] In the 1840s, too, such men as Herzen and Belinsky valued and defended the "individual human personality,"[18] while in the 1830s N. V. Stankevich and his circle explored their own individual psyches in search of metaphysical truths.[19] The interest in the individual in politics as well as literature persisted into the 1860s when the so-called men of the sixties "strove to affirm the individual as a moving historical force and as a philosophical principle."[20] Among the nihilists, D. I. Pisarev was the most radical individualist, arguing in his first article on Bazarov that Turgenev's hero "is guided only by his own whim or calculation. He recognizes no regulator—whether above him, outside him, or within him—no moral law, no principle. He has no noble aims and for all that represents a powerful force."[21] And when populism replaced nihilism as the leading political movement in the 1870s, Mikhailovsky took as one of his basic principles the defense of the individual against society.[22]

There was, moreover, a general predisposition in nineteenth-century Russia to see the individual as the embodiment of the spirit of the time. This belief, which persisted in Russia up until the revolution and which was particularly strong during the so-called Silver Age, inspired Gershenzon's splendid book *The History of Young Russia* [*Istoriia molodoi Rossii*], in which succeeding historical periods in Russia are represented by the biographies of prominent members of each generation.[23] Tolstoy himself stated his adherence to this doctrine in his 1862 article "Education for the People" [*O narodnom obrazovanii*]. He wrote there that each thinker can express what his epoch knows, but there is no need to teach it to the younger generation, which already knows it (8:8). Even here, however, Tolstoy was not simply a historicist. He went on to state that there was no need to teach virtue either: "The understanding of virtue either remains the same, or is infinitely developing, and despite all theories, the decline and the flourishing of virtue does not depend on education" (8: 8–9). The individual embodies or has access to moral and perhaps metaphysical truth as well.

Here Tolstoy revealed his connection to a general European nineteenth-century philosophical position that Maurice Mandelbaum has called metaphysical idealism. Nineteenth-century idealists turned traditional metaphysics on its head. Whereas before the human individual was understood as part of a metaphysical whole, now the individual encapsulated that whole in himself. Hence: "the metaphysics of idealism finds man's own spiritual nature to be the fullest expression of that which is to be taken as basic in reality."[24]

Metaphysical idealists, Mandelbaum writes elsewhere, can believe in ideas either of reason or of will (ibid., 7). So to turn against Hegelianism (a rational idealism) was not necessarily to turn against idealism itself. One could be, like Apollon Grigor'ev, a Schellingian idealist who attacked any rationalism as false. The main belief that Tolstoy shared with other metaphysical idealists of his century was that to study himself was the only possible way to study metaphysics. If he spoke authentically, he would speak authoritatively, in the "absolute language" that Morson has shown to be so important for him.[25]

In Russia Tolstoy was connected to the metaphysical idealism of earlier generations through friends like Annenkov and critic V. P. Botkin. It was Annenkov, for instance, who wrote in his memoirs of how the whole generation of the 1830s considered themselves chosen ones.[26] These men "especially valued Fichte's idea that the *individual* is rooted in the transcendental sphere; this doctrine made possible their emancipation from romantic subjectivism."[27] Spiritual descendents of the men of the 1830s and others were active in the 1860s and 1870s as part of a reaction against positivism. Wayne Dowler has written of these Russian writers and thinkers that

> The idealist looked on reality as a unified whole and regarded the human soul as the highest manifestation of the whole. Whereas the positivist searched for truth in nature through the accumulation of scientific evidence, the idealist turned his inquiries inward to the human soul where he sought to unlock the secret of the whole of reality. The idealist attached great significance to the autonomy of the soul and demanded freedom for the fullest development of the personality in all its facets. For it was in the unfolding of the individual and collective human experience that the ultimate truth and reality resided.[28]

As we shall see, Tolstoy took his own unique and independent position among the metaphysical idealists of his time. Like them, however, he asked what man was and what he ought to be, and like them he studied himself to find an answer. Taking this attitude toward himself, Tolstoy could elevate a natural predisposition to individualism into something of general, indeed universal significance.[29]

The final general and related consideration that has guided me is that the synthesis that Tolstoy sought was always a moral one. Like Russian thinkers as a group, his concerns were at base ethical, not metaphysical.[30] He needed a moral synthesis because, as Zenkovsky says, the Good for Tolstoy must be absolute or it is not the Good (ibid., 399).

For Tolstoy's contemporaries it was not necessary to explain why a human being needed moral standards; in fact, it was more difficult for them to grasp that people might live without them. (Dostoevsky's characters grapple with this possibility.) For us the opposite tends to be true, and indeed the Berlin school of thought on Tolstoy sees relativism—the idea that there are no fixed moral standards—as a possible basis for Tolstoyan morality. This position, however attractive it may be in and of itself, and despite the fact that it does properly attempt to account for Tolstoy's love of diversity and particularity, is based on a fundamental misunderstanding of what Tolstoy himself intended.

Like most *Tolstovedy* [Tolstoy scholars], I am fascinated by the character of the man whose works I study. I am under no illusion, however, that I can completely reconstruct either the circumstances of Tolstoy's life or his responses to those circumstances. I have had to pick among many, even myriad possible paths of exploration, and, like previous critics, my choices have been dictated by my own interests and the interests of my own time. I want to interpret his works, which, unlike their author, are still living today and influencing those who read them. I am convinced that a necessary step in doing this is to understand Tolstoy's intentions in writing them, but I wish to distinguish my use of those intentions from the task of biography as such.

For the biographer, Tolstoy's works are signposts along the road of Tolstoy's life. I see them as living entities with which we readers interact as we would with a powerful personality. To the extent that each of them is a provisional resolution of conflicts within Tolstoy, each has a "personality" more integrated and less contradictory than Tolstoy's own.[31] The key to the meaning of each work lies in the intentions of the author who created it, but only and especially in his intentions as an author and at the time. The works succeed because they are whole: like children, after their birth they take on a life of their own independent of and sometimes antithetical to their parents. Unlike human beings—for this analogy between poetic texts and living beings can be taken only so far—the works live only in the consciousness of their readers. My critical objective is to clarify the original meaning of Tolstoy's works to make it easier for contemporary readers to understand and learn from them.

Rather than call Tolstoy a moralist, perhaps it is more helpful to call him a *mathematician* as Pascal used the term in one of his *Pensées*:[32]

> *Submission.* One must know when it is right to doubt, to affirm, to submit. Anyone who does otherwise does not understand the force of reason. Some men run counter to these three principles, either affirming that everything can be proved, because they know nothing about proof, or doubting everything, because they do not know when to submit, or always submitting, because they do not know when judgment is called for.
>
> Sceptic, mathematician, Christian; doubt, affirmation, submission.[33]

Tolstoy was obsessed with numbers. He studied for a while at the faculty of mathematics at Kazan University. As a young man he gambled obsessively at cards and even, as is well known, gambled away his ancestral home at Iasnaia Poliana. He played solitaire while he was thinking about his work, and he loved the mathematical and warlike game of chess. His oldest son Sergei recalled how superstitious he was about numbers. So, for instance, he considered the year 1877 to be crucially important for him because every seven years the body changes completely, and in 1877 he was forty-nine years old, or 7×7.[34] Like Pascal's mathematician, Tolstoy wanted to affirm the ultimate reasonableness of life even if it would be unreasonable to do so.

Although Tolstoy recommended submission to others, he himself vacillated between scepticism and affirmation. Only when things made sense to him could he be happy, and he was ultimately willing to sacrifice a great deal in order to live by what he called common sense [zdravyi smysl]. Tolstoy's passion for mathematics was rooted not in reason, I think, but in a subrational need to understand and thereby control his own life and fate. It is connected, in other words, with that same individualism that colored every aspect of his life. Indeed, it is possible that Tolstoy's individualism, understood for the moment simply as a personality trait, arose from a combination of great passions and a powerful mind that made him distinguish himself sharply from others. As Tolstoy taught, the mere possession of the ability to reason does not make us rational beings. He himself possessed to the highest degree what he called, in a letter of 1865 to A. A. Tolstaia, the "Tolstoyan wildness [tolstovskaia dikost'] common to all of us" (61:123). This made his reason, in the words of Romain Rolland, "a passion, no less blind or jealous than the other passions which had possessed him during the earlier part of his life."[35]

I offer this psychological explanation of Tolstoy the moralist as a speculation that gains some credibilty from the fact that the psychologizing is "Tolstoyan." I do not, however, approach Tolstoy's oeuvre in a psychologizing spirit. If Tolstoy's rationalizing moralism worked against him in the later part of his life, his passion for reason and morality is also one of the personal factors that made him a great writer. His preoccupation with a philosophical and moral justification of the life of the individual seems in our own time to be the most old-fashioned part of his art. His attempt in the later part of his life to combine reason and revelation in his rational religion seems especially lame today. If he had not written great works of art, few today would read the many tracts written after 1880. The reader of this book would be justified, therefore, in wondering about the importance of its subject. Why should we care about Tolstoy's intentions in producing his masterpieces if they are irrelevant to our enjoyment of the works?

The answer to this question is twofold. First, one must distinguish between the products of Tolstoy's old age and those of his youth and maturity. They are different responses to the same problems. Second, as I will attempt to show, those very preoccupations that seem unimportant at first thought are, in fact, the source of the intensity of Tolstoy's art. Take them away, and you have books about Karenin's shoulders and the high jinks of Stiva Oblonsky. At the same time, too, Tolstoy is determined to keep his feet on the ground. He is at his best when he has created a structure within which both body and soul can be seen to thrive, struggle, and grow. His major theme was not, as it seemed to a post-Victorian like Merezhkovsky, a celebration of the body; rather, it was the struggle to accommodate body and soul, earth and sky, real and ideal in the life of the individual.

Part One

THE 1850s

One

Analysis and Synthesis

The Hegelian Atmosphere of the 1850s

In the early 1880s, in *What Then Should We Do?* [*Tak chto zhe nam delat'*], Tolstoy wrote that in his youth the influence of Hegel was all pervasive (25:332). Because of his loudly trumpeted dislike of Hegel, many critics have either ignored the possible effects of this atmosphere on his early writing or they have limited those effects to what they regard as the Hegelian period in Russian literature, the 1840s.[1] A small group of Soviet critics, beginning with the respected A. Skaftymov, have, by acknowledging and examining Hegel's influence on *War and Peace*, reopened the question of Hegel's place in Tolstoy's development during the previous decade. So Skaftymov takes Tolstoy's reminiscence about Hegel in *What Then Should We Do?* to refer to the fifties, and he writes that "the young Tolstoy's closest interlocuters on questions of world view at that time [B. Chicherin, V. Botkin, A. Druzhinin, Iu. Samarin, and K. Aksakov] were Hegelians."[2]

All thinking Russians in the 1850s were children of the Hegelian forties.[3] Ivan Kireevsky remarked during that decade that he knew several hundred Russian Hegelians of whom only three had actually read Hegel (ibid., 210). Nowhere else, in fact, was the Hegelian tradition as uninterrupted as in Russia (ibid., 239). Certain Hegelian ideas, having lost their immediate connection to Hegel himself, simply became part of Russian philosophical culture (ibid., 241–43). Principal among these were the ideas of dialectic and concreteness, and the related notion that truth is a merging of real and ideal.[4]

Analysis and synthesis became the related methods in Russia by which truth, understood in this Hegelian sense, was achieved. Analysis meant the dissection of compound reality into simple parts by critical reason, while synthesis meant the reconstition of reality thus dissolved into a whole, a truth, in accordance with ideal standards. Chizhevski emphasizes that a yen for synthesis, or "wholeness," as Zenkovsky calls it, was a Russian proclivity before Hegel. And Russians, Tolstoy among them, were looking for a synthesis that provided moral guidance. Even if Hegel did not provide the synthesis Russians wanted, however, his philosophy fostered their yearning for one. Hegelian thought created the formal structure, if not the content, of the standards according to which others and Tolstoy himself judged his work.

In the 1850s, when Tolstoy was getting his start, Russian literary criticism already enforced Hegelian criteria, due to the influence of Vissarion Belinsky in the previous decade. The mainstream of Russian criticism, including socialist realism, descended from Belinsky's Hegelian, so-called organic aesthetics.[5] The organic work of art became canonic for Russian literature: "The organic model of the work of art, as reflected in Belinsky's critical method, is dualistic: the work of art is seen as the realization of an idea, or a fusion of the 'ideal' and the 'real'" (Ibid., 210). All artistic material within a given work, be it form or content, comprised an "organism" which embodied the artist's original idea. All details produced by analysis had eventually to lead to a synthesis which gave them life. Even those who openly attacked Hegel in the fifties did so by reinterpreting these terms rather than by abandoning them.[6]

Chernyshevsky

N. G. Chernyshevsky, who in the fifties spearheaded the attack on Hegel, was a member of the younger generation, a "scientific" socialist, and a follower of the new materialist ethics and aesthetics emanating mostly from France. Those on the other side—V. P. Botkin, P. V. Annenkov, critic and prose writer A. V. Druzhinin, A. A. Grigor'ev, I. S. Turgenev—were and remained men of the forties, under the influence of German idealism (although not necessarily Hegel). Chernyshevsky fired the opening salvo in the war of the two generations with a review in the March 1855 issue of *The Contemporary* [*Sovremennik*], which was, in fact, an attack on the writings of his colleagues in the journal.[7] He followed this with the publication, in May 1855, of his dissertation, *The Aesthetic Relations of Art to Reality* [*Esteticheskie otnosheniia iskusstva k deistvitel'nosti*]. Here he introduced an aesthetics which was, in his own words, "an application of Feuerbach's materialistic philosophy to aesthetic reality,"[8] and he attacked the Hegelian aesthetics of the preceding generation.[9] While applauding Hegel's emphasis on reality, he denied the existence of any absolute spirit informing or transforming it.[10] Chernyshevsky followed the materialist credo that "there is an independently existing world; that human beings, like all other objects, are material entities; that the human mind does not exist as an entity distinct from the human body; and that there is no God (nor any other non-human being) whose mode of existence is not that of material entities."[11] At the same time, however, like other members of his generation, he believed in the dialectic,[12] and even in the interaction of real and ideal in art. The ideal for him was not Hegelian Mind, but rather the conclusions of human reason, itself part of the material world. Nature was nothing but matter, and our ideas, themselves the product of reason interacting with experience, should mold nature. The moral goals of the artist-moralist, not reality itself, generate artistic form.[13]

Soon after Chernyshevsky's dissertation was published, in 1855–1856, there appeared a series of ten articles entitled *Studies of the Age of Gogol* [*Ocherki gogolevskogo perioda russkoi literatury*], in which Chernyshevsky set about to practice what he had preached. Citing Belinsky as his authority and spiritual teacher, he argued that Russian prose, founded by Gogol, should be didactic; that is, it should serve the cause of social justice. In the first article he credited Gogol with having introduced the "critical mode" [*kriticheskoie napravlenie*] into Russian literature.[14] This was neither as extreme as the satirical mode, which had existed before Gogol, nor was it merely analytic. To analyze, argued Chernyshevsky, means to reproduce and study details without thought or direction; while the critical mode "is penetrated by consciousness of the correspondence or lack of correspondence of the examined phenomena to the norm of reason and noble feeling" (ibid., 18). This noble feeling, Chernyshevsky wrote, is aroused by a comparison of the phenomena described with "the demands of reason." He attributed the weakness of Gogol's ideal characters not to Gogol's failings as a writer, but to the absence in Russia of undistorted ideals (ibid., 10–11). True to his aesthetics, Chernyshevsky held that Gogol could not describe what was not present in the surrounding reality. So he had to write critically, subjecting the image of reality provided by imitation to moral principles supplied by "reason and noble feeling." These principles, the writer's "ideal," give form, or meaning, to reality. As Belinsky had required, real and ideal would fuse into a synthesis. Hegelian dialectic, if not Hegelian ideas, was at work.

To Chernyshevsky's opponents, he was a mere pretender to a throne which they, by virtue of their friendship with Belinsky and their understanding of his ideas, deserved to inherit. The best critic among them, a man himself destined to have a large and largely unacknowledged influence on Russian criticism,[15] was Apollon Grigor'ev. A Hegelian in the forties who became a Schellingian in the fifties,[16] Grigor'ev objected to the Chernyshevskians on two counts: their materialism and their rationalism. Turning their own attack against idealism and abstraction in art against them, Grigor'ev came to the defense both of reality—nature—and art. From his Schellingian perspective, nature was all feeling, which flees from or dissolves under the cold gaze of reason. Chernyshevsky and the Left were *teoretiki*, theoreticians. They denied reality any moral significance in itself and then applied an abstract and inadequate meaning (what Chernyshevsky would call reason and noble feeling) to it from the outside. Grigor'ev also criticized their "rational, mechanistic and analytic conception of art." He defined art as "synthesis and inspiration," and the criticism of the theoreticians as mere "analysis."[17] His own version of synthesis was based neither on reason nor on Hegelian Mind, but on feeling, "inspiration," and he rejected Chernyshevsky's distinction between criticism and analysis because he believed that reason by itself can produce only analysis, not synthesis.

The Contemporary Reception of Tolstoy's Work

Both the so-called Left (Chernyshevsky) and Right (Grigor'ev) believed then in dialectic and the interaction of real and ideal in art. It was within this framework of Hegelian, organic criticism that Tolstoy's contemporaries understood his work. His gifts as an analyzer were universally acknowledged, but sometimes feared. Turgenev's awestruck "a fearsome thing"[18] after he read the second Sevastopol sketch ("Sevastopol in May") exemplifies the respect contemporaries felt for the writer who described what lay behind the trappings of war, even down to the last moments of consciousness of a dying man (chap. 12). It was precisely as the writer of "Sevastopol in May" that Tolstoy arrived in Petersburg in September 1856, and began to subject his new friends to those same lethal doses of psychological analysis. He especially singled out Turgenev as a lover of what in the language of the day were called *frazy*, fine sentiments that Tolstoy regarded as hypocritical.[19] He admitted in his diary how he loved to attack the sacred cows of his contemporaries (47:88).

The camps of Left and Right took differing views of Tolstoy's psychological analysis. Chernyshevsky defended it against attacks from the Left in a famous article in the December 1856 issue of *The Contemporary* [*Sovremennik*].[20] He coined the famous expression "dialectic of the soul" (*dialektika dushi*; ibid., 423) as a metaphor for the fundamental psychological process, the interaction in the psyche of past and present sensations, that Tolstoy was exploring in his art. Along with the "dialectic of the soul," the second distinct quality of Tolstoy's art, in Chernyshevsky's opinion, was its moral purity, its "chistota nravstvennogo chuvstva" (ibid., 427). Psychological analysis and moral purity: these are the "norms of reason [science] and noble feeling [morality]"—the ideals necessary for synthesis—underlying Chernyshevsky's brand of organic art. Although Chernyshevsky admitted in a letter to Nekrasov that he had deliberately overpraised Tolstoy in his article,[21] he obviously did so in the belief that Tolstoyan analysis, in fact, lent itself to the radical rationalist ideals that he himself espoused.

Apollon Grigor'ev, representing the older tradition of philosophical idealism, also praised Tolstoy's writing, but he complained that it lacked synthesis. In an essay published in two installments in *Time* [*Vremia*] in 1862, Grigor'ev formulated his reservations about Tolstoy's art within the Hegelian framework typical of the age.

When *Childhood, Adolescence*, and the war stories appeared, everyone hailed them as "the first full and complete artistic expression of the psychological process."[22] Attempting to isolate what was unique in Tolstoy, Grigor'ev compared him to other outstanding writers. He was "close to Turgenev in poetic tenderness of feeling and deep sympathy for nature, but diametrically opposed to him in the stern sobriety of his view, which is merciless to all sensations even the slightest bit outside the quotidian, [and] in his hostility to everything false, however brilliant it may be." In these last qualities he would be closer to Pisemsky if his realism were "innate" and not the child of his analysis. (Grigor'ev meant here that Pisemsky lacked a sense of anything higher than the merely physical which was his theme.) Tolstoy and Goncharov shared an external enmity to idealism, but, unlike Goncharov, the practical was not Tolstoy's ideal. In his hatred of "banality" [*poshlost'*] he followed Gogol, but, unlike Gogol, he did not weep over a lost ideal. What he shared with all these writers was their "negativity," the result of their alienation from the "soil" (Grigor'ev's beloved *pochva*).

Tolstoy, Grigor'ev maintained, wanted to find his ideal both within himself, and in reality, in Grigor'ev's "soil." So he analyzed himself and his surroundings, digging deeper and deeper, but unable to find the bottom. The result was the "pantheistic hurt" [*skorb'*] of "Lucerne"; the suspicion of anything false (hypocritical) so extreme that in "Three Deaths" the death of the tree is higher even than the death of the peasant; and the "stern submission to fate" that spares not even human feelings in "Family Happiness." After this last work—Grigor'ev referred here to the fact that at the time he was writing Tolstoy had published nothing since 1859—came "an apathy, no doubt temporary and transitional."[23] For Grigor'ev Tolstoy was an analyst looking for an ideal, and hence a synthesis, that he had not yet found.

Tolstoy and Chernyshevsky

The Soviets, beginning with Eikhenbaum, who resurrected Chernyshevsky's 1856 article and adopted the phrase "dialectic of the soul" to describe Tolstoy's psychology,[24] have uncovered many similarities between Tolstoy and Chernyshevsky.[25] Like Chernyshevsky, Tolstoy was much more wedded to analysis and reason than were his older friends.[26] He was also, as Grigor'ev feared, more of a moralist, dissecting souls and reassembling them to make them serve the practical aims of morality. He most definitely resembles Chernyshevsky in this endeavor.[27] Tolstoy, moreover, attacked civilization with the same Rousseauist fervor and reliance on radical, rational solutions as Chernyshevsky's followers, Dobroliubov and especially Pisarev (ibid., 338). In this respect, in fact, he was more radical than Chernyshevsky and akin to the nihilists of the succeeding generation.

Where Tolstoy and Chernyshevsky differed was on the role of human reason in creating the conditions necessary for a social morality. Human reason, the human mind without any divine or metaphysical support, was Chernyshevsky's bridge between the natural egoism of man and the needs of society. Rakhmetov—Chernyshevsky's ideal character in *What Is to Be Done?*—develops his rational principles into "a finished system to which he adhered absolutely." With a single weakness (cigars), Rakhmetov lives "by conviction," not by "passion," so as to prove the disinterested truth of his theories of human happiness.[28] For Tolstoy, human reason, while powerful in the human soul, could never dominate it to the extent that it does in Chernyshevsky's novel. Human reason serves the passions without reforming them. In the progression in the fifties from the uncompleted *Novel of a Russian Landowner* [*Roman russkogo pomeshchika*], which was conceived in 1852 as a rational model of philanthropy, to the "Landowner's Morning" (*Utro pomeshchika*; 1857), Tolstoy demonstrated to himself, as well as to others, that reason acting on its own simply masks a selfishness worse because it is more tyrannical than that based on natural self-love. The experiences of his character Nekhliudov constitute a refutation before the fact of the very possibility of a Rakhmetov.

This disagreement between Tolstoy and Chernyshevsky came into the open in the 1860s. In his play *The Infected Family* (*Zarazhennoe semeistvo*; 1864) Tolstoy set out to demonstrate that the rational egoism of the new generation inspired by Chernyshevsky was egoism, pure and simple.[29] At the center of the play is the eighteen-year-old Liubov' Ivanovna, or Liubochka. Liubochka, whose name means "love," is the personification of spontaneity and feeling. The male nihilists in the play desire her, but they do not deserve her because they deny the role of feeling in human life and therefore really despise her. As rationalists, moreover, they themselves never rise above egoism, and want to possess her without really loving her. Liubov' Ivanova closely resembles Natasha Rostova: she talks like Natasha and her first entrance in the play could have been written for the heroine of *War and Peace*. Through this link of the play and the novel, *War and Peace* itself may be seen as a response to *What Is to Be Done?* with its overweening faith in human reason.

Tolstoy rejected Chernyshevsky's rational individualism. It is important to grasp, however, that in doing so he was not simply rejecting either reason or individualism. His fundamental quarrel with Chernyshevsky was over materialism. Tolstoy himself was always a dualist, who believed in the existence of both rational self-interest and an inner spiritual principle that allowed human beings to direct or even contradict it. Thus the soul, or psyche, as he first described it in his diary, contained both self-love and "love of everything" (46:267). He built his psychology, following principles that he held in common with Chernyshevsky, on dualist assumptions that Chernyshevsky rejected. Because of his dualism, he required a synthesis that differed from the one Chernyshevsky espoused.

It is most significant in this context to observe the differences between Tolstoy's pedagogical theories and those of the radical democrats in the 1860s. The radical democrats advocated education of the peasant as the only route to equality and social justice.[30] Dobroliubov, for instance, while he defended nature and attacked anything artificial, also said that he did not trust the heart. Natural impulses had to be strengthened by a developed reason (ibid., 584–85). It is no accident that Chernyshevsky scoffed at the theoretical articles in Tolstoy's pedagogical journal *Iasnaia Poliana* and compared their author to a "half-educated assessor of a county court" who thinks he knows enough to write laws.[31] Without reason, and the "development" that Chernyshevsky so vigourously defended in *What Is to Be Done?*,[32] man is no better, in fact worse by virtue of his superior ability to calculate, than the beasts.[33]

"Education for the People" [*O narodnom obrazovanii*], the article in *Iasnaia Poliana* that Chernyshevsky scorned, applies to pedagogy Tolstoy's insight about tyranny masquerading as reason. It argues that traditional methods of education merely subject the student to the will of the teacher. The problem of human selfishness was more intractable for Tolstoy than for Chernyshevsky, and therefore a real basis for a social morality was more elusive. Tolstoy's dualism was the source of a belief in human goodness whose condition was not, as it was for Chernyshevsky, merely the presence of developed human reason. In "Who Should Be Teaching Whom to Write: Should We Be Teaching the Peasant Lads, or They Us?" [*Komu u kogo uchitsia pisat', krest'iankim rebiatam u nas, ili nam u krest'ianskikh rebiat*], Tolstoy claimed that virtue was natural and that education corrupted it.

Tolstoy agreed with the men of the forties that feeling was primary both in nature and in man. Art, as the voice of feeling, more truly repre-

sented reality in its deepest manifestations than could science, the voice
of human (logical and dialectical) reason. When Apollon Grigor'ev attacked Chernyshevsky as a "theoretician," he was referring to the as-
sault by rational philosophy using rational analysis on both poetry and
reality. When he called poetry "synthesis and inspiration," he was defending it as the true representative of and avenue to a higher reality
inaccessible to rationalism. It was Tolstoy's accommodation to and exploration of this reality that distinguished him both as a writer and as
a psychologist from Chernyshevsky. But as we shall see, Tolstoy's natural morality was rooted in an idealism that took both feeling and reason into account.

Subjective Reality for the Early Tolstoy

Tolstoy truly was, as Chernyshevsky, Eikhenbaum, and others have
contended, a kind of scientist who explored nature and especially
human perception and psychology as boldly as any nihilist. He believed both that reason was natural in human beings, and that the material world, which is indirectly accessible to us through our senses and
reason, really existed. As a young man, he loved the part of the material world nearest to him, namely, his own body, and perhaps it was
through it that he came to love nature so much. In any case, in late 1856
(18 December) he wrote in his notebook that "no form of idealism
[*ideal'nost'*] is harmful, so long as there is sensuousness [*chuvstvennost'*].
If you hold firmly to the earth, it stretches out the soul" (47:201).

Following this dictum, Tolstoy's understanding became a blend of
the "concrete" or "sensuous"—that is, a realism based on analysis that
gives rise to the modern scientific understanding of nature and human
nature derived by reason from the evidence of the senses—and an "idealism" that gives spiritual meaning to the physical world. This "idealism" comes not from analysis but from intuition. It is ultimately "subjective"; that is, we "know" it through inner feeling rather than through
analysis of sense data. Tolstoy's version of subjectivity, however, embraced reason as well as feeling. Indeed it—subjectivity—was understood to be the only avenue to the higher reason that makes sense of the
world.

Soviet critics, following Chernyshevsky's and then Eikhenbaum's
lead, have concentrated on the "scientific" Tolstoy, the brilliant psychological analyst and social critic. As Marxists, they believe in a dialectic
based on materialism and evolved through "the tools of formal and
dialectic logic."[34] Marx declared that "the beyond of truth having van-
ished,"[35] philosophy must serve history and establish the truth of this

world. To Marxists, Tolstoy's belief in an absolute is simply a form of subjectivity, by which they mean that the individual's natural but mistaken perception stems ultimately from feeling, not reason. This is the approach taken by E. N. Kupreianova in *The Aesthetics of L. N. Tolstoy* [*Estetika L. N. Tolstogo*]. She argues in chapter 1 that the knowledge of psychic life which underlies Tolstoy's artistic genius makes him a bad thinker when he mistakes the yearnings of the psyche for metaphysical truths.

As a student of philosophy, Kupreianova is herself certainly aware that Tolstoy's "poetic" confusion of subjectivity and objectivity had strong philosophical support in the nineteenth century, in the movement that Maurice Mandelbaum calls metaphysical idealism.[36] To get at the essential differences between a metaphysical idealist and a materialist, it is useful to compare what Chernyshevsky actually says about Tolstoy's "dialectic of the soul" with a similar description of Tolstoyan psychology from an article by metaphysical idealist P. V. Annenkov that appeared two years earlier than Chernyshevsky's. (Annenkov's article, entitled "Descriptions: I. S. Turgenev and L. N. Tolstoy (1854)" [Kharakteristiki: I. S. Turgenev i L. N. Tolstoi], originally appeared in the first issue of *The Contemporary* [*Sovremennik*] for 1855; Chernyshevsky's appeared in the same journal in December 1856.)

> CHERNYSHEVSKY: Count Tolstoy's attention is focused most of all on how certain feelings and thoughts develop from others. He observes with interest how a feeling *which arises directly from a given situation or impression*, being subjected to the influence of memories and to the force of other feelings, then returns to its former starting point and again and again wanders, altering along a whole chain of memories; how a thought, born of a first sensation, leads to other thoughts, is carried farther and farther away, merges daydreams with real sensations, hopes for the future with reflection on the present. Psychological analysis can take various directions ... Count Tolstoy concerns himself most of all with the psychological process itself, its forms, its laws—the dialectic of the soul to use a defining phrase.[37]

> ANNENKOV: He believes in *the living activity of the organism* and with the genuine feeling of a poet he catches that moment when nature itself, with no help, emits the first spark of thought, the first trace of feeling and the first inclination [of will]. He then follows their progress in its whole winding flight through a multitude of sensations and circumstances which they embellish.[38]

Chernyshevsky appreciated Tolstoy's prose because it was based on the same associationalist—Lockean—psychology that he practised himself.[39] For Chernyshevsky, the origins of human behavior are external to man, in "a given situation or impression." Only thought is internal, and even it, "born of a first sensation," comes originally from the outside. There is no soul in man, only a dialectic between new sensations and thoughts and previously internalized ones. True to Chernyshevsky's materialism, everything is reduced to physical laws—chance—and we are left wondering with Dostoevsky's underground man how human beings could be capable of any freedom, let alone moral responsibility. Annenkov, on the other hand, believed in a real dialectic between soul (the "living organism") and the external world ("sensations and circumstances"). His description of Tolstoy's art resembles Hegel's definition of what poetry can and should be, namely, "that principle of the self-apprehension of the inner life as inner . . . [broadening out] into an objective world [and] completely unfolding the totality of an event, a successive series and the changes of the heart's movements, passions, ideas, and the complete course of an action."[40]

Tolstoy was as committed to the existence of the external world as Chernyshevsky was, but he also believed in the real existence of an inner life independent of, though interacting with, external reality. The inner self is active: it chooses among the myriad sensations, feelings, and thoughts flooding our souls. These choices are not random: they reveal the moral character of the individual who makes them.

To demonstrate the workings of the "dialectic of the soul," Chernyshevsky cited the death of Praskukhin in the second Sevastopol sketch. Gustafson has shown in persuasive detail how the scene does, in fact, proceed according to the principles of associationalist psychology.[41] Praskukhin, Gustafson concludes, dies without discovering his "true self" and so, especially if the body is regarded as external, he seems the perfect example of the human self as passive receptacle of outer sensations (ibid., 297). As such he attracted Chernyshevsky's attention as proof of the close connection between himself and Tolstoy.

Given just how clear the connection is in the case of Praskukhin, however, it is important to note the peculiar Tolstoyan emphasis, even here, on an active inner life. Praskukhin's feelings and thoughts before the bomb goes off are not random. They all relate to the inner principles—a tangle of ambition, vanity, self-love, justice (payment of debts), and love—that have guided his life. Praskukhin does have an inner life, then, although it is chaotic and seems to have no independent existence outside of concerns for the body (self-preservation) and for the opinions of other human beings (*amour propre*).

Moreover, Praskukhin's death does not end the sketch; it is followed directly by a chapter on Mikhailov (chap. 13), which serves as its counterpoint. The first lines of the chapter assert that Mikhailov and Praskukhin undergo exactly the same experience.

> Mikhailov, having seen the bomb, fell to the ground and squinted just the same way, opened his eyes and closed them twice just the same way, and just like Praskukhin thought and felt an immense amount in the two seconds the bomb lay unexploded.

Mikhailov even thinks that he has died and so, with Praskukhin, passes into death. If he reacts differently to identical circumstances, it is because his inner life differs from Praskukhin's. For one thing, Mikhailov, unlike Praskukhin and Kalugin, whose completely self-centered reaction to Praskukhin's death is recorded at the beginning of the previous chapter (he sees it as a career opportunity for himself), has a strong sense of duty. Tolstoy emphasizes the word *duty*, twice applying it to Mikhailov. Connected to this feeling is Mikhailov's simple religiosity. When he is facing death, he thinks of God and the afterlife. And, unlike Praskukhin, Mikhailov's soul seems ordered, so that better impulses can overcome worse ones. Like the others, Mikhailov has feelings of fear and ambition; he may have felt all the emotions that visit Praskukhin in the seconds before his death; but he *overcomes* his fear and other feelings to force himself to check up on Praskukhin back where the battle rages, because "it's my *duty*."

Praskukhin, like the other officers at headquarters, is a creature of *amour propre*. He thinks only of himself, and yet his self-esteem depends entirely on what others think of him. His gaze remains directed outside himself and toward the world of men. He compares his situation with Mikhailov's; he hopes for honors in the future; he remembers slights and debts in the past. His last words are addressed to the fleeing soldiers: "Take me with you." Praskukhin's *amour propre* diminishes his reality, both for himself and for Tolstoy's readers. He is more a shadow than a man.

Mikhailov looks inside himself to God: his last words are: "Lord, forgive my sins!" His self-esteem, also important to him, depends on what God, not men, thinks of him. Asking for forgiveness of sins, he conceives of himself as an independent individual capable of moral responsibility. He is therefore in touch with God's law, and so is able to act on a sense of duty rooted in something more than self-preservation. One can say of Mikhailov, then, as one cannot of Praskukhin, that he has fixed inner principles, or ideas, as well as an active inner life. These principles order his soul and make it independent, to a certain extent, of its circumstances.

The terrible description of Praskukhin's death probably did more than anything else in "Sevastopol in May" to establish Lieutenant Tolstoy's reputation in Petersburg as an unflinching realist, or analyst, of war and men's reaction to it. Tolstoy himself emphasized this aspect of his work by ending it with the famous declaration that the hero of his story was Truth, *Pravda*—the truth that the war had no real heroes. It is all the more striking, therefore, that the stern analyst found a sense of duty in an otherwise ordinary soul, which could not be traced back to motives connected with preservation of the body, to simple self-love, or to self-interest. This sense of duty does not, on examination, turn out to be a hidden concern for the body or even for the opinions of others. Looking into the soul, Tolstoy found the potential (and therefore the imperative) for moral law, moral freedom, and moral responsibility.

Mikhailov is not, like Praskukhin, simply reacting *to* his surroundings; he is acting *on* them in accordance with an inner impulse that can only be known through feeling. It has no empirical, that is, scientifically verifiable, reality. Tolstoy believes in this kind of feeling, and Chernyshevsky does not. It is the manifestation, in this particular story, of the "love of everything" that Tolstoy had detected in the soul already in 1847. This "love of everything" stems from a divine source that provides synthesis for Tolstoyan analysis. It gives direction and purpose to the soul. Without it, the individual is nothing but process; with it, the individual acquires real being, along with moral responsibility and freedom.

Tolstoy's Goethean Realism

The early Tolstoy sought to occupy the middle ground between subjective and objective experience. In the language of *War and Peace*, he wanted to make sense of freedom *and* necessity, the spiritual world that we know directly through consciousness, and the material world that we know indirectly, through experience and reason. To the extent that Tolstoy wanted to harmonize and unify the subjective and objective realms, he was undertaking a Hegelian project. It is doubtful, however, given his expressed hostility to Hegel, that he did so consciously. The intermediary between him and Hegel in this respect might have been Goethe, whom he read assiduously throughout his life.[42]

Russians in the 1840s, including Bakunin, Stankevich, Belinsky, and Herzen, had drawn the connection between Goethe and Hegel.[43] During that decade, Herzen, for example, whom Tolstoy met in 1861 and whom he admired, regarded the two Germans as possessing a complete understanding of life (ibid., 139). Herzen's "Dilettantism in Science" (1842) and *Letters on the Study of Nature (1844–1845)* are the most important productions of Russian Hegelianism of the 1840s.[44] In "Dilettantism in Science," Herzen quoted lines from Goethe's "Epirrhema," as part of his attack on both materialists and dreamers, who mistakenly took either the purely objective or the purely subjective sphere to be all of reality.[45] In 1844 he systematically studied Goethe's science as preparation for writing *Letters on the Study of Nature (1844–1845)* (ibid., 245). While attacking the romantic image of Goethe prevalent in Russia, Herzen discovered Goethe as "one of the greatest representatives of Realistic art" (ibid., 238). For him Goethe was the model for the "speculative empiricist," "who was able to combine in his work the spirit of the idealist tradition with the empiricism of the predominantly materialistic modern age" (ibid., 245). He meant by this that Goethe did not allow the evidence of empiricism to destroy his belief in human freedom. Herzen, through Goethe, is championing a realism that rejects neither freedom nor necessity, a realism subsequently embraced and developed by Herzen's younger contemporary Tolstoy.

In his book *From Hegel to Nietzsche*, Karl Löwith writes of the relation of Goethe and Hegel that

> What appealed to Goethe about Hegel was nothing less than the principle of his spiritual activity: mediation between self-being (*Selbstsein*) and being other (*Anderssein*). In Goethe's idiom, Hegel placed himself in the middle, between subject and object, while Schelling emphasized the breadth of nature, and Fichte, the height of subjectivity. . . . To discover and establish the mid-point between subject and object, between being *pro se* and being *per se*, between the internal and the external, was the motivating force behind Hegel's entire philosophy of mediation, from his first systematic fragment to the *Logik* and *Encyklopädie*.[46]

Löwith goes on to explain that Hegel, Goethe, and Schelling all start from the middle point between personal existence and the existence of the world. Löwith is writing within the German tradition stemming from Schiller's famous essay of "Naive and Sentimental Poetry," in which the natural, classical, and objective (the naive) is opposed to the willing, free, romantic, and subjective. Thomas Mann, in his essay on Goethe and Tolstoy, sees Goethe and Tolstoy as examples of naive (objective) poets to Schiller's and Dostoevsky's sentimental (subjective) ones.[47] Löwith presents Goethe as even greater because he is also attuned to the subjective experience in all its ramifications. In this he agrees with Karl Barth, who wrote that the return to man and the self inaugurated by Rousseau brought an end to the Enlightenment and ushered in the "age of Goethe."[48]

The difference between Hegel and Goethe, according to Löwith, is the allegiance of one to history and the other to nature. For both, "the affairs of men are subordinated to the service of a whole";[49] but Hegel sees unity, or the whole "from the point of view of the *historical spirit*," while Goethe sees it "from the point of view of nature as it is per-

ceived." For Hegel, there is a "cunning of reason," for Goethe—of nature. Tolstoy, of course, shared Goethe's attachment to nature.

For Goethe, to "mediate" between subjective and objective reality
was possible only if human freedom could somehow be reconciled
with the law that reason tells us governs all experience. Rather than
losing themselves in nature, human beings must be seen to fulfill themselves, and therefore to satisfy the requirements of their fundamental
need for freedom. Everything hinges here on the definitions of freedom, on the one hand, which, if freedom and necessity are to be reconciled, cannot be a simple rejection of all law, and nature, on the other,
whose law cannot be seen as simply mechanical and therefore inimical
to legitimate human aspirations. Goethe took nature as it presented
itself to reason and experience, but he searched for "the [higher and
unifying] reason behind everything that lives" (ibid., 9), and he assumed that such a reason was there.[50]

The "reason behind everything that lives": this was the element of
Goethe's worldview that allowed him to unite the subjective and objective. He early distinguished himself from the *Storm and Stressers* for
whom the essence of poetry was freedom defined as a lack of rules and
a concomitant formlessness.[51] So Goethe himself in *Dichtung und
Wahrheit* described the Bible of *Storm and Stressers*, his own *Sorrows of
Young Werther*, as a "general confession" that freed him from the movement (ibid., 89). His own classicism "rested upon his idea of 'inner
form,'" which for him was "the expression of an objective necessity" (ibid., 90). For him "only law can give us freedom" (ibid., 91). This
was true in man as in nature, and so the offensiveness for man of natural necessity is erased. In Goethe's own words, "The law appearing in
phenomena produces, in the greatest freedom and in accordance with
its own conditions, the objectively beautiful, which must indeed find
worthy subjects to grasp it" (ibid.). Those "worthy subjects" are human
beings, who freely submit themselves to law.

Like Tolstoy, Goethe stayed away from metaphysics and indeed
made it a fundamental principle of his scientific investigations never to
pass from "perception" to theory.[52] At the same time, he never questioned the unity and harmony of nature.[53] He was what Ernst Cassirer
has called an "intuitive thinker."[54] So, for instance, as Cassirer goes on
to explain, in his theory of color he bypassed Newtonian mathematics
"to include nothing but the world of the eye, which contains only form
and color." Thus, he wrote Schiller, "all reasoning is transformed into
a kind of representation." At the same time, he did not oppose theory.
Cassirer quotes him again, this time in the forward to the *Theory of
Colors*: "Merely looking at a thing can tell us nothing. Each look leads
to an inspection, each inspection to a reflection, each reflection to a

synthesis; and hence we can say that in every attentive glance at the world we are already theorizing" (ibid., 82).

In Tolstoy, too, looking and thinking are related. Marcel Proust forcefully describes the "theorizing" quality of Tolstoy's prose:

> This is not the work of an observing eye but of a thinking mind. Every so-called stroke of observation is simply the clothing, the proof, the instance, of a law, a law of reason or of unreason, which the novelist has laid bare. And our impression of the breadth and life is due precisely to the fact that none of this is the fruit of observation, but that every deed, every action, being no other than an expression of law, one feels oneself moving amid a throng of laws—why, since the truth of these laws is established for Tolstoi by the inward authority they have exercised over his thinking, there are some which we are still baffled by.[55]

Proust goes too far and thereby makes Tolstoy's prose more like his own completely controlled and subjective writing. The laws that Tolstoy discovered and used to create his complex structures were, in Tolstoy's mind, always the result of observation, either of himself or of external reality. So, in 1857, in a letter to Annenkov to be discussed at length in chapter 3, he was looking for the "dim law" in nature itself that would allow him properly to choose among and arrange a chaos of natural things (60:182); in 1873 he praised Pushkin for the unfailingly correct hierarchy of high and low things in his poetry (62:21–22). As for Goethe, laws for Tolstoy were embedded in reality and could never satisfactorily be expressed outside of concrete examples.

It was the Goethean ideal of reasoning as representation that inspired the young Tolstoy and allowed him to devote himself totally to nature and poetry. It is also the source of what Gustafson has called his "emblematic realism."[56] For Tolstoy as for Goethe, poetry celebrated nature, the life of the body, but it was nature redeemed by spirit. Goethe, like the young Tolstoy, regarded his way of thinking as "objective."[57] The world spirit appeared to man indirectly, through objects that were at the same time particular and each one symbolic of the whole.

> If everything real is a simile of the Absolute which appears in it, it must ultimately suffice us to speak of the invisible interior of Nature in pictures and similes. But the point is to find suitable, appropriate similes. The most valuable ones, says Goethe, are those "which cover the object completely and seem to become identical with it." (Ibid.)

Tolstoy, perhaps by virtue of his nationality and certainly of the time in which he lived, was more of a moralist than his German predecessor was. Even as, in the article "Who Should Be Teaching Whom to Write:

Should We Be Teaching the Peasant Lads, or They Us?" he celebrated the harmony of nature and spirit by declaring man, "just born," to be the very image of "the true, the beautiful and the good (8:321–22)," he varied the common formula to put the good in the place of honor above the beautiful. The world Tolstoy described in *War and Peace* is neither allegorical nor naturalistic. It can be both concrete and spiritually meaningful. Like Goethe and like Hegel, Tolstoy believed that the parts, either of the self or of nature, could not be defended without reference to the whole, a whole that for him had to be moral. One can describe his whole early project, culminating in *War and Peace*, as the search for a synthesis that would unify the self and nature. The next two chapters will explore how this early synthesis developed, first by looking at Tolstoy's understanding of the self, and then at his understanding of nature and of the relation of the two.

Two

The Young Tolstoy's Understanding of the Human Soul

> We have one, only one infallible guide, the uni-
> versal spirit, penetrating us all together and each
> of us as individuals, implanting in each of us a
> yearning for what ought to be; that same spirit
> which in a tree orders it to grow toward the sun,
> in a flower orders it to turn to seed towards fall
> and in us orders us to cling unconsciously to one
> another. ("Lucerne")

Tolstoy, the Psychological Analyst

In "Sevastopol in May," Mikhailov is an example of what Richard Gustafson has called the "active, willing" self.[1] Here, as almost everywhere
in Tolstoy, this active self is shown to be moral. I would maintain, however, that although the existence of this self was not in question for
Tolstoy, its morality was. For Gustafson, this self comes not from the
Western European tradition, but from Eastern Christianity. I agree
with Gustafson that in Tolstoy the striving self modifies the Lockean
empiricist psychology that Gustafson describes so well, but I do not
think that, for the first part of Tolstoy's life at least, the two models are
in conflict. I believe, moreover, that Tolstoy could have discovered the
striving self within the Western Enlightenment tradition itself, and that
his early philosophical writings suggest that he did so.

Tolstoy never practiced psychological analysis out of simple scientific curiosity. He began to analyze himself as part of an effort at self-
improvement. To this end, he needed to understand human psychology so as to manipulate it to achieve a perfection which at the time he
also defined as true freedom. "And so precisely *psychology* turned out
to be the basis of philosophy understood as the science of life."[2] Tolstoy's earliest writings include a discussion of the goal of philosophy
(1:229–32), a discussion of how the psyche works toward freedom
(1:233–36), and tables, admonitions, and plans relating to his personal
attempts at self-improvement (46:245–76). He explained in his first
diary that he was starting it, in the spring of 1847, in order to monitor

and to further his progress: "In the diary there have to be tables of rules and in the diary also my future activities have to be defined" (46:29).

The young philosopher defined analysis as "the replacement of a certain [*opredelennyi*] concept by the simplest concepts of which it consists" (1:230). He continued: "By means of the analysis of any concept, it is possible to go from the most complex to the most abstract, that is, to that which cannot be defined. A concept of that kind is called consciousness. What is consciousness? Consciousness is the concept of the self, in other words, *I*" (ibid.). The method of investigation that Tolstoy here described was Cartesian. When Tolstoy reread his early philosophical fragments and commented on them in the second, unfinished part of *Youth*, he remarked that in them he had corrected Descartes. He had replaced the Cartesian "I think, therefore I am" with "I desire, therefore I am," because, so he reasoned, to think, one has to want to do it (2:343). This statement written in 1857 did not mean that Tolstoy was outside the Cartesian tradition. On the contrary, it draws attention to the fact that at least by 1857, and perhaps earlier, he saw himself as maneuvering to find his own place within it. In 1873, in his diary, Tolstoy strongly reaffirmed his commitment to this method of analysis, writing approvingly of how from his youth he had "analyzed and mercilessly destroyed everything."[3]

Like Rousseau, and Thomas Hobbes,[4] in order to explore human things Tolstoy from the beginning practiced introspection, that is, analysis on himself, on feelings the reality of which he could know only in himself. When you get to consciousness [*soznanie*], or *I*, he wrote, analysis is no longer possible, because it is an act of the knowing self that cannot understand, or break down, itself in the same way. From the beginning Tolstoy took "an empiricist and positivist view of reality,"[5] but he concentrated on understanding the one thing that is not comprehended within that view, the thing that does the viewing—the self.

It was Rousseau who, from within the ranks of Enlightenment thinkers, first raised the possibility that the passive knowing and experiencing self of Lockean psychology might be a thing in and of itself.[6] The self according to Rousseau makes itself known in the "sentiment of existence," which, in turn, is proof of the reality of our individual being.

> Rousseau seems more inclined (albeit confusedly) to understand the "sentiment of existence" metaphysically rather than psychologically, to see in it not a mere feeling or particular experience but something that actually reveals and constitutes our true being. Somehow, a man exists not through his relation to God or to the essence of man but through a relation to himself. Our being *is* our presence to ourselves, our sentiment of existence.[7]

The young Tolstoy shared this belief in the reality of individual being. It was a belief that would have been reenforced, moreover, by his early immersion in the writings of Goethe, who tried to establish the worth of the individual with something prior to morality or mind. Goethe called this something *Charakter*, "the definite peculiarity, the *daimon* in him, which reaches out into the world 'with unconditioned will-ing,' the indefatigably vital activity and obstinacy whereby the monad seems to make its personal existence a reality."[8] Viëtor uses the term "monad" in order to signify Goethe's agreement on this point with Leibnitz. Both believed that "the universe organizes itself into countless independent single beings, which Leibniz calls 'monads.' These final, eternal units of spiritual character are active in an independent manner, like the 'entelechies' of Aristotle" (ibid., 68–69).

Even had he not read Goethe, or Rousseau and other writers in the Cartesian tradition of radical doubt, Tolstoy's own intense sense of self would have inclined him this way. Analyzing, Tolstoy moved, as he wrote in his early philosophical ruminations, from the most complex to the simplest, indivisible, and undeniable things. In human beings, what is basic and indivisible is the particular self, which may be compared, as Tolstoy did compare it in *War and Peace*, to the atom, understood in the mid-nineteenth century to be the smallest particle of matter. Once again he would have found his presuppositions confirmed in Rousseau, who, in *Emile*, wrote: "The sensitive being is indivisible and one. It cannot be divided; it is whole, or it is nothing."[9]

It is not surprising to find that the young Tolstoy, in his first writings, had a Rousseauist view of the human soul. Like Rousseau he believed that "two things primarily determine the degree of our existence: extent and unity" (ibid., 44). As Carden has pointed out, these two aims were potentially in conflict, since "extent," or what she aptly calls the "expanding plenitude" of the soul as Rousseau understood it,[10] can destroy unity. The young Tolstoy was aware of this tension already in his project of self-improvement. His goal was expansive: "the development of all my faculties" (46:29); but he was careful not to cultivate any one faculty at the expense of another.

When he analyzed human beings, Tolstoy found, adopting a "typically eighteenth-century model of human psychology," that they were made up of "four 'parts': the 'body,' 'feeling,' 'mind,' and 'will'" [1851; 1:292,339].[11] The goal of man is freedom (1:233) and his essence is the "unlimited will" that is truly free (1:234). Everything else has its cause outside him, in the physical world (1:233–34) and therefore in some sense is not him. The body is low because it is pure matter. Yet, Tolstoy did not reject the body. Given the low place he assigned it, it is striking how much effort he devoted to the cultivation of bodily virtues of health, suppleness, and endurance (44:212, 273–76). It is clear that the virtues of the soul as he understood them required a strong, healthy, and disciplined body. Although he wanted to have all the human "faculties" serve free will, he preferred to reform rather than reject the lower ones.

Tolstoy was naturally drawn to what Melzer has called Rousseau's "idealistic realism."

> To state it more formulaically: Rousseau's skepticism debunks all of the purportedly "higher" things in human nature and affairs and, more, actually blames them for causing all the evils they are supposedly needed to cure. But in doing so it *exculpates* man's *lower*, bodily nature, which had always been falsely condemned, showing it to have an unsuspected goodness upon which one might base the unity and happiness formerly sought in the "higher." This is the unique "philosophical chemistry" through which Hobbesian realism is made to issue in Platonic sublimity. Extreme skepticism is directed at the "high" for the sake of idealism regarding the newly exculpated "low." Such is the general philosophic spirit—idealistic realism—that lies behind Rousseau's system and his revolutionary new principle of the natural goodness of man.[12]

The principle of being of the self is its own particularity: it is itself and it wants to remain itself. This principle gives rise to Rousseau's first characteristic of the soul, namely, unity. Particularity, or unity, is protected by two seemingly opposite factors: a self-love that aims to preserve and unify the whole being, and a need for freedom from outside influences that might dilute its integrity or unity. We may speculate, therefore, that freedom for the young Tolstoy was in the service of the individual rather than the other way around. What this "atom," this particular being, wants is freedom from everything external (1:234). It is most unified, most fully itself when it is independent of all outside influence. Freedom is therefore prior to morality, but unity is prior to freedom.

The other Rousseauian principle, extent, is the source in Tolstoy (as in Rousseau) of the "striving self," which is already present in the philosophic fragments from the 1840s and which Gustafson correctly identifies as Tolstoy's answer to empiricism. This is a propensity toward growth, a "pure, goalless expansiveness, a formless energy, *élan*, or libido."[13] Gustafson draws attention to the predominance of will over intellect in the soul as Tolstoy understood it, and sees this will as the origin of the "striving self."[14] In fact, the opposite is true. Desire in and of itself, with no object, is the expression of the expansive, or striving self. To live is to move, and so the soul moves and expands because it is living. The will is the manifestation of the striving, not vice versa. This is the reasoning behind Rousseau's idea, which Tolstoy adopted.

But what is the soul striving toward? Although Tolstoy even in the 1840s gives a moral direction to the expansive self, as in Rousseau the expansiveness itself is submoral: "Man strives, that is, man is active. Where is this activity directed? How can one make this activity free? —is the goal of philosophy in the true sense" (1847; 1:229). The primary fact about the human soul is its dynamism. Philosophy has to make sense of this, and it also has a pedagogic role—the achievement of freedom and unity—from the beginning. According to Melzer, Rousseau suggested in different books several different moral ways of life that would utilize this natural propensity of the soul.[15] Tolstoy, too, changed his mind several times about how human beings could be moral. So, drawing on statements from Tolstoy's old age, Gustafson calls the willing self in Tolstoy a "particle of love" reaching out to others and striving ultimately to rejoin the Divinity from whence it came.[16] In the 1840s Tolstoy himself saw the self as striving toward divine or universal reason. In this model, reason had to reform will in order for man to be free and happy (46:3–4). What remains constant, what links these two dissimilar visions, is the existence of the striving self, pure and simple. Music represents this self. So Nikolai Rostov, listening to Natasha sing, "can kill and rob and yet be happy" (4.14). Even in Tolstoy's old age, on rare occasions, as in Fedia Protasov's love of gypsy music in *The Living Corpse*, the striving self, with its love of freedom, appears naked, without moral justification (34:22).

Tolstoy asserted even in 1847 that human beings love others as well as themselves (46:267) but, given his understanding of the soul as complete in itself and therefore essentially solitary, it is difficult to explain why that soul might want to sacrifice itself for others. The answer must lie, as Gustafson asserts, in the idea of the striving, active self that literally takes an individual out of himself. There is no theoretical reason, however, to consider this striving self moral. Psychological analysis had led Tolstoy to it. In both cases just cited, in youth and old age, Tolstoy was looking for a moral law or synthesis to harness the striving.

Precisely *because* Tolstoy was a product of the Cartesian tradition, it was difficult for him to establish a basis of human community. The freer, the more particular a being is, and hence the more it is itself, the weaker are the ties that bind it to other human beings. Tolstoy struggled his whole life with this problem inherent in the Western philosophical tradition, which he never entirely abandoned.[17] At different times he suggested different solutions to it. Analysis, then, discovered the active self, and a synthesis was necessary to give it moral meaning.

Synthesis and the Influence of Rousseau

Categorizing him as an analyzer rather than a synthesizer, Tolstoy's older contemporaries naturally enough placed him among men of his own generation, the fifties, rather than among men of the forties. If Tolstoy accepted this interpretation, it was because it coincided with his own long-held opinion of himself. To this extent himself an unconscious Hegelian, he, too, accepted the need for synthesis. His personal history, interwoven with but always distinct from the history of his times, consists in a struggle to counter the unexpected but very real disintegrating power of psychological analysis as practiced by his generation. Unbeknownst to his new friends, he already had within his arsenal the means to accomplish this end when he arrived in Petersburg.

Perhaps the best way to gain access to this part of Tolstoy's private agenda is to try to reconstruct the early history of his relations with Rousseau. Tolstoy shared a fascination for Rousseau with the younger radical democrats, Dobroliubov and especially Pisarev.[18] For Tolstoy's older friends, Rousseau was old hat, an eighteenth-century philosopher whose teaching had been assimilated and corrected by the German philosophers whom they admired. Inasmuch as they recognized Rousseau's influence on Tolstoy, they condemned it. So Turgenev remarked to Botkin about "Lucerne": "I didn't like it: it's a mixture of Rousseau, Thackerey and the short form of the Orthodox Catechism."[19] Tolstoy himself, on the other hand, as he wrote to Bernard Bouvier in 1905 in response to his invitation to join the Rousseau Society, always regarded Rousseau as a living inspiration:

> Rousseau a été mon maître depuis l'âge de 15 ans.
> Rousseau et l'évangile ont été les deux grandes et bienfaisantes influences de ma vie.
> Rousseau ne vieillit pas. Tout dernièrement il m'est arrivé de relire quelques unes de ses oeuvres et j'ai éprouvé le même sentiment d'élévation d'âme et d'admiration, que j'ai éprouvé en le lisant dans ma jeunesse. (75:234)

> [Rousseau has been my teacher since I was fifteen years old.
> Rousseau and the Gospels have been the two great and beneficent influences of my life.
> Rousseau does not grow old. Just recently I happened to reread several of his works and I experienced the same sentiment of elevation of soul and of admiration that I experienced in my youth.]

At the end of his life he told A. Goldenweizer that he had left Kazan University after he had begun to read Rousseau and wanted for the first time to pursue his studies in earnest.[20] He claimed elsewhere that at age fifteen he wore a medallion of Rousseau around his neck, and that as a young man he read all the master's work, "including the dictionary of music."[21] He periodically reread his favorite works throughout his life. Rousseau's influence was, moreover, indirect as well as direct. Inasmuch as Tolstoy himself was an "expressivist" writer, Rousseauist ideas were "the medium in which he swam."[22] This tradition, going back to Rousseau's idea of the expansive soul, helps explain why Tolstoy could write that he felt he himself had written certain pages of Rousseau.[23]

All in all, one can say of Rousseau as of no other writer that he helped form Tolstoy's soul. It is difficult to assess this influence precisely because it was so all-pervasive. Its importance, however, led Tolstoy himself to ponder its extent and limits. His scattered comments, taken together, comprise a critique of Rousseau that explains the philosopher's place in the development of the writer as it concerns us here.

The second, unpublished part of *Youth*, written in 1857, contains an account of the narrator's, Nikolenka's, youthful reading of Rousseau:

> Besides that, in the same summer I read Weiss's *Principes philosophiques* and some works of Rousseau and made written comments on them. Feverish, intense work was going on in my head. I will never forget the strong and joyful impression and that disgust at how people lie and that love of the truth which the confessions of Rousseau produced in me. — "So all people are the same as I am," I thought with satisfaction: "I'm not the only one, such a freak, who was born on earth with an abyss of vile qualities.—Why then do they all lie and pretend, when everything has already been revealed by this book?" I asked myself. And so strong was my yearning for knowledge at that time that I almost didn't even acknowledge either good or bad. The one possible good seemed to me to be sincerity in the bad as well as the good. Rousseau's reflections on the moral advantages of the savage state over the civilized one were also very congenial to me. It was as if I were reading my own thoughts and in thought only added a little to them. (2:345)

Like other critics,[24] I take this account to be autobiographical. Tolstoy's commentary on the *First Discourse*, written sometime at the end of the forties, in fact survives, and helps clarify, the passage from *Youth*. According to the commentary, primitive man is better because he is not hypocritical: his vices are out in the open (1:233). If this is one of the sources of primitive man's superiority, then the *Confessions*, as a call for and an example of sincerity, may have been seen, by Tolstoy as well as by Rousseau, as an attempt to right that particular wrong in civilized man. The *First Discourse* and the *Confessions* would therefore be linked in Tolstoy's mind in the 1857 passage from *Youth*—and perhaps already in the late forties—as the presentation and solution of the same problem. This problem may also be seen as one starting point of Tolstoy's art: like Rousseau, he was disgusted by the hypocrisy of civilized life and was determined to present people as they really are. It is therefore not surprising that his first surviving artistic work, the so-called "History of Yesterday" probably written in 1851, takes as its avowed task "to narrate the inner [*zadushevnaia*] side of one day of life" (1:279). However many Rousseauist writers may have intervened between Tolstoy and Rousseau when Tolstoy wrote both this and his first published work *Childhood*,[25] as attempts at authenticity the ultimate inspiration of these works is Rousseau.

This connection comes out into the open on the first page of "A History of Yesterday," in a bit of advice from Book 5 of Rousseau's *Confessions* about how to behave in society. In recommending billiards to a youth who might otherwise be tempted to show off in society, Tolstoy slightly garbles Rousseau's text,[26] but he has the intention right. Rousseau actually says that if he went into society again he would carry a ball in his pocket and fiddle with it "so as not to talk when I have nothing to say" (ibid.). The problem in society, says Tolstoy, is not to be interesting, but to control one's foolish vanity, and to do this it is better to avoid idle conversation, which merely serves that deadly vice. Vanity, of course, is one great cause of inauthenticity, because it makes the sufferer care more about what others think of him than about what he thinks of or wants for himself. Behind Tolstoy's lighthearted opening digression on manners in "A History of Yesterday" lurks the obsession with vanity and authenticity that he shared with Rousseau, and the reference to the *Confessions* appears in the text along with the Rousseauian theme.[27]

In both the passage from *Youth* and elsewhere, Tolstoy praised Rousseau for his truthfulness, by which he meant his authenticity, or "sincerity." He wrote in 1889 that "I have loved it [the truth] since I was 15, when I was in ecstasy over Rousseau" (50:162). Rousseau's exclusive devotion to the truth, however, worried Tolstoy. Under the philosopher's influence, the youthful Rousseauist "almost didn't even acknowledge either good or bad. The one possible good seemed to me to be sincerity in the bad as well as the good." The moralist, unlike the philosopher, loves the good more than the truth, and so Tolstoy was uneasy at the destructive power of analysis and sincerity in the service of the truth alone. Tolstoy could not wholeheartedly embrace Rousseau's "antiteleological teleology," according to which "each thing exists most fully precisely by ignoring the call of 'order'—of 'ends' and 'essences'—by remaining free and wild, by cleaving to its inner unique-ness and particularity, by 'being itself.' "[28] Tolstoy, coming after a ro-manticism in part inspired by just this side of Rousseau, was looking for a teleology that Rousseau apparently did not need.

So, in 1857, Tolstoy implicitly distinguished himself from Rousseau precisely on moral grounds. Like the nihilists of the sixties, he identi-fied himself with the Rousseau of the *First Discourse*, the hater of hy-pocrisy. He feared, however, that this hatred would overwhelm any positive morality. It would reveal the truth about human beings, namely, that however much we hide the fact, we act exclusively out of self-love, without providing any principle by which this innate selfish-ness might be overcome. Long before he arrived in Petersburg in 1855 he was searching for an antidote to the destructiveness of psychologi-cal analysis.[29]

Love and honor are disguises for the selfish passions of lust and *amour propre*, and so the young Tolstoy scornfully debunked them in writings of the fifties.[30] Compassion could not by itself provide a suffi-cient base for human community. It would make us pity others, but not sacrifice ourselves for them. But what makes Tolstoy's relations with Rousseau so fascinating and difficult to grasp is the debt he owed pre-cisely to Rousseau in his search for a positive moral philosophy.

Tolstoy may have turned his back on idealism in 1847,[31] but he reim-mersed himself in it in 1852. While a young officer stationed in the Caucasus over the course of several months, he read the works of Plato in the translation of Victor Cousin.[32] Still reading Plato (he read the *Statesman* on 8 August 1852), he then turned to a rereading of all of Rousseau. It is not by chance that the work of Rousseau that most im-pressed Tolstoy this time around was not the *First* and *Second Dis-courses*, with their "negative" truths about the hypocrisy of civilized man, but the *Profession of Faith of the Savoyard Vicar*, from Book 4 of *Emile*. The Vicar addresses precisely those concerns—morality, free-dom, and the existence of the soul—that were troubling the young Tol-stoy. Tolstoy reported reading the *Profession of Faith* first on 27 June 1852 (finishing it on the twenty-ninth), then reread it on 8 July and 7 October of the following year.

The reasons for and the results of this intense intellectual experience he related in a letter to A. A. Tolstaia in 1859:

> I will try, however, to make my "profession de foi." As a child I believed
> fervently, sentimentally and without thinking: then at around age 14 I
> started to think about life in general and I ran up against religion, which
> didn't fit into my theory, so, of course, I considered it my duty to destroy it.

I lived very comfortably without it for about ten years. Everything was unfolding before me clearly, logically, it divided into categories, and there was
no place for religion. Then the time came when everything was revealed,
there were no more secrets in life, but life itself began to lose its meaning. At
that time I was alone and unhappy, living in the Caucasus. I started to think
the way people have the strength to think only once in their lives. I have my
notes from that time, and now, reading them over, I can't understand how a
person could rise to the level of mental ecstasy that I achieved then. It was a
torturous and a good time. Never, either before or since, have I risen to such
a level of thought, have I gazed *there*, as during that time, which lasted two
years. And everything that I discovered then will remain my belief forever.
I cannot do otherwise. From two years of mental work, I discovered a simple,
old thing, but one which I know as no one else knows it; I discovered that
there is immortality, that there is love, and that one must live for another in
order to be eternally happy. These discoveries amazed me by their resem-
blance to the Christian religion and instead of uncovering them myself I
began to search for them in the Gospels, but I found little. I found neither
God, nor the Saviour, nor the *mysteries*, nothing; and I searched with all, all,
all the strength of my soul, and I wept, and I tortured myself, and I wanted
nothing but the truth. For God's sake, don't think that you can understand
even a little bit from my words all the strength and concentration of my
searching then. This is one of those secrets of the soul which all of us have;
but I want to say that rarely have I met in people such a passion for the truth
as there was in me at that time. Thus it has remained with my religion, and
I have lived well with it.[33]

Tolstoy wrote this letter under the influence of his Caucasian diary,
which, as he told his aunt, he had just reread. We may assume, therefore, that he depended on the diary for help in this particular recon-
struction of his past. He had lost his faith in Christianity at age fourteen
(1842), and felt the need for faith only some ten years later, that is, in the
Caucasus, in 1852, when he began to read Plato and Rousseau. During
the two-year period from 1852 to 1854 he returned again and again in
the diary to the themes that his reading of the two philosophers inspired in him. His "profession de foi," as he himself called his tale of
the loss and renewal of his faith in his letter to his aunt, imitated the
Vicar's attempt to base a morality on common sense alone.

The Vicar delivers his confession to the young Rousseau to save him
from the "moral death" that threatens him because of misfortune and
disillusion with religion.[34] Jean-Jacques' radical doubt resembles Tolstoy's in the Caucasus as he described it in his letter to A. A. Tolstaia.
The Vicar turns to metaphysics only for "what was immediately related to my [and Jean-Jacques'] interest"(ibid., 269), that is, to ground

the possibility of morality in something other than hope or superstition. Tolstoy's reading of Plato and Rousseau in the Caucasus had the same purpose.

Misfortune has half ruined the young Jean-Jacques when the Vicar finds him, "heading . . . toward the morals of a tramp and the morality of an atheist" (ibid., 263). As Tolstoy's initial reaction to the *Profession of Faith* in his diary reveals, his own disillusion with religion was a result of bad thinking. In his diary he quoted without comment, and therefore presumably with wholehearted approval the following sentence from the *Profession of Faith*:

> Petite partie d'un grand tout, dont les bornes nous échappent, et que son auteur livre à nos folles disputes, nous sommes assez vains pour vouloir decider ce qu'est ce tout en lui-même, et ce que nous sommes par rapport à lui. (46:127)

> [We are a small part of a great whole whose limits escape us and whose Author delivers us to our mad disputes; but we are vain enough to want to decide what this whole is in itself and what we are in relation to it. *Emile*, 268]

This sentence is an attack on vanity [*tshcheslavie*].[35] As Tolstoy made clear on 8 July 1853, after rereading the *Profession of Faith*, it attacks specifically the vanity of mind: "I read the *Profession du Foi du Vicaire Savoyard* and, as always when I read it, an abundance of useful and noble thoughts welled up in me. Yes, my main misfortune is a big brain [*bol'shoi um*]" (46:167). Tolstoy was endorsing the Vicar's—and Rousseau's—attack on the Enlightenment's overweening faith in the power of reason. As Tolstoy recounted in his letter to A. A. Tolstaia, unguided reason, a *bol'shoi um*, had led him to analyze the traditional beliefs he had unconsciously held, and had thereby undermined his belief in them. When he trained his eyes on the heavens in search of new beliefs, however, he found that human reason alone cannot know God. ("How could I dare to think that it is possible to know the ways of Providence. It is the source of reason, and reason wishes to comprehend it" [12 June 1851; 46:63].) He concluded in *Adolescence* (written after his renewed acquaintance with the Savoyard Vicar) that the human mind can ask the highest questions but cannot by itself answer them (2:56).

Obviously the Vicar's taming of the vanity of the mind greatly impressed Tolstoy. For all their animus against metaphysics, however, neither Tolstoy nor the Vicar really abandoned it. On the contrary, as moralists they were more deeply wedded to certain metaphysical presuppositions than a philosopher, concerned only with the truth, would be. Although the Vicar restricts his metaphysics to what is necessary for his happiness, his conclusions are far-reaching enough. As Jean-

Jacques observes, he spins a whole "theism or . . . natural religion"[36] from the knowledge of the heart. The letter to A. A. Tolstaia attests that with the help of the Savoyard Vicar Tolstoy, too, found a natural religion complete with soul, immortality, and moral laws. In his own words from that letter, he gazed "there" [*tuda*], that is, at the metaphysical reality that underlies appearances.

Tolstoy was especially struck by the Vicar's defense of the conscience:

> the conscience is the voice of the soul; the passions are the voice of the body. Is it surprising that these two languages often are contradictory? And then which should be listened to? Too often reason deceives us. We have acquired only too much right to challenge it. But conscience never deceives; it is man's true guide. It is to the soul what instinct is to the body; he who follows conscience obeys nature and does not fear being led astray. (Ibid., 286)

The day Tolstoy finished his first reading of the *Profession of Faith* (29 June 1852) and summarized his impressions of the work, he paraphrased this passage (and the encomium to conscience further on that begins "Conscience, conscience! Divine instinct, immortal and celestial voice, certain guide of a being that is ignorant and limited but intelligent and free . . ." [ibid., 290]) by proclaiming the conscience to be "our best and truest guide" (46:128).[37] To escape from the philosophical and ethical crisis that a too active mind had precipitated, Tolstoy must have seized on the Vicar's definition of conscience as "an innate principle of justice and virtue according to which, in spite of our own maxims, we judge our actions and those of others as good or bad."[38]

Conscience is necessary for both the Vicar and Tolstoy precisely because they believe that human beings are independent "monads." But while it thereby guarantees their independence from everything outside them (even metaphysical truths), it limits that radical freedom bestowed by Rousseau on the individual released from the constraints of traditional metaphysics. A comparison with Dostoevsky points out the tension within the Rousseauian tradition itself. Dostoevsky's novels are polyphonic (to use the term popularized by Bakhtin) because individual characters within them are too free to be morally self-sufficient. They are essentially social, not solitary beings, because the moral truth they need for self-sufficiency only emerges from a comparison and merging of many voices. For Tolstoy, by contrast, conscience, if he will only heed it, provides the individual with everything he needs for moral guidance.

The other metaphysical concept that Tolstoy borrowed from the Vicar is that of the relation of the conscience to nature. The same crucial passage about conscience from the *Profession of Faith* that echoes repeatedly in Tolstoy's diary ends in the *Profession of Faith* with the words: "he who follows conscience obeys nature and does not fear being led astray."[39] The third draft of "The Raid," written in the fall of 1852 and therefore after Tolstoy's renewed acquaintance with the Savoyard Vicar, already reflects this lesson: "War! What an incomprehensible phenomenon. When reason sets itself the question: is it just, is it inevitable? An inner voice always answers: no. Only the persistance of this unnatural phenomenon makes it natural, and the feeling of self-preservation—just" (2:234). The "inner voice" active here is of course the conscience, speaking, as does the narrator in the published "Raid," for nature.[40]

The identification of conscience with natural law complicated Tolstoy's relations with Rousseau, who seems himself, in the person of the young Jean-Jacques, to disagree with the Vicar about it. Directly after the Vicar makes his point, Jean-Jacques attempts to interrupt him. The Vicar seems to interpret this interruption as an objection to his claim that conscience is natural. In response he spends several pages arguing that men naturally love the good. For this to be so, they would have to be naturally concerned with others as well as with themselves. Not surprisingly, then, the expansion of the Vicar's original point culminates in the contention that men are "made to become" social:

> Whatever the cause of our being, it has provided for our preservation by giving us sentiments suitable to our nature, and it could not be denied that these, at least, are innate. These sentiments, as far as the individual is concerned, are the love of self, the fear of pain, the horror of death, the desire of well-being. But if, as cannot be doubted, man is by his nature sociable, or at least made to become so, he can be so only by means of other innate sentiments relative to his species; for if we consider only physical need, it ought certainly to disperse men instead of bringing them together. It is from the moral system formed by this double relation to oneself and to one's fellows that the impulse of conscience is born. To know the good is not to love it; man does not have innate knowledge of it, but as soon as his reason makes him know it, his conscience leads him to love it. It is this sentiment which is innate.[41]

In the *Second Discourse* Rousseau had argued that natural man was solitary, and at the beginning of *Emile* itself he states as a general principle that "natural man is entirely for himself. He is numerical unity, the absolute whole which is relative only to itself or its kind" (ibid., 39). In the same Book 4 in which the *Profession of Faith* appears, Rousseau speaks of conscience as a product of the proper relation of the passions and reason. He ultimately grounds love of others in love of self alone, transformed by the power of compassion (ibid., 235). This position stands in direct contradiction to the Vicar's dualism: the Vicar argues that men *naturally* love one another as well as themselves and "It is from the moral system formed by this *double* relation to oneself and to one's fellows that the impulse of conscience is born" (emphasis mine).

On the other hand, the Vicar agrees with his creator that man is wholly and only natural: his social morality does not have a supranatural source. As a feeling, according to the Vicar, conscience depends for its power on "other innate sentiments relative to his [man's] species" in order to combat simple physical need when the two conflict. I would suggest that these "other innate sentiments" to which the Vicar refers are the sexual urges that are, in his words, "relative to the species": that is, they exist to perpetuate the species. This theory gains credence when one considers that the Vicar himself has strong sexual feelings that ruined his career because he could not keep his vows of celibacy.[42] He knows firsthand the power of sexual feelings, which are natural and cannot be denied. ("It was not long before I sensed that in obliging myself not to be a man I had promised more than I could keep" [ibid.].) The sexual urge is an expression of human libido, or expansiveness. If this is so, then conscience can be understood as a voice that derives its power from submoral but sociable sexuality, and its direction from reason which tells it that the good lies not in one man, but in mankind. "To know the good is not to love it; man does not have innate knowledge of it, but as soon as his reason makes him know it, his conscience leads him to love it."[43]

Like Rousseau, the young Tolstoy made a strong distinction between lust, on the one hand, and erotic love, on the other. Just as the young Rousseau in his *Confessions* was disgusted by the prostitutes who plied their trade in holes dug in the riverbank in Geneva and also by the proximity in the body of the sexual parts to those of elimination, so Tolstoy regarded sexual appetite pure and simple as bestial. But Tolstoy, too, at various times hinted at a connection between sexual love and the love of others which must be the basis of a true social morality.

A striking case of this occurs in *War and Peace*, in the love scene between Natasha and Pierre that ends part 8. Pierre declares his unconditional love for Natasha and thereby summons her back to life and feels himself spiritually renewed as well. Rushing from the house and riding through the streets of Moscow with open coat in subzero weather, he sees Halley's Comet in the middle of the sky.

> [The comet] foretold, so it was said, all sorts of horrors and the end of the world. But in Pierre this bright star with its long shining tail did not arouse any kind of terrible feeling. On the contrary, Pierre joyfully, with eyes wet

from tears, gazed at this bright star, which seemed, with inexpressible speed having flown through immeasurable spaces in a parabolic line, suddenly, like an arrow having pierced the earth, to have fastened itself in one place selected by it in the black sky and to have stopped, energetically having raised its tail upward, shining and playing with its white light amidst innumerable other twinkling stars. To Pierre it seemed as though this star responded fully to what was in his softened and encouraged soul, which had bloomed into new life. (8.22)

Precisely because this scene seems to make the most elevated claims for love, it is necessary first to establish exactly what Pierre is feeling. He tells Natasha that he would marry her if he could. Later, when he finds himself about to repeat this, he decides to stop visiting the Rostovs because he cannot conceal his love and, as a married man, cannot pursue it to a natural conclusion (9.20). When he meets her after his imprisonment, the same love for her wells up in him again, and this time, with Helene dead, he is able to court her (15.15). Their married life, briefly illustrated in the first epilogue, is distinguished by many children—she spends all her time "carrying, giving birth to [and] nursing children"—and, it seems, by a happy and vigorous sex life. (When he returns from a long absence, she drags him off to the bedroom posthaste.) There can be no doubt, then, that his newly discovered love for her at the end of part 8 is both exclusive and sexual.

At the same time, both his initial pity [*zhalost'*] for her, and the fact that his sighting of Halley's Comet occurs on Prechisten'kii [Most Pure] Street indicate the purity and elevation of his feeling. The combination of earthiness and spirituality in his love is emphasized in the magnificent description of the comet, which seems to Pierre to embody what he is feeling. It is thrice called a star, but unlike stars it moves through the sky. As a heavenly body, it is related in the novel to the higher morality of disinterested and ultimately divine love of mankind;[44] and, at the same time, by its motion and especially its seeming closeness to the earth it is more akin to the human feeling of exclusive love.

Unlike this and other descriptions in the novel of the stars, the description of the comet is erotic: thus it seems to Pierre, pierced to the heart by Cupid's arrow, to be like an arrow piercing the earth. It is no accident that the same elements in the comet that seem to Pierre to correspond to his love have seemed to others "to foretell all sorts of horrors and the end of the world." Here, the novel hints at the connection at the highest level between erotic love and the forces behind war and destruction. In both cases the very foundations of life seem to move as individuals and peoples change and couple according to God's dynamic harmonious plans.

Like other heavenly bodies in *War and Peace*, the comet represents ideals informing nature and the human soul. In this case, however, the ideals are of feeling rather than reason. So in part 9, when Pierre analyzes what has happened to him, he sees his love for Natasha not as an answer to the questions that plague him during his periods of doubt, but as an alternative to questioning at all.

> This terrifying question Why? For what?, which before had presented itself to him in the middle of every activity, now was replaced in him not by another question and not by an answer to the previous question, but by a representation of *her*.... All his doubts would disappear, not because she had answered the questions that had presented themselves to him, but because the representation of her carried him instantaneously into another, light sphere of spiritual activity, in which there could not be either innocent or guilty, into the sphere of beauty and love, for which it was worth living. (9.19)

For the time being and in this specific instance in the novel, Tolstoy separated genuine love and beauty, on the one hand, from reason, freedom, and moral responsibility, on the other. Or did he? The "representation" [*predstavlenie*] of Natasha that replaces thought makes life "worth living," and life is not worth living when Pierre or Prince Andrei see reality in the cold light of reason. Princess Maria or Platon Karataev, on the other hand, see a silver lining in every cloud and goodness even in the worst human beings. Is not their love for humankind related to, if not greater than, Pierre's love for one human being? At this point in *War and Peace* erotic love would seem to be depicted as pure expansiveness of soul endowed with the purposefulness of divine love. (It differs from divine love in its exclusiveness.) Thus did Tolstoy connect real and ideal in one feeling.

Moral synthesis came for the young Tolstoy from an idealism incorporating both reason and feeling in a divine being whom he in fact defined, in a diary passage of 1860, as "law and force" (48:23). In human life higher reason and feeling (law and force) meet and mesh in conscience. On the one hand, conscience is a feeling. As such it can be primary in man, understood as a sentient, not a rational being. It can influence a simple man like Mikhailov in "Sevastopol in May" through what seems like an almost mechanical sense of duty. On the other hand, it also collaborates with reason for both the Savoyard Vicar and Tolstoy. In 1847, while reading Rousseau, Tolstoy, in a passage that begins with the crossed-out phrase "I am completely in agreement with Rousseau," wrote that reason, "the pre-eminent faculty of man," can provide moral guidance if the individual withdraws from society and listens to its voice. And he proceeded to equate the principles of true reason with "everything that exists" (46:3). The Savoyard Vicar says that reason makes us know the good, and conscience makes us love it.[45] In the third draft of "The Raid" from the fall of 1852, in a passage that reads like an illustration of the Vicar's point, reason asks a question that conscience answers (2:234). For Tolstoy, then, and perhaps for the Vicar, too, conscience is the voice of divine reason. The two only seem to be opposed because, as Tolstoy had remarked in 1851 about the presumption of human reason, Providence "is the source of reason, and [human] reason wants to comprehend it" (46:62). He wrote also, this after his close study of the *Profession of Faith*, that metaphysics is "the study of thoughts which are not liable to expression in words" (25 November 1852; 46:150). Words, as creations of human reason, cannot encompass the divine. Conscience is a feeling, not a thought, precisely because the highest thought is not directly accessible to mankind. We must intuit God's reasons. So, according to the Vicar, conscience "is to the soul what instinct is to the body":[46] the one conveys physical law, the other moral law to man.

For the Savoyard Vicar, God Himself is both intelligent and good, but goodness in man is "the love of his fellows"; in God it is "the love of order" (ibid., 285). In a reasonable and free universe love of others helps keep order: it serves Goethe's "reason behind everything that lives." For both the Vicar and Tolstoy, harmony (order) in nature fosters peaceful, even loving coexistence among human beings. It is the ideal that provides synthesis for the analysis in works like "The Raid" and "The Woodcutting."

The whole purpose of education in *Emile*, as Rousseau makes clear in the opening paragraphs of the book, is to preserve the natural wholeness or unity of man within civil society. It thus may be said to address the problems of the disunity and alienation of civilized man raised the *Second Discourse*. In Tolstoy's articles on education written for *Iasnaia Poliana* in the early sixties, he also made unity and the natural harmony of the different parts of man the goal of education. In "Who Should Be Teaching Whom to Write: Should We Be Teaching the Peasant Lads, or They Us?" [*Komu u kogo uchitsia pisat', krestianskim rebiatam u nas ili nam u krestianskikh rebiat*], he acknowledged Rousseau as the source of these ideas:

> Man is born perfect—this is the great word uttered by Rousseau, and this word, like a rock, remains hard and true. Just born, man is the very image of the harmony of the true, the beautiful and the good. But every hour of life, every minute of time expands the spaces, the quantities and the time of these

relations, which at the time of his birth were in perfect harmony, and every step and every hour threaten the destruction of this harmony, and every successive step and every successive hour threaten new destruction and do not hold out hope for the restoration of destroyed harmony. . . . *Our ideal is behind, and not ahead of us.* (8:321–22)

Written just before he began *War and Peace*, Tolstoy's articles on education may be regarded as programmatic for the novel. As Patricia Carden has shown persuasively in "The Expressive Self in *War and Peace*," (psychological) unity is one goal of the education the various characters receive in the novel. This unity is natural and needs only to be restored: *"Our ideal is behind, and not ahead of us."*

So Tolstoy borrowed Rousseau's emphasis on unity while subscribing to the Savoyard Vicar's dualism. He reconciled these antimonies— one might say that he squared the circle—by claiming, like the Vicar, that conscience is natural and therefore, like self-love, tends toward the happiness of the individual. As self-love is an expression of the fundamental need of the soul for unity, so love of others and then conscience arise from a combination of its natural expansiveness and natural reason. Hence, in the musings inspired by reading the *Profession of Faith* in July 1853, Tolstoy could write about the *happiness* of soul and body.

And this explains, too, how, in a famous passage from "Lucerne," he could write:

> We have one, only one infallible guide, the universal spirit, penetrating us all together and each of us as individuals, implanting in each of us a yearning for what ought to be; that same spirit which in a tree orders it to grow toward the sun, in a flower orders it to turn to seed towards fall and in us orders us to cling unconsciously to one another. (5:25)

Carden calls this sentence a non sequitur because it moves "from the idea of growth to the idea of community."[47] It would have been more logical, she says, for Tolstoy to have ended the sentence "paraphrasing his favorite Rousseau, 'and which in us directs us to fill the sphere in which we live with our affections'" (ibid.). Carden attributes this inconsistency to Tolstoy's unthinking acceptance of the ideas of expressivism. In fact, the seed of the inconsistency that she correctly discerns is to be found in Rousseau himself, in the *Profession of Faith*. The Savoyard Vicar is the indispensable link between Rousseau the philosopher, for whom every truth could be disputed, and Tolstoy the poet and moralist, in whom the need for things to make moral sense was stronger than the need for truth itself. The universal spirit manifests itself in the *Profession of Faith* both as growth in nature and as conscience in us, the conscience that "orders us to cling unconsciously to one another." Indeed, inasmuch as conscience is fueled by natural love of others, it bespeaks a moral direction inherent within the motion of life itself, which therefore can be seen to express itself equally in growth and in community. Tolstoy, as we shall see, was not able to sustain his belief in the morality even of physical life. But *War and Peace* could not have been written if its author had not inherited, both directly and indirectly, this faith in the natural source of conscience and sociability from the Savoyard Vicar.

Three _____

The First Synthesis: Nature and the Young Tolstoy

> Everything spoke to me of beauty, happiness
> and virtue, [saying] that both one and the other
> were easy and possible for me, that one could
> not be without the other, and even that beauty,
> happiness and virtue were one and the same.
> (*Youth*)

BY NATURE Tolstoy meant everything outside the human soul that was made by God and not by man. This included the body, so that human beings are connected to nature in a way that they are not to civilization. In one sense, then, and in part, we *are* nature. Tolstoy saw that we *know* nature only indirectly, through our physical senses, and he revolutionized landscape description to bring it in line with this fact. Nature in his fiction is always drawn from the perspective and through the senses of a viewer present at the site. The effect is wonderfully vivid and concrete: the reader feels transported in body, as well as imagination, to the scene. The fine work done on this aspect of his writing has made his view of nature seem more modern, more like ours, than it in fact was.[1]

The purpose of this chapter is to reconstruct the young Tolstoy's attitude toward nature and particularly to explain what he meant by nature's goodness. The chapter is less an argument and more a description of the process of Tolstoy's development than others in the book. The reason for this is to show how Tolstoy's thoughts grew from relatively simple and perhaps one-sided beginnings to complex structures that more nearly evoke the complexity of the world as Tolstoy understood it. In at least one respect my task is an impossible one. I must arbitrarily choose one simple beginning point; whereas, in reality, Tolstoy was always juggling several perspectives at once.

I begin, then, with the relation of conscience and nature as it grew out of Tolstoy's reading of the Savoyard Vicar. Tolstoy's diary during the two years after he read the *Profession of Faith* is full of passages working out the implications of conscience and its place in the soul. Directly preceding his proclamation (on 29 June 1852) of conscience as mankind's moral guide, he pondered the question of immortality. And then immediately after it, and again obviously in response to the same key passage in the *Profession of Faith* about the conscience as voice of the soul (*Emile*, 286), he began to wrestle with the difficulty of distinguishing the voice of conscience from others in the psyche (46:128–29). This problem was resolved two weeks later (13 July 1852).

> *The yearning of the flesh is for personal good. The yearning of the soul is for the good of others.* It is impossible to assume the immortality of the soul, but it is possible not to assume its destruction. *If the body is separate from the soul and can be annihilated, what then proves the annihilation of the soul? Suicide is the most striking expression and proof of the soul; and its [suicide's] existence is proof of its [the soul's] immortality.* I have seen that the body dies; therefore I assume *that mine will die too; but nothing has shown me that the soul dies, therefore I say that it is immortal—so far as I can understand. The concept of eternity is a disease of the mind.*[2]

Tolstoy aggressively asserted the existence of the soul. He developed his argument about the soul's immortality using the Vicar's method of philosophically minding his own business; that is, metaphysics provided the foundation for morality and otherwise was left mysterious. The soul was necessary both to provide a moral guide and to make us free, morally responsible beings and Tolstoy proved its immortality "*so far as I can understand [po moim poniatiiam].*" Beyond that, "*the concept of eternity is a disease of the mind.*" Tolstoy disciplined his "big brain" not to overstep its natural powers. Not it, but morality was to be served in Tolstoyan metaphysics, which would be limited to the assertion that the existence of the soul cannot be empirically disproved.[3] He defined the message of conscience, the voice of the soul, as "the good of others." This conformed both to his understanding of morality from his earliest writings (March–May 1847; 46:267–68) and to the Vicar's elaboration of his position in the paragraphs following the passage cited above.[4] It also carried the notion of conscience beyond standards of reasonable justice based on what is owed each individual to a more Christian standard of love of others. This standard was "to the soul as instinct is to the body": it was implanted in us by God to allow us to overcome self-love when necessary.

The two goals of soul and body could obviously come into conflict. To avoid this and to keep the self unified, the young optimist set out to prove two maxims. "Happiness is virtue": this was to be the "main idea" of the didactic novel (*Four Epochs of Life*) that he set out to write in 1852 (4:363). The lesson of *Youth* was to be similar: "beauty, happiness, and virtue were one and the same thing" (2:82). This lesson, significantly, comes to Nikolenka, the narrator and hero of the story, from nature. Tolstoy's second and related maxim was that civilization has made us bad; by nature we were good. He wanted to show that the natural way of life includes both our desire for personal happiness and our desire for self-sacrifice. Only then could he portray human beings as unified within themselves and unified with nature. Nature therefore became the first grand synthesis within which the contradictions inherent in human nature, as Tolstoy understood it, could be reconciled.

Tolstoy's Understanding of Nature in the Early 1850s

Tolstoy's contemporaries welcomed in his art and in the man himself a kinship to nature that made him well suited to carry the banner of the new realism. Grigor'ev's comparison between Turgenev, who worships, and Tolstoy, who wants to *be* the "soil," echoes contemporary opinion about the two writers. We need only substitute the word *nature* for *soil*, for instance, to grasp what Nekrasov found so compelling in the chapter "Thunderstorm" in *Adolescence*. (He wrote Tolstoy that "such things as the description of the summer road and the thunderstorm . . . will give this story a long life in our literature."[5]) Turgenev might gaze at a storm and describe it reverently, while noting its cruel inhumanity.[6] In Tolstoy Nekrasov sensed a new force in Russian literature that would embrace the storm itself, as Nikolenka does in "Thunderstorm."[7]

Tolstoy's "naturalism" could take more than one form, however. It fueled that "nihilism," that rejection of culture that so aggravated the cultivated leaders of the Russian intelligentsia when Tolstoy appeared among them. In the two works before 1856 in which nature plays a decisive role, "The Raid" [*Nabeg*] and "The Woodfelling" [*Rubka lesa*], nature and human life are contrasted, not likened. In both works Tolstoy emphasized "naturalness [*estestvennost'*]" in the world of nature and artificiality in the world of man."[8] In the imagery of darkness in "The Raid," for instance, Tolstoy contrasted the real unity of nature with an illusory unity in human life (ibid., 44–47). The narrator of "The Raid" speaks of "the conciliatory beauty and strength" of nature (chapter 6); "The Woodfelling" ends in the "tranquil harmony" of the night (chapter 13). In both stories human life with its wars and senseless deaths seems estranged from or alien to the harmony of nature. The stories reiterate the cry of the Savoyard Vicar that: "The picture of nature had presented me with only harmony and proportion; that of mankind presents me with only confusion and disorder! Concert reigns among the elements, and men are in chaos!"[9]

Tolstoy wrote "The Raid" from 7 April to 24 December 1852. The theme of nature emerged only in the third redaction,[10] that is, after the summer when Tolstoy reread all of Rousseau. As we have seen in the previous chapter, the twin themes of conscience, the "inner voice" that links us with nature, and harmonious nature itself, contrasted with the chaos of human life, date from this crucial renewed acquaintance with the writings of Rousseau. Nature plays a similar role in the Sevastopol sketches—the most striking instance of this is chapter 14 of "Sevastopol in May"—and indeed throughout Tolstoy's career. The opening paragraph of *Resurrection* is a tribute to the persistence of this Rousseauian theme.

A Maturing Philosophy of Nature (Tolstoy and Fet)

The lover of nature who arrived in Petersburg in 1855 could not have been attracted by mere aesthetes. The men of the forties did not think of themselves as enemies of "reality": indeed when Chernyshevsky first published his thesis, Botkin welcomed it in a letter to Turgenev precisely because it made nature, or reality, the basis of art. Botkin agreed with the "realist school" [*real'naia shkola*], by which he meant Chernyshevsky's so-called critical realism, that art is not absolute, not opposed to nature. "Poetry is insight into the innermost essence of things . . . that is, reality."[11] What offended Botkin and the others was Chernyshevsky's narrowing of the definition of reality, his "biologism."[12]

This crucial disagreement about what comprises "reality" comes out in those passages in P. V. Annenkov's and Chernyshevsky's articles about Tolstoy in which they described the psychological process.[13] It is clear from Annenkov's description of Tolstoyan psychology that Annenkov, like Chernyshevsky, believed that nature and the self were fundamentally the same. This is what he meant when he wrote that "nature itself, with no help from the outside, emits the first spark of thought, the first trace of feeling and the first inclination [of will]." The principles of nature, as opposed to their concrete realizations, are ideals, and these ideals are expressed (in different ways) both in nature and in the human psyche.

It was the combination of their belief in the soul *and* their belief in the inner relation of the soul and nature that made the aesthetes so attractive to the young Tolstoy when he arrived in the capital. The terrible "troglodit" who exposed the hypocrisy of human life in light of the truths of nature was ready to take a stand against Gogolian or Thackerayan "critical realism" in favor of positive ideals based on nature. We cannot understand either *War and Peace* or the author's positive striv-ings in the fifties unless we can recapture his vision, shared with and encouraged by his friends, of the direct, beneficial relation between man and nature, the subjective and objective worlds. The contempo-rary whom he most resembles in this respect is the poet Fet, who be-came Tolstoy's closest literary friend during the writing of *War and Peace*. Perhaps the best way to illustrate the importance of nature for Tolstoy at this time would be to contrast present day readings of A. A. Fet with Tolstoy's understanding of his friend's poetry. We will see at the same time how the idea of the direct relation of man and nature was translated into art, and how Tolstoy learned not only from critics but from his fellow writers as well.

In a letter to Botkin dated 9 July 1857, Tolstoy praised the *liricheskaia derzost'*, the "lyrical daring," of two lines from a new poem, "Eshche maiskaia noch'" [May Night Once Again]:

> v vozdukhe za pesn'iu solov'inoi
> Raznositsia trevoga i liubov'.
>
> [in the air after the nightingale's song
> Uneasiness and love resound]

The Fet scholar B. Ia. Bukhshtab in a long quote from *Lev Tolstoy: The Seventies* [*Lev Tolstoi: Semidesiatye gody*] borrows Eikhenbaum's defini-tion of lyrical daring as "grasping subtle shades of psychic life and interweaving them with nature description."[14] Elsewhere Bukhshtab writes of Fet's poetry that "lyrical emotion as it were expands in nature, infecting it with feelings of the lyrical 'I,' unifying the world by the mood of the poet" (ibid., 82). Nature description for Fet "despite all its accuracy and concreteness . . . always serves as a means for the expres-sion of lyrical feeling" (ibid., 102).

The modern reader may accept this purely psychological reading of Fet's poetry. For Tolstoy himself and his friends in the fifties the poetry meant something more. For them the lines that so struck Tolstoy were examples of a direct interaction of the self and nature possible because both were emanations of the same metaphysical essence. Tolstoy would have interpreted the two lines from "May Night Once Again" to mean that the nightingale's song sparks "uneasiness and love" in the soul of the poet. The final verse of the poem indicates that Fet himself intended it to be read this way:

> Het, nikogda nezhnei i bestelesnei
> Tvoi lik, o noch', ne mog menia tomit'!
> Opiat' k tebia idu s nevol'noi pesnei,
> Nevol'noi—i poslednei, mozhet' byt'.

[No, never more tenderly and incorporeally
Could your face, o night, torment me!
Again I approach you with an involuntary song,
Involuntary—and perhaps the last one.]

The poet has become the nightingale, but a conscious, speaking one, responding to the night with a song that has lyrics of "uneasiness and love," as well as melody. Fet repeats the word *involuntary* to stress how the spring night "torments" him, evokes his song in him, how, in other words, nature itself is singing through him. The "lyrical daring" of this poem consists precisely in Fet's having transcended the merely psychological to create a poetic image of the self and nature as really the same.

Fet wrote and published this poem in 1857, after the appearance in *The Contemporary* [*Sovremennik*] of Botkin's article "A. A. Fet" (January 1857). Botkin, as he confided to Turgenev, used this piece to make a programmatic statement about the nature of poetry and art.[15] In this spirit he divided it into two parts: the first, a general discussion of art and philosophy; the second, a discussion of Fet's poetry. Botkin was the first to write of what became known as Fet's lyric subjectivity, saying of Fet's poems about nature that "the main thing consists not in the picture of nature itself, but in that poetic feeling that is aroused in us by nature; thus nature appears here only as the occasion, the means for the expression of poetic feeling."[16]

This statement can be understood only within the philosophical framework elaborated in the first part of Botkin's article. Sounding there very much like Tolstoy in the second epilogue to *War and Peace*, Botkin wrote, "Those same laws that produce the phenomenon of nature also establish the basis of phenomena occurring in our psychic life [*v nashem dukhe*]." This did not mean that human beings are animals, but that

> all phenomena of the human spirit [*dukh*] take place according to laws inherent in it [and] profoundly related to the common life of the universe. We live by the same spirit as nature—we are that very same nature, but animated [*odukhotvorennye*] and conscious of ourselves. The dumb poetry of nature is our conscious poetry: it is given to us to express this dumb poetry of nature. (Ibid., 358)

Botkin was speaking here as a student of Schelling's *Naturphilosophie*, according to which the essence of nature is to be found in "unifying, 'living' forces,"[17] which also animate human beings. Nature sings through us and we give it language. The "poetic feeling" that dominates nature in Fet's poetry is therefore itself an emanation of nature.

Botkin did not see Fet's poetry as self-consciously philosophical. In a sentimental, that is, self-conscious, world it was naive. Fet captured the inner workings of the soul but did not reflect on them; in this sense he was a naive child.[18] As a rare example of a poem that actually depicts the creation of poetry, Botkin cited the closing stanza of "Ia prishel k tebe s privetom" [I came to you with a greeting; 1843]:

Rasskazat', chto otovsiudu
Na menia vesel'em veet,
Chto ne znaiu sam, chto budu
Pet',—no tol'ko pesnia zreet.

[To say that from all around
Merriment is wafting over me,
That I myself don't know what I will
Sing—but only that a song is ripening.]

As in "May Night Once Again," nature imparts a feeling to the poet (" . . . from all around / Merriment is wafting over me"), and then the poet to his own surprise becomes the voice of nature. I have remarked the repetition in "I Came to You with a Greeting" of the word "involuntary." This emphasis no doubt reflects Fet's own reading of Botkin, who described Fet's poetry several times in his article as "involuntary" [nevol'no, nevol'nyi]. I leave aside whether the poetic voice of a man who got his start in poetry under the tutelage of Apollon Grigor'ev could truly have been naive.[19] An intimate of the Contemporary circle from 1853 on, inspired then by his friends to an unprecedented outpouring of poetry (ibid., 31), Fet certainly learned from his brother-in-law Botkin's understanding of his poetry. If not philosophical itself, his "lyrical daring" can hardly be considered naive. It was nurtured under the same philosophical influences that Tolstoy felt after his arrival in Petersburg. The poem that Tolstoy so admired reads like a poetic illustration of Botkin's thesis.

Tolstoy himself certainly read Fet's poetry with Botkin's article in mind. He greeted the article with the greatest enthusiasm, calling it in a letter to the author a "catechism of poetry." He wrote further that "if you don't take up criticism seriously, then you don't love literature" (20 January 1857; 60:152). And he remembered the article long after, praising it in a conversation with V. F. Lazurskii in 1894.[20] Eikhenbaum says of Tolstoy's acquaintance with Fet's poetry that "it imparted to this 'dialectic of the soul' a special lyric tone which it had lacked before."[21]

The second chapter of Youth ("Spring") ends with a fine example of this tone and with an explanation for it:

Some kind of feeling new to me, extremely strong and pleasant, suddenly penetrated my soul. The wet earth, on which here and there bright green blades of grass with little yellow stems had pushed through, the little streams, sparkling in the sun, along which pieces of earth and woodchips were swirling, the reddening twigs of lilac with swollen buds, swaying under my very window, the busy chirping of little birds stirring in this bush, the blackish fence, wet from snow melting on it, but mainly—this fragrant damp air and joyful sun spoke to me audibly, clearly about something new and beautiful, which, although I cannot transmit it as it was spoken to me, I will try to transmit as I perceived it—everything spoke to me of beauty, happiness and virtue, [saying] that both one and the other were easy and possible for me, that one could not be without the other, and even that beauty, happiness and virtue were one and the same. "How could I not have understood this, how bad I was before, how I could and can be good and happy in the future!" I said to myself. "I must quickly, quickly, this very moment become a different person and begin to live differently." Despite this, however, I still sat for a long time at the window, dreaming and doing nothing. Have you ever during the summer lain down to sleep during the day in cloudy, rainy weather and, awakening at sunset, opened your eyes and, in the widening quadrangle of the window, from under the linen shade, which, billowing, beat like a switch against the windowpane, seen the shady, violet-coloured side of the avenue of lime trees, wet from rain, and the damp garden path, illuminated by bright slanting rays, heard suddenly the merry life of birds in the garden and seen insects, translucent in the sun, which hover in the window opening, felt the scent of air after a rain and thought: "How could I not be ashamed to sleep through such an evening"—and hurriedly jumped up to go into the garden and rejoice at life? If this has happened, then it is an image of that strong feeling which I experienced then.

A feeling "penetrated" Nikolenka. The air and sun "spoke" to him "audibly, clearly." Here is that direct relation between the human soul and nature of which Botkin had written in his article. Then—beginning with the words "Have you ever"—comes the lyric "image [*obrazchik*] of that strong feeling which I experienced then." It is clear from the context that in writing this Nikolenka is not merely using nature subjectively, to express a feeling. It almost seems as if the opposite is true: that nature uses him. The physical awakening and resurrection that takes place in spring is equivalent to a moral awakening in the soul and can inspire it. This little vignette invites the reader to share Nikolenka's direct communication with nature detailed in the first half of the paragraph. It also fosters an unprecedented closeness between writer and reader. If the writer can exactly re-create what he perceived, then he and his reader can receive the same feeling from nature.

In an important sense the experience Tolstoy described in this passage was understood by him as objective. Any uncorrupted human being, and even a sensitive corrupted one, would be moved as Nikolenka is. A subjective, that is, inner, experience of goodness has a corresponding, objective reality in nature. The belief in the possibility of such communication with nature and between writer and reader lays the groundwork for Tolstoy's own version of "lyrical daring." Eikhenbaum's definition of this phenomemon is not daring enough. Technically, Tolstoy did, as Eikhenbaum says, "grasp subtle shades of psychic life and interweave them with nature description." What Tolstoy meant by doing this, however, was to show the meeting and intermingling of nature and the self at the exact point where they are the same and cannot be separated.

What was unique about Tolstoy's "lyrical daring" and differentiated it from Fet's was the belief that the conscience was natural and that feelings of goodness (self-sacrifice), as well as feelings connected with healthy self-love, could come from nature. Hence the difference between the morality of the "lyrical daring" illustrated in the passage from *Youth* and the pure sensuality of Fet's poetry.

Botkin and the Exploration of the Feelings

With the exception of Annenkov, Tolstoy's new friends believed that the basis of the interrelation of the self and nature was purely sensuous. As illustrated in Botkin's article, human beings lend consciousness, or higher reason, to nature, giving it a perfection in art that it did not possess in reality. But nature, in turn, inspires human beings with the passion and truth necessary for life and art. Consciousness without nature was "abstract" or too theoretical, as Grigor'ev complained apropos of the Chernyshevskian radicals. It created Turgenev's superfluous man, whose excessive consciousness and alienation from nature made him, in Turgenev's vivid image, like a dog whose back legs have been run over by a cart.[22] It is therefore not surprising that the so-called aesthetes emphasized feeling in contradistinction to the critical reason of the radicals. This emphasis had its effect on Tolstoy.

The young officer rode into Petersburg astride his moral high horse. The last entries in his diary before arriving in the capital were written in the mood of moral purity supported, as we know although Tolstoy's friends did not, by a moral idealism which he had already embraced. In September 1855, Tolstoy declared that he intended to write only with "thought" and with a [moral] "goal" (47:60). Here spoke the voice of the stern judge of Sevastopol, who exposed the base motives of heroes with Thackerayan irony and precision (Tolstoy had read *Vanity Fair* in June [47:45]) and celebrated Truth from the vantage point of Higher Reason. Tolstoy's new friends espoused an idealism based more on feeling than reason and so, during the early Petersburg years, the focus of his interest shifted, from reason to the feelings. Briefly, but with lasting results for his art, Tolstoy explored, without disapproval and usually approvingly, the whole range of possible sensations, from the physiological reactions of the body to ecstasies of romantic love.

V. P. Botkin became and remained one of Tolstoy's closest Petersburg friends. Botkin was an erudite man who had played an important role in the intellectual life of the forties. He had been an intimate of Belinsky, who had relied extensively on Botkin's knowledge of German philosophy in developing his own theoretical positions.[23] In the fifties Botkin regarded himself and was regarded by others of his generation as the one among them who had best understood Belinsky. He was also a hedonist who took paganism as his religion.[24] He loved everything sensuous, from the simple pleasures of nature—he recommended to Turgenev that for the purest happiness he should become a plant[25]—to escapades in Paris so debauched that they shocked even his sophisticated friends.[26] Turgenev once said of him that he should be buried with a truffle in his mouth (ibid., 104). Botkin's sensitivity to all stimuli of spirit and flesh extended to a great love and understanding of the arts, of philosophy, poetry, and music. The high and the low were united in him by his sensuality: he loved the combination of sumptuous dinners and conversation whose high tone he set himself. The son of a wealthy merchant, Botkin fit perfectly into an aristocratic milieu that valued intelligence, good taste, and sensitivity. He was not nobly virtuous—he was famous for his fearfulness, for instance[27]—but nothing beautiful was alien to him. Even in his old age, when Tolstoy claimed to have forgotten everything he had learned from his friends in the fifties, he still recalled Botkin's unfailing artistic taste.[28]

Tolstoy and Botkin were already close friends by May 1856. At that time, during Tolstoy's short stay in Moscow (from May 17 to 27) on the way to Iasnaia Poliana, he visited Botkin twice at his dacha in Kuncevo, the first time on the day of his arrival. Likewise, in November 1856, on his first day in Moscow he went straight to Botkin's. During December and January of that winter, whenever the two men were in the same city they saw each other almost every day.[29] They remained close at least until 1859, when Tolstoy consulted frequently with his friend about *Family Happiness*. No letters between the two survive after 1862; but Sreznevskii is so impressed by the intensity of their friendship that he speculates that their correspondence in the sixties must have been lost (ibid.). In any case, Tolstoy still felt close enough to Botkin in 1865 to invite him, through Fet, whom Botkin was visiting, to visit Iasnaia Poliana (61:83). For his part, Botkin followed Tolstoy's career up to the end of his life. Annenkov reports that during his last winter, spent in Rome, he listened to *War and Peace* with great pleasure and praised it highly.[30]

In trying to understand Tolstoy's attraction to Botkin, we must remember two things: Botkin was no ordinary hedonist, but a philosophical one; and Tolstoy himself had a sensual nature. The theoretical justification that Botkin provided gave Tolstoy a unique chance to explore his sensuality as something positive in itself. The diary of summer 1856 reveals that Tolstoy took full advantage of this opportunity. It begins during his first visit to Kuncevo, Botkin's dacha outside Moscow:[31] "After dinner I rode to Kuncevo. I found an empty and most charming dacha—books, cigars, a glass of water sweating from the ice that was melting in it" (47:73). These lines, especially the image of the glass, jump from the page because they are so uncharacteristic of Tolstoy, who almost never tries to capture tactile beauty for its own sake. During the summer at Iasnaia Poliana that follows directly on Tolstoy's visits to Kuncevo, he kept a notebook with nature description more extensive than any in the diary since the Caucasus in 1851 (47:177–96). The Caucasian diary had been remarkable for its elevated tone (46:61– 66). The diary of the summer of 1856 is earthy. Tolstoy's notebook contains observations of the intimate functions of his own body and their place in nature (47:177, 179), and the diary comments on Pushkin, Gogol, and Goethe's *Sorrows of Young Werther*, as Tolstoy read the poets most admired by his friends.[32] During this period Tolstoy indulged without stint his love of music, most frequently with Botkin, with whom he shared this passion.[33] And finally there were women. During the winter season of 1856–1857, he even kept a mistress, one A. P., "a clever girl and a passionate one."[34] Beginning in the summer of 1858 he had a torrid love affair with a married peasant woman named Aksinia Bazukina from a village near Iasnaia Poliana, an affair that produced an illegitimate son.[35]

As Tolstoy himself had written in 1847, the source of all feeling is love (46:267). From the beginning of 1856 on, Tolstoy was in love with love, physical and spiritual alike. On 21 March 1856 he wrote that his main mistake in life had been to allow his mind to replace feeling (47:68). On 15 April, during Easter, he wrote "Christ is risen [the Orthodox greeting at Easter], all who love me. And I love everyone" (ibid.). His infatuation with love continued into the fall, when he wrote (on 16 December) that "love, love, it alone unerringly gives happiness" (47:100). During his trip abroad in 1857, in Clarens, Switzerland, where he stayed from 9 April to 15 May (Old Calendar), he declared that "love is choking me, physical and ideal love" (47:129).

N. V. Stankevich, whose influence on Tolstoy I will discuss below, had written in 1835 that

> Love is a chemical process in the nonorganic kingdom, becomes occasionally a sensation in plants, grows broader and more powerful in animals, and in man receives its highest significance—as does everything in nature . . . Christianity in its purest form is the religion of love . . . for me, love is a religion.[36]

Tolstoy did not actually read this passage, because it did not appear in Annenkov's 1857 edition of Stankevich's correspondence. What a "chemical process" has to do with love in man becomes clear from a document by Stankevich which Tolstoy probably did read, entitled "My Metaphysics," written in 1833.[37] There Stankevich states that growth is the main principle of nature, and human will is linked to nature because it, too, is motion (ibid., 17, 21–22). Tolstoy, too, from his earliest writings, believed the essence of man to be will, not reason (because "to think you have to want to think" [2:343]). From Stankevich and his heirs he came to understand the connection of will with life in general: will is the form that motion takes in self-propelled beings. As Tolstoy put it in *War and Peace*, "The forces of nature are outside us and not known to us through consciousness and we call these forces gravity, inertia, electricity, animal vitality, and so on; but we are conscious of the force of life in man and we call it freedom" (second epilogue).

The essence of man and nature is motion. This motion expresses itself as various forces (including "animal vitality") in nature and as "freedom," or the will in man. But it is, in fact, the same thing, in Turgenev's words from *Fathers and Children*, "a wide wave of life, ceaselessly rolling both around us and within us" (chapter 26). Feelings, as motions, arise from this "wide wave of life . . . within us" and therefore have an intimate connection with nature. It is not surprising then to find that the Petersburg Tolstoy exalted nature along with love. Tolstoy began his new series of notebooks with their detailed nature descriptions on 23 May 1856. On the same day he wrote, "At Botkin's, at Kuncevo and on the road there, I reveled in nature to the point of tears" (47:75). The next day he continued, "Four feelings have possessed me with unusual force: love, the melancholy of remorse (which, however, is pleasant), the desire to marry (in order to escape this melancholy) and—[the feeling of] nature" (ibid.). Feeling united man and nature, and under the influence of his Petersburg friends Tolstoy explored the artistic and philosophic implications of this unity.

Sterne

Botkin's celebration of sensuousness as a good in itself may have reminded Tolstoy of an earlier stage in his education, namely, his fascination with the works of Laurence Sterne. This may be why a phrase from Sterne floats into a diary description of a minor episode involving Botkin and Apollon Grigor'ev. Returning home from a reading of "Two Hussars" [*Dva gusara*] at the home of A. A. Tolstaia,

> [I found a note] from Vas'ka [Botkin] and Apoloshka [Grigor'ev] and rejoiced exceedingly, like a man in love. As if everything became light. — Yes, the best means for true happiness in life is this: without any laws to let out from oneself in all directions, like a spider, a sticky web of love and to catch in it everything that comes along, an old woman, and a child, and a woman, and a policeman. (5 May 1856; 46:71)

The sticky web of love comes originally from Sterne's *Sentimental Journey Through France and Italy* where Sterne justifies his hero's, Yorick's, lust for a chamber maid as a feeling inseparable from all the others, including kindness:

> "If nature has so wove her web of kindness, that some threads of love and desire are entangled with the piece—must the whole web be rent in drawing them out?—Whip me such stoics, great governor of nature!" said I to myself—Wherever thy providence shall place me for the trials of my virtue— whatever is my danger—whatever is my situation—let me feel the movements which rise out of it, and which belong to me as a man—and if I govern them as a good one—I will trust the issues to thy judgment, for thou hast made us—and not we ourselves.[38]

Morson shows clearly how Tolstoy imbibed Lockean psychology from his study of *Tristram Shandy*. At every moment a number of impressions and sentiments flood our souls. Only a healthy reason, or in Sterne's terms, judgment, can select from among these sentiments so that we can act, but, as Morson says, that reason, which was so important to Locke (and Sterne), is not us, at least as we are in the present moment.[39] We *are* our impressions and feelings. It is this understanding of the self as all sensitivity that welled back up in Tolstoy under the influence of Botkin and his circle.

In 1851 Tolstoy wrote "A History of Yesterday" with Sterne in mind, and he translated the *Sentimental Journey* when he was beginning work on *Childhood*.[40] In 1853 he borrowed the passage from Sterne about the web of kindness (from "If nature" to "in drawing them out") as the epigraph to an early draft of "The Maids' Room," a chapter (17 in the final version) of *Adolescence* (2:366). Here he depicted Nikolenka's mixed feelings of lust and love for the servant girl Masha. The web of love then appears on its own and translated into Russian in 1856, in the diary entry about Botkin and Grigor'ev, and again in *The Cossacks*, where Olenin, in an ecstasy of self-sacrifice, conceding Marianka to Lukashka, vows to capture all around him in "a web of love" (chap. 28). When Tolstoy wrote about Botkin and Grigor'ev, he was evoking the moral power of feeling itself, as he said, "without any laws."

It is not clear from the *Sentimental Journey* as we have presented it so far, however, why feeling itself, without benefit of judgment, should be moral. The fact is that, in Russia as in England, the Sterne who parodied English novels coexisted with a more sensitive, or sentimental Sterne. Tolstoy revealed his proclivity for this Sterne by choosing to translate the *Sentimental Journey* rather than the more satiric *Tristram Shandy*,[41] but even in the latter novel he loved the sentimental passages.

This point is important enough to warrant an example. On 4 June 1851 Tolstoy copied the following passage from *Tristram Shandy* into his diary:

L'esprit délateur, qui alla porter a jurement rougit en la deposant et l'ange chargé de tenir les registres laissa tomber une larme sur ce mot en l'inscrivant et l'effaça. (46:79)

[The ACCUSING SPIRIT which flew up to heaven's chancery with the oath, blush'd as he gave it in; — and the RECORDING ANGEL as he wrote it down, dropp'd a tear upon the word, and blotted it out for ever.]

These lines come from chapter 168, or volume 6, chapter 8, of *Tristram Shandy*, from the story of Captain LeFever, in which Uncle Toby's generosity most clearly emerges.[42] Clear parallels exist between the scene of the dying Captain and Uncle Toby, and that in "The Raid" of the dying Alanin and Khlopov. A sentimental angel like those in the passage from Sterne appears in *Childhood* in the chapter of the same name in which Tolstoy eulogized childhood: "Where are those burning prayers? Where is the best gift—those pure tears of ecstasy? An Angel-Comforter flew down, with a smile he wiped away those tears and called up sweet visions to the unspoiled childish imagination" (1:45). For Tolstoy, the "flux of feelings," while not itself moral, had a moral function because the world itself was a moral place, organized by moral ideals. The lines from *Childhood* illustrate precisely this moral function. Because they submit so completely to the natural flux of feelings and sensations, children are naturally moderate and naturally good. No matter how powerful any one feeling may be, an "Angel-

Comforter," that is, the simple flux of feeling in the child's soul, will carry it away and other feelings will replace it. The child lacks a negative attribute of adults, a strong ego, which could stem the flow of feeling in the soul.

The sentimentality of Sterne appealed to Tolstoy, indeed he may have exaggerated it, because of the young Tolstoy's own attraction to a metaphysical idealism that did not belittle the physical world and the body. He thus no doubt attentively read a later passage in the *Sentimental Journey* in which Yorick again finds strands of lust and compassion intertwined in his soul. Yorick addresses first his "sensibility" and then its source directly:

> Dear sensibility! source inexhausted of all that's precious in our joys, or costly in our sorrows! thou chainest thy martyr down upon his bed of straw—and 'tis thou who lifts him up to HEAVEN—eternal fountain of our feelings!—'tis here I trace thee—and this is thy divinity which stirs within me—not, that in some sad and sickening moments: '*my soul shrinks back upon herself, and startles at destruction*'—mere pomp of words!—but that I feel some generous joys and generous cares beyond myself—all comes from thee, great - great SENSORIUM of the world! which vibrates, if a hair of our heads but falls upon the ground, in the remotest desert of thy creation.[43]

When Tolstoy proclaimed his intention of capturing everyone in a "web of love," he believed for the moment at least in an ideal based on feeling alone, a "great Sensorium" that makes moral sense of our lives "without any laws," that is, directly through feelings, without recourse to human reason. At this moment Tolstoy was at the peak of the wave of feeling unleased in him by his contact with his Petersburg friends.

N. V. Stankevich

For all his enthusiastic espousal of feeling during the Petersburg period, however, Tolstoy even then did not forsake his ideal of reason. Grigoriev warned Fet against this side of Tolstoy's nature when he wrote on 4 January 1858: "If one looks at his nature through his works, [one sees that] Tolstoy has set himself the task of *persecuting*, even with a certain violence, the musically elusive in life, in the moral world, in art. In this for the time being lies his strength, in it is his weakness as well."[44] The "musically elusive" [*muzykal'no neulovimoe*] is the pure feeling that Grigor'ev as a Schellingian[45] wholeheartedly embraced. As Pavel Gromov writes in distinguishing Tolstoy and Fet, the novelist was too rational and too moral for the poet: Fet wanted to expel from his art what was essential to the art of Tolstoy.[46]

If Grigor'ev and Tolstoy's other friends disapproved of his love of reason and morality, he found an ally in someone else whom he knew only through his writings: N. V. Stankevich. Like Tolstoy, or perhaps, more precisely, as Tolstoy aspired to be, Stankevich was an idealist who never lost faith in the existence of absolute truths.[47] He headed a literary and philosophical circle at Moscow University from 1832 to 1834, and then, after graduation, continued his studies, consulting with and advising his friends, until his death in 1840. Chizhevski calls him the "boss of the Russian Hegelians."[48] During his first years at the university he studied the German poets, especially Goethe and Schiller[49] and then took up philosophy, going from Schelling to Kant, and on to Hegel. Stankevich published very little, but, as a mentor of Bakunin, Belinsky, Turgenev, and others, he affected the development of Russian culture.

Stankevich exerted, moreover, a direct as well as an indirect influence on the fifties. During that decade, concern that the lessons of German idealism, exemplified in the character and thought of Stankevich, might be lost led Annenkov to collect Stankevich's letters and a few writings and publish them. *Nikolai Vladimirovich Stankevich: His Correspondence and Biography* [*Nikolai Vladimirovich Stankevich: Perepiska ego i biografiia*] came out in 1857 to universal acclaim from the Left as well as the Right.[50]

As an intimate of Annenkov, whose biography of Pushkin he had read enthusiastically in the summer of 1856 (47:80), Tolstoy was no doubt initiated into the cult of Stankevich soon after his arrival in Petersburg. He also would have learned about Stankevich from Turgenev, who had known him in Berlin and Rome during the last months of Stankevich's life. Annenkov, who had not known Stankevich personally, asked Turgenev to write up his reminiscences for use in the biography. Turgenev obliged, and Annenkov made extensive use of the short memoir that resulted.[51]

The editors of Turgenev's *Complete Works* [PSS] speculate that he wrote this memoir during the summer of 1856 because Stankevich, as Turgenev described him, physically resembled Tolstoy (ibid., 606). That summer—the summer of Tolstoy's greatest ecstasy over love—Turgenev and Tolstoy were very close, and Tolstoy visited the older man on his estate. Turgenev's confounding of the physical appearance of Tolstoy and Stankevich no doubt reflects his belief that the two were spiritually akin. Tolstoy amazed his older friend by his ability to enter into the inner lives even of animals. On a walk with Turgenev Tolstoy stopped before an old gelding and began to tell him about the animal: "He not only put himself in the horse's place, but he drew me into the position of the unhappy creature. I couldn't contain myself and said:

Listen, Lev Nikolaevich, really, you were once a horse. You really ought to depict the inner state of a horse."[52] Stankevich, according to Turgenev, also empathized strongly with others. In the same paragraph in which Turgenev later described Stankevich's physical appearance, he actually mentioned Tolstoy:

> Stankevich had such an effect on others, because he didn't think about himself, he took a genuine interest in each person and, seeming himself not to notice it, drew him after himself into the realm of the Ideal. No one argued as humanely, as beautifully [*prekrasno*] as he did. There wasn't a trace of phrase-mongering in him—even Tolstoy (L. N.) wouldn't have been able to find any in him.[53]

The memoir, written for Annenkov's use rather than for publication, contains a private joke: Tolstoy often questioned Turgenev's own sincerity and accused him of "phrase-mongering." Perhaps Turgenev intended implicitly to criticize Tolstoy here by juxtaposing the younger man's harshness with Stankevich's humanity. But elsewhere, as in the anecdote about the horse, it is clear that Turgenev admired Tolstoy for some of the same qualities he praised in Stankevich. Like Stankevich, Tolstoy was perfectly sincere, and, like him, he "took a genuine interest in each person."

Whether on his own, or more likely from the suggestions of his friends, Tolstoy himself felt close to Stankevich. When, in the summer of 1858, he himself finally read the *Correspondence*, he wrote A. A. Tolstaia: "I have never loved anyone as much as this man whom I have never seen. What purity, what tenderness, what love he is full of . . . " (60:274). It is not by chance, of course, that Tolstoy praised Stankevich for his love. Critics have long used this letter (and one to V. N. Chicherin from the same time [60:273]) to point out the similarities between Tolstoy's and Stankevich's "religion of love."[54] Kupreianova, who devotes twelve dense pages to the relation between the social thought of the two,[55] states categorically that "Stankevich and his circle were of all the tendencies in Russian social thought the closest to Tolstoy."

Love occupied a central place in the thought of both Tolstoy and Stankevich: through it alone the individual is united with other people and with nature (ibid., 75). For both, however, "love is not opposed to 'reason' [*razumenie*] but is its 'instinctive' manifestation" (ibid., 76). Motion or feeling in lower beings turns into love in man because, according to Stankevich, man is both a microcosm of nature and the only direct (conscious) expression of higher reason.[56] For Stankevich, physical love was only an occasion for experiencing the higher love released by higher reason. So in all three of Stankevich's romances (discussed in

Annenkov's biography), he sought "prekrasnye prizraki" [beautiful spirits], but found instead "zemnoe chuvstvo" [earthly feeling] and broke off with his beloved.[57] Stankevich kept falling in love, but he battled with "the offensive perfection of nature" (ibid., 77) that makes us go from the spiritual state of being in love to the physical act of consummation. He especially loved Schiller's poem *Resignation*, in which hope and pleasure are mutually exclusive states (ibid., 80).

In the letter to A. A. Tolstaia, Tolstoy exclaimed over Stankevich's "purity . . . tenderness . . . [and] love" (60:274). For Tolstoy, as for Stankevich, that love was purified and made disinterested by reason. So Tolstoy himself distinguished between "ideal and physical love" (47:129). He differed from his hero, however, in his definition of nature. When Stankevich visited the Caucasus in 1836, its wildness overwhelmed him.[58] "Under this beautiful sky there is not one being with whom you could identify, there is no love, no thought (ibid., 176)." "There, not a single fine expectation of your soul, not one high human dream, will be realized, . . . but you will have your fill of diverse scenes, remembrances (ibid., 187). Nature for Stankevich was characterized by raw feeling and by the diversity caused by chaotic motion, but it lacked harmony. Like Botkin, Grigor'ev, and Turgenev, Stankevich distinguished between nature and reason.[59] So in *My Metaphysics* he remarked that man was a replica, a microcosm of nature *and* reason.[60] History for Stankevich, following Schelling, became a "second nature," in which man overcame his natural egoism and thereby achieved "full reasonableness."[61] Stankevich recognized the necessity of nature—as he put it in 1835, between self-knowledge and "full reasonableness" lies nature—but he feared its raw power.

Unlike Stankevich and the others, Tolstoy, while fearlessly embracing the forces of nature, also saw it as the domain of reason. As I have discussed already, in his early nature stories, following Rousseau, he contrasted the reasonableness, the harmony of nature with the irrationality of human life. His study of the Savoyard Vicar in 1852 helped him develop ideas that were already present in his diary in 1851, during his first days in the Caucasus. There he worshipped a God of Love *and* Reason who appeared to him in nature.[62]

Comparing Botkin's metaphysics as elaborated in his article on Fet with Tolstoy's treatment of nature in *The Cossacks*, one can clearly see the difference in views between Tolstoy and his mentors. Botkin wrote that "we live by the same spirit as nature—we are that very same nature, but animated [*odukhotvorennye*] and conscious of ourselves. The dumb poetry of nature is our conscious poetry: it is given to us to express this dumb poetry of nature."[63] Nature is dumb: it lacks spirit [*dukh*] and higher reason as expressed in consciousness [*soznanie*].

Bilinkis has observed that in *The Cossacks*, Lukashka has a dumb sister, which indicates that the *narod*—by which he means the cossacks—personify nature as force or feeling alone.[64] Conscience and the need for personal perfection are present only in Olenin. Unlike other commentators, however, Bilinkis realizes that for Tolstoy this conscience is also part of nature. This is what Botkin, Turgenev, and Stankevich did not believe, and why the first two considered Olenin to be superfluous in a work they otherwise regarded as Tolstoy's masterpiece. They ignored or misunderstood the moment in the stag's lair when conscience and consciousness come directly to Olenin from nature. (More on this in chapter 4.) For Botkin and his predecessor Stankevich, man *added* spirit and consciousness to nature; for the Tolstoy of *War and Peace*, man *expressed* what was already present in nature. This difference is crucial for understanding the early Tolstoy: for him nature was moral, so no distinction had to be made between art and morality. The "true, the beautiful, and the good" (8:321–22), celebrated by him in his early works and *War and Peace*, could all be the same.

Nature, Reason, and the Feelings ("Lucerne")

We come now to the second stage of Tolstoy's new appreciation of nature during the Petersburg period, a stage in which he consolidated his new insight into nature and the feelings and incorporated it into his earlier understanding. The first attempt to incorporate his new ideas in art came in "Lucerne," whose first draft was written in the form of a letter to Botkin on 26 June 1857 (60:199–211). In nature nothing stands still, all is motion, the ocean of which Turgenev had written in *Fathers and Sons* (chap. 27). Thus, after a lengthy description of the view from the town, Nekhliudov concludes:

> Neither on the lake nor on the mountains, nor in the sky, was there a single precise [*cel'naia*] line, or one precise [*cel'nyi*] colour, or one identical moment: everywhere was motion, irregularity, fantastic shapes, an endless intermingling and variety of shades and lines, and over it all lay tranquillity, softness, unity and the inevitability of the beautiful. (5:4)

Nekhliudov contrasts this nature with the offensive mathematical precision of the townscape. Here nothing moves and everything is so complete that it cannot blend with other things.

> And here, in the midst of this undefined, tangled, free beauty, right in front of my window, stupidly, making itself the focus [*fokusno*], jutted the white

stick of the quay, lime trees with braces and little green benches—poor banal human works, not drowning as did the distant summer places and ruins, in the general harmony of beauty, but, on the contrary, crudely contrasting with it. (Ibid.)

In "Lucerne" nature and civilization thus depicted correspond to a natural and a civilized, "English" state of the human psyche. English landscaping and architecture reflects English character as Tolstoy understood it: rational individualism makes each Englishman an island unto himself, with nothing connecting him to the inner life of any other individual.[65] So at the dinner table Nekhliudov finds only "strict decorum taken as law, a lack of communication based not on pride but on the absence of the need for closeness and the solitary enjoyment of the comfortable and pleasant satisfaction of their needs" (5:4). Intercourse with the English makes Nekhliudov as "dead," as "frozen," as they are.

The natural landscape has the opposite effect:

I felt an inner agitation and the need to somehow express an excess of something suddenly overfilling my soul. At this moment I wanted to embrace someone, to embrace him tightly, to tickle, to pinch him, in general to do something unusual with him and with myself. (5:4)

The most basic definition of life as motion and feeling is thus a direct expression of life in human beings. Motion in nature both corresponds to and awakens feeling in Nekhliudov. Feeling "overflows" and generates the need for communication lacking in the English.

Of all the arts, music best expresses feelings and hence our kinship with nature.

[The itinerant singer in "Lucerne" awakens in Nekhliudov] the need for love, fullness of hope and a causeless joy of life.

"What do you want, what do you desire?" came to me involuntarily. Here it is, beauty and poetry surround you on all sides. Breathe it into yourself in great full gulps, enjoy yourself to the limit, what more do you need! Everything is yours, everything is good." (5:8)

The music expresses the feelings that nature has inspired in Nekhliudov. By so doing it also releases him into the flux of nature and makes him feel that nature belongs to him ("Everything is yours, everything is good"). Especially during the period of his infatuation with feeling, Tolstoy valued this shedding of the conscious, rational self. He called for self-forgetting pure and simple (29 April 1857; 47:206), and claimed elsewhere (on his hike through Switzerland from 27 May to 6 June) that it released limitless physical strength (47:196). We join with the forces of nature, and they belong to us just as we are part of them.[66]

This creates "the need for love, fullness of hope and a causeless joy of life."

In *The Cossacks* Olenin temporarily joins the cossack community by succumbing to his love for Marianka.

> Perhaps I love nature in her, the personification of everything high and beautiful in nature; but I don't have my own will, but through me some kind of elemental force loves her, the whole of God's world, all of nature is crushing this love into my soul and saying: love. I love her not with my mind, not with my imagination, but with my whole being. Loving her, I feel myself an inseparable part of the whole world of God. (chap. 33)

This love is a force of nature like the one that affects Nekhliudov in "Lucerne." Olenin becomes an "inseparable part of the whole world of God," relinquishing both his conscious will and the promptings of his moral reason to do so.

The forces in nature are governed by physical laws that regulate each moving thing. When we join nature, we abandon ourselves to laws of necessity that rule the living just as surely as the laws of physics rule matter. In the well-ordered traditional society, they are in full force. Thus in *The Cossacks* Olenin describes the life of the cossacks: "people live here the way nature lives: they die, give birth, couple, again give birth, fight, drink, eat, rejoice, and again die, and [there are] no conditions except those unchanging ones which nature has laid down to the sun, the grass, the animal, the tree. They have no other laws" (chap. 26).

Tolstoy "discovered" the laws of nature, that is, he discovered their relevance for his art, during the Petersburg period. Adherence to them is the moral of several stories written at this time. In "Three Deaths" (1858), whose pagan flavor offended A. A. Tolstaia,[67] Fedor and the other peasants accept necessity while the lady dying of consumption does not. The most uncomplaining member of the dying trio is the tree. It is cut down by the young carter Serega, who fashions a cross out of it for Fedor's grave. Serega thereby fulfills his part of a bargain with Fedor, but only partially. Fedor had given his boots to Serega in exchange for his promise to erect a stone over Fedor's grave. To avoid buying that stone, Serega cuts down and kills the tree instead. But even this all too human peccadillo has its place in the larger scheme of things: the tree's death makes way for new growth in the forest. This latter theme finds harsher expression in "Polikushka" (1863). There both the weak Polikushka and his innocent infant die because the sentimental lady interferes with the law of the stronger that decrees that Polikushka should be sent as a soldier. Turgenev was particularly horrified by the death of the baby in "Polikushka,"[68] while Grigor'ev called Tolstoy a "nihilist," for having placed human beings and a tree on the same level in "Three Deaths."[69]

Stories from the Petersburg period stress how dangerous it is to flout the laws of nature. Especially striking in this regard are the unpublished group of stories, all variations of the same plot, entitled "Tikhon and Malan'ia," "The Idyll," and "Fragments of Tales from Village Life" (1860–1862). In them a peasant woman whose husband does not live at home teases and resists a farmhand, and then succumbs easily to an experienced womanizer. The title of one part of "The Idyll" also expresses its moral: "Don't play with fire, you'll get burned." Malan'ia gets burned—her husband beats her when he finds out about her lover and she has an illegitimate son—but not burned to death. Thirty years later her son has become a "big shot—an overseer," and she is admired by all for her virtue. Like Olenin when he falls for Marianka, Malan'ia is not to blame for the lapse in her youth. Passion forced her to be unfaithful to her husband. So Malan'ia's tale contains another moral for absent husbands (like the husband in Tolstoy's own affair with the peasant woman Aksinia which produced an illegitimate son): nature abhors a vacuum. Husbands who leave their wives in order to work in the city can expect someone else to occupy the empty marital bed.[70]

The nature description in "Lucerne" as we have discussed it thus far spells out Tolstoy's new discoveries about the laws governing motion in nature and the human soul. There is something about the landscape in this work familiar to readers of "The Raid" and "The Woodcutting," however, and that is the insistence on unity and especially harmony ("this inexpressibly harmonious and soft nature"; "the general harmony of beauty"). Tolstoy had not abandoned either this harmony nor the divine reason with which he associated it.

Through music "Lucerne" articulates the relevance of harmony for human life, as well as for nature:

> I distinctly made out the distant full chords of a guitar, sweetly trembling in the evening air, and several voices which, interrupting one another, did not sing a theme, but here and there, singing out the most prominent parts, made you feel it. The theme was something like a sweet and graceful mazurka. The voices seemed now near, now far, now you heard a tenor, now a bass, now a throaty pipe with cooing Tirolean modulations. This was not a song, but a light masterful sketch of a song. (5:7)

The "voices" of the musician's song do not speak, of course, but sing. Music, not words, is the language of feeling, and we learn that the musician, in fact, did not compose the words of his second song (5:16). What is important and original is his melody. Nothing is complete in itself, and so unity and harmony among all the parts is possible. As imprecise colors and broken lines complement one another in the landscape at the beginning of "Lucerne," so here living beings interact to form a complete whole, a melody. This melody is the harmony produced and understood by divine reason.

The melody is only hinted at, never played outright, and it is transmitted through individual voices. This signals Tolstoy's adherence at this time to the Goethean belief in the real existence of individuals, who "at the same time . . . are members of a universal harmony, in which every individual substance has a share. . . . Each one [monad] is in its way a small image of the universe, a microcosm."[71]

Tolstoy did not claim that feeling itself was necessarily moral. So, having been awakened to feeling by the Swiss landscape, Nekhliudov would as soon pinch someone as embrace him (5:4) and in Tolstoy's diary self-forgetting may be for the sake of malice, as well as for sacrifice (47:206). But God's world is moral even if participants in it are not. We cannot expect reason from the parts of a rational whole, but inasmuch as the parts derive their meaning from the whole, they are reasonable. Some human beings some of the time sense their relationship to this whole. To act in accordance with the reasonable whole, whether consciously or unconsciously, is to be both true and good. This is why Olenin feels morally justified in abandoning his inner desire for "self-abnegation" for the "beauty" of nature epitomized in Marianka. Unlike his friends, who do not believe that either nature or human feelings are governed by divine reason, Tolstoy derives morality from nature.

The musical theme in "Lucerne" expands on the one in "The Woodcutting," which ends with Antonov's mournful song. This ending, in turn, recalls that of Turgenev's "The Singers," from which it differs significantly. The brutal words of the echoing exchange that closes Turgenev's story ("Papa wants to beat you") emphasize the essential amorality of nature and of the poetry (music and feelings) that links us to her. In Tolstoy the music of divine reason sweetens the austere laws of necessity by which God orders life.

The culmination of this theme comes in *War and Peace*. The night before Petia Rostov is sacrificed to these laws, he hears a heavenly chorus, which his imagination fashions from the night sounds of the camp, including the sound of his own sword being sharpened with a steel. Petia himself directs the chorus, and this joyful participation in inhuman forces presages his death. A lively adolescent and a Rostov, Petia is all vitality. Disobeying the orders of Dolokhov to wait for the infantry, he rides this vitality to his death. Petia's death, heartrending though it may be, is part of a mysterious harmony or balance of human individuals in the universe as presented in the novel. It is no accident that it occurs during a raid in which another Peter, Peter Bezukhov, is rescued.

Objective and Subjective Poetry

On 22 April (4 May, New Calendar), 1857, about two months before he sent his letter containing the first draft of "Lucerne" to Botkin, Tolstoy wrote a letter to Annenkov reporting on the progress of his manuscript about cossacks:

> That serious thing that I've spoken about with you once I've begun in four different tones, I've written about 3 publisher's sheets in each—and I've stopped; I don't know which to choose or how to merge, or whether I shouldn't throw the whole thing out. The thing is that this subjective poetry of authenticity—an inquiring poetry—both has become a bit offensive to me and doesn't suit the task or the mood in which I find myself. I've set off into the infinite and firmly positive objective sphere and I've gone crazy: in the first place because of the abundance of subjects or, better, sides of subjects which have presented themselves to me, and because of the variety of tones in which it is possible to display these subjects. It seems to me that a dim law is stirring in this chaos according to which I might be able to choose; but up to now this abundance and variety have added up to impotence. One thing that comforts me is that thought hasn't arrived at the point of desperation in me; on the contrary some kind of commotion is going on more and more intensively in my head. I'm going to hold to your wise law of chastity and will show no one and will leave it to myself to choose and discard. (60:181–82)

The Cossacks was Tolstoy's novel about nature, and the "objective sphere" to which he referred in this letter was the natural world. He contrasted it with the "subjective" sphere, the inner life of the psyche, about which he had just published (in *The Contemporary* [*Sovremennik*], January 1857) the not very well received *Youth*. *The Cossacks* he would write in a different way. Subjective poetry has one subject: the inner self which the poet studies in himself simply because his is the only self he can really know. The objective sphere, by contrast, has an infinity of subjects. Even more puzzling, these subjects can be viewed from many and various perspectives. Hence the problems that had arisen in writing what would become *The Cossacks*. A combination of introspection, psychological analysis, and moral judgment was the "inquiring poetry" that had been Tolstoy's preferred and dominant method in all three books of his autobiographical trilogy (*Childhood*, *Adolescence*, and *Youth*). Another method was needed to join the subjects and perspectives present and swarming in nature.

What Tolstoy was looking for, as he wrote to Annenkov, was a "thought" that would organize the material present in nature. If he set aside "inquiring poetry," it was not because he rejected reason simply. He needed to find the reason *in nature*. Such a thought was already buzzing in his head, but it came *from* nature: it represented the "dim law" stirring in nature itself. It was not by chance that Tolstoy broached this subject with Annenkov. Unlike his other Petersburg friends, Annenkov was a champion of reason even in nature. He was a Hegelian whom the late-nineteenth-century positivist critic Ivan Ivanov took to task precisely for writing, in his first review of Tolstoy's work, of the *thought* that comes from nature. Nature, wrote Ivanov, can emit feeling, but not thought.[72] The young Tolstoy would disagree with Ivanov. He was looking precisely for the thought in nature.[73]

In the summer of 1856 Tolstoy read through Annenkov's three-volume 1855 edition of Pushkin.[74] The first volume of this edition, which contains the famous *Materials for a Biography of Pushkin* [*Materialy dlia biografii A. S. Pushkina*], is preserved in Tolstoy's library at Iasnaia Poliana. Tolstoy read this biography "with pleasure" (47:80), and marked places that particularly interested him. He bracketed a passage discussing the poem "Razgovor knigoprodavca s poetom" [Conversation of the bookseller with the poet] as the prologue to *Eugene Onegin*, and within the brackets he underlined Annenkov's assertion that Pushkin spoke for himself in the following lines[75] (these lines also comprise the epigraph to the fifth chapter of Belinsky's 1843 book on Pushkin):

V garmonii sopernik moi
Byl shum lesov, il' vikhor' buinyi,
Il' ivolgi napev zhivoi,
Il' noch'iu moria gul glukhoi,
Il' shepot rechki tikhostruinoi.

[My rival in harmony
Was the noise of the forest, or the wild wind
Or the lively melody of the oriole,
Or the muffled boom of the sea at night,
Or the murmur of the quietly flowing stream.]

Like Botkin, Annenkov understood the poet as the voice of nature. The poet derived his wisdom directly from observation of nature as it expressed itself both in outside reality and in the inner life of the human psyche. In marking Annenkov's comments on these lines, Tolstoy was agreeing with him.

In another part of his critique, Annenkov drew attention to Pushkin's rejection of the confusion of ecstasy [*vostorg*] with inspiration [*vdokhnovenie*]. Inspiration for Pushkin included thought and reason, and required calm and planning. Annenkov went on to say that "calmness and judgment" [*spokoistvie i obsuzhdenie*] informed many of Pushkin's own works and made them like classical antiquity.[76] Just as poetic inspiration included these things, so did the beauty in nature that poetry transmits. That Tolstoy accepted this interpretation of Pushkin and of the Beautiful is clear many years later, when, rereading Pushkin in the early 1870s, he praises him precisely for his understanding of the natural "hierarchy" of high and low things and the perfect arrangement of these things in his poetry.[77]

So thought expressed itself in nature as the proper order of things, an order the young Tolstoy sensed as a "dim law" stirring in "chaos." In "Lucerne" this order appears as "tranquillity, softness, unity and the inevitability of the beautiful" [*neobkhodimost' prekrasnogo*] and the "general harmony of beauty" (5:4).

In his letter to Annenkov, Tolstoy contrasted subjective, or inner, poetry with objective poetry and said that for the time being he felt himself tilting toward the latter. Although objective poetry contained a reasonable and moral element that made it acceptable to Tolstoy, it was not the "inquiring" poetry of thought. What it might have been we may gather from another letter written a week after the letter to Annenkov to A. A. and E. A. Tolstaia in which Tolstoy praised the Swiss landscapist Alexandre Calame (1810–1864). Calame was limited, even obtuse, but had a talent that Tolstoy had not until then appreciated. "There is an abyss of poetry in all his things, and it's harmonic poetry." Perhaps, Tolstoy speculated, his talent had crushed his mind. "In general, either very little of his mind comes out in his talent or his talent has crushed his mind—he can't define himself. But you have to love these people" (60:189).

The "mindless" artist, be he writer, painter, or musician, precisely because he is not bound to standards of human reason, has access to the Goethean "reason behind everything that lives," the reason that operates through dialectic and synthesis to create the harmonious universe that first bursts into print in "Lucerne."

The Metaphysics of Opposites and Goethe Again

The material to be studied in this section has already been collected by Eikhenbaum, in an addendum to his book on the 1870s entitled "Tolstoy in *The Contemporary* (1856–1857)" [*Tolstoi v 'Sovremennike' (1856–1857 gg.)*][78] Eikhenbaum comments on Tolstoy's unwillingness to adopt any one ideological position among the warring sides on *The Contemporary* and in Russian society at large in the mid 1850s and on his desire instead to use love to unite all sides. He quotes two passages from Tolstoy's notebook of April and May 1857:

> There are two minds. According to one, the logical, small mind, for civilization to advance is a good thing; the good according to the other, which looks down from above, is an equal compensation in the absence of civilization. According to a third, even higher, into whose realm I can glance only for a moment at a time, both together are just. (47:203–4)

> Reading the logical, materialistic Proudhon, his mistakes were clear to me just as the mistakes of idealists were to him. No matter how many times you see the powerlessness of your own mind, expressed always in one-sidedness, you see even better this one-sidedness in past thinkers and doers, especially when they complement one another. From this [one can conclude] that love, joining all these views into one, is the single infallible law of mankind." (47:208–9)

I agree with Eikhenbaum that we are in the presence of a kind of dialectic here, but one cannot possibly understand it—and Eikhenbaum does not really attempt to explain it—within the terms he uses to discuss it. Eikhenbaum (ibid., 288–90) turns to Chernyshevsky for an explanation of the "love" that will reconcile seeming contradictions: this love is the "purity of moral feeling" that Chernyshevsky described as one of the two distinguishing characteristics of the young Tolstoy. (The other was his method of psychological analysis, the "dialectic of the soul.") Chernyshevsky was able to detect this "purity" in Tolstoy because he himself possessed it (ibid., 289). In both men, according to Eikhenbaum, this highmindedness went back to utopian socialism. Eikhenbaum shows, here and elsewhere,[79] that Tolstoy was interested in and sympathetic to certain aspects of socialism. But Eikhenbaum links Tolstoy to Chernyshevsky through their socialism only with one very important caveat, the significance of which he does not elaborate, namely, that Chernyshevsky was a materialist.[80]

Tolstoy, Eikhenbaum implicitly admits, was not a materialist.[81] While Chernyshevsky tried to derive all morality from self-interest rightly understood by human reason,[82] Tolstoy distinguished human from divine reason and denied that the former enjoys direct access to the latter. It is within the context of Tolstoy's idealism that one must interpret the passages from the 1857 notebook cited by Eikhenbaum. The narrow "logical" truth of which Tolstoy wrote so disparagingly is one of the attributes of human reason. The second truth is divined by dialectic, also accessible to human reason, but not itself the source of synthesis. Truths discerned by human reason are partial, while divine reason comprehends and unites all these partial truths. The love that Eikhenbaum associates with the "web of love" by which Tolstoy hoped to capture his friends Botkin and Grigor'ev (ibid., 287) is Stankevich's reasonable love, love informed by divine reason.

In *Lev Tolstoy*, responding to the same body of material considered in "Tolstoy in *The Contemporary*" [*Tolstoi v 'Sovremennike'*] Eikhenbaum calls Tolstoy a "nihilist" or "cynic" who dissolved all theories of positive knowledge in the acid of analysis and countered this nihilism only with "instinct" and "conviction," which, moreover, were almost "biological."[83] Eikhenbaum at this point misunderstands Tolstoy's position in just the same way Grigor'ev had. Not acknowledging Tolstoy's peculiar form of idealism, neither sees how higher reason, which speaks through feelings in man and orders the chaos of motion in man and nature, both redeems human reason and puts it in its place as "one-sided."

The theory of knowledge put forth in the 1857 notebook bursts into print at the end of "Lucerne," when Nekhliudov attacks the adequacy of any system of positive beliefs:

What an unhappy, pitiful creation is man, with his need for positive decisions, thrown into this eternally moving, infinite ocean of good and evil, of facts, views and contradictions! People labor and struggle for centuries to move the good to one side and the bad to the other. Centuries pass, and no matter where, no matter what a dispassionate mind might throw upon the scales of good and evil, the scales do not move, and on each side there is as much good as there is bad. If only man could learn not to judge and not to think harshly and positively and not to give answers to questions given him only in order that they remain eternally questions! If only he understood that every thought is both a lie and just! It is a lie by virtue of its one-sidedness, because of the inability of man to embrace the whole truth, and just because it expresses one side of human aspirations. They've made categories for themselves in this eternal moving, infinite, infinitely mixed chaos of good and evil, they've traced imaginary lines along this sea and waited for the sea to divide itself the same way. Precisely as if there were not a million different categories from an entirely different point of view, on a different plane. True, these categories have been worked out over centuries, but centuries have passed, and millions will pass. Civilization is good; barbarism is evil; freedom is good; lack of freedom is evil. It is precisely this kind of imaginary knowledge that destroys the instinctive, most blessed, primordial demands of good in human nature. And who will define for me what freedom, what despotism, what civilization, what barbarism are? And where are the boundaries of one and the other? In whose soul is the measure of good and evil so steadfast that he can measure fleeting tangled facts with it? Who has so great a mind that he can embrace all the facts and weigh them even in the immobile past? And who has seen a situation in which there was not good and evil mixed together? And how do I know that I see more of one than the other because I'm not standing in the right place? And who is able even for an instant to tear his mind away from life so as to view it independently from above? We have one, only one infallible guide, the Universal Spirit, penetrating us all together and each of us as an individual, implanting in each of us a longing for what ought to be; that same Spirit which in a tree orders it to grow toward the sun, in a flower orders it to turn to seed toward autumn and in us orders us to cling unconsciously to one another. (5:25)

Even N. N. Strakhov, whose interpretation of Tolstoy's works Tolstoy himself so valued,[84] regarded Nekhliudov's speech as an example of the dispairing nihilism that had so troubled Grigor'ev in Tolstoy's writings of the late fifties.[85] Nekhliudov is long-winded, because he enunciates ideas that his creator is just in the process of digesting. Far from being nihilistic, however, his speech attacks the narrow or partial truths, the truths of "logic," in order to defend the comprehensive truth of divine reason. To do this successfully, he must banish the anger of simple moralism (Chernyshevsky's "purity of moral feeling"). And so Nekhliudov goes on to attack his own anger, an anger that comes dangerously close to an attack on God for His injustice. He must, he tells himself, accept the contradictions of human life and treasure even the souls of "lords," as well as those of itinerant minstrels. The love that he should feel instead of anger is precisely a form of *understanding* more complete and therefore closer to God than understanding based on human reason alone. So Nekhliudov's diatribe against human pride turns into a hymn to God: "Endless is the goodness and wisdom of He who has allowed and ordered all these contradictions to exist. . . . He looks mildly down from his radiant, immeasurable height and rejoices at the endless harmony in which you all contradictorially, endlessly move."

The story ends with one more twist, or one more step in the dialectic that leads to perfect, divine understanding: an acceptance even of Nekhliudov's anger as a response to "the harmonious need for the eternal and infinite . . ." All anger, even anger at anger, is banished as the condition for perfect harmony. Through a comprehensive divine love, that same love, itself a synthesis of love and reason, discussed in the 1857 diary, God presides over all the oppositions which, through their interaction, create motion or life.

Throughout most of "Lucerne" Nekhliudov rails against the cold rationalism of civilization as epitomized by the English and defends the "chaos" of nature and feeling. The epistomology advanced in the same story is the ontological or metaphysical equivalent of this chaos. Just as nature, human life, and feeling contain nothing complete, but altogether form a complete whole, so knowledge itself is made up of opinions which each "express one side of human aspirations" and so are one-sided or even contradictory, but which all together make up the truth. There is dialectic in this metaphysics of opposites, and there is the grand synthesis that occurs in a comprehensive God.

At the very time Tolstoy wrote "Lucerne" his diaries reveal that he had been reading Goethe intensively.[86] It should come as no surprise, then, that, for Thomas Mann, Nekhliudov's final encomium to love was not utopian socialist, but "Goethean."[87] As Mann correctly discerns here and throughout his essay, what seems most Goethean about Tolstoy's art, and especially *War and Peace*, and what most distinguishes that art from his later writings is its "adoration of nature," or sympathy for *everything* real and natural. For Tolstoy as for Goethe, the condition of this adoration was the existence of synthesis in nature, the "reason behind everything that lives."[88] This synthesis encompasses in itself both good and evil, but for "the true, the beautiful and the good" (8:321–22) to be present and unified in man and nature, one must be able to determine the usefulness even of evil. The God who presides over "Lucerne" and stills even the righteous anger of Nekhliudov is like God in *Faust*, who defends the necessity even of Mephistofeles.[89]

Of himself Mephistofeles says to Faust that he is "Part of that force which would / Do evil evermore, and yet creates the good."[90] In an "Oration on Shakespeare," delivered when Goethe was twenty-one years old, he made this point in his own voice: "What noble philosophers have said of the world, applies also to Shakespeare;—namely, that what we call evil is only the other side, and belongs as necessarily to its existence and to the Whole, as the torrid zone must burn and Lapland freeze, in order that there may be a temperate zone."[91] This idea means that the negative, even as it is expressed in human evil, is thereby not simply negative. Instead it is seen as a necessary part of universal law.[92]

Tolstoy himself, in *War and Peace*, took a similar position. He believed that in the whole world, to use Carden's felicitous image of the holidays at Otradnoe, "the dark and the light are folded into each other like a marble cake."[93] The "metaphysics of opposites" itself, which creates an all-inclusive harmony, may derive from Goethe's theory of polarity, which Goethe had deduced from the working of a magnet, and which, in the form of polar opposites, he believed comprised the unity of nature.[94] Von Gronicka speculates that the Goethean idea of "Systole und Diastole" had been the inspiration for Turgenev's vision of the universe as composed of the two fundamental forces, centripetal and centrifugal.[95] Turgenev had elaborated his thought in "Hamlet and Don Quixote," which Tolstoy read in manuscript while the two writers were living together in Dijon in 1857 (47:117). While the rivalrous younger man was somewhat snippety about the manuscript ("good material, but not of much use and clever in the extreme") he subsequently praised it highly—and may have borrowed some of that "good material" for his own use.[96] Both indirectly, then, and directly through Goethe's work Tolstoy knew of the theory of polarity as a primal phenomenon of life. *War and Peace*, from the two socks that the nanny in the first epilogue knits on one set of needles up to the title of the novel itself, is saturated with the idea.[97] His adaptation of it is one more proof of his determination to depict nature there as a totally good opposition to civilization.

Tolstoy remained as attached to nature in the 1860s as he had been in the 1850s. Annenkov was right when, in "Russian Belles Lettres in 1863" [*Russkaia belletristika v 1863 g.*], responding to the publication of *The Cossacks*, he wrote that Tolstoy, the "psychologist and skeptic"[98] who had produced such works as *Childhood* and *Youth*, attacked civilization from the point of view of a positive ideal. As revealed in his articles on education, it was "a passionate attraction to the simplicity, naturalness, strength and truth of the spontaneous [*neposredstvennye*] phenomena of life" (ibid., 289).

   Having quite properly begun by affirming Tolstoy's love of nature and the natural, it is important to reiterate that, fundamental as it most certainly was, it never was the primary inspiration for the man or his art. Tolstoy was never like Trigorin in Chekhov's *Seagull*, who says he really loves and understands only nature, and includes other things in his writing only out of duty. Although he loved nature and had a good eye, Tolstoy considered landscape in and of itself to be the lowest form of art.[99] If he could indulge his love of nature unreservedly in the 1850s and 1860s, that was because nature included—had to include—the spiritual, moral realm that was always primary for him. Tolstoy's first extant diaries consist not in paeans to nature, but in schemes for controlling his own rich, often contradictory and unruly nature. It is true that from the beginning he was enthralled by the works of Rousseau, and especially by Rousseau's attack on civilization from the point of view of nature. His very attachment to nature as opposed to civilization, however, implied for him the necessity of finding a natural ideal. Grigor'ev had understood this in his 1862 essay on the works of Tolstoy. In Annenkov's article on *The Cossacks*, he took up this argument and extended it, claiming to find in this latest work the synthesis that the young skeptic had long sought in nature. But Annenkov was wrong when he contended that Tolstoyan aesthetics even in *The Cossacks* put nature ahead of morality, and therefore that the Tolstoyan ideal of nature was "poetic," not "moral."[100] As had been true in the fifties, nature according to Tolstoy *was* moral. This was what Tolstoy meant when he himself announced in "Who Should Be Teaching Whom to Write: Should We Be Teaching the Peasant Lads, or They Us?" that *"Our ideal is behind, not ahead of us"* (8:323). We had it at birth ("Who Should Be Teaching Whom to Write?") and we see it around us in nature, "which continually displays that truth, beauty and goodness which we seek and desire" (8:322).[101]

Part Two

THE 1860s

Four

Nature and Civilization in
The Cossacks

THE HARMONIOUS universe of living reason discovered in "Lucerne" receives its apotheosis in *War and Peace*. Before turning to that most expansive of all Tolstoyan novels, however, we need to examine *The Cossacks*, to see how Tolstoy solved the problem of nature and morality there. This novel, published in 1863, makes the case for a natural morality as far as Tolstoy had developed it in the fifties. The work most admired by his Petersburg friends,[1] it reflects their teaching more than any other major work of Tolstoy, but also takes issue with that teaching on the crucial point of the relation of nature, reason, and morality.

The Cossacks compares civilization and nature; but, first impressions to the contrary, it is not simply a rejection of the former for the latter. Tolstoy had first conceived it as a celebration of the "savage state." As it and he grew through the fifties, however, he came to see savage man as worse and civilization as better in one crucial respect than he had thought at first. The fly in the natural ointment to heal civilized woes was the seeming absence in savage man of love of others, the basis of the "self-abnegation" touted by Olenin as true morality. Morality among the cossacks seems to extend to justice as moderation of self-love, but not beyond. Although willing to sacrifice himself for the community, the cossack, it turns out, is not truly social, and therefore ultimately cannot be a model for the civilized and selfish young man who comes from Moscow at the beginning of the book.

Natural Necessity in *The Cossacks*

There were two levels of morality as Tolstoy came to understand it: that of moderation and justice, and that of self-sacrifice. The first and lower morality depended entirely on reason, both as it manifested itself in the laws of natural necessity and in human beings. These comprised the "bridle" by which God restrained vitality in nature.[2] In *The Cossacks*, these natural laws are enforced by a physical necessity that the high-born Olenin has not known before. They order the lives of sentient beings so as to achieve an overall, reasonable harmony which is not the aim of each individual. The individuals are not reasonable in their essence, but nature is.[3]

All living beings except humankind live by the laws of reasonable order. Freedom and pride have led human beings to aggrandize themselves, collectively and individually, at the expense of the whole. In this sense human beings are worse than other creatures, and civilized ones are worse than those who, like the cossacks, live in a more natural state.

Tolstoy's rationality, his belief in a natural morality based on the laws of biology, linked him through Rousseau to Chernyshevsky and such radical democrats of the sixties as Dobroliubov and Pisarev. It was his call for submission to physical necessity as a cardinal principle of morality in stories like "Three Deaths" and "Polikushka" that caused friends on the Right like Grigor'ev to consider him a kind of nihilist. The nihilists, however, were determinists who believed in the absolute power of circumstance.[4] Unlike them, Tolstoy insisted that it was natural for human beings to reason to the extent necessary for morality. In *The Cossacks* this is true even of Lukashka, who acknowledges the validity of Olenin's condemnation of killing even as he shrugs it off as an unacceptable limitation on his freedom (21).

Older cossacks like Eroshka are more moral than young bucks like Lukashka because experience of necessity has moderated their natural pride. One can speculate that Lukashka, if he survives the wound he receives at the end of the book, will be chastened by it.[5] From it he would learn suffering and fear of death and be able to extrapolate from his own experience to the experience of others. He would no longer kill in ignorance of the sufferings of others and with innocent joy in his own power, and, like Eroshka (15), he would remember his youthful love of killing with revulsion.

The Morality of Self-Sacrifice in the Stag's Lair

Tolstoyan morality grounded in the laws of nature and effected through compassion and conscious submission to necessity is not new in *The Cossacks*. Neither is the dependence of both of these moral principles on the power of reason. These arguments Tolstoy had developed in his early war stories.[6] The new feature here is an argument for the naturalness of a higher morality of self-sacrifice. Tolstoy did not attempt, as in *War and Peace*, to give this argument a metaphysical support. He appealed simply to individual experience and placed that experience at the heart of his book about nature, in the stag's lair.

Olenin's name is of course based on the Russian word for stag, *olen'*, and he himself identifies with the stag. When it escapes, something in his heart "tears," as if his own natural essence were fleeing him. He returns to the stag's lair the day after the hunt with Eroshka in search of that essence.

To be at home in nature, Olenin must put aside the natural dislike of physical discomfort that may have caused human beings to separate themselves from nature in the first place. He must accept the stifling atmosphere of the dense forest and especially the blood-sucking mosquitoes that almost drive him back to the village. He overcomes, indeed he embraces, his pain and with it the natural principle that legitimates his own love of hunting. In nature, living things mingle without regard for individuals, as the wild grape near the stag's lair winds round a tree. They eat and are eaten. The mosquitoes feed on Olenin as he hunts and shoots pheasants, whose brothers—in Olenin's imagination—sense their dead fellows without grieving for them.

It is interesting to compare *The Cossacks*'s complete acceptance of what some might regard as the harshest law of nature with Tolstoy's criticism of this same law as it operates in human society, even in *War and Peace*. In nature as in high society people live for themselves alone. Olenin, as he rests in the stag's lair, is, in his own mind, "Dmitrii Olenin, a being completely distinct from all others." The two situations differ because in human society people prey on one another to satisfy illegitimately inflated passions, and these passions cause them to ride roughshod over the legitimate needs of others. Olenin's desires in the stag's lair have been reduced to such a minimum that, paradoxically, his bare, bestial self-love becomes the ground for understanding others. They, those simple beings, the pheasants or even those mosquitos that hound him, are each "just such a Dmitrii Olenin, distinct from all others, as I am myself." Olenin can now flow, in imagination, into the place of a mosquito and see himself from the mosquito's point of view. Having perceived the mosquito as a "Dmitrii Olenin," he can turn this insight upside-down, to perceive himself as "not a Russian gentleman at all, a member of Moscow society, friend and relative of so-and-so and so-and-so, but simply just such a mosquito, just such a pheasant, or stag, as those who were living now around him." So he comes to Eroshka's insight, the source of the old man's morality of moderation and compassion, about the similarity and mortality of all physical beings: "Just like them, like Daddy Eroshka, I'll live, I'll die. And he spoke the truth: only the grass will grow up."

It is easy to see the operations of reason at work as Olenin makes his way toward Eroshka's wisdom. Both to imagine someone else to be you and to imagine yourself as someone else takes comparison, an action of reason. To generalize from your observations and imaginings also requires reason. There is, however, an initial moment in the stag's lair before reason begins. To understand the place of reason in natural man as portrayed in *The Cossacks*, one must examine this primal state of pure feeling, pure life.

At midday Olenin seeks out the stag's lair to find rest and shelter from the sun. In this place he gazes at the mingled signs of his and the stag's presence here the day before, and, Tolstoy intended his reader to understand, he becomes just such a stag as the one that lay here then:

> He felt cool and comfortable; he wasn't thinking about anything or desiring anything. And suddenly there came over him such a strange causeless feeling of happiness and love for everything, that he, out of childhood custom, began to cross himself and thank someone.

In the first sentence Olenin is the physical being in complete repose, with sensation ("cool and comfortable") but without thought or even desire. Then, out of this passive state—unsummoned, as indicated by the impersonal construction [*vdrug na nego nashlo*][7] and without any external cause ("causeless")—comes the primal feeling of "happiness and love for everything." The stag, without reason, so without thought and imagination, cannot put the feeling that he may share with Olenin into words. In Olenin at this moment Tolstoy depicted what an animal who could express himself and thereby express nature might be and feel.

Olenin's "happiness and love for everything" is one feeling (*chuvstvo*, not *chuvstva*) with two parts. There is both unity here and a potential, in the complexity of the one feeling, for disunity. As I noted in the previous chapter, Tolstoy especially admired Turgenev's essay "Hamlet and Don Quixote," which was published in 1860, and which Turgenev was writing when the two writers lived together briefly in Dijon, France, in 1856.[8] Tolstoy was working at this very time on the manuscript of *The Cossacks*. In Turgenev's essay the centripetal force of egoism is epitomized by Hamlet, and the centrifugal force of "devotedness and sacrifice, illuminated in a comic light," by Don Quixote (ibid., 184). The two feelings are seen to be in conflict. In the stag's lair Olenin has found in a single feeling not only happiness, the centrifugal self-love natural to physical beings, but the centripetal love of others natural to the spirit. The Goethean "Systole" and "Diastole," the contraction and expansion of the heart, speak in one being and even at the same time.

One may also understand the two parts of Olenin's feeling as the manifestations of those two fundamental characteristics of the soul as

Rousseau understood it: unity and extent, or expansiveness. The feeling points both inward, fostering happiness and unity, and outward, fostering love of others. If this feeling in fact expresses the natural tendency in the soul toward unity and extent, then Tolstoy in this work gave the natural expansiveness of the soul a moral meaning that it did not necessarily have in Rousseau. Once again, he followed the Savoyard Vicar in arguing for the natural sociability of man. In any case, there can be no doubt that Olenin is experiencing here a distinctly Tolstoyan and moral variation of the Rousseauian "sentiment of existence" that makes life so sweet.

Reason will foster the development of both self-love and love of others. Olenin remains in repose for only an instant. He moves from physical sensation ("cool and comfortable") to feeling ("happiness and love for everything"), and then to thoughts that come over him as independently of will as do those feelings that precede them and indeed lead to them.

> Suddenly with particular clarity it came to him that here I, Dmitrii Olenin, a being so very distinct from all others, now lie alone, God knows where, in that place where a stag lived, an old stag, a beautiful one who possibly never saw a human being, and in such a place where no human being ever lay before and thought such thoughts.

Once again Tolstoy indicated an absence of active will in the subject with another impersonal construction: "There suddenly came into his head . . . [*Emu . . . prishlo v golovu*]." With reason, however, come form, limits, and distinctions. For the first time in the revery Olenin knows who he is ("Dmitrii Olenin, a being distinct from all others") and he also, by extrapolation, knows the inviolable particular being of others (the stag who had never seen a human being). It is the knowledge of his own particularity that makes compassion possible, and so there then follow the reasonings and imaginings that culminate in Eroshka's wisdom. ("Just like them, like Daddy Eroshka, I'll live and die," etc.)

But Olenin does not stop at this plateau. He goes on to construct a doctrine of self-sacrifice that later in the novel strikes even him as "one-sided, cold, intellectual" (33). When Turgenev in a letter from 1863 to Fet called Olenin a man "preoccupied with himself, boring and sick,"[9] he was no doubt referring to passages such as this one. Turgenev and even Olenin to the contrary, however, this part of Olenin's revery is not simply outside nature and therefore irrelevant to the work. *The Cossacks* is not just, as Turgenev called it, a "contrast of civilization with original, untouched nature" (ibid.), but a clash between the two played out in the heart and mind of Olenin. The two are among those "categories" or contradictions of which Nekhliudov, in "Lucerne," says that each contains good and bad.[10] At the end Olenin appears irresolute because he really cannot choose one of the two without losing something that his creator regarded as fundamentally necessary to his happiness and goodness.

Olenin returns to nature in the stag's lair, but the return occurs through a leap of the imagination that requires a somewhat developed reason. Thus he does not shed reason with the trappings of civilization, nor does he for more than a moment shed the self-consciousness made possible by reason. Until he begins to think in his revery, he has been a kind of passive observer as nature—or Tolstoy—seems to build him from the ground up, from sense to feeling to thought. Even at the most primitive layer, however, that of the passive body [*Emu bylo prokhladno, uiutno; ni o chem on ne dumal, nichego ne zhelal*; He felt cool, comfortable; he wasn't thinking about anything, desiring anything], the self, he, *emu*, even if only as the subject of physical sensations, is still present. Having felt, Olenin starts to think, and the sentence structure changes accordingly, from the impersonal "Emu . . . prishlo v golovu" [it came into his head] in the previous paragraph to the active "dumal on dal'she" [he continued to think] in this one. The conscious, active self, the will of this self, makes its appearance. It states what it wants: "I want only one thing—to be happy"; and it reasons about how to achieve true happiness. What has already happened to Olenin, the way he has stripped down to the bare essentials of his being, has revealed to him the folly of inflated passions, and so he is able to reason his way to the threshold of his revelation.

Olenin reasons that other desires—wealth, fame, comfort, love—can be thwarted by circumstance and must be illegitimate. He therefore directs his natural desire for happiness toward the one thing that would bring him happiness completely within his power: self-abnegation. It is this kind of calculation, of course, that later strikes him as inadequate because it appears to be rooted entirely, not in real love of others, but in self-love. He, and those readers who have agreed with him, have forgotten the "love of everything" that he felt at the first stage of his revery. The contented self-love and love of others that he felt then go back to the self-love and love of others mentioned in Tolstoy's first diaries. They are phenomena which Tolstoy explained in different ways at different times but the existence of which he seemed determined at all times to defend. Here he suggested that self-abnegation will make Olenin happy because it satisfies the love of everything that is part of his original, primitive sentiment of existence.

I said earlier that Tolstoy avoided metaphysics in *The Cossacks*. A slight but crucial exception to this occurs in the stag's lair as Olenin works out his argument for self-sacrifice.

"But so what if the grass will grow up?" He thought further. "It's still neces-sary to live, it's necessary to be happy; because I only want one thing—happiness. It doesn't matter what I may be: whether I'm just such an animal like all the rest over which the grass will grow up, or whether I'm a frame into which a part of the One Divinity is put, nonetheless it's necessary to live the best way. How ought I to live in order to be happy, and why haven't I been happy before?"

Resting in the heart of nature, and at the core of his own being in nature, Olenin plots the course of his future life in order to satisfy the desire for happiness that is fundamental to all natural beings. At the same time he inserts into his argument a metaphysical possibility—that he may be "a frame into which a part of the One Divinity is put"—that Daddy Eroshka would never entertain. This possibility, which could underlie and unify all of nature without being anywhere directly acces-sible there, could fuel a real desire for self-sacrifice in the individual, who might find it in and of itself necessary to his fulfillment. The natu-ral tendency of the part to return to the whole could be the origin even of the centripetal force depicted in Turgenev's essay; nature itself could be seen, as it is to a large extent in *War and Peace,* as a dynamic equilib-rium of the two forces of self-love and self-sacrifice. If this desire for self-sacrifice does exist, it comes from within the same individual who loves himself.[11]

Olenin's desire for self-abnegation, though hedged around in the stag's lair with an equally natural egoism, is thus natural. Its effect, however, is to cast Olenin out of nature. Olenin's musings bring with them a change in the weather and in Olenin's mood. The sun goes behind a cloud, the wind comes up, and the man who had accepted the natural laws of life and death suddenly fears for his own life. Olenin's will has revived (*He* thought; *I* desire one thing only) and, lawful though its cogitations and desires may be, it makes nature seem "gloomy, stern, wild." The reason for this is that nature cares nothing for the fate of the individual self, on which, for better and for worse, Olenin's attention is now focused.

Only other human beings care about this, and so the "new light" of Olenin's revelation corresponds to the "sun [that] bursts into light in his soul" when he eventually stumbles on the place where Lukashka and his fellows are encamped (21). Eroshka's wisdom is solitary, like the old man's life: it moderates an essentially solitary self-love. Only love of others makes human beings social, and it has that effect on Olenin. Like the sexual passion to which it may be related, it forms a natural social bond because it requires other human beings for its ful-fillment.

When Olenin discovers the encampment and recovers his spirits, the sun briefly emerges again from behind the clouds to illuminate the scene. Its reappearance is meant to suggest, I believe, the naturalness of human sociability. In a sentient being such sociability must be based on feeling: the necessary feeling in Olenin comes from a glimmer of divine love in his soul. This love, it will be recalled, is *reasonable*. Hence the greater self-consciousness and capacity for reason of civilized or at least Christian man is necessary to cultivate the natural but exceedingly weak seedling of self-sacrificing love.

If the morality of self-sacrifice has a natural justification, and for that reason occurs to Olenin in the stag's lair, that does not mean that Olenin's own desire to sacrifice himself is purely selfless. In the civilized human being, self-love and self-sacrificing love both flourish under the liberating influence of greater reasoning power, so that in the self-conscious human being they may be present at the same time and affect one another. So in Olenin the desire for self-sacrifice mingles with a desire for glory. Like Prince Andrei he both wants to sacrifice himself for others and to have others love him as a result: "And is it worth living for yourself," he thought, "when you come to die, and you'll die without having done anything good, and *in such a way that no one will know?*"[12]

To put Eroshka's wisdom in the Rousseauist perspective that was so crucial for the young Tolstoy, one can say that the natural morality of Eroshka attains the desired unity of soul by taming its expansiveness through exposure to natural necessity. Inasmuch, however, as unity is achieved by limiting expansiveness, it also limits and even distorts human nature. The desire of the self-sacrificing Olenin to "cast out on all sides" a Sternian "web of love" to "catch" his friends (28) is an expression of the expansive self, which first speaks in the stag lair to rebel against Eroshka's morality of necessity ("But so what if the grass will grow? . . . It's still necessary to live, it's necessary to be happy; because I only want one thing—happiness.") The predatory flavor of Olenin's image of catching his friends in a web of love is deliberate: it makes the connection between the amoral expansive self in the state of nature and the moral use to which such energy might be put in a civilized human being. Constrained in natural morality resting on moderation, the expansive self hunts again, this time for souls, in the higher morality of civilized man in touch with his natural beginnings.[13]

Olenin's discovery "is revealed [*otkrylsia*]." Once again, this time with a reflexive verb form, Tolstoy indicates Olenin's passivity, which assures the reader of the real existence, undistorted by subjective blinkers, of the revelation. The self-sacrificing love to which Olenin proceeds to reason his way is surely related to the "love of everything" that he felt during the sentimental, feeling stage of his experience. When Olenin's active and self-conscious self has reasoned its way back to this love, it can draw on nature in the form of instinctive feeling to confirm its reality.

The Cossack as Savage Man

The work that over a period of eight years became *The Cossacks* was originally conceived as a continuation of Tolstoy's autobiographical trilogy. This thread in the work's history was important enough that the final extant copy of the manuscript in 1862 was entitled "Mar'iana. Molodost' (Kavkaz 1853)" [Mariana. Youth (The Caucasus, 1853)] (changed on the manuscript to "Kazaki. Kavkazkaia povest' 1852-ogo goda" [The Cossacks. A Caucasian story from 1852]).[14] Tolstoy's belief that ontogeny recapitulates phylogeny made the switch from the youth of an individual to the youth of mankind an easy one. At the same time *The Cossacks* remains a story about Olenin and *his* youth. Olenin discovers the source of his youthful vitality in the Caucausus, but he must leave it behind in order to achieve manhood. The suggestion is that the maturity of mankind itself lies outside and beyond the cossack world.

The question is to what extent that cossack world is synonymous with the world of nature. To describe the cossacks, Bilinkis uses Belinsky's characterization of Pushkin's gypsies as "unconsciously reasonable" [*bezsoznatel'no razumny*].[15] One could say the same thing of beasts, of course, that they live by the laws of nature even though they live by feelings alone. To the extent that it is completely unconscious, the cossack life is unspoiled and natural, but not fully human.

The cossacks are not intended to be full grown human beings, but neither are they merely beasts. They are sentient beings endowed with a potential for reason that remains mostly undeveloped. Yet, they do have consciousness and they do know right from wrong. Olenin completes his youth among them and in the stag's lair he discovers the all-important natural sentiment of "love of everything" that will inspire his adult morality. He also reasons there, and his reasoning up to a certain point—to Eroshka's wisdom, the wisdom of the mature cossack—does not conflict with nature. But despite their potential for selfless love, a potential expressed in their community solidarity, the cossacks cannot follow Olenin beyond Eroshka's wisdom to a creed that would elevate selfless love above self-love.

What fatally divides Olenin from the cossacks, as he admits even as he finally gives into his passion for Marianka, is self-consciousness, the self that asks "who am I? and why am I here?" (23). His morality of self-sacrifice is "conscious" (*soznatel'noe*; 26), the product of a self that has developed beyond the limits imposed by nature on all nonhuman beings. The development of the self is fostered by reason.

Like all human beings, the cossacks have reason. They have achieved the level of development at which Olenin in his revery in the stag's lair recognizes his own particularity. One can say that human beings, unlike other animals, *know* (because they can think) that they are distinct from all others. This is the fundamental knowledge of the cossack, and Eroshka's old man's wisdom consists precisely in reasoning his way back from cossack community based on passions like honor and love of family to the essential solitariness of man and its implications. But Tolstoy wanted more than this. He wanted a real community based on love of others as well as self, and he wanted this community to be natural.

As always in Tolstoy, the presentation of reason's role in morality is complex. In his revery Olenin feels both happiness and love of everything together *before* reason enters the picture to make him distinguish his own particular being. In this sense reason, with its connection to form, shuts off the insight of feeling (content) about the basic similarity of all living things.[16] The sense of particularity imposed by reason becomes a barrier between a living being and the "content" of which it is composed. But objective and universal reality, a reality accessible to feeling but not to reason, is reasonable. It is both harmonious and governed by laws.

Once individuals have become conscious of themselves as discrete beings, their energy, their love becomes focused on themselves. Human beings are naturally (though not primarily) reasonable, so this awareness of self is natural—it occurs to Olenin in the stag's lair—and it corresponds to the real nature of things. In the imagery of *War and Peace*, we are atoms indivisible in ourselves but subject to the influence of general laws. One can say, then, that because the cossacks are authentic, they are *too* unified to be capable of higher morality.

There is a curious moment in *The Cossacks* that, properly understood, sheds light on what Olenin and his creator find problematic for human community and morality in cossack life. It occurs as the stage is being set for the bloody encounter between the cossacks and abreks. Olenin has ridden out onto the steppe with the cossack posse. When the abreks come into view, "Olenin was struck by the place where they were sitting."

The place was just like the whole steppe, but because the abreks were sitting in this place it seemed suddenly to be distinct from all the rest and somehow marked. It even seemed to him to be just precisely the spot in which the abreks ought to have been sitting. (41)

The place acquires a uniqueness because of the presence in it of the abreks. Like Olenin in the stag's lair, they are completely and distinctly themselves, "being[s] so very distinct from all others," and they therefore impart their particularity to their surroundings. As Olenin did in the stag's lair, they blend completely with the setting because they acknowledge and totally accept the death that awaits them. This is the law of nature lived by mosquitoes and pheasants and understood by men in touch with nature. The cossacks who will kill the abreks are committing a natural act which the abreks themselves, were the situation reversed, would as willingly commit. Passions, particularly the passion of honor, have taken these men out of themselves and caused them to band together, but what holds each warrior here now is the belief that it is better to die than to compromise his individual dignity.

What Olenin finds frightening in this eery and powerful moment is the irrationality of the participants, their obsession with personal honor, on the one hand, and their complete and almost inhuman acceptance of the laws of nature, on the other. If nature is nothing but particular individuals and laws that limit their expansion, then it can harbor no real freedom and no morality. This is not Tolstoy's position, but to the extent that the cossacks remain completely immersed in nature, they cannot see their way to its moral and reasonable heart.

Consciousness, possible only because we are reasonable beings, makes us more concerned with ourselves, but also, through that selfsame reason, aware both of our own limits and of the particular being of others. It can turn self-love toward love of everything and unify it with love of others by purifying that self-love to the extent that, for all intents and purposes, the general and the particular meet in a particular being. He becomes a microcosm of the macrocosm, as is the case with Platon Karataev.[17] When this happens the natural love of everything can flourish, as it does in Platon.

There is no such character in *The Cossacks*. The work is more "realistic" than *War and Peace*. (For this reason many readers have preferred it.) It expresses a comparison of civilized and savage man,[18] from which nature emerges as the source of feelings fundamental to civilized life. Nature displays incredible variety and vitality along with laws of necessity, which are required to keep order. Civilization as Olenin sees it after his encounter with the cossack world has succeeded in banishing or ignoring the laws of necessity, but without moderating self-love. As a result, untried self-love flourishes in civilization without the natural restraints that lend the cossacks their dignity and depth.

But if nature is so much better than civilization, why then does Olenin choose to leave the cossacks? The simple answer is that he cannot participate wholeheartedly in the bloodshed that is required of every male member of the community.[19] The cossacks are *too* natural for him, too determined to kill and be killed. There is something claustrophobic about their world, epitomized by the jungle where Olenin finds the stag's lair. Natural morality is not enough.

In *War and Peace*, Tolstoy would argue that a real free and self-sacrificing morality can be derived from nature. Only civilized human beings can know this, however. Only they can find their way through the (real) fact of human particularity to the (ideal) similarity of all. The savage cossacks, midway between nature and civilization, do not get beyond a self-love grown stronger because of a developing reason. Civilization brings with it, for better as for worse, a more developed reason, and makes possible a glimmer of higher reason necessary to find one's way to the "reason behind everything that lives" and to the "love of everything" that is its expression in feeling.

Tolstoy did not emphasize this ultimately positive core of civilized life in *The Cossacks*, but he does acknowledge it. Olenin has it strengthened and even confirmed by his experience at the heart of nature, in the stag's lair, where he remembers his childhood prayers. Daddy Eroshka, on the other hand, has no knowledge of this higher reason. When, in chapter 27, he finds Olenin at work on his diary, he assumes he is writing "slanders" [*kliauzy*] and persuades him to set the diary aside. Eroshka obviously takes a dim view of writing altogether, as another tool by which human beings manipulate one another. For Tolstoy, however, writing, an act of communication and therefore fundamentally social, can have another, higher function. In fact, at the very moment Eroshka is making fun of him Olenin is penning an affirmation of his love of others. In this case, Olenin is communicating with himself, in diary writing that is meant to discover and firm up the moral contours of his life:

> "I've thought a lot and changed a lot in the past while," wrote Olenin, "and I've come to what is written in the primer. To be happy, one thing is needed—to love, and to love with self-abnegation, to love everyone and everything, to throw out all around a net of love: whoever falls into it, take him. Thus have I snared Vaniusha [his manservant], Daddy Eroshka, Lukashka, Mar'ianka."

Even after he seems to reject civilization, Olenin is caught between two worlds, the real one of the cossacks based on healthy self-interest moderated by necessity, and an ideal one of his imagination. Daddy Eroshka, for all his wisdom, has no access to the ideal world. This chapter ends with his bursting into tears because he and Olenin are "unloved" [*neliubimye*]. What he cannot conceive is the potential in Olenin, let alone in himself, really to love others.

Tolstoy's original idea in writing *The Cossacks* was to show that "the good is the good everywhere, that there are the same passions everywhere, that the savage state is good" (18 August 1857; 47:152). In the second part of 1857, partly under the influence of *The Iliad* and *The Odyssey*, he rejected this intention as inadequate. In drafts of his work written around this time the cossacks were portrayed as Homeric heroes.[20] Homer's world was good: as an antidote to modern times it was "soothing, calming, harmonious";[21] but, despite his greatness, Homer had one flaw: "I read the Gospels, which I haven't done for a long time. After the Iliad. How could Homer not have known that the good is love! Revelation. There is no better explanation" (29 August 1857; 47:154). Before Tolstoy read Homer, he had portrayed Lukashka (then called Kirka) in a draft entitled "Beglyi kazak" [The Fugitive Cossack] as romantically in love with Mar'ianka.[22] This he exchanged in drafts after Homer for his ultimate depiction of Lukashka as in control of his feelings for Mar'ianka. His freedom is more important to Lukashka than any passion. In this respect, he resembles Olenin before he comes to the Caucasus. Like Lukashka, Olenin had given in to "passions" [*uvlecheniia*], but only until they had seemed to threaten his freedom (2). Similarly, Lukashka will not give up his freedom for Mar'ianka. It is not that he does not desire her. Like Olenin when he finally surrenders himself to his love for Mar'ianka, Lukashka clutches her hands and tells her to do what she wills with him; but when she will not sleep with him, he spends the night with his mistress (13). His favorite song, which he sings at the end of chapter 27, in which, in his own mind, he discharges his debt to Olenin for the gift of a horse, is about a falcon that will not be captured and kept in a golden cage.

The cossacks are passionate, but they retroactively explain their passions away. Eroshka is swept away by one passion after another, the narrator tells us, but he always gets his feet back on the ground by interpreting his passions "practically," that is, as servants of his own rational self-interest (16).

So it is Olenin rather than Lukashka who in the final version of the novel is carried away by his passion for Mar'ianka. As he had hoped, he learns in the Caucasus what it means to love. His love, like what

Pierre and later Levin feel for their beloveds, is akin to, though more egoistic than, the "love of everything" that it dispossesses in his soul.

Olenin possesses the secret of love that he had absorbed with his first education. At the very heart of nature, in the stag's lair, it comes back to him just after he experiences the natural "love of everything" in the form of memory of childhood prayers. The cossacks, although nominal Christians, have forgotten this secret, and so they remain in the "child-like" world of Homer.[23] The secret itself is natural, but it takes civilized men raised as Christians to rediscover it in nature. Natural or savage men suppress it. This is why the book in which Tolstoy most glorified nature is not *The Cossacks*, but his book about the Russian nation, *War and Peace*.

Five

The Unity of Man and Nature in
War and Peace

The artist's goal is not to resolve a question irre-
futably, but to force [the reader] to love life in all
its innumerable, inexhaustible phenomena. (Letter to P. D. Bobyrykin [unsent], July or August
1865)

Life is everything. Life is God. Everything shifts
and moves, and this movement is God. And
while there is life, there is the pleasure of the self-
awareness of Divinity. To love life is to love God.
It is hardest and most blessed to love life in its
sufferings, in the innocence of sufferings. (*War
and Peace*, 14.15)

WAR AND PEACE is uniquely optimistic and "open" among Tolstoy's
works. Like the Savoyard Vicar, and like Nekhliudov in "Lucerne," in
this work for the time being Tolstoy swallowed his anger (or spent it on
smallfry like politicians and intellectuals) and left morality to Providence. To a greater extent here than anywhere else, he conceived of
himself as a poet who celebrates life "in all its innumerable, inexhaustible phenomena," as it is, not as it should be.

To do this, he had to regard life as fundamentally happy and just.
During the years when he was writing *War and Peace*, someone remarked that happiness is the most unjust thing on earth. Tolstoy responded: "Human happiness, like water in a pond or lake, is spread
out absolutely evenly up to the edge."[1] Happiness, of course, was what
Tolstoy wanted. Perhaps the most fundamental requirement of this
happiness was unity with nature. Without it human beings could not
be whole: they would have to tear away half their lives in order to
satisfy the other half. Yet, as I have argued earlier, Tolstoy could not
embrace nature wholeheartedly without believing that the natural life
was moral. Turgenev may have preferred *The Cossacks* to *War and Peace*
because the earlier work seemed to praise nature for its beauty and
"wholeness" (or unity) without claiming that it was moral. Turgenev

must have agreed with Annenkov's review of *The Cossacks* that in it Tolstoy distinguished "poetic" from "moral" truth.[2] From the previous chapter it must be clear the extent to which Turgenev and Annenkov misunderstood the work. Tolstoy had, in fact, argued in that work that the higher morality of self-sacrifice is incipient in nature, but that natural or at least savage man[3] would not act according to this morality even if he acknowledged its superiority. *War and Peace* is more radical. There everything real and good is seen to be natural, and so the unity of the self and nature is realized to the greatest possible extent.

Tolstoy needed many and diverse things for his happiness, and it was not easy for him to assemble, let alone unify them in his greatest novel. Indeed, when it was all over, and he was rereading the book in order to republish it in the early 1870s, it seemed to him that he was inspecting with a sober eye the aftermath of an orgy: so artificial and tawdry did the results of his passionate exertions on behalf of natural goodness seem in the cold light of Schopenhauerian reason. "The one thing that comforts me," he wrote to A. A. Tolstaia, "is that I was completely carried away by this orgy and thought that nothing else existed" (62:9).

What seemed excessive to Tolstoy in his sceptical mood was the theoretical argument necessary to sustain a vision of the world that corresponds so much to human expectations that readers of *War and Peace* often say that they find it completely "realistic." The purpose of this chapter is to reconstruct that argument part by part.

Nature and History in *War and Peace*

To achieve unity of man and nature within the novel, history, in which love of others comes into its own, had to be included within nature's compass. Properly interpreted, political history becomes a part of God's will which affects every individual (and which every individual affects) but which remains ultimately mysterious. Its meaning lies hidden in that part of metaphysics—by far the greater part—that the student of the Savoyard Vicar regarded as inaccessible to human reason. It was when Tolstoy reached this outer limit of the conceivably natural and discovered the natural equivalent of what historians call history that his novel took off.

In a progression typical of him from radical negation to a positive new ideal, Tolstoy arrived at the idea of political history as a mysterious force of nature. This he did in the wake of his rejection of the idea of progress. This last was the false ideal to which Tolstoy had referred in "Who Should Be Teaching Whom to Write: Should We Be Teaching the Peasant Lads, or They Us?" In another article published in *Iasnaia Poliana* entitled "Progress and the Definition of Education," [*Progres i opredelenie obrazovaniia*], Tolstoy blamed the moral relativism fostered by the idea of progress on Hegel (8:326). Historicism, invented by Hegel, holds that "everything historical is rational," and that therefore the only absolute good is progress. To this Tolstoy responded that the only real law of progress is that of the potential for perfection that resides in each individual soul(8:333). The law of progress in the soul transported into history "turns into idle empty chatter, leading to the justification of all sorts of nonsense and fatalism." The perfection we should pursue in our personal lives is within us. Although Tolstoy did not explicitly make the connection—his particular purpose in "Progress and the Definition of Education" did not require it—there was no reason to believe that this perfection sought by the soul was any different from the ideal "behind us" that he had lauded in nature and in the uncorrupted soul in "Who Should Be Teaching Whom to Write: Should We Be Teaching the Peasant Lads, or They Us?"

The very first reference to what was to become *War and Peace* occurred in February 1863, just after Tolstoy had finished "Progress and the Definition of Education."[4] The novel was conceived as a continuation of the attack on progress and history launched in the pages of *Iasnaia Poliana*. It can therefore be no accident that this attack surfaced again in the very draft in which, after thirteen attempts, Tolstoy found the beginning of his novel in a salon run by the as yet unnamed Anna Pavlovna Sherer (13:72–73). The historian, Tolstoy wrote, does not understand how human life really proceeds. History is the story of human "disfigurements" [*urodstva*]. Real life, the same everywhere, goes on outside of history: "They [the historians] see the trash that the river throws up onto its banks and sandbars while the eternally changing, disappearing and emerging drops of water which make the riverbed remain unknown to them." This crucial early draft reveals that Tolstoy's novel about the greatest event of nineteenth-century Russian history was conceived in an important sense as antihistorical.[5] Tolstoy was planning to write not a history, and not an idyll (from which public life would be excluded or left in the background), but a kind of epic. In it everything important in human life would be revealed to have a natural justification.

It is typical of Tolstoy's youthful energy and ambition, however, that he was not content in *War and Peace* simply to debunk something as important as history. Instead, he set out to supply a natural equivalent for it. The crucial metaphor of the river itself, both in its entirety and made up of individual drops, individual human beings that comprise and shape it, stands for history in the novel. A natural force whose real purpose is known only to God, the river represents the herd life of mankind, serving goals beyond the ken of individuals. This is how I interpret the parallel drawn between the Enns River and the army in part 2, chapter 5. In this way Tolstoy supplied a natural explanation even for such "unnatural" human phenomema as war, which in "A Few Words about *War and Peace*" he called "biological law."

Freedom in *War and Peace*, as elsewhere in Tolstoy, is to be understood in the sense enunciated by the Savoyard Vicar: "My being able to will only what is suitable to me, or what I deem to be such, without anything external to me determining me."[6] Free human life therefore by definition exists only outside of history, which is conceived either as the trash thrown up onto the banks of a flowing river or as the river itself, the metaphor for legitimate "natural" history. To the extent that leaders willingly give up their freedom to become creatures of the mysterious force behind the river, they are "disfigured." In Tolstoy's peculiar argument broached at the beginning of part 9 and expanded in the second epilogue, leaders serve the needs of their followers, who, while obeying the inhuman dictates of war to slaughter their fellows, slough off moral responsibility for their acts upon these leaders. Individual soldiers, who kill because they want to do so, remain free in the sense that they are acting according to an inner compulsion. But since this compulsion contradicts the voice of conscience in each soldier, he relinquishes his *moral* freedom in this specific matter to leaders in whom ambition has stilled conscience.[7]

It is useful to compare Tolstoy's understanding of the relation of the self and history with that of Herzen. For Herzen, according to Patricia Carden, the self affects history inasmuch as it is part of a collective.[8] Carden quotes a famous passage from Herzen about human beings as both determined by history and determining it (ibid., 524). Within the passage, in an elaborately developed metaphor comparing history to a carpet, the individual self figures as both "woof and weaver" (ibid., 525). Like Carden (and N. N. Ardens, whom she credits),[9] I am struck by the relevance of this passage to related arguments in *War and Peace*. One difference between Herzen and Tolstoy seems crucial for understanding the latter's position. While granting the power of historical forces and the seeming weakness of the individual in the face of them, both men were concerned to defend the existence of human freedom and responsibility. Herzen, however, did this from an avowedly atheistic perspective, while Tolstoy remained a kind of believer.

Herzen's passage ended with the following words: "And that is not all: we can change the pattern of the carpet. There is no master, there is no design, there is only the warp (foundation) and we all alone by ourselves." The passage comes from "Robert Owen" [*Robert Ouen*], part 6, chapter 99, of Herzen's wonderful memoirs *My Past and Thoughts* [*Byloe i dumy*; 395]. "Robert Owen" was published in the sixth issue of the journal *Northern Star* [*Poliarnaia zvezda*] in 1861, and Tolstoy read it there.[10] Tolstoy's argument about history in *War and Peace* may even have been, at least as he first conceived it, his response to the extended discussion of history in this article.

In any case, he wrote to Herzen about this very passage that the "pattern" of the carpet, in comparison with the ideas—immortality, historical laws—that it replaced was "a button in place of a colossus": "So it would have been better not to give them this law [of the pattern and the possibility of changing it]. Nothing in place [of these other laws]. Nothing but that force that topples colossuses" (14 March 1861; 60:374). Tolstoy did not believe that human beings are "alone by [them]selves" in the universe or, as Herzen put it elsewhere in his article, that "neither nature nor history *are going anywhere*."[11] He took the Pascalian mathematician's view that things ultimately must make sense even in the senseless barbarism of war. He therefore, as Boris Sorokin has noticed, depicted war as senseless slaughter and at the same time hinted that it might have had another, hidden meaning.[12] For him there *was* a God who operates as a kind of puppet master in *War and Peace*, pulling the strings of the Napoleons who mistakenly believe themselves to be shaping history. What leaders and historians call history is merely "trash," that is, the stuff of politics which, in reality, depends on a combination of human ambition and chance. When human beings do go to war, however, they are obeying natural, if inhuman laws. Because this real history is ultimately determined, the individual human freedom that Tolstoy valued no less than Herzen did can exist only outside of it.

Real history, as defined in *War and Peace*, is "the life of nations and humanity" (second epilogue, 1). As such, it interested Tolstoy because in the grip of historical forces people do things, good and bad, that contradict both self-love and conscience.[13] These forces, and war itself, are "biological," but they are guided by a divine being.

The 1868 notebook contains a curious example of the biological thinking underlying *War and Peace*: "History.—families fulfill their destiny: the continuation of the human species. Conflicts. Each [family] wants world domination" (48:108). In this passage, families, and by extension, nations, are like the expanding and contracting drops of water in Pierre's dream of the liquid globe. The notebook continues with an outline for the argument about history in the second epilogue (48:108–11). "The purpose of living, that is, of moving, is to find an activity," and the more this activity accords with "general laws," that is, "the continuation of the species," the happier will be the individual actor. A brief theory of history based on these ideas and others derived from them follows, with one caveat, namely, that we do not necessarily know God's original purpose or intention from the "conflicts" and motion of history. Although we may "feel" it at times (as does Kutuzov), we cannot know the objective truth of history, and therefore we cannot base our historical theories on it (48:111). All we can really know in history, as elsewhere, is the subjective world of feeling, which in these pages of his notebook Tolstoy presented as biologically driven.

This notebook thus states explicitly the crucial idea that Gary Saul Morson has developed in *Hidden in Plain View*. If ultimate laws govern history, only God, with whom the notion of determinism is associated, can comprehend them. This, Morson shows, is how Tolstoy drew the line in *War and Peace* between the objective and determined sphere, on the one hand, and the subjective and free one, on the other.

> Tolstoy refuted the usual interpretation of determinism not on metaphysical but rather on epistemological grounds. He believed that, by their very nature, the principles governing human events are incomprehensible to the human mind. To be sure, all events are determined; and, to be sure, if it is once conceded that life can be governed by reason, then life is impossible. But life *is* possible, because reason cannot understand the principles of events and therefore cannot predict as the underground man fears ... determinism ... is totally irrelevant to human life and the practice of historiography.[14]

Therefore, Morson concludes, "A wise man believes and behaves as if events happen just 'for some reason'" (ibid., 90). Morson wisely stops short of denying the existence in Tolstoy's world of *metaphysical* determinism, but if it does exist it cannot be *totally* irrelevant to human life. Humankind must recognize the limits of its legitimate freedom. When a man like Napoleon oversteps its boundaries he becomes a pawn of Fate. Like the Savoyard Vicar, Tolstoy insisted that mankind must mind its own business, leaving God to mind His. Political men must know enough to acknowledge their lack of freedom, as Kutuzov does. We are not ultimately responsible for what happens in the "swarm," or political, life of mankind, although we must participate in it; but we are responsible for our private lives, which Tolstoy took some trouble to keep separate from "swarm" life.[15]

Divine history, then, mysterious but real, replaces manmade political history in *War and Peace*. And in a related development, the false ideal of history, progress, also really exists.[16] The idea of rational progress is a distorted shadow of the potential for perfection within the human soul.

One of the things that separates the late-twentieth-century reader from Tolstoy is his very nineteenth-century preoccupation with what he called *usovershenstvovanie*. In note 46 of chapter 3 I have translated this as "pursuit of perfection," because this phrase captures the sense of process in the Russian word, which, in its philosophic meaning, has no exact equivalent in English.[17] To the extent that *usovershenstvovanie* was Tolstoy's goal for himself and for mankind as a whole, he himself participated in that optimistic belief in progress that may have been finally discredited by the horrors of our own century.[18] Tolstoy's very first diaries made "the development of my faculties" his goal (46:29), and he early on created the character Nekhliudov in order to dramatize this side of his nature and to impart "pursuit of perfection" to Nikolenka Irten'ev, his narrator in the trilogy. It is significant that Nikolenka does not discover this goal himself: this natural man needs a Nekhliudov, who has little appreciation of nature and much *amour propre* (an unnatural passion associated with a developed reason), to reveal it to him.[19]

"The pursuit of perfection" as a natural human faculty implies that man, as nature made him, is not good enough. It is a quality inherent in natural man that makes a certain kind of progress necessary. From Tolstoy's earliest philosophizing, he seemed to have associated "the pursuit of perfection" on the highest level with two different things: love and reason. To perfect oneself was to shift the balance in the human soul from the natural love of self to an equally natural but naturally weak love of others, and the way to do this was through reasoning. So, as we have seen in the previous chapter, Olenin is different from the cossacks both by virtue of his more developed powers of analysis, or reason, and because of his adherence to the doctrine of self-abnegation, which, moreover, he justifies as the only reasonable way of life. And although the source of Olenin's love of others is natural, when he tries to apply it, it separates him from nature.

In *War and Peace* the right kind of progress is seen to have occurred within the Russian people, whose highest exemplar, Platon Karataev, has achieved human perfection. Like other human beings, he loves himself and desires happiness. More than any other character in the novel, however, Platon sees his life in terms of the general, rather than the particular (12.13). "But his life, as he himself regarded it, had no meaning as a separate life. It had meaning only as part of a whole, which he continually sensed." Platon ultimately and perhaps to an inhuman extent identifies his own interests with those of humankind. The story that Platon tells of the wrongly accused merchant illustrates the way each life, even one sorely wronged, makes sense only with reference to God's purpose (14.13). As Platon tells the story, he sits "covered with his soldier's overcoat as with a priest's vestments": he is God's messenger to Pierre, who stands in relation to him as Peter does to Christ in the New Testament. (The man of the earth, Pierre, will put Platon's teaching into practice so far as is humanly possible.) Platon is a fatalist, but one who believes both in God and in human responsibility. This perspective reveals the injustice of the merchant's story to be justified and transforms what might be anger into religious ecstasy at the revelation of God's plan, or the Goethean "reason behind everything that lives."[20] It is only by experiencing the most terrible injustice that the merchant achieves the ultimate human satisfaction of knowing that his life has meaning beyond his own happiness. Unlike in history, God is shown here to be concerned with the fate of the individual (both the falsely accused murderer and the real one), whose salvation is His aim.

There is another important difference between external and internal history. The latter, unlike the former, is within the realm of individual responsibility. Thus, the merchant in Platon's story claims responsibility for his own fate. He takes as a general principle that all, including himself, have sinned and therefore deserve whatever unhappiness life brings them. This point of view is the opposite of the one expressed in Princess Maria's "Tout comprendre, c'est tout pardonner" [To understand everything is to forgive everything] (1.25), but in Platon's story, as in the novel, both sentiments are seen to be true. We are not responsible for what happens to other people, even as we inevitably participate in their fates, but we are responsible for ourselves. Thus, Princess Maria is as strict with herself as she is forgiving of others.

It is no accident that Platon refers to peasant ways as Christian ones. (He uses the adjective *khristianskoe* in place of *krest'ianskoe* [12.13].) Unlike the cossacks, whose Christianity is only skin-deep, the peasants of *War and Peace* have had the benefit of revelation, and hence of human history. This is the only plausible explanation, according to Tolstoy in the diary entry from 1857 quoted above in chapter 4, of how love of others came to vie with self-love in the course of civilization. In "Education for the People" (1862), he suggested that "the understanding of virtue [in the human soul] either remains the same, or is infinitely developing" (8:8). There is, significantly, no suggestion of conflict between natural and civilized man in this second explanation, proffered just before Tolstoy began *War and Peace*. In the novel of unity, the inner history of the human soul, like external history, is the natural direction taken by life, which Tolstoy understood as informed and formed by divinity.

"The pursuit of perfection" is the moral force within each individual soul, and, as such, it parallels a presumed but unprovable divine goal for the world as a whole. The behavior of human beings both when they surrender themselves to general forces and when they heed the voice of conscience is similar: in both cases they sacrifice what would seem to be their undiluted self-interest for the goals of all.[21] In this the human individual is no different from any natural being, or from nature itself as the novel portrays it. In all cases, the individual, willy-nilly, serves the whole, which subsumes everything, all those opposites that comprise the world, within it. And a dynamic view of nature includes even the history of individuals and nations within it.

Circular versus Faustian Reason in *War and Peace*

Nature in *War and Peace* is ruled by harmonic reason, which operates through the metaphysics of opposites. Sergei Bocharov has also called this form of reason "circular," in contrast to what he calls the "Faustian," or "linear" reasoning characteristic of Pierre or particularly Andrei. Circular reasoning he associates with the round Platon Karataev.[22] As an example of circular reasoning, Bocharov compares the question *zachem* (why) of Torzhok with the *zachem* of Mozhaisk as reflections of one another. In the first one there is a simple sense of contradiction, which is replaced in the second by a productive opposition [*protivorechie*]. At Mozhaisk *zachem* becomes not just a question but the answer, an answer connected to the patriotic war and to the peasant *mir* [commune].[23] But, Bocharov points out later (ibid., 97), the question *zachem* reawakens later in Pierre. So one provisional title of the novel—*All's Well That Ends Well*—turned out to be inappropriate: at the end *mir* [peace] is being destroyed again.[24]

Precisely because of the "circular" or open structure of *War and Peace*, the truths of Andrei and Platon are intended to complement rather than simply contradict one another.[25] Bocharov's reference to Faust is helpful for understanding this, because the Faustian element in *War and Peace* functions just as it does in *Faust* itself. From God's point of view, Faust's energy is one element in a living harmony made up of elements, all legitimate, which (as in the liquid globe of Pierre's dream) clash, couple, and disappear. The equilibrium and family happiness established at the end of *War and Peace* is no more the goal of life than the state of motion and war that precedes it. One leads to the other in an unending circular motion which, in *War and Peace*, Tolstoy sanctified as itself moral.

The unconscious life of a Platon Karataev is governed by laws, and, as such, has as much to do with reason as does the life of Prince Andrei.[26] One could even say that Platon's way of life is more reasonable than Andrei's, although Andrei strives to be rational. In fact, what makes Platon a less believable figure than Andrei is his extreme, in Tolstoy's view Platonic, reasonableness. Platon is so reasonable, so naturally moderate, that, as I have said before, he lives according to the laws that govern the whole: "But his life as he himself looked on it did not make sense as an individual life. It made sense only as part of a whole which he felt continuously" (12.13). To "make sense" [*imet' smysl*] is to be reasonable, which Platon is so long as he, and the reader, regard his life as "part of a whole."

The so-called unconscious life, ordered by the harmonic reason that rules the universe, makes more sense than Andrei's life, in which he seeks a reasonable existence for his individual self. Andrei, who begins by regarding his own body as a temple[27] and whom his wife justly accuses of egotism (1.4), is initially like the Kuragins in his selfishness. Bocharov rightly points out that the world of selfish wills spawns the crisis of *zachem*.[28] Unlike the Kuragins, however, Prince Andrei, selfish and willful though he be at the beginning of the novel, has the higher reason and hence concern with nobility to ask *zachem* in the first place, and then to try to answer the question. Andrei's life becomes fully reasonable only when he is willing to relinquish his individual existence, his physical life, in order to rejoin the fully rational essence toward which he is driven. He has to will his own death, and then he can speak, without compassion but without bitterness, in biblical parables about the sparrows of the field being cared for by God. At that point he cares no more about human love than Platon, in his story of the unjustly accused merchant, cares about human justice. The fates and the reason of the two characters converge: both speak from the lofty and inhuman perspective of Providence.

Tolstoy wrote in the first epilogue (1) that "If one allows that human life can be guided by reason, then the possibility of life is destroyed." Every human individual encapsulates in himself the principle of harmony and moderation by which Providence rules the whole, but if each individual simply lived by that principle, there would be no life, because there would be no motion. It is more natural, and necessary from the point of view of divine reason, for living beings to care irrationally for themselves above all others. So irrational particularity has its sacred place in the reasonable universe that Tolstoy so carefully constructed in his novel. The moment when death in the form of an exploding shell comes to Andrei, an intense love of life wells up in him in opposition to it (10.36). Even Platon loves his own life. He keeps busy fulfilling his simple needs, which beyond food, warmth, and rest include music, storytelling, and the company of other human beings. Unlike Andrei, Platon does not will his own death: he weeps and beckons to Pierre for companionship when he sees it coming (14.14).

After his liberation from captivity, Pierre, taught by Platon and adversity to live moderately within himself, practices the kindly distance from other people that distinguished Platon's relations with others.

Only after he meets Natasha and his passion for her reawakens does the action of the novel move forward once again. The family scenes in the first epilogue are parts of the alternation of peace and war that make up the process of life. The Faustian quest for answers and justice is, as it was in "Lucerne," one manifestation, an intellectual one, of life's energy as it expresses itself in the individual. Like Pierre's love for Natasha, it is one of the passions that cause things to happen. Everything that happens, happens according to the laws of harmonic reason.

Harmonic, or circular reason, as I have argued, takes place through the interaction of opposites. This is what distinguishes it from logic. The inadequacy of logic to comprehend life is exposed in Tolstoy's wicked portrait of Speransky, who "would use all possible weapons of thought except comparisons [or similes—*sravneniia*] and would move too boldly, so it seemed to Prince Andrei, from one to another" (6.6). Tolstoy's own writing abounds in metaphors and similes, and this is as true of his polemics and essays as of his fiction. Indeed, the most conspicuous failing in his nonfiction may be his overuse of these devices. Where the reader requires argument, he often finds a simile that irritates by attempting to convince him more by analogy than by logic. We may better understand Tolstoy's attraction to comparisons by reflecting on Speransky's failure to use them. As a logician, Speransky sees only the differences between things so that he can distinguish one from another. He connects them only by contiguity in time and space and through cause and effect. In their essences they remain distinct. The poet—Tolstoy—sees things in their interconnectedness, until, through harmonic reasoning, he understands the unity of all things. The reasoning behind the metaphysics of *War and Peace* is the same as that expressed and illustrated in "Lucerne." *Physically* we are separate, and this is a necessity of spiritual as well as physical life; but *morally*, or spiritually—Tolstoy did not distinguish the two—everything is interrelated.

The Morality of Nature in *War and Peace*

Harmonic, or circular reason requires that some die so that others may live. So Petia's death destroys his mother and restores his sister, Natasha, to life as she nurses her grieving mother (15.2). Andrei's death, similarly, creates a vacuum that is filled by the marriages of Natasha and Pierre and Nikolai and Maria. The war, which brings about Andrei's death, also plays an important role in these marriages. Here one is reminded, not by chance I think, of Goethe's poem *Herman and Dorothea*. In his well-known letter to Lederle of 25 October 1891, Tolstoy placed this work at the top of the list of books that had affected him from age twenty to age thirty-five, in other words, while he was writing *War and Peace*.[29] In chapter 2 I remarked on the connection between Pierre's love for Natasha and the destructive forces unleased in 1812. As in *War and Peace*, in *Herman and Dorothea* war brings the lovers together. Goethe underlines the importance of this fact by remarking that Herman's parents also fell in love as a result of a catastrophe, a disastrous fire that destroyed their city. Tolstoy, too, explicitly linked eros and war in *War and Peace* in his description of fall 1806 (4.10).[30] Amid feverish preparations for war, an "atmosphere of being in love" prevails in the Rostov household as never before. In human life as in nature, according to the metaphysics of opposites, the old gives way to the new.[31]

Tolstoy did more in *War and Peace*, however, than demonstrate the place of destruction in the cycle of life. He argued there that death and even war are good, because without them there would be no morality. This is essential to the success of Tolstoy's whole endeavor. For, I repeat, if mortals, even the greatest heroes, are not individually responsible for war, then God, who put in place the laws that cause it, must be. When individual human beings "will" the death of themselves and others, as Tolstoy's narrator says they do in more than one place, they are following the commands of God, who actually appears in *War and Peace* as He does in the Old Testament. He is the *Rasporiaditel'*, the Master of Ceremonies, who unmasks the Napoleons, saying "'Look who you have believed in! Here he is! Do you see now that it is not he, but I who have been moving you?'" In his epic Tolstoy defended everything natural as part of a cosmic world order. This includes even the savage laws that cause war (10.39). In so doing, he goes beyond the Savoyard Vicar, who contrasts human disorder with order and harmony in nature.[32] So at the end of the battle of Borodino, the narrator declares outright that God is responsibile for it: "And there continued to its completion that terrible event [Borodino] which happened not by the will of human beings, but by the will of He who rules human beings and worlds" (10.39).[33]

It is strange but true, I think, that part of the greatness of *War and Peace* resides in the fact that Tolstoy was willing to accept war as natural without providing a humanly comprehensible justification for it. At the same time, and perhaps as shockingly for the modern sensibility, he did argue that war can play a salutary role in the moral education of the individual.[34] Pierre learns about the necessity even of war from the sequence of events connected to Mozhaisk. He discovers a metaphysical principle at Mozhaisk that justifies even the greatest cause of death and evil.

In "The Woodfelling" (1855), the brightest moments in the generally gloomy life of a soldier occur in combat before the fatal wounding of Velenchuk.[35] In *War and Peace* this strange fact of war psychology leads one eventually to reflect on the relation of alternating rhythms of necessity and freedom in the novel. Pierre first observes the two moods of war at Mozhaisk, before the battle of Borodino.

> On the morning of the 25th Pierre drove out of Mozhaisk. On the winding road which led from the city down an enormous steep hill past a cathedral on the right in which a service was going on and bells were chiming, Pierre climbed out of his carriage and went on foot. Behind him a cavalry regiment was descending the hill with its singers in front. Coming up towards him was a train of carts with the wounded from yesterday's engagement. The peasant drivers, shouting at their horses and lashing them with whips, ran from one side of the road to the other. The carts, in which wounded soldiers were lying and sitting in threes and fours, bounced over stones which had been thrown along the steep incline to make it something like a road. The wounded, bandaged with rags, pale, with compressed lips and knitted brows, holding onto the sides, bounced and jostled against one another in the carts. Almost all of them stared with naive childlike curiosity at Pierre's white hat and green swallow-tailed coat.
>
> Pierre's coachman shouted angrily at the convoy of wounded to keep to one side of the road. The cavalry regiment with its singers, descending the hill, overtook Pierre's carriage and blocked the road. Pierre stopped, pressed to the edge of the road cut out of the hill. Because of the slant of the hill, the sun did not reach the inner part of the road; there it was cold and damp; over Pierre's head was the bright August morning, and the church bells rang merrily. One of the carts with the wounded stopped at the edge of the road near Pierre. A driver in bast shoes, puffing, ran up to his cart, placed a rock under its tireless back wheels and began to adjust the breeching on his little horse, which had halted.
>
> A wounded old soldier with a bandaged arm, walking behind the cart, took hold of it with his sound hand and glanced at Pierre.
>
> "What do you think, countryman, will they place us here or take us on to Moscow?" he said.
>
> Pierre was so deep in thought that he did not hear the question. He looked now at the cavalry regiment which had met here with the convoy of wounded men, now at that cart near which he stood and on which two wounded men were sitting and one was lying; and it seemed to him that here, in them, lay the answer to the question that preoccupied him. One of the soldiers sitting in the cart had no doubt been wounded in the cheek. His whole head was bandaged in rags and one cheek had swollen to the size of a child's head. His nose and mouth were shoved to one side. This soldier was

looking at the cathedral and crossing himself. The other, a young boy, a recruit, blond and so white that his sensitive face seemed to be drained of blood, was looking at Pierre with a fixed, kind smile. The third man lay prone so that his face was not visible. The cavalry singers were passing close by.

Ah lost, quite lost . . . is my head so keen,
Living in a foreign land . . .

they sang their soldier's dance song. As if repeating them, but with a different sort of merriment, the metallic notes of the church bells reverberated high above. And with yet another sort of merriment, the hot rays of the sun bathed the top of the opposite slope. But under the slope, at the cart with the wounded, near the panting little horse where Pierre was standing, it was damp, sombre and sad.

The soldier with the swollen cheek gazed at the cavalry singers.

"Oh those dandies!" he muttered reproachfully.

"These days it's not only soldiers I've seen but peasants as well! They've rounded even them up," said the soldier behind the cart, turning to Pierre with a sad smile. "These days they're not particular . . . they want to fall on them with the whole nation—in a word, it's Moscow. They want to make an end to it."

Despite the lack of clarity in the soldier's words, Pierre understood everything that he wanted to say, and nodded his head approvingly. (10.20)

In "The Woodfelling," the moments of joyous vitality and fear of pain and death during wartime were consecutive (3:57–58). Here, in a brilliantly conceived landscape, Tolstoy portrays them both at once. Though contiguous in space and simultaneous, the two moments are absolutely discrete. The physical setting, with the wounded climbing under the slope of the hill and the healthy descending in full sunshine, emphasizes this.

Talking some four hours later to a doctor who is grimly preparing for tomorrow's slaughter, Pierre at last formulates the question inherent in the Mozhaisk landscape.

"They may die tomorrow, why [*zachem*] are they thinking about anything else but death?" And suddenly, by some secret connection of thoughts, the descent from Mozhaisk, the carts with the wounded, the church bells, the slanted rays of the sun and the songs of the cavalry vividly came into his mind.

"The cavalry are going into battle and meet wounded men, and they do not reflect for a minute about what awaits them, but go past and wink at the wounded. And from all of these, twenty thousand are fated to die, and they marvel at my hat! Strange!" thought Pierre, continuing on his way to Tatarinova. (10.20)

The meaning of the Mozhaisk episode is not exhausted by Pierre's discovery of the patriotism that animates army and peasants alike. If Tolstoy had wished to express in it only the Russian patriotism of 1812, he would have made the wounded cheer the healthy, as they do in the first Sevastopol sketch (4:15).[36] How the original identification of an individual with his homeland takes place is not at issue here. If one accepts it as the basis of patriotism, then the question of Mozhaisk still remains: why do the cavalry men seem oblivious to their own impending deaths? Even if they accept the necessity of the upcoming battle, why do they not display the grimness of condemned men?

On the battlefield Pierre observes the *"chaleur"* of patriotism at work. He joins an artillery unit in the thick of the action and becomes absorbed in the "family circle" which the unit comprises (10.31). Twenty men have fallen and been removed by ten o'clock, but the unit does not lose heart. "Merry talk and jokes were heard from all sides" (ibid.).

> Pierre noticed that after each shell had fallen, after each casualty, the general animation blazed up more and more. As from an approaching thunderhead, more and more frequently, brighter and brighter there flashed in the faces of all these people (as if in opposition to what was taking place) lightning bolts of a hidden blazing fire.
>
> Pierre did not look ahead at the battlefield and he took no interest in what was happening there. He was completely absorbed in the observation of this fire, blazing up more and more, which was burning in just the same way (he felt) in his own soul. (Ibid.)

The gunfire becomes so intense and men fall so frequently that stretcher bearers cannot remove all the wounded and dead. The worse the fighting, the more animated the men become.

> The young officer, becoming more and more flushed, commanded his soldiers more and more scrupulously. The soldiers handed up the charges, turned, loaded and did their job with strained dash [*shchegol'stvo*, a form of the same word that the wounded soldier at Mozhaisk used to describe the singers (*"Okh, shchegol'ki!"*)]. They jumped about as if on springs.
>
> The thunderhead had arrived and in every face the fire which Pierre had watched kindle burned brightly. (Ibid.)

Once again, it is certainly true that these soldiers feel the justice of their fight against the invaders. But the internal fire described here flames up not merely as a reflection of patriotism. It develops "as if in opposition to what was taking place." The more terrifying the situation becomes, the more the men respond with heightened energy—"as if on springs"—to danger. The cold winds of threatening death fan into flame the life spark in each man's soul. The greater the danger, the more intensely each man feels his own vitality.

The men whom Pierre sees descending the hill at Mozhaisk are not thinking about death, but they are preparing to face it. The suppressed knowledge of the danger that awaits them (along with the certainty of the justice of their cause) inspires their liveliness. War and hardship teach us what real vitality is. Only in facing death does each man learn how much he loves his own life and what living means to him.

At the moment of highest tension in the battle, when all the soldiers move as if on springs, the youthful officer is killed. "Everything became strange, unclear and cloudy in Pierre's eyes" (10.31). Now Pierre springs into action himself. He rushes to the reserves for ammunition. A shell explodes near the ammunition boxes, flinging him to the ground and seriously wounding a horse that lies near him, squealing from fear and pain. Himself now infected with panic, Pierre rushes back to his artillery unit, his home on the battlefield, and discovers it occupied by the French. After grappling with a Frenchman as disoriented as he is, he rushes out onto the battlefield in complete terror.

There is no place for Pierre to hide. "*Not remembering himself* from fear" (emphasis mine; 10.32), he cannot call forth in himself the inner resistance necessary to survive on the battlefield. Having abandoned all hope of saving himself, he now sees all the horrors of the chaos around him and submits to them. He is now in the position of the wounded soldiers at Mozhaisk. At the end of the day, still in this state, he himself starts to ascend the hill at Mozhaisk only to be called back by his coachman (11.8). Pierre's return to this site also brings the reader back to Mozhaisk. The reader, too, can now envision that scene before the battle from the points of view of the healthy and the wounded.

The Mozhaisk sequence suggests a paradoxical truth about reality. The appeal of war is not simply diminished by exposure to its very real horrors. Life and death are both real, and one cannot be appreciated fully without knowledge of the other. What the soldiers descending and ascending the hill at Mozhaisk feel are two sides of the same coin. Both states depend on an awareness of necessity common to all soldiers and expressed in the landscape at Mozhaisk. As Pierre comprehends in his dream in the inn yard nearby, war represents natural necessity, "the harshest subordination of human freedom to the laws of God" (11.9). This accounts for its positive role in the psychological drama of the novel. The resigned fatalism of the wounded soldiers reflects their conviction that the external force [*sila*] with which the cavalry must presently do battle is stronger than the strength [*sila*] which they, on the basis of their disastrous experience, attribute to the cavalry. Their situation recalls the atmosphere at the end of "The Woodfelling," and the sympathy of the slightly wounded soldier (who still has energy enough to feel it) arises from the same process of identification illustrated there.[37] The healthy soldiers do not identify with the wounded. Their own *sila* is aroused in anticipation of the struggle ahead. Only the man who has faced adversity knows his own strength and the life within him. Necessity inspires joyful freedom.[38]

We are now in a position to understand Pierre's dream in the inn yard of Mozhaisk, which is the culmination of the whole Mozhaisk sequence (11.9). First, Pierre thinks how brave the simple soldiers were, and he wishes he could be like them. His duel with Dolokhov comes into his head, and then his meeting with his benefactor, Bazdeev, at Torzhok. The raw contradictions of life and death, which at Torzhok stopped Pierre's life cold, turn in Pierre's dream into a fruitful opposition. He dreams of a banquet in which such men as Dolokhov and Anatole sit on one side of the table, and simple soldiers sit with Bazdeev on the other. Bazdeev speaks "and the sound of his words was as significant and uninterrupted as the roar of the battlefield, but it was pleasant and comforting." Bazdeev is identified with war because both bring the salutary message of mortality to Pierre, who up until his meeting with Bazdeev has never thought of death as it applied to himself. This is true even though Pierre has witnessed his own father on his deathbed. The terrible, simple gaze of death that old Bezukhov directs toward his son had meant nothing personal to the young lover of life.

Pierre tries to call the soldiers' attention to himself. What separates Pierre from the soldiers, and unites him with Dolokhov, Denisov, and Anatole, is an unnaturally exaggerated individualism that creates a need for attention. He cannot give himself sufficiently to the "common life" [*obshchaia zhizn'*] to which they belong. One cause, or effect, of this individualism is a heightened sexuality, which is often in Tolstoy represented by images of a man's legs. (An example is the sexual importance of Vronsky's legs in *Anna Karenina*.) Rising from his seat to speak to the soldiers, Pierre feels that his legs (from which, in fact, his overcoat has slipped) are uncovered. He is ashamed and covers them. So on the symbolic level of the dream, consciousness of himself as a sexual being interrupts the first part of the dream.

Pierre opens his eyes, but he is unwilling to leave his dream without hearing Bazdeev's words. He sleeps again and dreams not images but "only thoughts, clearly expressed in words, thoughts which someone uttered or Pierre himself thought up."

> "War is the most difficult subordination of human freedom to the laws of God," said a voice. "Simplicity is submission to God; you won't get away from Him. And *they* [the soldiers] are simple. They don't speak, but do. A spoken word is silver, but an unspoken one is gold. A person cannot possess anything while he fears death. But whoever does not fear it, to that person

everything belongs. If there were not suffering, a human being would not know his own limits, he would not know himself. The most difficult thing (Pierre continued to hear or think in his dream) is to be able to unite in your soul the meaning of everything. "Unite everything?" said Pierre to himself. "No, not unite. It is impossible to unite thoughts, but to *wed* all these thoughts—that's what's needed! Yes, *you've got to wed, you've got to wed!*" Pierre repeated to himself with inner joy, feeling that precisely with these and only these words was he expressing what he wanted to express and the whole question torturing him was resolved.

"Yes, you've got to wed [*sopriagat'*], it's time to wed."

"You've got to yoke up [*zapriagat'*], it's time to yoke up, your honor," repeated some voice. "You've got to yoke up, it's time to yoke up." (11.9)

Metaphysics, Tolstoy wrote in 1852, is "the study of thoughts which are not liable to expression in words" (46:150). Pierre's thoughts are metaphysical truths which are both *in* him—he thinks them himself—and not accessible to his conscious mind. Hence they make no sense to him when he wakes up. This episode illustrates how the truth comes to us only indirectly, through Goethean representation in reality.

The soldiers are *simple*: they know ineffable things simply by living them, by *doing*. Their simplicity consists in their ability to accept equally both suffering and pleasure. When you give up fear of suffering, everything belongs to you; that is, you become an integral part of the illogical but ultimately harmoniously reasonable process of life, what I have been calling the metaphysics of opposites. You submit your individuality to the "common life" of mankind.

At the same time the experience of suffering teaches us that we are individuals by revealing our limits to us. "If there were not suffering, a human being would not know his own limits, he would not know himself" [. . . *chelovek ne znal by granic sebe, ne znal by samogo sebia*]. The word used here is *znal*, not *soznal* [be conscious of], and not *feel*. We live before we suffer, but we neither know it nor know ourselves. Suffering brings knowing, and ultimately individual morality, into being.

So the "simple" truth comes to Pierre: "*you've got to wed! You've got to wed!*" [*sopriagat' nado, sopriagat' nado*]. I translate *sopriagat'* as the transitive verb "to wed" because according to Dal' this is what it means in church language. To be "simple," one must "wed" in one's life what cannot be logically united or joined [*soedinit'*] in one's thoughts. To reach divine, or metaphysical truth requires a leap of faith based, not on revelation, but on inner knowledge and experience.[39]

It is extremely important that Pierre *wills* himself back to sleep in order to learn the secret of the soldier's simplicity. At the beginning of the novel Pierre, in contrast to Andrei, lacks will. He can neither choose a career for himself nor resist the temptations of the flesh. Moral (as opposed to carnal) will begins to develop in Pierre when, after vicariously experiencing the suffering of the soldiers, he begins to "know his limits" and "know himself." This process will not be complete until Pierre has himself faced first execution and then the hardships of a prisoner-of-war. He then reveals a capacity for decision making and moral judgment, which he had previously lacked (13.12).

It is clear from the Mozhaisk sequence how the objective can fundamentally influence the subjective sphere: the human subject comes to *know himself* through the experience of suffering. This means that reason and moral judgment latent in the soul develop in response to what we have called nature or necessity. Tolstoy's point in *War and Peace* is that knowing, like everything else in life, is not static. It grows from the interaction of the sentient being with the limits imposed on it by the outside, objective world. In response to these limits, the soul discovers its own boundaries, and morality becomes possible. This process takes place through the mechanisms of circular reason, which is thus shown to be fundamental in the creation of human morality.

The Importance of Spirit in Wartime

It is important to emphasize that the justification of war in *War and Peace* goes beyond the motives of self-defense of individuals or nations, which Ginzburg rightly sees in it,[40] or even of self-knowledge and morality as discussed in the previous section. God works his will, whatever may be its ultimate purpose, through impulses in men that make them perform criminal acts of slaughter and destruction.

In one place in the domestic side of the novel Tolstoy made it perfectly clear that he understood and accepted those impulses as a necessary part of life. In part 4, chapter 15, Nikolai Rostov, home on leave, has lost a considerable sum at cards to Dolokhov. While waiting to confess his loss to his father, he listens to Natasha sing, and, not even noticing it himself, he sings in harmony with his sister.

> Oh, how that third vibrated and how something was touched that was best in Rostov's soul. And this something was independent of everything in the world and greater than everything in the world. What do gambling losses mean here, and Dolokhovs, and your word of honor! . . . It's all nonsense! You can kill, steal and still be happy!

Tolstoy could associate the "best in Rostov's soul" with permission to kill and steal in this astonishing passage precisely because in it Rostov momentarily relinquishes his individuality with all its trappings, good and bad. He unconsciously joins his voice in harmony with his sister, and with a feeling of relief at the shedding of responsibilities he descends below honor and pride, the attributes of dignity in the individual, to the level of pure feeling. This is also the level of the *dukh*, or spirit, that animates an army and each individual soldier in it. Individual morality is shed with individuality itself in this prime example of *obshchaia zhizn'* [common life], and the individual is willing to sacrifice both himself and others to the will of God that remains incomprehensible.

"Spirit" is a manifestation of life (self-propelled motion) pure and simple. If there is a reasonable element to it, it is one of which spirited human beings are unaware. One can say, indeed, that spirit opposes and overcomes reason in the form of rational self-interest. It is one of those irrational impulses that makes life as we know it possible.

N. N. Strakhov was the first critic to discern the importance of spirit in Tolstoy's war stories. In December 1866 he published a review in *Notes of the Fatherland* [*Zapiski otechestva*] of Tolstoy's collected works, which had come out in 1864. Strakhov, an admirer of Apollon Grigor'ev who after the latter's early death undertook to preserve his views of Russian literature,[41] elaborated Grigor'ev's treatment of Tolstoy but in a more positive vein. Grigor'ev had made the relationship between real and ideal in Tolstoy's works the subject of his 1862 article. By *real*, in this context, Grigor'ev had meant human actions taken for the sake of rational self-interest; by *ideal* he meant those actions that transcend and even contradict self-interest. For Strakhov, as for Apollon Grigor'ev, psychological analysis, which can issue in temporary despair or cynicism, permeated Tolstoy's work,[42] but he believed that Tolstoy, unlike Turgenev or Pisemsky, never gave up his search for the ideal (ibid., 174–78). This Strakhov discerned most clearly in the heroic spark in the souls of the soldiers in "Sevastopol in August." All Tolstoy's analysis and debunking of the phenomenon of courage in the various war stories of the fifties had not, wrote Strakhov, succeeded in extinguishing this spark.[43] When Strakhov came to write on *War and Peace* (in January and March 1869, in *Dawn* [*Zaria*], he proclaimed its main "*idea*" to be that of "*the heroic life*" (emphasis Strakhov's; ibid., 196). Tolstoy had not abandoned his search for "truth" [*pravdivost'*] in his latest work, said Strakhov. On the contrary, he had carried his psychological analysis farther than ever (ibid., 190–95). Against the backdrop of a somber realism, however, his idealism, the spark of heroism flickering in the soul, shone all the more brightly.[44] Both realism and idealism received their apotheosis, according to Strakhov, in the battle of Borodino, where animal baseness alternated with the "spark of heroism" (that spark from Sevastopol) which may flare up even "in the pettiest and most depraved souls." This spark represented the spirit that animated the troops.

Tolstoy considered Strakhov's articles to be the best ones written about *War and Peace*,[45] and he singled out both Strakhov's 1866 article on his collected works and its author for the highest praise: "This is the only man who, never having seen me, has understood me with such subtlety. His previous article in *Notes of the Fatherland* already showed me that" (ibid., 309). Since he commented later in a letter to Strakhov that he rejected the latter's application of Grigor'ev's humble and fierce types to *War and Peace*, what Tolstoy must have liked most about Strakhov's three articles was their common thread, namely, their exposition of the "heroic idea" and its relation to psychological realism. One can even speculate that Strakhov's 1866 article may have helped Tolstoy perfect the metaphysics of *War and Peace*. In any case, Strakhov had pinpointed the element in Tolstoyan psychology that compelled human beings to sacrifice their lives in war.

As a metaphor, the spark of courage is one of a family of fire images in *War and Peace* and elsewhere. On the one hand, it is connected to the metaphor of the pipe, which from "The Woodcutting" on symbolizes life in Tolstoy's soldiers.[46] This metaphor achieves its most developed expression in the scene during the battle of Shöngraben where Tushin's battery saves the Russian army. To keep his courage up, Tushin imagines there that his guns are great smoking pipes. On the other hand, the spark of courage is related in *War and Peace* to the fire that destroys first Smolensk and then Moscow. In the case of Smolensk, a man is shown torching his own property in response to the French invasion of the city (10.4). When Pierre, as part of his education at the battle of Borodino, himself feels this hunger for sacrifice (10.18), he later in a series of memories and observations connects it to the spark of courage which burst into flame in the artillery where he found a "home" during the battle.[47] So the spark unites in itself both the tiny flame of life in each individual that he cherishes above all else, and images of conflagration that engulf and unite many individuals.

The spark represents one of those phenomena in the soul, of which Tolstoy said in the second epilogue that they resolve by their wholeness the clash between freedom and necessity, between feeling and reason, content and form. As fire, it is an essence, like water, which Tolstoy also used to represent life or content in the human soul. These psychological metaphors are connected to other images in the novel that occur in the objective sphere, like the fire in Moscow and the great river that the Russian army must cross at Enns. Human will is the direct manifestation of life which, when he wrote *War and Peace*, Tolstoy believed to be but one expression of an essence underlying other motions in nature (second epilogue, 10). An example of another, "inhuman" force related to fire and mentioned in the second epilogue is electricity (ibid.). It is essential here to realize that of the two Russian words for freedom, *svoboda* and *volia*, Tolstoy says that the second, not the first, is the "essence of life" (second epilogue, 8). The primary meaning of *volia* is "will," and it is this will which, Tolstoy goes on to argue, we experience as "free" (*svobodnaia*). To be free is to do what one wills, but if one's will stems ultimately from forces that are part of God's world and governed by Him, then the distinction between this kind of freedom and necessity indeed disappears.[48]

The positive aim of Tolstoy's philosophy of history was to discover the real mover, or cause, of events,[49] and the answer to this question, according to him, was that, first, each participant in an event causes it. The soldiers of Napoleon's army fight not because he wants them to, but because each man wants to himself (9.1; 13.1). And what does he "want" to do, according to Tolstoy? To sacrifice himself and all he possesses (9.23) and to commit "mass crimes, wars, murders and so on" (second epilogue, 7). This recurring and amoral "will" among humankind to kill and destroy others and even oneself is represented poetically by Tolstoy as the spark in each individual soul.

As always in Tolstoy's fiction, in *War and Peace* it is bad to live within the parameters of one's individual life narrowly defined. The willfulness of the Kuragins, as opposed to that of the plundering Russian soldier during the war, is bad because it serves only the Kuragin appetite. The evil of this kind of will directed to personal gratification is personified in Dolokhov, whose chief appetite is for personal power. This flaw is exposed in Dolokhov when he holds back out of fear during the partisan raid to rescue Russian prisoners.[50] Dolokhov is afraid because, unlike those who temporarily relinquish their individuality to kill and be killed, he remains preeminently himself and therefore afraid of death while making war.

We are meant to compare Dolokhov with the peasant Tikhon, "the most useful and bravest person in the group" of partisans (14.5). Tikhon is likened to an animal, to a horse for his endurance, and especially to a wolf, for his ferocity.[51] He is a beast, a carnivore, with corresponding virtues and limitations. Tikhon's surname, *Shcherbatyi*, translated "Gap-toothed" by Maude, is drawn from a physical characteristic, like an animal's name.[52] His chief weapon is an ax, which he uses as dexterously "as a wolf uses its teeth." He is innocent and self-centered. Like the young fillies who torment "Strider" [*Kholstomer*] in Tolstoy's later story of the same name, Tikhon's chief characteristic is "merriment" [*vesel'e*] and, like them, he lacks imagination and therefore compassion. He feels no personal animosity against his prey until one of them shoots him in "the fleshy part of the back." "This incident had only one effect on Tikhon, that after it he rarely brought back prisoners." As this anecdote attests, Tikhon has self-love and the need to preserve himself: hence his anger. But his willingness to tell the story and laugh at it is proof that he lacks *amour propre*. He is "self-satisfied" [*samodovol'nyi*], but not vain or even proud. He willingly plays the jester to amuse the partisans, and he tells stories with illustrations beneath the dignity of a proud man: in one he crawls on his belly to show how he evaded the enemy. He confronts the enemy fearlessly and eagerly, but he will escape harm in any way possible, no matter how undignified. Tikhon is truly brave because he lacks all the virtues and vices associated with reason. Unlike Dolokhov, he has no interest in power. He kills out of high spirits, and because the leaders of the commune have sanctioned the killing of Frenchmen, thereby "unshackling" his natural and amoral energy. It is a wonderful detail of Tolstoy's characterization of this man-beast that he has all of Tikhon's comrades laugh at him. The wolfman is funny rather than sinister, because he kills innocently.

It is the "unshackling" of the energy of individuals like Tikhon—who is all energy—that fuels armies and makes war possible (48:88,89). Without "higher" inhibitions, the individual becomes capable of heroism (self-sacrifice) and crime (slaughter and destruction). The individual is free [*svobodnyi*] in the sense that he does what his unbridled will wants to do, but that will itself is seen as ultimately determined. Nowhere in the relevant section of the second epilogue (8) did Tolstoy write about the existence of freedom [*svoboda*] pure and simple. He wrote, instead, of the "consciousness of freedom," by which he clearly meant the freedom of the will to do what it wants. The will itself does exist, and, as it is presented in *War and Peace*, is subject to divine law. The actions of this will, independent of the will of the individual, create history.

Reason, Morality, and Nature in the Human Soul

In *War and Peace* Tolstoy extended his definition of nature to include peoples as well as individuals, and he went to extraordinary lengths to justify every universal and therefore natural human activity, including war. At the same time, he remained faithful to a moral code that could not possibly sanctify the killing that goes on in war. People like Tushin in the lower part of the "cone" (note 7) find courage to face death and even to protect others within their little bailiwick and they leave the ultimate justification to others for what they have to do to the enemy during battle.

As Nikolai Rostov turns from a recruit into a veteran, we see him learning this lesson. He tastes fear in his first skirmish (2.8), and he is wounded and terrified at Shön Graben (2.19). His love for Emperor Alexander and his willingness to fight do not thereby diminish, however, and even reach a climax when he sees Alexander alone and in trouble on the battlefield (3.18). Later, when Napoleon and Alexander make peace at Tilsit, Nikolai is depressed at what he allows himself to suspect was a useless loss of life on both sides. He draws back from this terrifying prospect to affirm loudly that the soldier's job is to fight, not to think (5.21). Henceforth, Nikolai will depend on his beloved Emperor to make the big decisions. In the theoretical language of the novel, he will loosen his personal energy to flow into the current that for humanly inexplicable reasons carries the Russian army westward as it had compelled the French and their allies to the east. At the same time, and like Tushin, he will remain responsible for his own personal conduct, in battle as elsewhere.

Tolstoy distinguished between what he called the "laws" of war and its actual causes.[53] Causes reside in individuals like Nikolai Rostov who lend their particular energy to the biological "force" that moves armies. Why they do this remains inexplicable, although historians might, if they used the mathematical approach recommended by S. S. Urusov and Tolstoy, lay out the "laws" of war, or how it works. As Tolstoy explained in his 1868 diary:

> The movement of a people is the freed force of a bonding [of individuals, seen as atoms, into a nation] in the literal sense. . . . We don't undertake, like Hegel, from pure reason, or like Wundt, from sensation, to prove everything, but we undertake, with axioms of motion, to prove certain theories of motion. . . . The human being, the personality, is an atom. He is necessary, as necessary as is the atom for a theory of physics, but his definition can lead only to the absurd.[54]

Historians must be careful, however, not to extend their studies to the life of the atom itself, which remains distinct from history proper ("the life of peoples and humanity"). Within the Rousseauist terms employed in earler chapters of this book, one may understand the swarm life of nations[55] as one mysterious use to which God puts the potential for extension in the soul. But at the same time that Tolstoy made his first foray into what Ginzburg calls "obshchaia zhizn'" [common life],[56] he still defended the reality and moral freedom of the individual. Thus, Tushin and Nikolai Rostov are "atoms" who, while participating in the swarm life of humanity in war, also remain responsible for their personal conduct. And one must not lose sight of the fact that even in depriving the individual of a certain part of his freedom in wartime in *War and Peace*, Tolstoy was defending his autonomy vis-à-vis other individuals.

People believe and feel that they are free, morally autonymous beings. What allows them to act morally is the faculty of reason they possess. The significance of spirit in *War and Peace*, and the attack on rational self-interest both here and elsewhere in Tolstoy's writings, should not blind us to the vital importance of reason within the soul. This is one of the least understood and yet most "Tolstoyan" elements of Tolstoy's psychology. If spirit in its natural state takes us out of ourselves and makes us know ourselves as part of a nation and humanity, reason is what allows us to know ourselves as individuals. In its natural state reason cooperates with feeling (which supplies the actual goal) to make human beings both truly moral and free (*svobodnyi*, not *vol'nyi*) to the extent necessary for individual moral responsibility. It is both part of consciousness—the inner knowledge that includes the totality of a person's feelings, thoughts, and impressions—and what makes consciousness possible. We cannot be conscious of ourselves without distinguishing ourselves from the external world. Even as he explored the roots of "obshschaia zhizn'" [common life] in *War and Peace*, Tolstoy extended his understanding of how reason helps assure the moral autonomy of individuals.

The Rostovs and "Living Life"

As Pavel Gromov has astutely observed,[57] the Rostovs, who represent the principle of feeling in *War and Peace*, have intellect, as well as feeling. The difference between them and, say, the Bolkonskys, according to Gromov, is that Rostovian intelligence is always "part of a whole, and the important thing is the whole, and not its parts."[58] A crucial example of reason at work in Natasha's soul is "that barrier of modesty that she had always felt between herself and other men," but which she does not feel between herself and Anatole (8.10). This "barrier" depends on the natural distinction, based on consciousness, between the self and others. When, in the depraved company of the Kuragins, the barrier vanishes, Natasha loses her natural good sense. She becomes all drive (like the Kuragins), and she takes up with one of them. It is no accident that her seducer is Anatolii, whose name closely resembles hers. Tolstoy drew attention to this similarity at the moment of greatest physical intimacy between Anatole and Natasha, when he is about to kiss her (8.13), by having Anatole call her Natali, the Russian version of her name in French. He himself is regularly called by his French name in the Russian form—Anatol'—and Anatol' and Natali, like Anatolii and Natalia, are almost perfect anagrams of one another.

Morality requires the same consciousness of self, the same line between the self and others, that the exercise of reason does. Although they have cunning aplenty, the Kuragins are amoral because they lack natural reason and hence self-consciousness.[59] One of them, *le charmant Hippolyte* as he is called, simply lacks reason: he is an idiot, Tolstoy tells us, but that goes mostly unnoticed. Since natural reason is lacking in court society at large, Hippolyte's dumb jokes pass there for wit (for instance, 1.4). The Kuragins all pursue their careers through greed and lust. Hippolyte is chasing the pregnant Lisa Bolkonskaia as the novel begins, Anatole goes after Natasha, and his father uses his still sexually attractive children to advance himself. When Vasilii Kuragin uses a low form of reason, a cunning, to advance his interests, Tolstoy calls this cunning "instinct" (3.1). Yet, Prince Vasilii's reason is lower than instinct in that it is simply in the service of self-love. It lacks the infusion of natural laws which compel even beasts to serve their species. Among the Rostovs, only Vera consistently shows this cunning.

At the same time, it is important to note that the Rostovs can be not only sly or, as in the case of Madame Rostova, for instance, narrowly concerned with family interests to the detriment of others, they can be criminal as well, at least in intention. Thus Nikolai Rostov, listening to Natasha sing while he waits to tell his father of his gambling losses to Dolokhov, experiences the relief of descending from moral concerns to pure amoral energy and the feeling that "one can kill and steal and still be happy" (4.15).

The difference between the Kuragins and the Rostovs—and the potential in the Rostovs to become like the Kuragins—solves a puzzle posed long ago (1909–1910) by V. Veresaev in his influential book *Living Life: On Tolstoy and Dostoevsky* [*Zhivaia zhizn': o Dostoevskom i Tolstom*]. Like many critics before and after him, Veresaev distinguished between the artist and moralist in Tolstoy (180). The artist is the voice of "living life," which reaches its zenith in *War and Peace*. The message of this work, and of the artist in Tolstoy, according to Veresaev, is that we need not try to be good; we must be ourselves and nature will take care of the rest (ibid., 183).

Veresaev observed that Tolstoy loved the animal in man, Daddy Eroshka for instance, but that he distinguished men from animals. Daddy Eroshka has pity, and animals do not.[60] Comparing the horse Strider [*Kholstomer*] and its owner Serpukhovskii in the story "Strider," Veresaev observed that the two are equally self-absorbed, but the horse is portrayed as good, while the man is bad (ibid., 124–25). And while sexual appetite, such as that which the stallion feels for the mare in "Master and Man," is acceptable in animals, it is base in humans (ibid., 129–33).

Yet, the meaning of life for Tolstoy, according to Veresaev, was life itself (ibid., 121–24), not goodness, which is but one manifestation of life (ibid, 107). To make the argument that Tolstoy preferred life to the good, Veresaev had to and did give examples of positively portrayed lust in human beings—Count Turbin in "Two Hussars"—and of Tolstoy's own preference for "living life" over the good, for Stiva Oblonsky over Koznyshev, for instance. And if this is so, Veresaev asked, how does nature make human beings good?

The answer to Veresaev's query is "living reason," the Goethean "reason behind everything that lives." Veresaev himself saw that for Tolstoy there was meaning in life, mind [*um*] in nature (ibid., 78–86). It permeates not only men and animals, but trees as well. But in his opinion, however, Tolstoy, although he wanted to believe that this meaning is the good, or self-sacrifice, never succeeded in making it the essence of his characters (ibid., 91). As a post-Nietzschean, Veresaev underestimated and even misunderstood the importance and status of "mind" for Tolstoy.[61] Even and especially while he wrote *War and Peace*, Tolstoy was a moralist who required that things make good sense. His early optimism depended on a belief that the true, the beautiful, and the good were truly the same, and were embodied in both nature and the soul. Even when Nikolai seems to shed moral responsibility as he sings with his sister, he descends to the legitimate "common life" in which human beings act in concert and leave the reasons for their behavior to God. The duet that Nikolai and Natasha sing is therefore linked to the harmonies that Petia hears the night before his death. And, at the same time, Nikolai's escape into the "common life" when he harmonizes with Natasha is only momentary and is followed immediately by his return to moral responsibility and his confession to his father.

There is a curious passage in the drafts of the novel that makes Tolstoy's intentions perfectly clear. In a description of Natasha's face that is too obviously symbolic to be included in the final text, Tolstoy drew a map of nature and "living reason" as he understood it.

> But the imperfections of her face could only be discerned in a portrait or a bust, in the living [*zhivoi*] Natasha it was impossible to discern this, because as soon as her face came alive [*ozhivlialos'*], the stern beauty of the upper part blended with the somewhat sensual and animal [*zhivotnym*] expression of the lower part into one brilliant eternally changing charm. And she was always lively [*ozhivlena*]. (13:626–27)

The keynote of this passage is the root *zhiv*, meaning life, in Russian as in English a verbal root, because life is an action rather than a thing. The physical nature of all life is also stressed by the connection, also true in English, of animal with animation, Natasha's "animal" expression with her liveliness. Natasha, as the personification of life, is both mind and feeling, ideal and real, with the one corresponding to the upper and the other to the lower part of her face. These two only come together when Natasha is animated: so do they in the "brilliant eternally changing charm" of nature.

The "mind" that Veresaev rightly said existed in everything for Tolstoy functions differently in different things. In an unspoiled human being it makes "life" good, and when it is missing, as in the Kuragins, life becomes monstrous. Life in the Kuragins more resembles an impersonal and amoral force like electricity than the force infused with moral feeling that Tolstoy believed natural to human beings. In wartime, all human beings may participate in impersonal and amoral forces. But even these forces are ultimately under the control of God for his own purposes. And the faculty of reason that makes human beings conscious of themselves and concerned with morality and freedom also has its place in nature.

The Bolkonskys

Especially in his depiction of the character and education of Prince Andrei, Tolstoy defended the *naturalness* of reason and morality in the individual soul. In the Rostovs, and in Natasha especially, feeling predominates and can overwhelm natural reason perhaps too easily. The opposite is true of the Bolkonskys. The old man lives by logic alone, and, as a result, is painfully alienated from all "living life." He despises all feeling, repressing it in himself and ridiculing it in others. In nature and in himself he accepts only the three laws of reason, of time, space, and cause (as defined in the second epilogue, 10), and he seeks to control all three. But old Bolkonsky's rationalism does not mean that he loves himself less than do the Rostovs. More self-conscious than they, he loves himself as much or more, and his will, armed with logic, is stronger than it would be in a man of feeling. He spends his time vainly erecting a barrier against the death he sees rushing toward him—a death that, as an individualist and an atheist, he regards as total annihilation. He admires honor above all other virtues: he fights inevitable death by valuing his dignity and reputation over his body. Instead of loving and accepting others, he judges them according to ideal standards he sets for them, as well as for himself.

Prince Andrei entered the novel as a younger version of his father. As is well known, he was to be a man of honor whose death at Austerlitz would end his dreams of becoming a Napoleon. In an early draft when Prince Andrei (here called Volkonsky) was dying on the battlefield, he looked at Nikolai Rostov (called Tolstoy) and in his gaze was "peace, and love and meaning" [*mir, i liubov' i znachenie*].[62] As he had lived, so he was to die like his father, who also awakens to love, the source of unconscious morality, at the moment of his death.

When Prince Andrei fell in a first variant of the scene of his wounding at Austerlitz, all he noticed was "a small patch of stubble-field with crumpled straw" (ibid., 184). This was an epic image of the death, the "harvest" to which his reasoning nature had brought him. In a later draft the mood of this episode, and with it what Andrei sees, changes: "And suddenly there was nothing but the high sky, but there was not even that, there was nothing except quiet, silence and calm" (ibid.). The first book of the novel came together only when Tolstoy realized that Andrei must not die at Austerlitz (ibid., 22). The dramatic change in poetic imagery as Tolstoy rewrote the scene explains why. Reason, applied only to personal goals, however noble, sees only the physical death poetically represented by the harvest field. In the rewriting of this scene Andrei's eyes and his soul soar upward to eternity, which defines all motion while itself remaining "nothing except quiet, silence and calm." Wounded, he turns from action on his own behalf to contemplation of the whole, from practical to theoretical reason.[63] Tolstoy rewrote this scene because he realized that Andrei, the man of reason and *amour propre*, whatever his faults, was destined in his novel to be the seeker after general principles of morality. Such a man, he realized, would concern himself with the eternal in his own soul because by virtue of that propensity to reason he would care more about the terms of his individual existence than the man of feeling who slips back and forth between conscious and unconscious life. Such a man would both yearn to escape from his own imperfections and would be driven to perfect himself.

This is the point where Tolstoy moved beyond *The Cossacks* to explore more thoroughly the links connecting morality, the man of reason, and nature. What is especially significant for the novel as a whole, and what cements its unity on every level, is that Andrei finds the ideal he seeks in nature. This is clear in a notebook entry from 1865. Andrei is conversing with Pierre after the death of the little Princess and Andrei's subsequent disillusionment with his early ideals. Pierre speaks, and "Andrei smiles, *the sky is resurrected*" (emphasis mine; 48:85). In Tolstoy's imagination as he jotted down this note the sky simply stands for Andrei's ideals: it is the representation in nature of "living reason."

Unlike her father and brother Princess Maria, from the moment of her appearance in the novel, lives by consciousness, not logic. Hence she ultimately becomes friends with Natasha and marries Nikolai Rostov. While the Rostovs are sensual, however, Maria remains spiritual and reasonable. In the first epilogue, while Natasha nurses her little Petia and changes diapers, Maria worries about the moral education of her children (15). The higher side of the Rostovs, what one might call the spirit of the flesh, is expressed through their musicality. The image of Bolkonskian reason is light, also the symbol of reason in the later Tolstoy.[64] (The absence of reason is darkness, the *zatmenie* that Natasha feels when she violates natural law by thinking of loving and possessing both Andrei and Anatole [8.14].)[65] This light shines in Maria's eyes, transforming her plain features and, incidentally, making Nikolai Rostov love her. Maria's reason transforms feeling in her without transcending it. She tells her brother, "Tout comprendre, c'est tout pardonner" [To understand everything is to forgive everything] (1.25): like Andrei, she sees human weakness, but unlike him, she does not despise people. She forgives them because "they know not what they do." Like Platon Karataev she is both a stern judge of her own conduct and a Christian determinist, who believes that "les malheurs viennent de Dieu, et . . . les hommes ne sont jamais coupable" [Misfortunes come from God, and people are never guilty] (9.8).

The comparison of Maria to an illuminated lantern (12.6) is especially helpful in grasping the difference between her and her brother. Before his fatal injury, Andrei sees everything in "a cold white light": "All of life seemed to him like a magic lantern, into which he had long gazed through the glass and under artificial lighting. Now he suddenly saw, without glass and in the clear light of day, these poorly painted pictures" (10.24). In his despair Andrei's reason deadens life in him and puts him outside it, making *it* into an artifact. This is an image inspired by Plato's cave in the *Republic*.[66] In the sun of pure reason the philosopher sees that what he had taken for true reality was merely a shadow cast on the wall of the cave. By elsewhere likening Maria to a lantern, Tolstoy took issue with this Platonic view of truth. Reason should not dissect and thereby kill the object it seeks to understand. It must view life from within, not from without: so Maria *is* the lantern which the light of her reason lights up. She knows that she is weak and imperfect, and, like her brother, she longs for spiritual perfection. (Hence that touch of melancholy that characterizes her.) Unlike Andrei, however, Maria also frankly if sadly acknowledges her desire for "earthly love" (3.3). While ashamed of this desire, she accepts it as God's will. She thereby accepts as divinely ordained the life of the body that so disgusts her brother. In the world of the novel it, too, partakes of the Goethean "reason behind everything that lives."

Tolstoy did not here deny the existence of ideal or Platonic reason. Rather he poetically indicated his Goethean preference for reason in its representations rather than in itself. Reason by itself reveals, as Morson says, the "truths of negation . . . the cold love and indifferent euphoria of a skeptic's apocalypse."[67] The truths are negative in Andrei when he separates himself from life and judges it because they lack the content that life gives them. Without these truths, these forms, on the other hand, pure energy would yield only the heartless melodrama of Andrei's nemesis, Anatole Kuragin.

From his role in the early drafts of the novel as a man of *amour propre* and therefore of society, Prince Andrei evolved into a man of nature, who seeks and most loves the natural ideal of reason or law in and of itself. He thereby discovers what he and all the Bolkonskys really want, namely, the secret of eternal life. But to the extent that he wants to and does separate the thing itself from its manifestations, higher reason, for instance, from the sky that represents it, this discovery comes at the cost of his individual, irrational existence. Indeed, all the Bolkonskys are associated with death in the novel. This is true even of Maria, whose yearning "for the infinite, the eternal and the perfect" in the first epilogue makes her husband fear that she might die (15), and of the adolescent Nikolenka, who is depicted there as high-strung and "sickly" (14). Prince Andrei's association with reason and perfection threatens the metaphysics of opposites that underlay Tolstoy's attempt to unite happiness and morality, body—or nature—and spirit in humankind. Another hero, as noble as Andrei or Maria but less rational than they, is needed to confirm in his person the validity of the philosophy of living reason. This is Pierre Bezukhov, in the language of Turgenev's famous essay, Don Quixote to Andrei's Hamlet.

Pierre

As has often been suggested, Pierre Bezukhov stands between and unites the Rostovian and Bolkonskian principles. For all his warmth and spontaneity, however, Pierre is as much a man of mind as of feeling. In a letter to Fet of 1867, Tolstoy thanked him for the terms *heart's mind* and *mind's mind* [*um serdtca, um uma*], saying that they had taught him a great deal.[68] The "mind of the heart," Fet had written to Tolstoy, is "the inner sum of convictions," while its counterpart and opposite *um uma*, the "mind of the mind," only serves the heart, whatever it desires. You can have a good head with a bad heart, or vice versa; as an example of a man with both good head and good heart, Fet had adduced Goethe.[69] Like his friend Andrei, Pierre cannot live without thinking, but unlike Andrei he thinks with his heart's mind, that is, with the reason inherent in consciousness that does not separate itself from what it observes. Pierre is the most perfect representative of what I have been calling the Goethean side of *War and Peace*. In a letter to Fet of May 1866, Tolstoy revealed that he had been reading Goethe and *Don Quixote*, both influences in creating Pierre.[70] And in a discussion of favorite writers in an early draft of the novel, Pierre says that he likes Goethe and the more poetic works of Rousseau, while Andrei dislikes Goethe and *La Nouvelle Heloise* and likes Racine and *Le Contrat Social*. Pierre responds that, on second thought, he likes them all (13:230–31). He epitomizes the accommodation of opposite principles necessary in life.

Pierre is natural, and, to the greatest extent possible, he is meant to combine the two principles of nature in *War and Peace*, earth and sky, real and ideal. When M. S. Bashilov, the first illustrator of *War and Peace*, sent Tolstoy his sketch of Pierre reclining and reading on a couch, Tolstoy suggested changes to emphasize both Pierre's thoughtfulness and his earthiness: "His face is good (if only there could be more of a tendency to philosophizing in his forehead—little wrinkles or bumps over his eyebrows), but his body is small—it should be wider and stouter and more massive" (61:134). Pierre was to be, like the Caucasian mountains as Olenin first saw them, a massive physical presence, but, unlike them, he was to be animated by spirit. He was to be that reason that Goethe preferred to see in, rather than separately from, its manifestations. In Tolstoy's portrait of Pierre there is, in fact, a hidden reference to Goethe's theory of colors, itself an example of how the sensual was in Goethe's mind permeated by the spiritual, or reasonable. In 1861 Tolstoy had visited Goethe's home in Weimar and observed a pyramid made of cardboard that illustrated the theory of colors. He wrote in his diary: "Goethe's house. Yellow—Vernunft; green—Sinnlichkeit; red—Phantasie; blue [*sinee*]—Verstand."[71] In *War and Peace*, Natasha confides to her mother that Pierre is "blue and red and square" [*sinii, temno-sinii s krasnym, i on chetverougol'nyi*] (6.13). Gromov has recognized that Natasha's peculiar intelligence speaks here.[72] Using the entry from Tolstoy's diary, one can decode Natasha's message: Pierre is the embodiment of Imagination and Understanding and, I would suggest, Earthiness.[73]

Natasha's remark thus interpreted provides much food for thought. Goethe distinguishes *Vernunft* from *Verstand*, and Tolstoy chose blue,

Verstand, to characterize Pierre. These words have a complicated history in German philosophical thought. For Kant, *Vernunft* represented the higher faculty of reason by which human beings thought about things beyond experience. *Verstand* was lower than *Vernunft*. It referred to the a priori concepts of logic, such as causality or substance, by which we organize sense perceptions, and it never transcended this relation to sense perception. *Vernunft* would then be associated with speculative metaphysics, and *Verstand* with science. Hegel adopted Kant's use of these terms with certain twists of his own, and the usages spread thence throughout German philosophical thought.[74] Before Kant, however, in classical philosophy, these words were used differently, and their status was reversed. Kant believed that only God was capable of intuitive thinking. Human beings could speculate about the absolute truth using *Vernunft*, but they could not know it. For the Greeks, and preeminently for Plato, intuitive thinking (*Nous*) about the basic ideas that underlay reality *was* possible, and the German translation for the Greek word meaning intuitive thinking, *Nous*, would be *Verstand*. Therefore, in German philosophy before Kant or outside of Kantian influence, *Verstand* would be a higher faculty than *Vernunft*. In this Platonic view, *Vernunft*, translated into German, had more the sense of analytical or deductive reason such as human beings practice and understand; *Verstand* meant something closer to intuitive intellect through which we gain access to the fundamental ideas in nature and human beings according to which God rules.[75]

Goethe understood his theory of colors to embody his belief in the natural coincidence of reasoning and representation possible because of the "reason behind everything that lives." Well aware of the Kantian tradition, he nonetheless used *Verstand* and *Vernunft* in something like the traditional sense. *Vernunft* was pure reason, a category of mind by which we organize or systematize external events or objects. *Verstand* was the intuitive understanding by which we penetrate to their essential reality.[76] Hence yellow, which Goethe associated with *Vernunft*, was the primary color closest to light, or spirit, whereas blue, which in the pyramid represented *Verstand*, was closest to darkness, or matter.[77] The "ideas" that we intuit and that give form or meaning to objects but that do not exist outside of them are what has been described as "a fusion of two traditions, the Platonic and the empirical, in Goethe."[78] So there arose that antecedent to Tolstoy's emblematic realism, what Viëtor variously refers to as Goethe's "objective idealism" and his "symbolic idealism."[79] The ideal and the physical or material merge or co-exist in reality.

I would suggest that the young Tolstoy, with the idealism that he had absorbed from Plato in the early 1850s, and with his subsequent love of intuitive truths encouraged by Goethe, used *Verstand* and *Vernunft* in the Goethean sense.[80] This may explain why in his list in the diary *Verstand*, as the highest faculty, comes at the end and next to *Phantasie*, or Imagination. Likewise, in *War and Peace*, Natasha's remark couples Imagination, *Phantasie*, with *Verstand*, and makes *Verstand* Pierre's dominant quality.

Verstand, then, would be the intuitive reason, the "mind of the heart" by which an individual could have direct access to what we have been calling living reason. In keeping with Tolstoy's Rousseauist education, his familiarity with Goethe's poetic works, and his own sympathy for the physical world, intuitive reason in his conception has something physical about it, as if it can only be known through the physical world. This would explain why such characters as the old roué Kutuzov (and, for that matter, Pierre) possess it, while a pure intellect like Andrei glimpses it only sporadically. The "mind of the heart" is a partner of poetry, especially poetry understood as the voice of the feelings. Because of his knowledge of movements of the heart, the poet has direct access to the great motions of the universe as well. Thus, as in the passage from Pushkin that so struck Tolstoy in Annenkov's biography of the great poet, poetry imitates the music of nature.[81] So Pierre has both *Verstand* and *Phantasie*, intuitive reason and higher feeling as they express themselves both in consciousness and in nature. Pierre's third feature in Natasha's trenchant description, his physicality, his "squareness," or perhaps, in Goethean terms, his *Sinnlichkeit*, anchors his spiritual qualities in reality, fulfilling Tolstoy's dictum that everything ideal must be rooted in the real (sensual) world (47:201).

"Lyrical Daring" in *War and Peace*

In March 1861 Tolstoy was reading *Faust* and wrote to Herzen that it was "the greatest drama in the world."[82] In March 1865 he was reading it again, and wrote of it in his notebook on 9 March that it was "Poetry of thought, poetry having as its subject what no other art can express. But we interrupt [*perebivaem*], tearing from reality painting, psychology and so on" (48:59). The "we" of the second sentence refers to lesser writers who do not grasp the whole of reality, and therefore "interrupt" it to take a piece of art, be it "painting" or "psychology," out of the whole; whereas Goethe in *Faust* has penetrated reality to the "thought" that holds everything together. His "poetry of thought," therefore, does not "interrupt" or dissect reality, but instead expresses it whole.

A few days and two diary entries later, on 17 March, Tolstoy was ready to formulate what the thought of the whole might be:

> Yesterday I saw in the snow, on a human track that had broken through it, the track of a dog that had not. Why is its [the dog's] fulcrum [*tochka opory*] so small? So that it doesn't eat all the rabbits, but only as many as it needs. This is God's wisdom; but it is not wisdom, not mind. It is the instinct of the Divinity. This instinct is in us. But our mind is the faculty by which we deviate from instinct and grasp these deviations. With terrible clarity, force and pleasure these thoughts came to me. (48:59–60)

Fresh from reading Goethe, reminded perhaps by his reading of his trip to Weimar, Tolstoy translated into his own terms the difference between *Vernunft* ("mind") and *Verstand* (intuitive thinking, or "instinct") as it was relevant for his novel. As is typical of the novel, he moved directly from an example of divine harmony in nature—the dog made small enough not to devour all rabbits—to inner harmony as it speaks in the voice of conscience. But conscience is not itself *Verstand*. The example of *Verstand* in this passage is Tolstoy's own penetration and grasp of the meaning of the tracks in the woods, which came to him "with terrible clarity, force and pleasure." He felt that he, too, was writing "poetry of thought." On 20 March, working out the historical scheme for his novel, he referred to it as a *poema* [a long and ambitious poem] (48:61). He was now approaching the historical material he was amassing from the point of view of the "poetry of thought," and he could proudly designate the genre of his work as on a level with *Faust* in its "objective idealism." It was a modern epic that unified the natural and human spheres precisely through its grasp of the "thought" encompassing both. This harmony of real and ideal, in turn, made it possible for Tolstoy to stretch his early form of "lyrical daring" to its outer limits.

Not surprisingly, Pierre, the man of mind and feeling, has the greatest range of experience with nature of any character in the novel. In chapter 2, we saw how he identified with Halley's Comet. In this case nature expressed the feeling that his love for Natasha had awakened in him. There are two examples of "lyrical daring" during Pierre's captivity in which nature actively participates in his education.

The first takes place the morning after Pierre meets Platon Karataev, and Karataev revives him by his kindness and his example.

> When, on that first day, having risen early in the morning, he came out of the shed at dawn and he saw at first the dark cupolas and crosses of the Novodevichii Monastery, he saw the frosty dew on the dusty grass, he saw the slopes of the Sparrow Hills and the woody bank winding above the river

and disappearing into the lilac distance, when he felt the touch of the fresh air and heard the sounds of the jackdaws flying from Moscow across the field, and when then suddenly light spurted out from the east and the edge of the sun sailed triumphantly out from behind a dark cloud, and the cupolas, and the crosses, and the dew, and the distance, and the river, all began to play in the joyful light—Pierre felt a new feeling, not experienced before, of the joy and strength of life.

And this feeling did not leave him during the whole time of his imprisonment, but, on the contrary, grew in him the more the difficulties of his position increased. (13.12)

The second landscape comes after Pierre has tried to visit other prisoners and a soldier has forbidden him to cross the road to do so. Pierre goes off by himself, sits down and thinks "for over an hour." Suddenly he bursts into laughter.

— Ha, ha, ha! — laughed Pierre. And he muttered aloud to himself. — The soldier wouldn't let me. They caught me, imprisoned me. They're holding me in captivity. What me? Me? Me — my immortal soul! Ha, ha, ha! . . . Ha, ha, ha! . . . — he laughed until the tears came out of his eyes.

Someone rose and came up to see what this strange large person could be laughing about alone. Pierre stopped laughing, rose, moved farther away from the curious man and looked around himself.

The huge endless bivouac, formerly loud with the crackle of campfires and human conversation, had fallen silent; the red flames of the campfires were dying down and turning pale. High in the light sky stood the full moon. Forests and fields, beyond the camp and previously invisible, now appeared in the distance. And still further beyond these forests and fields the light, wavering, beckoning, infinite distance was visible. Pierre looked at the sky, into the depths of the receding, playing stars. "And all this is mine, and all this is in me, and all this is I!—thought Pierre—And all this they captured and imprisoned in a shed boarded up with planks!" He smiled and went to settle himself down to sleep among his comrades. (13.14)

In the first example of "lyrical daring," nature literally builds "a new feeling . . . of the joy and strength of life" in Pierre. Step by step this feeling enters him through his senses; first sight, then touch, then hearing, and finally a sense of motion, as the sun rises and makes everything shimmer. The nature portrayed here is that ruled by necessity and known to us through perception and reasoning based on it. Pierre directly interacts with nature through feeling, rather than analyzing it by reason, but it is still the physical world, the world that science knows, that Pierre confronts here. We see it "poetically," through an appeal to our own senses, in its diversity, in its motion, and in the unity imposed on it by the sunlight which, animating diverse things, makes them into parts of a whole. Tolstoy believed that the same metaphysical force that animates nature animates the soul as well, and so this landscape can pour a feeling, a motion, into Pierre's soul. Like Nikolai's vision of the sunlit world during the crossing at Enns, or in the descent from Mozhaisk, the landscape contains a church (the cupolas of the monastery), because in *War and Peace* the purely physical world is infused by God's presence. The physical world, communicated to Pierre through his body, is capable of inspiring what the next paragraph describes as "this feeling of being ready for anything, of moral composure." The Russian word that I have translated as *composure* [*podobrannost'*] conveys a sense of putting things in order. The "new feeling . . . of joy and strength of life" and the feeling of "moral composure" are the same because Pierre is now in direct communication with the laws of nature that govern its forces and order its parts just as conscience does in the soul. When the feeling of physical life ("joy") reawakens in Pierre, so does "moral composure," because in this man of *Verstand*, feeling (life) and thought (law) are one. As the sun brings movement and unity to the landscape, Pierre's feeling both animates his soul and makes it whole.

This parallel is reminiscent of the moment in *The Cossacks* when the sun comes out both in the forest and in Olenin's soul. It is a striking example of Tolstoy's version of "lyrical daring" which, morever, demonstrates once again the connection between him and Goethe and between the two of them and the Savoyard Vicar. For Goethe:

> the autonomous conscience is the sun of the moral life. It is the same power, creating according to law, which gives to the life of Nature, as to the moral-spiritual life in us, both norm and form . . . [Goethe doesn't try to explain how this can be.] . . . The experiencing of God in Nature and in the conscience stand side by side here as equal in importance and value. The idea of order, of law, unites the moral with the cosmic. But many another secret remains unrevealed.[83]

Pierre is in touch with higher, divine reason. His soul is in order; he is a man of action who knows what he should do and can do it ("ready for anything") for the first time in his life. In prison Pierre becomes what he could not be when he earlier sought to slay Napoleon and so influence the course of history: a leader. The narrator says that he has become "almost a hero" to his fellow prisoners, and "this view bound him"; he feels a duty to be a good example. Pierre feels himself part of well-ordered nature, bound by its laws, and thereby bound to his fellow men as he has never been before. This is the direct effect of living reason on the soul, as it enters the soul through sense perception of nature. It is the kind of morality that Nikolai Rostov can appreciate, and it is an example for the reader of how nature in *War and Peace* can stimulate moral consciousness.

In the second landscape, Pierre thinks instead of feeling. Sitting motionless, he seems to leave his body, and when he does return to contemplate nature, he does so wholly through sight, the most spiritual sense. He is reflecting, as Prince Andrei did when he listened to Natasha sing, on the difference between the body and soul.

> [Andrei had felt like weeping over] the terrible opposition, of which he was suddenly vividly conscious, of something infinitely great and indefinite dwelling in him, and something narrow and physical, which he was himself and even she was. This opposition oppressed and rejoiced him during her singing. (6.19)

Properly viewed as a counterpoint to this earlier episode, the scene in the night camp acquires the metaphysical overtones that Tolstoy intended. The bivouac becomes a metaphor for all of human life, whose size and importance diminish when placed in comparison to the night sky, and the shed becomes a metaphor for the body, seen here as a prison of the soul. This symbolism, so different from the realism of the diurnal landscape, is appropriate because it occurs during Pierre's introspective mood. In the first landscape, nature influences an essentially passive soul, revived by Platon Karataev but as yet without content. Here, Pierre actively projects his idea on nature. In this respect, the scene is akin to Andrei's perception of the oak tree, first as a symbol of age and death and then of renewed life. Make no mistake, however: Pierre is not creating a linkage where one would otherwise not exist. As in the diurnal landscape, he is affirming the real underlying connection between himself as individual and the world, between the microcosm and the macrocosm. In this case it is human contemplation and the world's harmony that merge. Pierre is like the poet in *Faust*.

> Is it not, streaming forth, the concord of his art
> That carries back the world into his heart?[84]

The differences between Andrei's and Pierre's experiences are, of course, crucial. Andrei senses eternity in another person, and then contrasts it to physical life ("something narrow and physical"). Pierre senses it in himself and finds its corresponding image in nature, in the physical world. With consciousness—Tolstoy uses the word *soznan* to describe the way Andrei knows what is in Natasha—Andrei recognizes the coexistence of opposites in himself and Natasha, but he regrets it, as if the physical somehow imperiled or impeded the spiritual. Unlike Andrei, Pierre does not grieve over the imprisonment of his soul. He laughs. He is struck by the absurdity of the idea that something infinite and free could really be enslaved. What Andrei knows through consciousness he nonetheless subjects to logic, which decrees that one-half of an opposition must diminish or destroy the other. Pierre knows through inner, intuitive reason, which accepts opposites as part of a larger truth.

Having used *Verstand* to comprehend his situation, Pierre turns to the night landscape surrounding him. As George Steiner has observed, Pierre, unlike Andrei, draws the infinite sky into himself rather than being drawn into it.[85] Pierre can identify with the sky because his "immortal soul" is the human manifestation of the same organizing harmony that underlies nature, the sky as well as the earth. It is the "infinite spaces" that Botkin saw shining in the eyes of the young Tolstoy.[86]

Carden has compared Pierre's vision of the sky with that of Andrei and Nikolai Rostov.[87] One can also compare it with Natasha's reaction (overheard by Andrei) to the moonlit night at Otradnoe (6.2). The night makes Natasha want to fly, and Andrei actually hears a scuffle as the level-headed Sonia wrestles with her friend to keep her from flinging herself from the window. Thus, Natasha responds directly to the "light, wavering, beckoning, infinite distance," which Pierre also sees. This is feeling yearning to return to its source. Pierre contains himself (Carden makes subtle use of the word *self* in her article) because in him feeling is more tempered by contemplation than in Natasha.

Pierre is alone, and when someone approaches him to find out why he is laughing, he moves away. This landscape is one not of necessity and morality, but of freedom, which Tolstoy said in the second epilogue is purest when we are alone (9).[88] The two landscapes, considered together, are another example of the metaphysics of opposites in the novel. In the first landscape Pierre, through feeling or sense, acquires morality, law, from nature. In the second, *Verstand*, higher reason not expressed as instinct or conscience or sense of duty, but as conscious thought, allows him to contemplate and even experience pure feeling, free will, in himself.

So the book of nature replaces Kabala as a guide for Pierre. At the same time, and as is typical of Tolstoy, Pierre's "education" in these two encounters with nature is actually a voyage of discovery of what already exists within him. It is inaccurate, therefore, to say that nature in the first landscape actually inculcates morality in Pierre. The example and the kindness of Platon Karataev has stimulated Pierre to restore his soul to pristine orderliness, and therefore Pierre is prepared the next morning to receive "the new feeling . . . of the joy and strength of life" and a concomitant moral "composure." It is equally true, however, that the night landscape has a real underlying moral similarity to

Pierre's "immortal soul" that allows him to proclaim that it and he are one. Tolstoyan "lyrical daring" in *War and Peace* proceeds from the premise that man and nature, subjective and objective, can intermingle freely because they are based on the same laws and forces.

The Rousseauist understanding of the soul as both unified and expansive receives its greatest Tolstoyan expression in *War and Peace*. Pierre is Tolstoy's Jean-Jacques, a character who by the end of his education combines earthiness, rootedness in himself, and the ability, in his most contemplative, expansive moments, to embrace and encompass the whole world. Pierre achieves personal happiness in his private life, and even in his public life, inasmuch as he now knows what he should do there. He deserves this perfect happiness because his soul, in that scene in the bivouac, has been shown to be a miniature copy of the macrocosm, and therefore both as directed and as good as it.

Nature and the individual human soul are related to one another as macrocosm to microcosm, because in *War and Peace* God is manifest in nature. As a result, the novel contains a system of imagery drawn from nature that symbolizes the different parts of the soul and also joins the soul to nature. Images of water, all related to that vision of the great flowing river in the draft in which Tolstoy found the opening scene of *War and Peace*, represent vitality, *sila*, the source of all motion and feeling. The river of history and mass movements is mysterious and, from the point of view of the individual, amoral. The sky and celestial images of light—the sun, the moon, the stars, Halley's comet—represent the laws that give form and unity to vitality. At crucial moments, Prince Andrei, Pierre and the Rostovs, Natasha and Nikolai, are drawn in different ways to these images. All of them, even the sun, the source of physical life, suggest a parallel between the laws governing nature, and moral law.

In one scene, a young Nikolai Rostov looks longingly from the battlefield to the sun in search of the naturally good family life that he fears to lose along with his life. In another, in the presence of the overflowing river and the setting sun, Pierre tries to convince Andrei that real life takes place not on earth, by which he means the realm of mere physical existence, but in the whole world, the *mir*, by which he means the spiritual realm represented by the sky (to which Pierre in his impassioned speech points). As Andrei listens to his friend, he gazes at the sun reflected in the rippling water at the ford, and the waves splashing against the ferry seem to speak to him: "Really [*pravda*], believe this." The nature imagery of the scene seconds Pierre's belief in the reality of the life of the spirit, but corrects his temporary denigration, made under the influence of Bazdeev and the masons, of the vital in favor of the spiritual. Pierre's words summon Andrei from spiritual death, and water, the symbol of vitality, speaks to him. Andrei, I repeat, gazes not at the sky but at the river. Only after his return to life, in the final stage of his resurrection, does he renew his contact with the sky. In this scene at the ford, the interaction of light and water, the reflection of the sun in the water, is meant to suggest the presence in vitality itself of a spiritual or intellectual principle that beckons Andrei back to life. Pierre's dream of the liquid globe, an image that merges together sun, or light, and water, is the ultimate expression of this belief.

It is Pierre's Swiss geography tutor who, in his dream, reveals the liquid globe to him. This mysterious figure from Pierre's past may be intended as a reference to Jean-Jacques Rousseau, Swiss tutor to and creator of Emile, or possibly to the Savoyard Vicar. Had he lived, Rousseau would have been a very old man during the time of Pierre's youth in Switzerland.[89] (The fact that Rousseau actually died in 1778 is not relevant in a dream.) The globe itself recalls the setting of the Vicar's confession to the young Jean-Jacques. The Vicar takes the youth to a mountain top at dawn, and delivers his *Profession of Faith* as the sun rises in magnificent testimony to the truth of his natural philosophy. At the end of the first half of the Vicar's speech, Jean-Jacques compares him to "the divine Orpheus ... teaching men the worship of the gods."[90] There can be no doubt that the sun, unifying the landscape with its light and bringing it to life, is meant in this passage to symbolize the presence of God in nature. The existence of a rational and loving God ultimately both redeems the selfish part of man and grounds the conscience, "divine instinct, immortal and celestial voice" (ibid., 290) in nature. The old man in Pierre's dream shows him an image that combines two truths absorbed by Tolstoy from the Savoyard Vicar: the drops represent individuals who act in their own self-interest without seeking harm for others, and the globe represents the universe, which is made up of the drops, but in its entirety has a purpose ultimately mysterious to humankind. God is depicted as being at the center of the globe, and individual souls emanate from Him in the shape of miniature globes themselves.

Prince Andrei and Platon Karataev, the two characters in *War and Peace* who in very different ways strive for perfection, both die. This signifies that despite the potential and inherent perfection of each individual soul, the actual life of each individual, intertwined as it is with the lives of others and diluted by circumstance, including even the circumstance of a particular character, is necessarily imperfect. Pierre recognizes this fact when he laughs at the mental image of his soul imprisoned in his body.

In "Who Should Be Teaching Whom to Write: Should We Be Teaching the Peasant Lads, or They Us?" Tolstoy attributed the notion of the perfection of each human being to Rousseau. He then went on to explain the inevitability and hence the naturalness of human imperfection. In chapter 2, I quoted this passage to illustrate Tolstoy's concern with the principle of unity and its source in Rousseau. Rereading it in this context, one can see that that unity extends in principle, though not in practice, even to perfection, so that "just born, man is the very image of the harmony of the true, the beautiful and the good." This means that each individual is the very image of God Himself.

The equally natural destruction of our original perfection described in the passage, however, receives a metaphysical justification in the novel. It makes us need one another and gives us an inner goal toward which to strive. But if expansion in time and space destroy our original perfection, it remains latent within us to link us to other souls and to nature and to ground in each individual the sturdy reality of the characters in *War and Peace*. Because Tolstoy saw each individual as a microcosm of the whole, he believed when he wrote *War and Peace* that individuals had direct access through *Verstand* to the living reason that shapes and governs everything. When he came to write *Anna Karenina*, as we shall see, he no longer believed this to be true.

Part Three

THE 1870s

Six

From Nature to Culture in the 1870s

Mourir vient de soi-meme.
N'en ayons point souci.
Bien vivre est le probleme
Qu'il faut resoudre ici.*
(Béranger, quoted by Tolstoy in a letter to Fet
dated 28–29 April 1876; 62:272)

Art celebrates the passions, the beauty of life,
and therefore it is always a companion of the
pleasures, as music is an invariable accessory of
bawdy houses. But when *you* begin to create images, you have an infinite, incomparable sensitivity to their moral meaning; you are a judge, at
one and the same time both relentlessly penetrating and completely merciful, able to assess
everything according to its desserts. (Strakhov
to Tolstoy, 16–23 November 1875)

ALTHOUGH *War and Peace* and *Anna Karenina* share many of the same
themes, their treatments of these differ markedly. The later novel is less
enthusiastic, "cooler" as Strakhov remarked in a letter to Tolstoy.[1] Tolstoy had, in fact, in his own perception, stepped back from his subject
and now stood on the edge of a precipice separating life from those
ideals with which he had earlier felt life to be permeated. He wrote in
1876 to Fet that "['real' people] despite a healthy attitude toward life
are always standing at the very edge and they see life clearly only because they are gazing now into Nirvana, into Limitlessness, the Unknown, now into Sansara, and this gaze into Nirvana strengthens their
vision" (62:272).

Whereas in *War and Peace* life required only to be revealed and celebrated by the poet, in *Anna Karenina* the poet has to show his reader

* Death comes by itself. / We needn't worry about it. / To live well is the problem /
Which we must resolve here.

how to live well. Life had been the answer to mankind's problems in the first novel. In the second one it itself becomes the problem for each individual and for the author to solve.

In the 1860s, before turning to *War and Peace*, Tolstoy had set up and run a peasant school on his estate and published the journal *Iasnaia Poliana*, in which he had set forth his own theory of education. In the flagship article, entitled "Education for the People" [*O narodnom obra-zovanii*] and published in January 1862 in *Iasnaia Poliana*, he concluded that the one criterion of pedagogy must be freedom. As he put it in this particular context, the pupil must be able to reject what he knows will not satisfy him (8:29). The student knows instinctively what good and evil are, because "the consciousness of good and evil, independent of the will of any one human being, lies in all of humankind and develops unconsciously together with history" (8:24). Although Tolstoy wrote of history here, he was not promoting what he disdainfully called else-where "the religion of progress." In *War and Peace*, he went on to assim-ilate "real" history to nature.[2] The consciousness of good and evil is also, therefore, natural, and in another article in *Iasnaia Poliana*, "Who Should Be Teaching Whom to Write: Should We Be Teaching the Peas-ant Lads, or They Us?" [*Komu u kogo uchitsia pisat', krestianskim rebiatam u nas ili nam u krestianskikh rebiat*], written after mid-October 1862, he could write that "Man is born perfect" and that the purpose of educa-tion was either to maintain or to return to that natural perfection.

In the 1870s Tolstoy took up pedagogy again and published his *Primer* [*Azbuka*] in 1872.[3] Accordingly, he published another article en-titled "Education for the People" [*O narodnom obrazovanii*] in *Notes of the Fatherland* [*Otechestvennye zapiski*] in 1874. It is most enlightening to compare the principles of this article with those expounded in *Iasnaia Poliana* in 1862. The later article referred the reader to the earlier ones for the author's theory of education and claims that that theory re-mained the same (17:105). In the later article, however, Tolstoy no-where reasserted the natural goodness of man. He, instead, summed up the results of his educational experiments in the 1860s as "the sole criterium of pedagogy is freedom, the sole method—experience" (17:105). In the later article, moreover, he no longer illustrated the idea of natural goodness by contrasting, as he had in "The Iasnaia Poliana School in November and December" (8:29–75), the purity of the peas-ant boys with the debased condition of their parents. (I refer to the lyrical scene in which he walks the boys home through a beautiful win-ter night and peers into the ugly huts to which they are returning.) Instead, he praised peasant culture and the values it inculcated, and he relied on parents to know what their children should be learning.[4]

In the eleven years between the two articles entitled "Education for the People" nature had ceased to be an absolute standard for good for

Tolstoy. A trend away from nature and toward moral freedom is visible in all the writing of this decade, in the pedagogical writing that precedes *Anna Karenina*, in various philosophical fragments, and in the drafts to the historical novel on Peter the Great that Tolstoy worked on for many years but never completed.[5] In a related development the peasant, as the embodiment not of nature but of tradition and convention, emerges in Tolstoy's writing as the repository of moral truth. Whereas in *War and Peace* the peasant way is one lesson joined with others in Pierre's soul, in *Anna Karenina* the narod have become the only moral way.[6] As Tolstoy perceived a split between nature and moral goodness, he turned from nature to culture—and peasant culture became his new standard for morality.

The new critical attitude toward nature and also the latter's residual goodness are reflected in the role of children in *Anna Karenina*. Here, as in *War and Peace*, children figure as innocent and pure, but prone to basic human weaknesses. What is different in the two novels is the narrator's attitude toward those weaknesses. Petia Rostov and Serezha Karenin are both shown to love sweets, for instance. Petia's sweet tooth is portrayed sympathetically. One of the most touching moments in the novel comes when Denisov, looking at the corpse of his young friend, remembers it. It is one instance of the vitality that also sends him on his reckless ride to death; nonetheless, we love the vitality in him as we love it in ourselves. Tolstoy's attitude toward vitality was more critical in *Anna Karenina*, and so even in children it is no longer shown as simply good. Like his Uncle Stiva, Serezha finds that he cannot resist forbidden fruit: he takes a peach the way Stiva would steal rolls (3.15) (or cheat on his wife). Serezha, however, unlike Stiva, is not corrupt. He cannot point, as Stiva does in the opening episode of the novel, to the "reflexes of the brain" to excuse his misbehavior. Serezha knows that he has been naughty and expects his mother to punish him. This is proof that conscience is as active as the voices of desire in Serezha's healthy, innocent soul. When Anna does not scold him, Serezha is "confused" as well as happy. He needs to be punished in order to have his own moral sense confirmed in him. He is not naturally sinful, as St. Augustine saw himself to be when as a child he stole fruit. He is pure and innocent, but naturally weak and prone to impulse.[7]

Anna fails to punish Serezha because, knowing herself to be guilty of a greater sin, she is more concerned that he love and forgive *her* than that she do what is best for *him*. In the next chapter, Anna herself cries "all out, as children who have been punished do." She has judged herself and is unhappy the way a Liza Merkalova, also compared to a child (9.8), can never be. When she judges herself, Anna is behaving like a responsible adult disciplining a child. Even as she judges, however, she knows that "she," the she who acts, cannot change her ways. Small wonder that when called on to act, as she sits weeping, she feels herself "dividing in two." Child and adult in her, vitality and morality or moral reason, are parting company.

Children in *Anna Karenina* are also seen as capable, in an innocent way, of the pride and consequent love of distinguishing themselves that are Levin's weaknesses. These are what Tolstoy called spiritual, as opposed to bodily vices. When Levin is condemning the excessive pride of philosophers, he uses an example from the behavior of Dolly's children to make his point (8.13). The children are trying to cook raspberries over candles and to pour milk into their mouths like a fountain. Their mother reprimands them by telling them that they are destroying what others have prepared for their nourishment. Remembering this incident, Levin reflects that philosophers are like children. Philosophers rely for their happiness on truths they have learned from others and, out of the need to distinguish themselves, they invent tortuous ways to arrive at these same truths.

In *War and Peace*, either chance comes to the rescue of foolish children (like Natasha in love with Anatole), or children like Petia die as part of a mysterious and harmonious scheme of balance in the universe. In *Anna Karenina*, children need adults, human wisdom, to correct them. Again I refer to a shift in emphasis, not a complete change in ideas. In *Anna Karenina*, human beings in their natural state are not simply moral. Happiness still comes from nature, but morality, especially the higher morality of self-sacrifice, is transmitted through tradition. And whereas in *War and Peace* tradition itself—present, for instance, in Platon Karataev's characteristic use of folk sayings—perfects nature, in *Anna Karenina* it corrects nature.

Tolstoy explored this theme in the drafts to the historical novel on the Petrine period that he attempted in the seventies. He did not claim there that children were evil. At birth they are "pure and without sin" (17:282) but ignorant of the essential truth that will keep them that way. The need for belief is one of two natural responses—the other being "desires and passions"—to the natural fear of death (17:226), a fear that is coeval with the consciousness of individual life that appears already in very young children. Tolstoy no doubt adopted this idea from Pascal with whom he became enamored around the beginning of 1876.[8] In the famous section of the *Pensées* entitled "Diversions," Pascal argues that the proof that human beings are fundamentally unhappy lies in the fact that all of them, even kings, seek diversions rather than confronting the reality of their lives, and especially the reality of "inescapable death and disease."[9] Following Pascal, Tolstoy wrote in the drafts to the Petrine novel that people could either try to forget death, as it was natural for children to do, by busying themselves with "desires and passions," or they could look for a meaning in life that would not be destroyed by death, a meaning supplied by faith.

And here at last is where the peasants come in. They alone of all the Russian people possess this faith and transmit it from generation to generation. They are different from other Russians because they still retain what other Russians lost at the time of Peter. Russian Christianity permeates every aspect of their lives. At the end of the 1870s, Tolstoy remarked in his diary (48:123) that Peter should have taken the same view of the West as the peasants did to this day: that Russia needed Western technology without Western beliefs. The beliefs were so important, so much the basis of a uniquely Russian solution to the philosophical questions of life, that Tolstoy agreed with the peasants that it would be better to reject Western science if it eroded traditional beliefs. These beliefs were the product of a culture, not of nature or of one individual. As Tolstoy remarked while he was preparing his primer in the early 1870s, the wisdom of the Russia people, expressed in folklore, was spread all over Russia. If you collected all the proverbs together, you would have this wisdom.[10]

This explains the attitude that, according to Tolstoy, peasants took toward the education being offered them by the Westernized upper classes. In "Education for the People"(1874), Tolstoy claimed that the peasants wanted to limit the curriculum in public education to Russian, Church Slavonic, and mathematics (17:107). This policy would allow students to advance in other fields and would limit the interference of outsiders to narrowly practical matters.[11]

Tolstoy agreed with the peasants that they possessed moral truths that needed protection from desecration by upper class do-gooders. As he wrote in a letter to Strakhov in early 1876, the peasants had less analysis, less science, than the educated classes, but a more healthy religious, that is, synthetic, view of the world.[12]

Tolstoy made fun of educational theorists who called their peasant pupils "savages" [dikari] and thought that they themselves knew the answers to the deepest philosophical questions. Adequate answers to those questions (48:123) were, in fact, already enshrined in peasant culture, and the peasants understandably resisted the efforts of narrow rationalists to reform it.

In a late (1879) draft of his historical novel, Tolstoy explained how peasants maintain their faith:

> The assimilation of certain beliefs is just as natural, even inevitable, as being carried away by desires and passions. Just the way desires and passions don't wait for us to make a choice, a certain explanation of the sense of our life—a sense that death would not destroy—is transmitted to us along with

our growth and upbringing. This explanation is called faith precisely because it is transmitted from one generation to another during childhood and
youth—on faith. It is not proven, not explained, because you can't prove or
explain things to a child, but transmitted as truth—the fruit of indubitable
knowledge of supranatural origin. (17:227)

Elsewhere in the drafts of his historical novel, Tolstoy illustrated the
transmission of knowledge, both practical and spiritual, from one generation of peasants to another. In one place old Ivan Fedotov teaches
his favorite grandson to plow (17:283). In another the father of little
Aniska, caressing him tenderly, teaches him his full name and his family affiliation ("*chei ty?*" [whose are you?]; 17:243–44). Aniska's grandmother, who is the main early influence on him because of his often
absent father and his busy mother, teaches him religion even before he
knows the basic facts of his own biography. ("His grandmother taught
him to pray even before he knew what to call his mother and father and
the place where he lived" [17:244].) His grandmother has him say his
prayers every morning, so that "Aniska had already known God for so
long that he couldn't remember when he had learned about Him." In
all crucial moral situations, the grandmother invokes God: "Grandmother gazed at the icon in a way that she gazed at no one and nothing
else and, understanding this gaze, Aniska himself always looked at the
icon and the candle with the same feeling that he saw on his grandmother's face" (17:244). In *Anna Karenina*, the main characteristic of the
peasants is no longer their naturalness, but their labor, which is not
seen as part of nature, but as a manifestation of their essence, of the
God in their souls. The peasants have "*chuvstvo nravstvennoi istiny*" [a
feeling of moral truth].[13] This accounts for the modesty of Ivan
Parmenov's relations with his wife; it explains why the peasant whom
Levin meets on the road wants farming that is rational, but not capital-
istic.

Peasants are natural in *Anna Karenina* in that they fully accept the
rule of nature over their physical lives. But although they are *in*, they
are not entirely *of* nature. The phenological landscapes in Tolstoy's
notebooks in the 1870s all mention peasant tools and specific peasant
tasks as part of the description of the time of year.[14] These landscapes
are as much descriptions of peasant culture as of nature.

Ivan Parmenov's previous restraint in sexual love, which we hear
about from his father, is higher, more spiritual, and less natural than
labor. It is the platonic love of which Levin felt himself incapable when
he discussed it with Stiva in the symposium, platonic love understood
as temporary and leavened in the telling with innocent sensuality to
make it realistic. The third manifestation of spirituality among the

peasants, Platon Kuzmich's "life for the soul" which restrains his money-making, is unnatural, because it simply contradicts the natural law of self-love. It is the fruit of a faith ("life for the soul") that Levin comes to recognize in himself. Levin says that he imbibed it "with his mother's milk." He says that even as a child he had joyfully believed what he was told because it had jibed with "what was in my soul" (8.12).

It is in his soul, but *not* in nature. Another way to put this is to say that the question of life—and death—comes from nature, but that one natural response, the response of faith, is itself, in its content, supranatural. In the draft to the Petrine novel quoted above, Tolstoy actually used this word, *sverkhestestvennoe*, to describe it (17:227). The need to respond to death is natural, but the content of faith comes not from nature, but from somewhere else.[15] In the reflections that end *Anna Karenina*, Levin follows his reconciliation with the imperfection of human life with an affirmation of his ability to "insert" [*vlozhit'*] a sense of good into life. Human weakness he passively accepts—goodness is his to "insert" (or not to insert) into his life. Morality comes from the truly free, reasonable, self-motivating part of his soul. The rest of his life is really just process which, in moments of reflection such as this one, he seems to examine from the outside, as if it were not really him.

The moral, free part of the soul governs peasant culture and makes it a properly spiritual response to nature. The peasants accept nature—life and death—as it really is, and they insert morality into it. Their right living, although it consists in the proper accommodation to nature, separates peasant life from nature and places it in historical time. History, having flowed in Tolstoy's conception in the 1860s into the great river of nature in *War and Peace*, in the 1870s divides again from nature. Thus, in one of the final drafts of *Anna Karenina*, written in April 1877, Tolstoy wrote of the *historical* destiny of the Russian people. Society is agitated by the problem of the Slavs: "Meanwhile the *narod* continued to live the same quiet life, with the consciousness that its historical destiny was taking place just as God pleased, and that to foresee and shape this destiny was not given to nor required of man" (20:549).

Finally, there is one more sea change in Tolstoy's art of the 1870s that is related to the tempest brewing in his soul. This one he makes explicit in *Anna Karenina* in the conversation in the restaurant between Stiva and Levin (1.10–11). I will discuss this scene at length in the next chapter. Here, I want to draw attention to one aspect of Stiva's defense of his own way of life. "All the variety, all the charm, all the beauty of life," says Stiva, "consists of shade and light." Stiva thus defines the metaphysics of opposites in a nutshell, but he derives that principle of any moral value. In *The Cossacks*, Olenin can justify his surrender to nature and "beauty" as epitomized in Marianka because nature as a whole has a moral worth equal even to the worth of self-sacrifice, the finest flower of his inner life. Levin, by contrast, appears in this scene as the champion of a wholeness that is somehow opposed to beauty. For the first time in Tolstoy's art, therefore, the good is arraigned against the beautiful. When this happens, in Strakhov's wonderfully precise description of the narrator of *Anna Karenina*,[16] art that "celebrates . . . the beauty of life" is subordinated to "moral meaning." Tolstoy does succeed once more in reconciling the two in the novel. The reconciliation is a shaky one, however, and one in which beauty must assume a subsidiary role.

Schopenhauer

Tolstoy's acquaintance with the philosophy of Arthur Schopenhauer was one big reason for the shift in emphasis in Tolstoy's writing from nature to culture in the 1870s. As early as 1868 Tolstoy began to read the German philosopher.[17] He spent the summer of 1869 reading all of Schopenhauer's works. At the end of the summer he wrote Fet:

> Do you know what the past summer has been for me? Constant ecstasy at Schopenhauer and a series of spiritual pleasures which I have never before experienced. I've ordered all his works and I've read them and am reading them (I've read through Kant too) . . . I don't know if I'll ever change my opinion, but right now I'm convinced that Schopenhauer is the greatest genius of all. You say that he's written a little on philosophic subjects? What do you mean, a little? This is the whole world in an unbelievably clear and beautiful exposition. I've begun to translate him. How about you taking up a translation? We could publish together. Reading him, I can't comprehend how his name could have remained unknown. There's only one explanation, the one that he often repeats; namely, that the world is made up mostly of idiots. (61:219)

Although his exposure to Schopenhauer's philosophy changed Tolstoy forever, his initial infatuation soon gave way to a more nuanced relationship. He spent the 1870s coming to grips with this powerful new influence, and the novel *Anna Karenina* may be understood as part of his struggle. Tolstoy found Schopenhauer irresistibly familiar. Like Tolstoy, he was the type of metaphysical idealist who identified "ultimate reality with the Will, and not with Reason."[18] Eikhenbaum shows that Tolstoy borrowed his argument on the relationship of determinism and freedom of the will in the second epilogue of *War and Peace*, written in 1869, from *The Two Fundamental Problems of Ethics*.[19] In this work Schopenhauer, like Tolstoy in *War and Peace*, both acknowledged the existence of determinism in the physical world, and nonetheless defended the possibility of free will in the spiritual world. Schopenhauer also resembled Tolstoy (and Rousseau) in his reliance on reason. He gave philosophy a privileged position, because he did not regard all aspects of thinking as expressions of will.[20] (Here is where Nietzsche parted company with Schopenhauer [ibid.].) Schopenhauer believed in ultimate standards—Platonic Ideas as he understood them—which gave reason real authority and independence from the passions (ibid., 318).

Although Schopenhauer's teaching helped Tolstoy resolve a central problem of his early thought (the relation of freedom and necessity), it differed from Tolstoy's early understanding in ways that created a crisis for the writer at the beginning of the 1870s. In the first place, Schopenhauer insisted on the tension, indeed the antipathy, between the natural freedom of man and the possibility of morality. *Natural* freedom, in the strict sense in which Schopenhauer understood it, is a product of will. It is purely a negative concept, signifying the *absence* of law, or reason. This freedom, far from bringing happiness, makes us miserable. "Our existence has no foundation on which to rest except the transient present. Thus its form is essentially unceasing motion, without any possibility of that repose which we continually strive after."[21] Life, "in the desire for which our essence and existence consists" (ibid., 53), has no positive content according to Schopenhauer. This is proved by the phenomenon of boredom; if life were positive, "mere existence would fulfill and satisfy us" (ibid., 54). So much for the "sentiment of existence" of savage man which for Rousseau was more satisfying than any feeling civilized man could know.[22] In order to have any real, extended existence, this sentiment, in Schopenhauer's analysis, would have to be based on some law in organic nature, some stable point that does not in fact exist. So much, too, for Goethean "living reason," at least as it may be understood to provide a foundation for the "sentiment of existence."

For Schopenhauer, in contradistinction to Tolstoy and Rousseau, man is naturally bad.[23] The following passage reads like a refutation of Rousseau's account of human history in the *Second Discourse*, where he had claimed that evil began only with the beginnings of human society:

> He who is capable of thinking a little more deeply will soon perceive that human desires cannot begin to be sinful simply at that point at which, in their chance encounters with one another, they occasion harm and evil; but that, if this is what they bring about, they must be originally and in their essence sinful and reprehensible, and the entire will to live itself reprehensi-

ble. All the cruelty and torment of which the world is full is in fact merely the necessary result of the totality of the forms under which the will to live is objectified, and thus merely a commentary on the affirmation of the will to live. That our existence itself implies guilt is proved by the fact of death.[24]

Natural man is "sinful" *because* he is free: he is completely without reason and is not governed by reason from without. As a result, he lives entirely for himself in a kind of Hobbesian war of all against all. It is useful to compare Schopenhauer's teaching on this point with that of the Savoyard Vicar. Schopenhauer regarded the *Profession of Faith* as the "prototype of all rationalism," which he criticizes for taking, not reason, but "theism and optimism" as its "presuppositions."[25] Schopenhauer will be more reasonable than the so-called rationalists. As an atheist he sees no necessary correspondence, implicit in the Vicar's arguments and especially in the natural setting he chooses for his profession of faith, between order in nature and morality. The Savoyard Vicar strives to prove that the conscience is natural. Schopenhauer declares that one fundamental condition for morality, the freedom to be reasonable and therefore moral, must be outside of nature: "It is metaphysical; in the physical world it is impossible" (ibid., 142–43). *Moral* freedom for Schopenhauer, then, in contradistinction to Rousseau, is freedom *from* nature, freedom *from* life.

Schopenhauer and Rousseau would both agree that man is naturally selfish. What Schopenhauer denies in Rousseau's, and especially the Savoyard Vicar's account, is the existence of any natural law, either negative or positive, that holds human selfishness in check. To put the Schopenhauerian view in Rousseauist terms, man is naturally all expansion, no unity. And, unlike the Savoyard Vicar, Schopenhauer does not see expansiveness as moral or reasonable in any way. For him Olenin's "web of love" would have been just another weapon in the arsenal of the lover of glory. And there could be no divine purpose behind the slaughter of war. Man is naturally sinful because he wants to expand to the greatest extent possible at the expense of his neighbor.

For all this, Schopenhauer is not rejecting the possibility of morality. On the contrary, as Tolstoy understood when he borrowed the Schopenhauerian position on freedom and necessity, Schopenhauer put morality on a firmer footing by insisting, in the first place, on natural man's complete freedom from natural law. Precisely because we are creatures of will, not of order, who can, nonetheless, choose order, we can be held responsible for our actions. We can *make* ourselves moral. This is a second, and positive, freedom, the freedom to conform to law. Tolstoy defines moral freedom in precisely this way in his notebook on 25 October 1868, when, according to an American visitor to his estate,[26] he was already enthusiastically reading Schopenhauer: "What does freedom consist in? In a correspondence with eternal laws" (48:111). Because this new reasonable freedom is not natural to human beings, however, it leads us eventually to reject life, understood as the action of the will, for "real," that is, reasonable existence. Schopenhauer argues that his philosophy represents the true meaning of Christianity. It "demonstrates theoretically the metaphysical foundation of justice and charity" in the denial of self, "the denial of the will to live" which denial is "the true soul of the New Testament . . . the spirit of asceticism."[27] Reason leads eventually to the "thing in itself, the will to live . . . present whole and undivided in every single being" (ibid., 142) and hence not destroyed by the death of an individual. We can be just and compassionate because we are, essentially, the same will to live as everyone else. Through reason, we see ourselves from an objective, not a particular point of view. We see ourselves as the idea of the will to live, not a particular and unself-conscious manifestation of it. Reason leads us out of our natural selves, out of natural selfishness, out of nature. It leads us from the seeming variety of appearance to the sameness of law.

Like Tolstoy, and perhaps more than Rousseau, Schopenhauer was concerned to defend the foundations of morality. Schopenhauer's moral philosophy grew out of Rousseau's teaching on compassion but was both more radical and more systematic than Rousseauian morality. In *On the Basis of Morality*, which was first published (in 1841) as part of *The Two Fundamental Problems of Ethics*, Schopenhauer acknowledged his debt to Rousseau, "undoubtedly the greatest moralist of modern times."[28] Like Rousseau, Schopenhauer understood pity, and morality altogether, as a product of comparison, and therefore of reason.

> What distinguishes a moral virtue from a moral vice is whether the basic feeling towards others behind it is one of envy or one of pity: for every man bears these two diametrically opposed qualities within him, inasmuch as they arise from the comparison between his own condition and that of others which he cannot help making; one or other of these qualities will become his basic disposition and determine the nature of his actions according to the effect this comparison has on his individual character. Envy reinforces the wall between Thou and I: pity makes it thin and transparent; *indeed, it sometimes tears the wall down altogether, whereupon the distinction between I and Not-I disappears.*[29]

These lines could have been written by Rousseau or, for that matter, by the later Tolstoy. They show clearly that Schopenhauer understood the connection between Rousseauian *amour propre* and compassion. They differ from the Rousseauist and the Tolstoyan teaching only at one point, in the lines that I have emphasized. Since pity for Rousseau was based on the fact that we have bodies and are therefore physically distinct beings, "the distinction between I and Not-I" could never completely disappear. Unlike Rousseau, however, Schopenhauer was a thoroughgoing subjectivist: for him the whole phenomenal world is a creation of the brain, and the body is an objectification of particular aspects of the will.[30] The body, therefore, exist though it may, need not stand in the way of a complete union of self and nonself.

Schopenhauer believed that the will to live, taken as a whole, had a moral function. He made his argument for morality, however, at the expense of the morality, and especially the possible happiness, of the individual. The natural desire for individual happiness was selfish and sinful, according to him, and therefore must be abandoned. If this proved impossible, then the individual must yearn for, indeed do all he could to bring about, his own death, even by suicide.

Tolstoy embraced Schopenhauer because the philosopher's more systematic thought gave structure to his own ideas. Like his teaching on freedom, Schopenhauer's teaching on compassion would have appealed to Tolstoy because it set the concept of compassion on a firmer theoretical footing. This clarification of thought, however, came at a steep price. The draught that Tolstoy gulped down so eagerly during the summer of 1869 contained a hidden poison that threatened to destroy all his happiness. As Sigrid McLaughlin has discerned, Schopenhauer's attack on the life of the individual as incorrigibly selfish and sinful at the core dealt a potentially mortal blow to Tolstoy's more Rousseauist, optimistic view.[31]

Schopenhauer and Arzamas

A famous incident in the fall of 1869 showed Schopenhauer's insidious poison already at work. The day after his ecstatic letter to Fet praising Schopenhauer (30 August), Tolstoy left Iasnaia Poliana for Penza Province on a business trip. On 2 September, in a hotel in a town named Arzamas, he had his first attack of what has come to be known as the Arzamas terror: he wrote to his wife on 4 September from Saransk that ". . . suddenly a melancholy, a fear, a terror such as I have never known came over me" (61:167). He continued that the terror returned the next night, while he was on the road, but that it was milder and, not taken unawares this time, he conquered it. Tolstoy described the terror in detail in an unfinished story called "Notes of a Madman," begun in 1884 and published only posthumously (in 1912). In this story, the first person narrator, like Tolstoy, is on a trip to Penza Province to purchase an estate. Awakening from a doze in his carriage, he cannot understand why he has undertaken the journey. He is suddenly afraid of dying on the road. Later, in Arzamas, in a hotel room that is white and square, with a little red curtain framing the lone window, the terror itself, "red, white, square," overwhelms him. With it comes a sense of approaching death that renders all the activities of life meaningless without either substituting anything in their place or becoming less frightening itself by virtue of life's meaninglessness.

In "Notes of a Madman" Tolstoy made the terror begin while his narrator is still on the road. As is typical of the way he used biography, he altered the details of his own experience to make it an illustration, cleansed of chance, of his explanation for his experience. He wanted the attack to interrupt a trip, to suggest symbolically the interruption of life by a crisis in belief. What makes the story especially appealing to the biographer, however, is that the explanation of the feeling in the story—madness and an attack on society—as opposed to its description there, does not do it justice. "Notes of a Madman" is an unsuccessful story in which Tolstoy tries to fit the genie of his inchoate fear back into a rather quaint little Victorian bottle. The experience itself, even at a distance of fifteen years, comes across as profoundly disturbing. Suddenly, for no easily discernible reason, Tolstoy lost the confidence, vital to all his actions, that his own life made sense. In the absence of any other goal, death loomed up as the inevitable goal or end of life. The real problem for Tolstoy, then, was not physical death, which as a soldier he had faced directly and even challenged, but that feeling of meaninglessness. It was this that brought on the religious crisis that culminated in Tolstoy's conversion, and it is therefore no accident that "Notes of A Madman" was the first work of fiction written after 1880.

Sergei Tolstoy (Tolstoy's oldest son, born in 1863) records another experience that he witnessed in 1875 that seems to support this interpretation. On his way to bed on the second floor from his first-floor study at around midnight, Tolstoy suddenly cried out to his wife in terror. He repeated his cry a few seconds later. Sof'ia Andreevna rushed to the head of the stairs with a candle, and Tolstoy responded to her anxious query, "It's nothing, I lost my way."[32] Sergei Tolstoy associates this experience with Arzamas, and I agree. Alone in the darkness in his own home, the fifty-seven-year-old Tolstoy again felt lost and confused as he had at Arzamas. In this case, unlike at Arzamas, we hear the story about Tolstoy rather than from him. But if Tolstoy had chosen to tell this story, he might have given his own fear of the darkness a meaning similar to that implied in the fear felt by Nikolenka Bolkonsky at the end of *War and Peace*.

Tolstoy needed meaning to affirm life, and on the road to Arzamas he temporarily lost it. When that happened, his own life became like that sterile room in the hotel in "Notes of a Madman": white and square, with a little window framed in red for entering and exiting this world. Once again we recall *War and Peace* and the Bolkonskys, this time Andrei's dream in which he overcomes his fear of physical death. Andrei's life, from which he is already alienated, appears to him as a large room in which he engages in empty society chatter. So in "Notes of a Madman," the terror eventually focuses not on death, but on "the room," life itself—"red, white and square"—which, in the absence of any redemptive meaning, stands only for approaching annihilation and present absurdity.

Tolstoy himself at the time saw the connection between Arzamas and his summer ecstasies over Schopenhauer. He ended the letter to his wife describing his experience by reassuring her that now (a day later) he felt fine. He had gotten over what had ailed him the day before: "there's one good thing—no thoughts about the novel or philosophy" (61:168). He referred here, as the editors of the Jubilee edition agree, to his work on the second epilogue of *War and Peace* (ibid.), that is, to the arguments on freedom and necessity that he had developed with the help of Schopenhauer. Arzamas served notice that these arguments were taking root in Tolstoy's soul, and their implications for beliefs already in place were beginning to be felt. In particular, they threatened Tolstoy's happiness by calling into question the status of the "living reason" that gave shape and meaning to the life of the individual in *War and Peace*.

As an event in Tolstoy's life, the Arzamas terror formed both a bridge and a divide between *War and Peace* and *Anna Karenina*. In the earlier novel the principal characters all endure crises in which their lives suddenly seem meaningless. But these crises are motivated: Arzamas differed from them because it came out of the blue. Prince Andrei's dream about dying most resembles Arzamas as a direct challenge to the sanctity of individual life. The Schopenhauerian idea that death is an awakening from the illusion of individuality to the undifferentiated source of all life first finds concrete expression in Tolstoy's prose in this dream.[33] Tolstoy left it unclear whether Andrei's decision for death comes before or after his illness worsens; it is possible but not certain that Andrei wills his own death instead of just accepting it. Levin's crisis at the end of *Anna Karenina* exhibits no such ambiguity. Perfectly healthy, happier than ever, he nevertheless so yearns to die that he must hide a rope to keep from hanging himself. Death—not the eternal life that Andrei believes awaits him, but simple oblivion—is preferable to mere life.

Arzamas joins and separates these two episodes, which represent different stages of Tolstoy's reaction to Schopenhauer's philosophy. Tolstoy composed the final scenes of Andrei's life in 1868, while becoming acquainted with Schopenhauer's philosophy. Yet Andrei's death is a happy event for him and, most strikingly, for the world of the novel as well. The realm of perfection accessible to Andrei only in death gives order and law to life. It is the ultimate source of the "living reason" manifest in Pierre. By contrast, the effect of Schopenhauer's philosophy on *Anna Karenina* is pessimistic. It makes Levin hate his life for its meaninglessness, and it gives him nothing positive with which to replace the "living reason" of *War and Peace*. In *Confession*, which Kathryn Feuer has called "a sequel or second ending to *Anna Karenina*," Tolstoy wondered why Schopenhauerians (including the philosopher himself) "who understand the senselessness and evil of life" do. not commit suicide (chap. 7).[34]

Nature after Schopenhauer

Schopenhauer did not make Tolstoy into a complete subjectivist in his relation to nature. I agree with Gustafson that Tolstoy remained a firm believer in the reality both of the human body and of the outside world of which it is a part and to which it connects us through the senses.[35] In this he was a faithful student of Rousseau and the Savoyard Vicar. The very nature and method of the Vicar's inquiry depends on a rejection of subjectivism. So, for that matter, did Tolstoy's ingrained individualism. He believed firmly in the reality and universality of his personal experience.

Beginning as Tolstoy subsequently did from a state of Cartesian doubt,[36] armed only with his own mind and his own sensations, the Vicar constructs both a harmonious universe determined and ruled by God (ibid., 272–79) and "man . . . free in his actions and as such animated by an immaterial substance" (ibid., 281). Like Tolstoy, he is looking for and finds the ingredients necessary to overcome a (Cartesian) skepticism that is conducive to philosophizing but that he regards as impossible to sustain (ibid., 268). To accomplish this end, he must venture into metaphysics, but even his metaphysics rests as much as possible on what he can sense or know himself. To prove that he is free, for instance, he simply says that he can move his arm if he wants to (ibid., 272). (Tolstoy regarded this example as so striking that he used it to prove this very point in the second epilogue [8].) Relying as much as he does on personal experience, the Vicar accepts the evidence of his senses that the world exists, and he proves his own existence by pointing to the inner judge, or knower, who puts the evidence of the senses together to form a single impression (ibid., 270–71).

Perhaps because he understands that the senses provide his only access to the reality of things, the Vicar is not a subjectivist. He accepts the reality of the data conveyed to him by his senses. He puts aside the arguments of materialists and idealists to declare that whatever his senses convey to him, whether it be an idea or not, is different from him because it comes from outside and proves to him that something besides himself exists (ibid., 270). Here again the young Tolstoy was in agreement with his mentor. In *Adolescence*, in the key chapter of the same name, he presented the Schellingian subjectivist doctrine that nothing exists except our perceptions as the most absurd aberration of adolescent narcissism and the "mind of man." Like the Vicar, then, and perhaps following the Vicar and Rousseau, the young Tolstoy did indeed see the world as "the mental representation of our sense experience."[37] Like the Vicar, however, he did not fundamentally doubt the validity of that experience. We experience nature through our senses in the early Tolstoy but what we experience corresponds to something real in nature. He resembled Goethe, who believed that nature reflects herself "everywhere in a manner analogous to our mind,"[38] and, like Goethe (ibid., 58), he did not worry about epistemology.

In *Anna Karenina* and the works that succeed it, however, under the influence of Schopenhauer, what we get from nature changes. In keeping with Schopenhauer's correction of the rationalism of the Savoyard Vicar,[39] Tolstoy withdrew all symbols of reason or structure from his nature descriptions. In place of the unifying, godlike symbols of sun and moon, he developed the phenological descriptions that appear at this time, first in his notebooks and then in fiction.[40] The regularity of the seasons testifies to the existence of natural law, but shows it only in its results, in action. In accordance with Schopenhauer's teaching about physical life, all life is in flux, all is will. And, also in accordance with that teaching, human beings are free of the instincts that regulate the behavior of other higher animals.

Tolstoy accepted Schopenhauer's radical interpretation of the soul because it did follow from his own (and Rousseau's) understanding of life as pure motion. Anna, "simple, natural" at the ball (1.22), and Stiva, with his natural freshness and emotional subtlety, do not depart from nature even if they both deny the voice of conscience in their souls— this is because the laws that keep order through instinct in other living beings no longer necessarily govern the human soul. Anna is "natural" [*estestvennaia*] and yet she sins. In *War and Peace* we would have attributed her fall to the artificial Petersburg world in which she lives. Exposure to this world deadens the voice of living reason in Natasha and makes her susceptible to Anatole's seduction. But although circumstantial evidence abounds that suggests the corrupting influence of Anna's milieu, no impartial jury could convict it of causing Anna's tragedy. The immediate villain is that "excess of something" which makes Vronsky look at her a second time at the railroad station. Ulti-

mately this excess of natural vitality—Schopenhauer's natural freedom—simply overwhelms Anna's conscience and sweeps her to her
death.

The vitality of nature can be innocent and gay, as it is in the opening
scene of *Resurrection*. And life lived in harmony with nature is still seen
as moral in *Anna Karenina*. But after Schopenhauer, vitality can also be
sinister if human beings see only it without the law that always regulates it in nature. When Anna on the way back to Petersburg identifies
with the wildness of the snowstorm, she is abandoning morality and
law. The wildness of nature is real, though its seeming lawlessness is a
figment of the imagination of the lawless individual.

Russian high society does set the stage for the crime that Anna's
natural vitality carries out. Nature is not bad in *Anna Karenina* and neither is Anna's energy: society has simply denied it its natural outlet in
work. Anna and Stiva, both plump to the point of chubbiness, behave
like children whose hands are idle. Energy is meant to be spent, as
Dolly, "a wasted, aged, no longer beautiful woman" (1.2), has spent
hers bearing and raising children. She has no time or energy for the
illicit love affairs pursued by her husband.

In *War and Peace* leisure has a natural attractiveness and even importance. Yes, idleness can be dangerous. Natasha, too, is suffering from
an excess of energy when Anatole seduces her. Andrei has proposed to
but not married her. Tolstoy emphasizes her restlessness at the Christmas celebrations at Otradnoe where she wanders, counting minutes
until her fiance's return. She passes the time by ordering the servants
around. This presages Anna's Cleopatra-like domination of Vronsky, a
key element in his attraction to her. But Platon Karataev's exemplary
life includes time for conversation and songs. The part that describes
the whole stay at Otradnoe, moreover, actually begins with a paean to
idleness in a military camp at peace (8.1). Like the military camp that
Nikolai reluctantly leaves to go home, Otradnoe is peace before war,
the lull before a storm. Old Rostov has moved his family to Otradnoe
in a last-ditch and ultimately futile effort to avoid bankrupcy (7.8), and
Nikolai's mother wants him to save the family by marrying, not Sonia,
but a wealthy heiress. Natasha is yearning for Prince Andrei and her
seduction by Anatole takes place in the following book, right after she
returns to Moscow. All the battles, all the disasters are, however, in the
future. The Rostovs take advantage of the lull at Otradnoe to enjoy the
fruits of enforced, and therefore legitimate, idleness: they hunt, philos-
ophize, make music and love, and celebrate a traditional, even magical
Christmas. Time seems to be suspended in the present, given structure
by activities outside those dictated by necessity. In the midst of this
book comes the visit to Uncle, who leads what seems to be an exem-

plary if pagan life of virtuous idleness. Lounging in his garden as if back in Eden, Uncle feels no guilt. His life is full, not of physical work, but of fulfilled obligations to himself and his neighbors that put his conscience at ease. Moderation draws him back within the limits of his own soul and he lives within them as self-sufficiently as Robinson Crusoe on his island. This independence is possible because living reason in *War and Peace* sanctifies the life of each individual. Each can retreat to a secure home within himself.

In *Anna Karenina*, after Schopenhauer, Tolstoy no longer felt free to celebrate the idyllic and natural sentiment of uncle's existence in his garden. He had adopted the Schopenhauerian view of life as ceaseless motion. Either this motion spends itself in service to the natural rhythms of nature and human life (as in the mowing scene), or it serves the individual's particular and insatiable will. When Anna gives in to her passion for Vronsky, she, like Levin as he mows or when Kitty accepts his proposal, is also possessed by "some kind of invisible force [*sila*]." But Anna's will becomes simply identical with the general motion of energy, because the will is no longer controlled and modified either by conscience or by natural necessity.

Control of the will, even if, as in the case of peasant culture, it results in a life spent interacting with nature, comes not from nature, but from tradition or individual, rational conscience, neither of which is of natural origin. The point that Tolstoy wanted to make about Anna, unlike, for instance, his point about the Kuragins in *War and Peace*, is not that she is alienated from nature, although that may be true, but that of the two choices life presents to individuals, she makes the wrong one.

In the 1870s as earlier, Tolstoy did not deny that nature is harmonious or that the laws of necessity enforce that harmony. What changed in his position as the result of reading Schopenhauer was his belief in the natural correspondence between harmony in nature and in human beings. It is precisely at this point that Schopenhauer corrects the "optimism" and "rationalism" of the Savoyard Vicar. A fundamental disharmony between man and nature replaced Tolstoy's earlier belief in their harmony.

As a result, in the 1870s Tolstoy, without abandoning "lyrical daring," moved closer to Fet (and Tiutchev) in his understanding of it. He adopted as a fact the position held in this Tiutchev poem, which in 1886 he marked with the words: "Tiutchev. Profundity!"[41]

Est un arundineis modulatio musica ripis.

[There is a measured music to the reedy shores.]

Pevuchest' est' v morskikh volnakh,
Garmoniia v stikhiinykh sporakh,

I stroinyi musikiiskii shorokh
Struitsia v zybkikh kamyshakh,

Nevozmutimyi stroi vo vsem,
Sozvuch'e polnoe v prirode,—
Lish' v nashei prozrachnoi svobode
Razlad my s neiu soznaem.

Otkuda, kak razlad voznik?
I otchego zhe v obshchem khore,
Dusha ne to poet, chto more,
I ropshchet mysliashchii trostnik?

[There is melody in ocean waves,
Harmony in the quarrels of the elements,
And an orderly musical rustle
Streams in the trembling reeds.

There is an imperturbable order in all things,
Full accord in nature,—
Only in our transparent freedom
Do we recognize discord between ourselves and it.

From whence, how did this discord arise?
And why is it that in the general chorus,
The soul does not sing the same thing as the sea,
And the thinking reed complains?]

In his account of the philosopher's influence on Tolstoy, Eikhenbaum emphasizes the part of Schopenhauer's teaching on the importance of will.[42] Eikhenbaum concludes furthermore that Schopenhauerian ideas provide the "metaphysical basis" for the poetry of Tiutchev and Fet which, he demonstrates, so affected Tolstoy in the 1870s and particularly in *Anna Karenina* (ibid., 176–85). Fet and Tiutchev share with and may borrow from Schopenhauer the idea of nature as will. To the extent that Tolstoy now accepted this concept, he moved even closer to Fet (and to Turgenev, for that matter) than he had been in the 1850s and the 1860s, when he had believed that reason, as well as feeling, joined man to nature.

   In the early 1850s Tolstoy had railed in the fashion of the Savoyard Vicar against the disharmony in civil society, as opposed to the harmony of nature. His new position was more ambiguous because he came to regard human freedom from nature as in some ways positive. Pascal's "thinking reed," with which Tiutchev ended the above poem, became, despite the weakness and unhappiness of this figure, the basis of Tolstoy's new morality. Thus, Tolstoy was to utilize Pascal's famous

passage about the thinking reed as the epigram to his philosophic exposition of rational consciousness, *On Life*. Man would be moral not
because he was natural, but because he was rational and free.[43]

I repeat, then: Tolstoy did not become a subjectivist under the influence of Schopenhauer, nor did he cease to believe in a moral universe.
What human beings are naturally, however, and what we get from
nature, narrowed and changed. Natural necessity retained its function
of making human beings better by reminding them of mortality, but
nature itself did not, as it did in Pierre during his imprisonment, simply
translate in human beings into a sense of moral "readiness."

The mysteriousness of nature, almost if not completely expelled in
War and Peace,[44] is a major theme in *Anna Karenina*. Even natural necessity, whose moral function in human life remains clear, is more mysterious. Perhaps the most interesting example of this in the novel is the
episode of the tree hit by lightning near the end of the novel (8.17).
Kitty and baby Mitia, who usually rest under the tree, are caught in the
storm, and Levin is afraid that they have been crushed. He finds them
safe at the other end of the woods, and he later confides to Kitty that the
incident and the fear it inspired in him have made him realize for the
first time how much he loves his son (8.18).[45] There is no suggestion in
the account of this incident that the tree being struck by lightning has
any moral significance. Neither, however, is it presented simply as an
illustration of the operations of chance. In this sense the episode stands
in interesting juxtaposition with the death of the tree in the 1859 story
"Three Deaths." There the death of a tree is seen in rather a Darwinian,
scientific perspective,[46] as making way for new growth in the forest.
The equation in this early story of the laws of nature with moral law
was perceived by Apollon Grigor'ev and other contemporaries as nihilistic; while for Tolstoy the tree's death, understood in this way, had
moral significance as part of his developing theory of living reason. In
Anna Karenina we see the tree struck by lightning in its human significance, entirely through Levin's eyes. In itself the event remains mysterious, while its moral repercussions for Levin are made clear, namely,
that Levin learns "to love that well what thou must leave ere long."

In *War and Peace*, human beings, Kutuzov most conspicuously, but
also Pierre and Andrei at certain moments, have intuitive knowledge
of the divine intention through what I have referred to in chapter 5 as
Verstand. Perhaps as a result of his reading of Schopenhauer and subsequently of Kant, Tolstoy had to abandon his belief in *Verstand* as *Nous*,
in intuitive intellect as a human faculty. We are left alone in the universe either to perish or to find and hold fast to moral laws that God
has put in place for us to follow.[47] The laws are still there; but in place
of the Platonic model of direct access to Truth, Tolstoy adopted a more

Christian and Pascalian one of the reasonable submission by reason to supranatural Truth.[48]

As nature is revealed to be fundamentally mysterious, the balance between the subjective and the objective elements of nature description shifts toward the subjective. This is especially true when a character must make a moral decision and seems to derive spiritual guidance from nature. The haystack scene in *Anna Karenina* (3.12) is meant to illustrate this change. Levin looks into the sky twice during the night spent in the haystack. The first time is after he has decided to abandon his dreams of gentry family life and become a peasant. He looks up a second time after he has seen Kitty and returned to his former hopes. The two moments are to be considered together:

> "How beautiful!" He thought, looking at a strange shell exactly like mother-of-pearl made of fleecy white clouds. It had stopped just over his head in the middle of the sky. "How charming everything is in this charming night! But when did this shell have time to form? I looked at the sky not long ago and there was nothing in it—only two white strips. Yes, in this very same way my views on life have changed too!"

> He looked up at the sky, hoping to find there that shell that he had admired and that had epitomized for him the whole course of his thoughts and feelings during this night. In the sky there was no longer anything resembling a shell. There, in the inaccessible heights, a mysterious change had already taken place. There was not a trace of the shell, and spread out over a full half of the sky there was a smooth carpet of fleecy clouds getting smaller and smaller. The sky was getting bluer and lighter and with the same tenderness, but the same inaccessibility, it answered his questioning gaze.

To appreciate the way in which Tolstoy's attitude toward nature had shifted by *Anna Karenina*, it is helpful to compare these two moments to Prince Andrei's two encounters with the oak tree. In the first one, Andrei identifies with an ancient oak which in the early spring has shown no signs of blooming. In the second, after his visit to the Rostovs and his first glimpse of Natasha, he passes the oak tree on his way back to his estate. It has leafed out now, and Andrei, in a different frame of mind, identifies again with the tree because he feels a renaissance of feeling and life in himself. In both cases, in *War and Peace* and in *Anna Karenina*, the character finds a confirmation of his own inner state in nature. In *War and Peace*, however, there is a real correspondence between what is happening in nature (the change from winter to spring) and what has happened to Prince Andrei. In *Anna Karenina*, what is actually happening in the sky has no real relationship to Levin's situation. Levin interprets a particular cloud formation as looking like a glis-

tening shell—a divine promise rather like the rainbow after the flood—
and he compares its appearance to the appearance of his new plans.
When, a little while later, he sees that the shell has gone, its disappearance represents to him the disappearance of his new plans after his
glimpse of Kitty. Even as the sky, and the changes in the sky "epito-
mize" [*olicetvorit*] Levin's experience for him, he acknowledges the essential mysteriousness of nature. It is *nedosiagaemyi*, inaccessible: the
word is repeated twice in the second paragraph. This inaccessibility
[*nedosiagaemost'*] goes together with and legitimates the subjectivity of
the skyscape in the haystack scene. For if we cannot really know what
is happening in nature, we must rely on our imagination to give it
meaning.

It is helpful, too, to compare the sky from the haystack with Pierre's
sighting of Halley's Comet in *War and Peace* (8.22). Pierre identifies with
the rush of the comet through the sky because it is like the swoop and
breadth of his exaltation. This identification, like Levin's in the haystack scene, is avowedly subjective: "it seemed" [*kazalos'*] this way to
Pierre. As in other subjective landscapes in the novel (Pierre's identification with the moon, Nikolai's with the sun, and so on), however, the
character identifies with a real object rather than a creation of his fan-
tasy, like Levin's shell. The comparison of Pierre's ecstasy to a comet,
moreover, is a poetic commonplace so universally accepted and experienced that it leaves open the possibility that there may indeed be some
higher, metaphysical connection between the real object and the character's state of mind. Pierre's positive impression of the comet hints at
the underlying theme of the positive repercussions of war. By contrast,
Tolstoy went out of his way in the haystack scene to emphasize the
split between reality, whatever it may be, and our perception of it. This
is particularly striking given that in most cases in the 1870s he used
only tropes hidden in folk language or linked to universal perceptions.[49] Both Pierre's identification with the comet and Levin's with
cloud formations in the sky are illustrations on a psychological level of
that Rousseauian expansiveness of soul which seeks both to extend
itself and to draw everything into itself. In *War and Peace*, Tolstoy had
seemed to suggest that our spiritual identification with nature may
have some justification beyond a psychological one. In *Anna Karenina*
he was not so bold.

Linking Happiness and Morality in *Anna Karenina*

The idea of the essential mysteriousness of the universe was not new in
Anna Karenina. It went back at least to the Caucasian landscapes in the
1851 diary (46:51) and was reenforced by the reading of the *Profession*

of Faith in 1852. At that time Tolstoy had agreed with the Savoyard Vicar that one should limit one's attempts to comprehend the universe to what is absolutely necessary for human happiness. As it turned out, of course, a great deal was necessary, including a vision of the role of Providence in human affairs in *War and Peace* that may have embarrassed Tolstoy by its comprehensiveness and explicitness when he reread the novel in 1873.[50] Yet, as he wrote Fet in 1875, a writer needs scaffolding [*podmostki*] in order to have the confidence to write (62:209). In the 1870s, as in the 1860s, Tolstoy had to have a structure, a vision of how the universe works, if he was to construct a new novel.

To do this Tolstoy did not simply adopt Schopenhauer's understanding of life. On the contrary, his struggles to distinguish himself from this new influence were as important in the 1870s as was the influence itself. Strakhov, in a letter to his friend dated 8 January 1873, rightly pointed out that in the face of Schopenhauer's pessimism, Tolstoy remained an optimist, that is, a believer in the possibilty of the concurrence of human happiness and goodness.[51] To hold his ground, however, Tolstoy had to change his position. In particular he had to revise his understanding of the relation of higher reason to life. He did this in *Anna Karenina*, where, if life itself is no longer understood as moral, it can still be made to serve morality.

Strakhov helped Tolstoy come to grips with Schopenhauer's ideas. Like Tolstoy, he was both immensely impressed and disturbed by Schopenhauer's thought, and he shared his impressions with Tolstoy. He credited Schopenhauer with teaching him the value of Christianity (ibid., 22). He wrote in one letter to Tolstoy that he preferred Tolstoy's writing to that of Schopenhauer because the former, unlike the latter, put beauty ahead of morality (ibid., 32–33). Elsewhere, however, he criticized Schopenhauer for being immoral. Schopenhauerian pessimism, he wrote, could be traced to "the rejection of everything solid in morality" (ibid., 21). Contrary to appearances, Strakhov was not inconsistent in these various statements. Schopenhauer pointed out that Jesus preached self-denial, which, in fact, is the basis of virtue both for Strakhov and for Tolstoy. For Schopenhauer, however, Christianity and self-denial are essentially life-denying. In the 1870s, when Tolstoy still hoped to combine happiness and morality, he was not willing to accept such asceticism. Nietzsche was the Hercules who in the next decade squeezed the life out of the morality lifted above the earth by Schopenhauer. During the 1870s Tolstoy fought a two-pronged campaign, against Schopenhauer on one front to keep morality's feet on the ground, and against materialist science on the other, to keep its head in the clouds.[52] Strakhov, with his love and knowledge both of science and of idealist philosophy, was Tolstoy's natural ally in this battle to keep real and ideal together.

In 1872, Strakhov published *The World as a Whole: Sketches from the Science of Nature* [*Mir kak celoe: cherty iz nauki o prirode*], a book of essays on nature. According to his own testimony, Tolstoy read this book pencil in hand, unable to put the book down, and he wrote a detailed critique of it in a letter to Strakhov (12 November and 17 December 1872; 61:345–49). There can be no doubt, moreover, that the book is an important subtext for *Anna Karenina*.[53] Tolstoy began writing the novel only a few months after reading *The World as a Whole*, and he reread it, again with enthusiasm, while finishing his writing of the novel, in late 1875 (61:235). Strakhov's book is divided into two parts, the first on organic and the second on inorganic nature. Tolstoy devoted most of his critique in 1872 to the first part of the book. It is clear from his approach that he accepted Strakhov's contention, put forth in the introduction, that we understand organic nature better than we do inorganic because it is closer to us.[54] Tolstoy insisted, seconding and even strengthening Strakhov on this point, that we cannot know what the outside world really is. For all we know, it "lives" just as we do. He therefore objected to Strakhov's use of the Hegelian word *dukh* [spirit] because to him it implies that we know ourselves by an "objective" standard rather than by a special and limited form of knowing called "soznanie" (61:346). *Soznanie* [consciousness] gives us direct knowledge only of our own inner life, and we extrapolate from this knowledge in various ways to interpret the outside world. We cannot know directly what the outside world is. This does not mean, however, that a healthy consciousness, with conscience intact, simply misinterprets the world; on the contrary, it alone allows us to distinguish the "whirlwind" of impressions from true life. Tolstoy took up Strakhov's distinction between "life" as understood by consciousness, and the "whirlwind" [*krugovorot*], which the outside world, perceived without consciousness, appears to be. The snowstorm in *Anna Karenina*, seen through Anna's eyes, is just such a whirlwind. When Anna allows herself to be tempted by Vronsky's slavish adoration, she shuts out the conscience that imparts form to her soul and order to her interpretation of the world. So Gustafson remarks that the death of the peasant at the beginning of *Anna Karenina* signifies the death of Anna's and Vronsky's conscience: "The tragedy of the watchman who does not watch is the emblem of that suppression of conscience which results in death."[55] Anna descends into a chaotic whirlwind of feelings. Without *soznanie* she no longer controls and orders the different voices in her soul. She feels herself "dividing in two," as different voices compete for supremacy. Hence the appropriateness of the snowstorm—total, aimless motion—to her state of mind on the way back to Petersburg.

The representative of consciousness in *Anna Karenina* is, of course, Levin. Stiva calls him "cel'nyi chelovek" [an integral, or whole person], and says that he believes that everything in life must have a (moral) goal (1.11). The English translation loses the connection between "wholeness" or [cel'nost'] and goal [cel'], and with it, the crucial philosophical point that Tolstoy wanted to make here. The "cel'nyi chelovek" has "cel'nost'" [wholeness] as his "cel'." Levin's consciousness orders his soul, gives purpose to his impulses, and demands moral coherence in himself and others.

Unlike Anna, Levin is in no danger of losing himself in a flood of passion. He experiences his love for Kitty as "some kind of *external* force" that has "taken possession of me" (emphasis mine; 1.10), and when Kitty refuses his proposal, he has himself to fall back on. "He felt that he was himself, and that he didn't want to be anyone else" (1.26). Despite his disappointment, the consciousness that regulates his soul and keeps him together is intact. Back at his estate, as he daydreams, "he felt that in the depths of his soul something was adjusting things, measuring them and fitting them in" (1.27). Consciousness is giving Levin's inner life a structure. It is making and keeping him himself. This is the same inner knowing, or living reason, that gives Pierre, Natasha, and others in *War and Peace* access to higher reason. The reason in consciousness in *Anna Karenina*, however, does not come from nature (though it may operate there as well). It is supranatural, and has an inner source only.

Consciousness, Tolstoy continued in his letter about *The World as a Whole* to Strakhov, gives access to a standard of absolute perfection, by which one can presumably both judge oneself and order the outside world (61:347). This "concept of good," not susceptible to rational categories or ordering, is the "essence of all life." Tolstoy criticized Strakhov for attempting to derive perfection, even if it be the developing principle of intellect, from below, from the "zoological." Such a perfection, which the human subject would find only in himself, would be only "relative." As examples of absolute, religious standards of perfection, Tolstoy cited Christianity and Buddhism. In his reply, Strakhov accepted his friend's criticism of what he, Strakhov, called his own "pantheism."[56] It was at this point that he remarked that Schopenhauer had taught him the value of Christianity. He went on, however, to defend pantheism as the only possible basis for science, and he asked Tolstoy to elaborate on his idea of absolute good as the essence of real life. He rightly discerned this as the major disagreement between Tolstoy and Schopenhauer, who saw life as the whirling vortex of wills, and Christian principles as the escape from the whirlwind.

Tolstoy and Strakhov were arguing a philosophic point of sufficient importance to require emphasis. Like Tolstoy, Strakhov welcomed Schopenhauer as an ally in the battle against positivistic and particularly materialist thought. At the same time, and again like Tolstoy,

Strakhov saw Schopenhauer's intransigent subjectivism as a threat to the essentially optimistic (and in Strakhov's case Hegelian) philosophy that he championed. The title of Strakhov's book suggests that he meant it, among other things, as a response to Schopenhauer. Schopenhauerian pessimism had split the "world as a whole" into the "world as will and idea" (the title of Schopenhauer's major work of philosophy, translated by Fet into Russian). Strakhov's pantheism would hold the world together by infusing matter with spirit, and his book argues that science, in order to make sense of what would otherwise be random matter, must proceed on the assumption that such a fusion exists. Science, in other words, must assume nothing more and nothing less than that the world makes sense. Strakhov saw the necessity for intellectual and especially moral certainty of the existence of absolute standards which science could not provide and which pantheism excluded.[57] He credited Schopenhauer with teaching him the value of such standards, evident in Christianity. Understanding the flaw in his pantheism, Strakhov welcomed Tolstoy's correction of it. At the same time, and in the respectful manner typical of him in dealing with Tolstoy, he challenged his friend to provide a philosophically satisfying elaboration of an absolute standard of good. Strakhov himself believed in the material basis of life,[58] and so saw the need for a spiritual justification of matter, and the life of the body.

As for Tolstoy, this "flaw" in Strakhov's argument would have particularly drawn his attention because it now must have seemed uncomfortably close to his own doctrine of "living reason." In *War and Peace*, in fact if not in theory, he, too, had concurred with pantheism in seeing God mostly in the totality of His works.[59] Following the Savoyard Vicar and Goethe, he had resolutely steered away from metaphysics to concentrate wholly on what he experienced himself. With magnificent results for his art, he had avoided the very question that he now directed to Strakhov.

So Tolstoy did not answer Strakhov's friendly challenge right away—Strakhov had to repeat it in a letter written in April[60]—and when he did so, on 11 June, he seemed to have shifted his ground. He no longer claimed that the principle underlying life was that of the good.

> A human being can't understand and express the objective essence of life—that's the first thing. The essence of life—that which makes us live, is the need for what we incorrectly call the good. Good is only the opposite of evil, as light is of dark, and as there is no absolute light and dark, so there is no good and evil. Instead, good and evil are only the materials from which beauty is formed: for the Greeks, physical, for the Christians, spiritual. To turn the other cheek when you've been struck on one is not intelligent, not

good, but senseless and fine [*prekrasno*], as fine as Zeus firing his arrows from Olympus. But let reason [*rassudok*] touch that which is open only to the feeling of beauty, let it make logical deductions from how you're supposed to sacrifice to Zeus, how serve and emulate him, or how you're supposed to celebrate mass and take confession—and there's no more beauty and there's no guide in the chaos of good and evil (62:24–25).

Tolstoy's claim in his earlier letter to Strakhov that an absolute good underlay and informed all life had been his response both to what he considered Strakhov's excessively rational pantheism and to Schopenhauer's attack on life as evil to the core. In between this claim and the June letter quoted above, Tolstoy had reread Pushkin's prose and, inspired, had started to write *Anna Karenina*.[61] In a letter to P. D. Golokhvastov tentatively dated 9–10 April 1873 (62:21–22), he wrote of the "hierarchy" of high and low things that great poets like Pushkin understand and faultlessly recreate in their poetry. This "harmonious correctness in the distribution of subjects" harkens back to the harmony in nature of which Tolstoy had written in his 1857 letter to Annenkov, Pushkin's biographer.[62] Goethe is here, too, the Goethe of "living reason" in Nekhliudov's final impassioned speech in "Lucerne," of which Thomas Mann wrote, "Could one express oneself more 'Goethically'? Even the *Harmonie des Unendlichen* is here."[63] Tolstoy himself, in 1870, had commented on how "well balanced" Goethe's writing was, going on to say that "when Goethe reasons, philosophizes, then he is great."[64] Strakhov recognized the writer of *War and Peace* in Tolstoy's new *profession de foi*. He called it "the true religion of the artist, the poet." This, he declared, was what he had sought and found in Tolstoy's [artistic] writings. It was the basis of Tolstoy's "compassion [*miloserdie*], which has so delighted me."[65]

Tolstoy's new formulation was reminiscent of the harmonics of *War and Peace*, but not simply identical with them. In *War and Peace* he had wanted to establish the justice of both nature and life through *soprianie* [linkage] so as to join himself (and his readers) the more completely to them. Not morality, but morally legitimate happiness had been his main concern.

In *Anna Karenina* he wanted, above all, to establish the conditions necessary for morality. As a result, although Tolstoy, in his new definition of life, crowned "beauty" and not the good as its essence, he still claimed that life itself is fundamentally concerned with morality: it consists in the interaction of good and evil. As he wrote in a draft to his novel on Peter The Great, "In this battle between these two directions of the will [of "lust" and "the law of the good"] lies the whole meaning and interest of each private life and of the life of nations" (17:233). Later in the decade, just after he had completed *Anna Karenina*, he reformulated his idea in a notebook in a way that shows the hidden link between the two letters to Strakhov that we have been discussing.

> Life is nothing more than the manifestation of freedom.
> This manifestation is only as regards good and evil. Knowledge of good and evil is faith—religion.
> The mysterious phenomenon of conscience is nothing more than the consciousness of the correspondence or lack thereof to the open law of the good—to revelation. (17 Dec. 1877; 48:349)

> Evil is an expression of freedom, a deviation from *law. Freedom is life itself.* (1 February 1878; 48:349).

The law of the good exists and gives meaning to life. In order to make good actions and evil actions possible, however, life itself in its essence needs to be and is free. God has given human beings the freedom to choose good—adherence to law—over evil. So we have two kinds of freedom, each necessary for morality: as living beings we are essentially free to do whatever we want, good or bad, and as moral beings we are free to choose law over chaos. In his first letter to Strakhov, Tolstoy had alluded to the law that defined morality. In the second, he referred to the condition that made morality possible, the essential freedom of life.[66]

Tolstoy was coming to grips with the knowledge he had gained from Schopenhauer's philosophy, and he was adapting that knowledge so as to salvage at least part of the joyful optimism of *War and Peace.* Under Schopenhauer's influence, he moved away from the doctrine of "living reason" and the artistic theory of "reason as representation." He now affirmed the existence of an absolute standard of good that gave meaning to physical life without, however, being itself an intrinsic part of it. At the same time, what for Schopenhauer was the essential evil of particular existence—its freedom and hence its deviation from law—became for Tolstoy a necessary condition for morality. The big difference between *War and Peace* and *Anna Karenina* is the relationship between freedom and law. In *War and Peace*, both are natural and coexist in the "living reason" that manifests itself in nature and in the human soul. In *Anna Karenina*, conscience, "living reason," is internal, and therefore potentially in conflict with nature, or "life" in its natural expression in the individual. Nature and higher reason in human beings are in tension, and create the drama that is the essence of the novel. "Culture" becomes the arena in which nature is either perfected or corrupted. The "metaphysics of opposites" still exists, but in a dramatic rather than an epic world.

Seven

Drama in *Anna Karenina*

TOLSTOY'S NEW attitude toward life and nature in the 1870s had repercussions for his fiction beginning at the level of genre.[1] If *War and Peace* is epic, *Anna Karenina* is dramatic. By this I mean that Tolstoy emphasizes the link between personal happiness and morality in the first novel, and the tension between the two in the second. In the first, as the Savoyard Vicar would have it, happiness and morality can coincide both in the individual and in nature. In the second, morality does not originate in nature, at least not directly, and its demands threaten individual happiness.

The most important philosophical word in *War and Peace*, the word that glues everything together, is *sopriaganie*, linkage.[2] This linkage exists among characters, families, and, for that matter, nations, and between humankind and nature. It is fundamental within the human soul as well. Tolstoy never mentioned linkage in *Anna Karenina*, and when he wrote of it in a famous letter to Strakhov, calling it *sceplenie*, he specifically restricted it to the level of thought (62:270). Instead of linkage, the key word in *Anna Karenina* is *drama*. First uttered by the comic character Stiva, in one of the most important philosophical scenes in the book, the symposium in the restaurant, this word sets the tone of the novel, which is, on every level, a struggle between the forces of good and evil. That struggle had become fundamental for Tolstoy's view of the world.[3] As I have argued in the previous chapter, it involved a certain overcoming of nature, or at least nature as it presented itself to human beings. It also reopened the question of the source of morality and its relation to nature.

The Symposium in the Restaurant

Tolstoy's two opinions about the essence of life, expressed in his two letters to Strakhov, contain the seeds of Stiva's and Levin's different positions in their conversation early in the restaurant in *Anna Karenina*. Even if Tolstoy intended Levin, not Stiva, as ultimately the more noble and sympathetic character, the reader would be wrong simply to take Levin's side in their discussion. Each of their beginning positions proves to be partially right and partially wrong. In Tolstoy's initial letter to Strakhov, when he wrote of an absolute standard of good as the underlying essence of life, he was taking Levin's position in the debate. In the June letter, when he equated good and evil with light and dark and said that life is a mixture of both, he was making an argument akin to, though not the same as, Stiva's. The symposium in the restaurant, so perfectly integrated into the realistic world of the novel, in fact introduces the reader to theoretical presuppositions that elevate it above Zola and the natural school.[4] It lays the basis for the mixture of compassion and judgment that Strakhov found to be typical of the novel's narrator.

The two men argue about the nature of love. Stiva explains his differing but equal love for his wife and his mistress, and declares that the tension between these two loves makes for "a terrible drama." Levin denies that there can be any drama about love and he cites Plato's *Symposium* to prove his point. Sexual love is mere appetite, concluding with "Thank you very much for the satisfaction, my regards"; while platonic love is pure and without dramatic tension. Levin makes his criticism of sexual love confidently, and there is no doubt that Tolstoy shared it. What Stiva calls a drama, Levin and his creator consider a mere melodrama. When Stiva has finished "with melancholy desperation" telling the story of his respect for his faded wife and his lust for a blooming maid, Levin laughs, and concludes his comparison of Stiva's appetite for women with his appetite for food with a bit of advice: "Don't steal rolls." Stiva is essentially amoral; for him there is no moral distinction between the play of feeling that he champions in his conversation with Levin and the contrasts of flavors and textures in the meal he has so carefully chosen in the previous chapter. Life for him is the flow of feeling, infinitely subtle, whose meaning derives entirely from the stimulating contrast of one feeling with its opposite. Drama in the life of such a man is purely external and fundamentally comic: Johann Strauss's *Die Fledermaus*, from which Stiva quotes in the symposium, is truly his opera.

In contrast to his confident disdain for sexual love, Levin flounders at the very beginning of his defense of platonic love. His own life has taught him that there is no such thing in actual experience as pure "platonic" love for a woman. He therefore implicitly acknowledges the possibility after all of drama in love, but he moves the drama from an external one, a choice between two equally good things, to an internal struggle, such as Stiva might feel but does not want to acknowledge, between good and bad. This internal drama is at the heart of *Anna Karenina*.

Levin's hesitation opens the way for Stiva's characterization of him as too "whole" [cel'nyi], too much in need of a goal [cel'].[5] Wholeness and platonic love are associated in this scene because both refer to that standard of absolute good which existed for Tolstoy and redeemed the necessary imperfection of life. Levin's mistake at this early point in the novel is to confuse love for any woman with that absolute good: he therefore does not contradict Stiva's declaration that "women are the axis around which everything turns." Kitty, during his courtship of her, becomes Levin's goal, the way Mar'ianka becomes Olenin's goal, his goddess, in *The Cossacks*. Just like Olenin (chap. 33), Levin feels that "some kind of outside force has taken possession of me" (1.10). This force, or "momentum,"[6] in all its authenticity is ultimately part of the power of the mountains, which represent the physical world, in *The Cossacks*; it can be the power of sexual attraction, the legitimate purpose of which is the continuation of the human race. It is the same force, in a different manifestation, as the one that Levin feels compelling him in the mowing scene. It overwhelms the mind to act on the body which, however, in both these cases is made to serve the common needs of mankind. Later, after marriage has changed Levin but not saved him from despair about the existence of a spiritual goal in life, a character named Platon Kuzmich, with his richly symbolic name,[7] shows him the proper role of platonic love in life. It is the authoritative voice in the healthy soul, the voice of absolute good, that keeps this character, "a rich and good peasant" who obviously knows how to acquire good things for himself, from "skinning" a man to get a few more cents out of him (8.6). The voice of the body has its place in the cosmic scheme of things; but when Stiva makes women his goal, or when Vronsky worships Anna, they are worshipping the goal of the body, not of the soul, whose voice they ignore.

Stiva laughs at Levin's joke about the roll, but he counterattacks by calling Levin a moralist. Eduard Babaev has discovered that Stiva's words—"o moralist"—are, in fact, a quotation from a poem by the Persian poet Hafiz which begins, in Fet's translation, "O moralist, don't be so stern!" [*o moralist, ne bud' tak strog*]. Babaev shows in his fascinating exploration of this particular subtext how Fet's translations of Hafiz played a part in debates in the late 1850s between Tolstoy and his Petersburg friends about the nature of poetry. In this polemic, according to Babaev, Tolstoy had played the moralist to the epicureanism of Fet, Turgenev, and others.[8]

Babaev takes this subtext to be a defense of Tolstoy's own moral approach to poetry. In fact, although there is indeed much to criticize in Stiva, at this point in the discussion he is in the right. Levin has absolutely condemned fallen women, but he does so from a position of purity which he twice in the symposium admits he cannot himself assume. Stiva, who lives in the glass house of impulse himself, does not throw stones at others. As Tolstoy put it in one of the drafts to the novel, Stiva, " . . . not considering himself to be perfection, . . . was full of tolerance for all" (20:95). When, earlier in the conversation, Levin chastises himself for past sins, Stiva responds that it could not be otherwise: "that's the way the world is made." When Levin rails against "fallen women," Stiva mounts the same defense based on his personal experience: sin is a fact of life that cannot simply be dismissed as an aberration.

Stiva uses an example from Dickens—the behavior of a "Dickensian gentleman" (Mr. Podsnap) from *Our Mutual Friend*—to make his point about ignoring facts, however unpleasant. The reference to Dickens in the symposium may also refer to those polemics of the 1850s in which Tolstoy sided with the so-called aesthetes against the Chernyshevskians. If this is so, then Tolstoy was setting the record straight about the exact nature of his attraction to the champions of positive rather than negative art. The crux of the issue for him was between "negative," or satiric, and "positive," by which he meant compassionate, art, which he favored. Dickens represented a poet of compassion for Tolstoy:

> The main condition of a writer's popularity, that is, the means to make himself loved, is the love with which he treats all his characters. This is why Dickensian characters are friends in common for the whole world, they serve as a connection between a person in America and one in Petersburg.[9]

Comedy and compassion in Dickens are closely related: the irresistible power of feelings over human beings as portrayed in his work inspires both pity and laughter. Stiva's knowledge of this power and his easy acceptance of it in himself makes this essentially comic character the champion of compassion against Levin's moralism in the symposium. For the reader, the category of "fallen women" includes not only the girl seduced by Stiva, but Anna as well. When Stiva corrects Levin's excessive moralism, he speaks for the author, who thereby indirectly indicates to his reader the proper attitude toward his fallen heroine.

Babaev identifies Stiva as "an epicurean and an aesthete,"[10] like the representatives of the defenders of pure art who influenced Tolstoy in the fifties. No Lucretius, Stiva is an epicurean of the vulgar sort, who prefers the pleasures of the body to those of the spirit.[11] Kathryn Feuer has interpreted Stiva's dream in the opening scene of the novel as a paean to wine, women, and song.[12] In the restaurant scene itself, Stiva quotes loosely from a Pushkin translation (entitled "Iz Anakreona" [From Anacreon]) of the poet of sensual pleasure, Anacreon.

Uznaiu konei retivykh po kakim-to ikh tavram
Iunoshei vliublennykh uznaiu po ikh glazam.

[Fiery steeds I know by certain brands they carry
Youths in love I know by their eyes.]

The implied connection in this poem between lovesick youths and horses draws attention to another characteristic that Stiva shares with the epicureans, their materialism. The unfortunate "stupid smile" which Stiva blames for the rift between himself and Dolly in the opening scene of the novel—without that smile he feels that he might have been able to bring Dolly around—is, in his opinion, an example of "refleksy golovnogo mosga" [reflexes of the brain]. This phrase refers to an article of that title by the Russian scientist I. M. Sechenov, which appeared in 1863 in *The Bulletin of Medicine* [*Mediciinskii vestnik*]. In this essay, which made Sechenov a "hero to radical youth," volitional acts were seen to be the result of physical reflex reactions.[13] Almost all educated people of the time had read it or were familiar with its contents.[14] Stiva adopts the language and ideas of fashionable materialism because it justifies his self-indulgent way of life and masks his inability to understand life "as a whole."[15] Since nothing but matter exists and everything happens according to predetermined physical laws, the life of the body, which Stiva lives to the fullest, is the only life possible. His body operates according to laws over which he has little, often no, control. At times parts of his body—that conditioned smile, for instance, when he confronts Dolly—even do things not in the interest of the whole. Stiva's response in these cases is simply to go with the flow. Like his sister he has both physical grace and a remarkable sensitivity to nuances of feeling. He would never have made Vronsky's unforgivably awkward move that breaks Frou-Frou's back. He is perfectly at home in the aimless flux of nature as envisaged by ancient epicureans and modern materialists alike.[16]

The fashionable determinism that Stiva introduces into the novel in a comic vein takes on darker tones in the story of his sister and of Levin. It is important to keep in mind, however, the extent to which Tolstoy himself believed in the power of both routine and outside influence over the human soul. Stiva's foolish smile recalls the inappropriate smile on Pierre's face at his father's deathbed, or, for that matter, the funny incident in Tolstoy's very first surviving work of fiction, the so-called "History of Yesterday," in which the narrator's feet convey him out the door when he still has something to say to his hosts. Constant motion in nature translates in human beings into the constant and often irresistible influence of feelings, sensations, and memories, Chernyshevsky's dialectic of the soul.

This state of being, moreover, when acknowledged by the individual, creates compassion for others whom the individual understands to be subject to the same whims as himself. As in Dickens and in Sterne, an understanding of the power of impulse over reason is related to an attitude of compassion toward human weakness. Levin is insufficiently compassionate in the symposium because he has not yet come to grips with this fact of human nature. In contrast to his attitude at the restaurant, Levin's final reflections, which end the novel, begin with an affirmation of his human weakness: "I will get angry at Ivan the coachman just as before, I will quarrel as before, I'll blurt out my thoughts inopportunely, as before there will be a wall between the holy of holies of my soul and others, even my wife, just as before I'll blame her for my fear and repent of it."

"That's the way the world is made": Stiva's response to Levin's confession of past sin in the symposium receives its ultimate vindication in these lines. By the end of the novel, Levin has accepted the fact, humiliating for mind and soul, that he has a body, which to a great extent goes its own way as part of a larger and seemingly random chain of causes and effects.

Levin, however, goes on in his final reflections equally to affirm the existence in himself of the "sense of the good which I have the power to insert into it [life]." Acceptance of the body is a good and necessary thing, then, but living simply for the body is not. The peak of Stiva's spirituality is a fleeting compassion which vies in him with other feelings. He lives only for physical pleasure. What Stiva totally lacks is moral freedom, the freedom to make moral choices among competing influences. Tolstoy's defense of the variety of life and its beauty, as developed in the letter to Strakhov, is based on the existence it implies of a freedom that makes both good and evil possible. But because the exercise of *moral* freedom depends ultimately on the moral sense that Levin possesses, Tolstoy's own position in the letter actually combines the points of view of Stiva and Levin. Thus Levin, in contrast to Stiva, regrets his sins, quoting famous lines from Pushkin's poem "Remembrance" [*Vospominanie*].

Stiva's conclusion, that the variety of life is a good thing, is correct, but his reason for drawing that conclusion—merely that it makes life beautiful and charming—is not. In making Stiva the champion of mere beauty, Tolstoy may indeed be taking issue with the aestheticism of his friends in the fifties, and in the process pointing out the connection between it and vulgar epicureanism. Living for the body, Stiva pities, but he does not judge either himself or others. Since he lives for pleasure, relegating his conscience to the status of other voices in his soul, he is not truly free, that is, free to follow moral law. Here he differs from his sister, who inhabits the same moral world as Levin. To appreciate the moral value of Stiva's defense of variety, therefore, one must step out of the symposium to compare Levin with Anna.

Anna Karenina was much criticized by contemporaries as containing two novels, one about Anna and the other about Levin.[17] When the publisher Katkov used this excuse to cut off publication of the novel in *The Russian Herald* [*Russkii vestnik*] at the end of part 7, after Anna's suicide, Fet came to Tolstoy's defense. In an unpublished response to Katkov's decision—a decision actually made for political reasons—Fet argued that "the inner, artistic link of Levin with Karenina stares you in the face throughout the whole novel." He jokingly suggested that to make his intention absolutely clear, Tolstoy should have entitled his novel *Karenina, or the Adventures of a Lost Lamb, and the Stubborn Landowner Levin, or the Moral Triumph of a Seeker after Truth.*[18] The novel can only end with part 8, where the parallel and contrast between the lives of the two characters is completed. Fet crosses t's and dots i's for the philistine reader who does not comprehend the dramatic structure of the novel.[19]

In order to encourage the reader to compare Anna and Levin, Tolstoy made them alike in certain fundamental ways. Although they meet only once in the course of the novel, and then only toward its end, they are spiritually akin. Both share an openness to influence and change that makes them potentially moral. It is important to note in this context that Levin makes his first appearance in the novel not as the moralist in the symposium, but as a skater famous for his skill and strength. Like Anna and Stiva, then, Levin has physical grace. Like Anna and unlike various intellectuals in the novel, he also has the ability to change his mind, even to the point of seeming illogical. Sergei Ivanovich criticizes his brother for "a mind although quick enough, nonetheless subject to the impressions of the moment and hence full of contradictions" (3.1). Levin and Anna are in touch both physically and spiritually with the illogical forces that govern life from minute to minute. Both differ from the two Alekseys, Karenin and Vronsky, in that they do not, cannot, lock themselves into a set of rules that would shield them from natural flux. It is precisely in the midst of the "krugovorot" [whirlwind], the wild snowstorm on the way back to Petersburg, that Anna has her first chance consciously to reject Vronsky. "Oblivion" [the rejection of moral consciousness] beckons her, "and she could as she willed [*po proizvolu*] give in to it or restrain herself"

(1.29). Real choices only present themselves when, for better or for worse, we step outside the house of rules we have built for ourselves or that others have built for us.[20]

At the same time and on the other hand, Levin and Anna are alike in that they both feel the influence of and need for moral law. They cannot simply go with the flow. The Petersburg fast set live quite comfortably in the "whirlwind" of passions that eventually sweeps Anna to her death.

Betsy explains Anna's problem to her: "You see, it is possible to look at one and the same thing tragically and make a torture of it, and to look at it simply and even merrily [*veselo*]. Perhaps you're inclined to look at things too tragically" (3.17). Anna's response, which follows immediately, links the tragic with the moral: "'How I wish I could know others as I know myself,' said Anna seriously and thoughtfully. 'Am I worse than others, or better? Worse, I think.'" Anna is worse than Betsy and the others only because, unlike them, she makes moral judgments about herself. She is a tragic heroine, unlike the comic Stiva, because she inwardly acknowledges the choice between good and evil. This similarity between Anna and Levin sets up the contrast that Fet observed. Both live morally: one chooses evil and dies, while the other chooses good and lives. This choice is possible only when both freedom and moral law exist. Drama, for Tolstoy, was therefore ultimately a didactic genre, in which, as he told P. A. Sergeenko in 1900, conflicting sides speak their pieces fully and as forcefully as possible, but "at the same time the main, basic thought is felt everywhere."[21]

In the symposium, Levin initially takes the side of law against freedom. Recollection in the middle of the conversation of his own past moral struggles makes him realize that he is somehow mistaken in his simple moralism. He eventually learns Stiva's lesson, that to live means to be tempted and often to fall. *Anna Karenina* teaches that the imperfection of human beings imposed on them by their bodies is necessary in a free and yet moral universe. Tolstoy has taken the atheist Schopenhauer's point about the irrational and hence fundamentally evil nature of human individuals and made it part of a budding theology.

Characters in *Anna Karenina* are necessarily imperfect, but they are capable of moral choices. Moral choice is the lynchpin around which *Anna Karenina* turns.[22] Corresponding to this shift in emphasis from what Mirsky calls the "vegetable" (in *War and Peace*) to the "moralistic" (in *Anna Karenina*),[23] the Goethean "metaphysics of opposites," still the skeleton of a living work of art, also evolves to acquire a moral function. Within the human soul, the opposites become choices for good or evil available to human beings by which they confirm or do not confirm their humanity and moral freedom.

Anna as Heroine of a Novel

Tolstoy called his work *Anna Karenina: A Novel*; in so naming it he was drawing attention to the fact that it was to be a case study dedicated specifically to the heroine of a *novel*.[24] He named the book after Anna because she, of all the characters in the book including Levin, most fully meets the specifications for such a heroine.

As he did in *War and Peace*, Tolstoy played with meanings in the title of his second novel. First Bilinkis and then other Soviets have explored the multiple meanings of the word for peace [*mir*] in the title of *War and Peace*.[25] The Russian word for novel [*roman*] also has more than one meaning. It can refer to a love affair. Kitty uses the word in this way in the novel, and precisely about Anna. Talking to this charming Petersburg lady for the first time, Kitty wonders about the history of her marriage to Karenin: " 'But how did she go through all this? How I would like to know the whole story of her romance [*roman*],' thought Kitty, remembering the unpoetic appearance of Aleksei Aleksandrovich, her husband" (1.20). The truth, as yet unknown to Kitty and Anna herself, is that Anna's romance, and with it the novel, have barely begun.

The first lines of the book fix its genre and also explain its relationship to *War and Peace*. Babaev has observed the connection between the happy and unhappy families of *Anna Karenina* and the French saying at the end of *War and Peace*: "Les peuples heureux n'ont pas d'histoire" [Happy peoples have no history]. [26] Rousseau's *First Discourse* may be the original source of Tolstoy's conviction that the happiness of nations and individuals alike lies outside of history, which is the record of mankind's unfortunate departure from nature. In families as in nations, in *Anna Karenina* as in *War and Peace*, the key to human happiness and freedom is moderation of the passions. Like history, novels occur when people do not moderate their passions. For this reason, Levin's successful marriage, and even Dolly's unsuccessful one, inasmuch as she holds the family together, cannot be the subject of a novel.

The aphorism about happy and unhappy families was originally conceived (late in the writing of the novel) as an epigraph to the first part. Only at the last minute did Tolstoy append the epigraph to the text and slightly alter the succeeding sentence.[27] This, according to Babaev, gave the novel two beginnings, a philosophic one (the epigraph about vengeance), and a narrative [*sobytiinoe*] one (ibid., 133–34). The philosophic beginning is outside the text because it provides a standard for judging events and characters. The second beginning belongs in the text rather than outside it because it generates the novel.

Both beginnings come from the objective narrator, whose authority and structural role have increased, Bilinkis notes, in comparison to *War and Peace*,[28] but the epigraph judges while the aphorism only comments. The epigraph takes the perspective of perfection, or law, the aphorism that of freedom from law and the consequent necessary imperfection of life. Novels begin with departures from the laws that give sameness, happiness, and sense to life.[29] This is why they, unlike epics, have beginnings as well as endings—endings that in the exemplary novel *Anna Karenina* are shown to be dead ends.

Anna's Radical Individualism

In the chapter at Betsy's salon, which was originally intended to begin the novel, Anna delivers her own striking aphorism. She is listening to a conversation about passionate love and whether it justifies unfaithfulness in marriage. Asked her opinion, Anna replies, "I think . . . if there are as many minds as there are heads, so there are as many kinds of love as there are hearts" (2.7). With her aphorism, Anna is declaring war on routine, and the conventions that sustain it. Vronsky shows he understands the aphorism as sympathetic to his pursuit of her when he "sighed as if after danger when she uttered these words." Anna speaks while "playing with the glove she has taken off." Here, as elsewhere in Tolstoy's fiction, the glove removed symbolizes a departure from conventional sexual mores. (Tolstoy used this gesture in the same way during the attempted seduction in Italy in *Family Happiness*.) On the face of it, this would seem not to be a bad thing. Routine in Petersburg society takes the place of moral laws. It imparts regularity to the lives of egotists Stiva and Vronsky without making them moral. Conventions are part of the moral hypocrisy of society, which allows any depravity so long as it is comme il faut.

It is crucial to remember, however, that in *Anna Karenina* not all convention is bad. The defense of culture that Tolstoy mounts in the 1870s gives convention a new legitimacy in his fiction. Good conventions supply the moral underpinnings of peasant culture and of the unhappy but morally fulfilling life led by Dolly Oblonsky. It is no accident that in a crucial scene in the novel Dolly discovers the kinship between herself and peasant women, a kinship based on their common preoccupation with children (3.8). Dolly is the standard bearer in this novel for unself-conscious morality. As Blackmur has written of her apropos of this very episode: "Dolly is the monitor of all that is living: she has paid the cost of goodness without ever having had it, and in so very deep a way that no fresh start—neither rebellion nor new effort along fresh lines—could ever get it for her. She is neither good nor evil; neither hopeless nor desperate."[30]

Nikolai Rostov plays a similar role—that of the ordinary decent man—in *War and Peace*, and therefore the difference between him and Dolly is symptomatic of the difference between the two novels as wholes.[31] Nikolai's goodness is rooted in nature, whereas Dolly finds her anchor in the conventions of family life. As the guardian angel of marriage and the natural momentum behind it she promotes the marriage of Levin and Kitty in the face of Levin's (natural) pride (3.10), but at the dinner party in part 4 she helplessly battles the same momentum, this time tearing apart the Karenins' marriage (4.12). In part 2, chapter 2, she herself does not let herself see obvious signs of Stiva's renewed infidelity, because it would deprive her of the "family habits" which she cannot do without. As Kitty tells her in anger, she humiliates herself to hold her family together (2.3). To protect the family Dolly practices a kind of hypocrisy that shields her from reality. In spite of this, however, she occupies a central positive place in the novel because she stands for "routine" as a bulwark against natural "force" when it threatens the family.

Anna's aphorism about hearts and heads is, in fact, connected to the one about happy and unhappy families. When she denies the existence of general truths, both for the head and for the heart, she implicitly denies that all happy families would be alike, that is, that they would conform to the same rules. At this crucial moment in her story, she chooses freedom—an absence of general laws—which will make her and those who depend on her unhappy. Her unhappiness, and that of her family, will be unique, precisely because she has turned her back on moral law. Without it, free will of the individual reigns supreme, and the individual is free to love as he or she wills. Sexual love exists for the pleasure of the individual rather than as a powerful natural force that channels the energies of the individual into preservation of the species.

Anna's embrace of radical individualism—for that is what her aphorism signifies—implies a rejection of *all* conventions that limit the will of the individual. She thereby separates herself from Dolly, as the latter perceives during her visit to Vronsky's estate. "She suddenly felt that she was already so far from Anna that there existed questions between them that they could never agree on and about which it was better not to speak" (6.23).

Birth control is the issue that reveals the newly formed rift between the two friends. Anna has rejected the natural consequence of sexual relations and family life, namely, pregnancy, because it would interfere with the pleasures of the individual on which her relationship with

Vronsky is based. Dolly, who has herself dreamed of freedom from motherhood and even of "the most passionate and impossible love affairs [*romany*]" on her ride to Vronsky's estate (6.16), is shocked into reaffirmation of her role as keeper of the hearth by the appearance of a truly "liberated" woman in the person of Anna.

For her part, Anna finds that despite her renunciation of society, she does not really succeed in liberating herself from it.

> She felt that that position in high society, which she had made use of and which that morning had seemed so insignificant to her, that that position was dear to her, that she wouldn't be strong enough to exchange it for the shameful position of a woman who had abandoned her husband and son and joined her lover; that no matter how hard she tried, she wouldn't be stronger than herself. She was never going to experience the freedom of love, but would always remain a sinful woman under the threat of being exposed every minute, deceiving her husband for a shameful liaison with another, independent man, with whom she couldn't live one life. (3.16)

Anna's truthfulness is impressive here and indicative of a strength of soul lacking in the corrupt women of Betsy's circle. At the end of these reflections, Anna weeps "as children who are punished do." She is experiencing and acknowledging part of the bitter truth of the novel's epigraph as Tolstoy himself explicated it many years after, that the evil deeds people do rebound upon themselves.[32] Seeming to turn her back on society, she, in fact, embraces the individualism that it both camouflages and defends. She finds that she needs society to justify the essentially amoral life she has chosen, and so she cannot simply ignore its condemnation of her.

This individualism, unlike the family life of Dolly, has no basis in moral law, so Anna finds herself without anything to replace the routine of her life with Karenin. At a crucial moment in Anna's story, after she has confessed everything to Karenin, the word *opredelit'sia* [to take shape] appears five times in a paragraph describing Anna's hopes for the future (3.15).[33] A few pages later, Anna acknowledges that a new life will not "take shape" [*opredelitsia*] to replace the old one. She is condemned to constant motion, which becomes a motif accompanying her until her death. This motion characterizes the world of individualism as a whole as portrayed in the novel, from Safo Shtolc's way of "rushing forward" (3.18), to Vronsky's estate named "Vozdvizhenskoe," suggesting motion, in comparison to Levin's estate "Pokrovskoe," suggesting shelter or protection, to the industrial development of Russia, with railroads both facilitating this development and symbolizing it in the novel.[34]

To Judge or Not Judge Anna

Tolstoy's attitude toward his heroine is complex. This is not because he himself has mixed feelings about her, but because she changes in the course of the novel, and the attitude of the narrator changes with her. Tolstoy did not intend simply to condemn Anna or her way of life. His book is a case study, undertaken with the cool detachment that Strakhov noticed was its dominant tone.[35]

Anna's appearance in the novel coincides with her first, barely noticeable straying off the path of virtue toward her death. Almost in spite of herself she basks in the warmth of Vronsky's initial attraction to her, so that by the end of the episode at the train station she weeps from a sense of foreboding about her own future. Yet, at the same time that Tolstoy displayed Anna's dangerous vitality in her first appearance and also recorded her first false step, he made a point of her virtue, emphasizing her attempts to restrain herself both physically and spiritually. Her glance is lively but "restrained" [*sderzhannaia*]; the "excess of something" in Anna peeks out "against her will" [*mimo ee voli*]; she "extinguishes" [*potushila*] the light in her eyes "deliberately" [*umyshlenno*], but it still shines "against her will" [*protiv ee voli*] in her smile. All these observations, crowded together in the first, one-paragraph description of Anna, qualify her vitality without banishing or even completely controlling it. The effect is one of "opposite forces of animation and restraint ('will') . . . in delicate equilibrium."[36] This "delicate equilibrium" extends even to Anna's physical bearing. "Karenina stood," the narrator informs us a little later in a one-sentence paragraph, "motionless, holding herself extremely straight, and her eyes smiled" (1.18).

We see Anna first through Vronsky's eyes. What Vronsky finds fatally attractive in Anna is precisely the tenuously maintained balance of forces that he senses in her almost immediately. He himself lacks this tension between body and soul. Vronsky is a rock of a man, "a short, well-built brunette, with a good-naturedly handsome, extremely calm and firm face" (1.14). Like his namesake Aleksei Karenin, Vronsky is an egotist, and therefore a creature of stasis, who strives above all to stay within himself and draw everything he wants into himself. In comparison with him, Anna, quick and open, is spiritual. But Vronsky misinterprets the tension in Anna, or perhaps it would be better to say that he sees in her only what a completely earthbound creature can see. Like Marianka for Olenin in *The Cossacks*, Anna for Vronsky represents the eroticism that makes otherwise self-centered, self-contained bodies come together. In this respect she resembles Pushkin's Cleopatra, whose fatal power she exercises.[37] In Pushkin's poem, Cleopatra's voice and gaze animate the whole palace. When she lowers her head and sinks into thought, the guests and chorus fall silent. Vronsky responds to Anna in similar fashion. At the train station, when she joyfully greets her brother, he "not knowing why himself, smiled." When she suggests that something must be done about the dead man's family, he rushes to obey, mechanically, as Jackson points out.[38] At the ball, Vronsky is fully in Anna's power.

> Anna smiled and the smile communicated itself to him. She grew thoughtful and he became serious. Some kind of supernatural force pulled Kitty's eyes to Anna's face. She was charming in her simple black dress, charming were her full arms with their bracelets, charming was the firm neck with the strand of pearls, charming was the curling hair of the disordered coiffure, charming were the graceful light movements of the little hands and feet, charming was this beautiful face in its animation; but there was something horrible and cruel in her charm. (1.23)

The ball resembles Cleopatra's feast in Pushkin's poem, and Anna resembles Cleopatra in this passage. Here, once again, Anna is seen from the outside, this time by Kitty. Anna's fascinating sensuality is serpentine. She weaves her spell over Vronsky, and for that matter Kitty, who continues to feel her power.

For Kitty and for Vronsky Anna is a goddess, but a pagan and even a chthonic one. Kitty, from inside the warm cocoon of her family and wrapped in her own virtue, is attracted but ultimately repelled by her. Anna, as Vronsky perceives her, represents the pinnacle, the spiritual apex of his world. This is why the "impression that she made on him" gives him "happiness and pride," and makes him feel like a "tsar" (1.31). Vronsky is matter waiting, yearning to be animated by the motion that is Anna. Her appearance sends an "electric shock" through his body that "with new force" makes him "feel himself, from the springy movements of his legs to the movement of his lungs as he breathes" (3.22).

In characteristic fashion, Vronsky wants Anna for himself. He wants to own the goddess that he worships so that he, too, can live with her intensity. One can say that this is a need, the natural goal of Vronsky's earthbound existence. Vronsky's belief in the nineteenth century ideal of progress and his adoration of Anna are connected.

> The belief in progress is lack of belief or incomprehension of the great God and faith in a little one. *They* have formed progress so that the *motion* of

everything, that is, the essence of life, is directed toward goals they desire—
or that they understand. There is no God except for our *desire*. It is the same
as idol worship. (19 March 1870; 48:121)

Vronsky is one of *them*, one of the idol-worshippers who for a time
worships Anna. The motion, the vitality behind his love for Anna and
behind the idea of progress is real, but the goals of each are false.

To possess Anna, however, Vronsky has to kill her: he has to make
her choose him, and hence her body, over her soul. Tolstoy therefore
compared the seduction scene to a murder. Vronsky misreads Anna.
Although it continues to fascinate him, he never understands the spiritual struggle that is the ultimate cause of the tension in Anna that at-
tracts him. At the height of the struggle that climaxes in the seduction,
as Anna and Vronsky talk at Betsy's salon, Vronsky is "struck by the
new spiritual beauty of her [Anna's] face" (2.7). But Anna's capitula-
tion to Vronsky is the beginning of the end of the moral struggle that
creates this beauty.

The first three parts of the novel chart Anna's spiritual struggle
against the evil demon in her soul that wants to occupy it exclusively.
Her conscience speaks many times (1.18, 20, 21, 28, 29; 2.7, 27; 3.15, 16,
17, 23 [her pity for Karenin]), making it possible for the reader both to
blame her (because she knows the good and still chooses the bad) and
to pity and admire her for her noble struggle.

In part 4, at the center of Anna's story, that division of her soul into
good and evil, which is mentioned three times in the space of a few
pages (3.15, 16) in the previous part, is complete. While she seems to be
dying of childbirth fever (4.7), she speaks "with extremely defined intonations" [*s chrezvychaino opredelennymi intonacionami*], with that definition [*opredelenie*] that otherwise eludes her. To emphasize the authority
and sincerity of her speech in this situation, the narrator repeats in the
same paragraph that she speaks "with unusually correct and heartfelt
intonations" [*s neobyknovenno pravil'nymi i prochuvstvovannymi intona-
ciiami*]. She is the completely good Anna who concerns herself with her
children—in the case of her daughter Anna, for the only time—and
penetrates to goodness in her husband that even he himself did not
know existed. She rejects the "other," who "fell in love with that one
[Vronsky]" and she desires only Karenin's forgiveness and then death.
Subsequently, however, the bad Anna is resurrected and comes to
dominate her soul again. In part 4 Anna is in flux, with the good and
bad parts of her soul presenting themselves in turn and without any
conscious effort on her part to explain the transitions. Most ominously
for her future, the reappearance of the bad Anna coincides with her

recuperation. Her surrender to Vronsky has meant the fatal dominion of body over soul, a dominion challenged only when Anna is dying— here in part 4 and in the final moments of her life, as she flings herself under the train.

Parts 5, 6, and 7 chronicle the events from Anna's spiritual death to her physical death. In these parts Anna, in outward appearance at least, becomes the almost completely reactive, manipulative creature that some critics see in her.[39] Vronsky possesses Anna, but at the cost of what he really wanted in her. "All is finished," says Anna at the seduction scene. "I have nothing but you. Remember that" (2.11). She adores Vronsky so much that she finds it frightening (5.8). She cannot find anything "neprekrasnoe" [not fine] in him, and she feels her own insignificance [nichtozhestvo] before him. Deprived of her own good self, Anna now worships Vronsky as he had worshiped her. As for Vronsky, "despite the full realization of what he had desired for so long, [he] was not completely happy" (5.7). Anna herself seems entirely of the earth now, and so unable to satisfy Vronsky's longings.

Tolstoy found the judgment inflicted by God on Anna self-evident in the obvious unhappiness that her conduct brings her. This unhappiness is intended in a straightforward way as a warning to readers of the novel. At the same time, though, that very unhappiness suggests that in parts 5, 6, and 7 Anna is not a pagan goddess, or, as Eikhenbaum would have it, a personification of Schopenhauerian will.[40] Even though she may appear so to others, she is not really earthbound even at the end of the novel. She remains, as she was in her conversation with Betsy, someone who is tragic rather than comic (3.17), someone who knows the good even as she does the bad. She makes Vronsky into her idol because, like Vronsky previously in his love for her, she needs something more than simple physical pleasure and fastens on Vronsky to provide it. Like Levin, Anna is and remains a seeker. In this sense, for Anna as for him, the future is "open" to the very end. Anna's options end with her suicide, of course, but that she draws back at the last moment from this fatal step is a testimony to the fact that spiritual (if not physical) choices remain for her.[41]

The voice speaking to Anna, even as she throws herself under the train, comes from inside her. It represents the part of her that is still free despite the fact that she has given herself utterly to her passion. Anna is still herself even at the nadir of her existence, and therefore her inner moral drama continues to the very end.

Anna does not totally disintegrate at the end of her life, and indeed if she did, her story would be as predictable and undramatic as Stiva's. As in his epic novel, though to different effect, Tolstoy's psychological drama requires that laws exist and that human beings feel the effects of these laws. It also depends on a belief in the potential "wholeness" of the human individual. It requires that Anna be able to take responsibility for her actions even at the end of her life. How this remains possible, given Tolstoy's altered understanding of human nature, is the subject of this book's concluding chapter.

Eight

Science, Philosophy, and Synthesis in the 1870s

The Enduring Importance of Unity for Tolstoy

During the 1860s science ceased to be peripheral in Russia.[1] Tolstoy, too, was affected by the general interest in science and felt the necessity in *War and Peace* of giving a "scientific" explanation for his ideas. His philosophical theories in the 1860s had depended on a belief in ultimately mysterious forces that fuel laws accessible to science (second epilogue, 7, 10). The existence of these forces in nature—in the second epilogue Tolstoy had used the examples of gravity, electricity, chemical affinity, inertia, animal force, and so on—parallels the existence of free will in the individual. All of the forces, moreover, are really the same. Natural forces "are only distinguished from one another in that they are differently defined by reason." What we call free will differs from the others only because we know it directly, through consciousness, not reason. Like the other forces, it is "free" in that it, in itself, cannot be explained by the laws of causation. We experience will as free, moreover, because "consciousness of freedom" is a necessary condition of our existence as human beings. One might say that we apply our "law" to the essence of life just as that essence is shaped in accordance with other laws (governing gravity, electricity, and so forth). All forces at bottom are the same "essence of life" that both unites man and nature and nature within itself.

As part of his emphasis on the unity of natural forces, Tolstoy had referred at one point in the second epilogue to the relationship between heat and electricity. This suggests that he may have been aware already in the 1860s of scientific experiments to prove the unity of natural forces.[2] In the early 1870s, as part of his work on his Primer [*Azbuka*], he read about and was intrigued by the work of such scientists as Humphrey Davy and especially Michael Faraday and James Prescott Joule (48:140). Over the course of the first half of the nineteenth century these men had evolved an electrical theory of chemical affinities that explained both the unity of natural forces and how they worked.[3] Tolstoy was especially taken with the work of Joule on the quantitative equivalence of heat and mechanical work, and, following Joule, he declared in his diary of 16 March 1872 that the sun was the source of all energy and that all energy (even, for instance, the force of gravity) was warmth and heat (48:149). In a philosophical fragment written in 1875, he wrote that everything was subject to "the laws of the conservation of matter and forces and their interaction" (17:345).

The law of the conservation of energy and matter made a unified theory of the physical world possible, and dispelled the notion of the "imponderability" of force, or energy. To the extent that Tolstoy in *War and Peace* relied on this idea in order to argue for the essential mysteriousness and even freedom of the human soul, his science was old-fashioned. At the same time, it is not surprising that Tolstoy found the work of Davy, Faraday, and Joule so appealing. The new theories that resulted in mid-century in the idea of the conservation of energy depended, in part, on ideas already current in the eighteenth century and dear to Tolstoy.[4] This connection between eighteenth- and nineteenth-century science meant that in the 1870s Tolstoy could remain faithful to and even embrace more firmly the underlying unity of nature, the "connection amongst all the forces of nature" which Levin finds in Tyndall and affirms (1.27).

Atomism

As part of this ever-intensifying commitment to unity, Tolstoy joined Strakhov in his battle against the widely held belief of nineteenth-century science in a world made up of fragmented matter—atoms—which moved endlessly and without any overarching purpose.[5] Thus, in 1872 Tolstoy praised without qualifications the second half of Strakhov's *The World as a Whole* [*Mir kak celoe*], entitled "Inorganic Nature: A Critique of the Mechanical View" [*Neorganicheskaia priroda: kritika mekhanicheskogo vzgliada*] (62:348). There Strakhov attempted to refute the theory of atoms, understood as irreducible bits of matter. While the theory itself in his opinion was a product of the legitimate desire to construct a whole from parts, it gave rise to the mechanical view according to which everything happened from random motion.[6] It seemed clear to Strakhov that this was not true and that atoms, as the "atomists" understand them, did not exist.

> Really, what ought to be clear to each and all is the unceasing changeability of matter, its mergings and transformations, its metamorphosis from dead bodies into living plants, from plants into animated animals, the metamor-

phosis of bread and wine into man—all of this is hidden from the atomist, as by a sorceror's cloud, by his atoms. He sees only one thing—atoms moving, turning, colliding—and this is the whole world in its grandeur. (Ibid., 381)

The modern theory of atoms, according to Strakhov (who also mentioned ancient theories), evolved from Descartes's separation of spirit and matter and would only be overthrown when the two were reunited, so that "the independence of the parts depends on the independence of the whole" (ibid., 378). He believed that what he called spirit, *dukh*, was inherent in matter and that all things ultimately were "modifications of one and the same element" (ibid., 479). To truly understand matter, one had to understand its essential motion (ibid., 443).

Clarifying his thought, and thereby threatening the balance between general and particular in his art, Tolstoy in the 1870s dropped his own use of "atomic" imagery. In *War and Peace*, drawing on the peculiar religious positivism of his friend S. S. Urusov,[7] he had articulated the laws of history cum nature which operated without negating human freedom. The argument in the novel for the possibility of human freedom had depended on a strict separation between the world of the soul and the outside world. To explain this separation, Tolstoy had compared individuals to atoms, and the laws that influenced them to the laws of motion governing atoms:

> As the sun and every atom of the ether is a sphere, complete in itself and at the same time only an atom of a whole inaccessible to a human being on account of its immensity—so every individual carries within himself his own goals and at the same time carries them in order to serve general goals inaccessible to a human being. (First epilogue, 4)

> The movement of a people is the freed force of a bonding [of individuals, seen as atoms, into a nation] in the literal sense. . . . We don't undertake, like Hegel, from pure reason, or like Wundt, from sensation, to prove everything, but we undertake, with axioms of motion, to prove certain theories of motion. . . . The human being, the personality, is an atom. He is necessary, as necessary as is the atom for a theory of physics, but his definition can lead only to the absurd. (48:88,89)

Everything that happens is determined by laws theoretically if not practically accessible to science. Science cannot explain historical events simply because it is not omniscient: it cannot discover every human being who contributes to them. Their combined actions have effects, not intended by them, that make history. Even if history could be explained, however, the human beings who caused it, the atoms, would remain mysterious. Within individual human beings, hemmed in as they truly are at every moment by causes that influence them and effects to which they unwittingly contribute, is something that allows them to choose among the many potential causes that besiege them at every moment.[8] They choose either wisely or foolishly with reference to their own individual needs, which have no direct or conscious relation to the laws that govern history. A lifetime of such moments creates the individual, who expresses himself fully in his choices freely made. Pierre Bezukhov, laughing at the enslavement of his "immortal soul," is just such an atom living in a determined world without being himself fully determined by it. The image of the liquid ball in Pierre's dream reveals the external relationship of each atom, each drop of water, to other drops and to God.

The atomic imagery in *War and Peace* had been part of Tolstoy's attempt, perhaps originally inspired by the Savoyard Vicar, to affirm the possibility both of human freedom and of a harmonious world governed by divine law.[9] It had depended, I would suggest, on the implicit assumption, borrowed from Rousseau,[10] that the human individual in his totality, as a physical as well as a spiritual being, had a metaphysical reality.

This assumption would have been affirmed and supported by Goethe's doctrine of the "living reason" that informs nature in its infinite variety rather than reducing seeming variety to an underlying sameness. Defense of natural variety is yet another striking similarity in the nature description of the young Tolstoy and Goethe. Compare, for instance, Werther's hymn to the variety of nature, to the "thousand familiar things" and "the countless indescribable forms of the worms and insects,"[11] with the descriptions of the garden in *Youth* (in the chapter of the same name) and of the forest in *The Cossacks*. In both *Youth* and *The Cossacks* Tolstoy emphasized the vitality of nature, the abundance of living forms, their actual and particular being,[12] and the way each stretched toward the sun and expanded to the greatest extent possible, even curling around its neighbors. Connected to this, of course, was that commitment to the real existence and legitimacy of the individual which Tolstoy also shared with Goethe.[13]

Tolstoy's reading of Schopenhauer, with his subjectivist claim that human beings must and could deny their separateness from others, weakened his philosophical if not his emotional commitment to a human individuality based on the obvious physical fact that human beings have bodies. And after reading Strakhov and after his readings in physical and chemical science for his *Primer*, Tolstoy dropped the comparison of human beings to atoms. The image of the individual as a single atom or drop of water appears only once in *Anna Karenina*, curdled, in Levin's bitter summary of the achievements of Western philosophy: "In infinite time, in infinite matter, in infinite space, a little bubble-organism is formed, and this bubble will hold itself together for a little while and burst, and this bubble is—me" (8.9).

In the 1870s Tolstoy no longer conceived of nature as composed of atoms governed by laws. All things were, in fact, made up of both earth (matter) and sun. The sun was the source of all energy, which in all its diverse permutations was some form of heat, or warmth (16 March 1872; 48:148–49). This energy interacted with matter in order to create a balance. Everything moved (May 1870; 48:135). If this were not so, all things would merge in stable equilibrium. As it was, everything shifted as both the sun and the earth moved (April 1872; 48:158–59). In this vision, as in Strakhov's idea of the "beautiful harmonic sphere," all the seeming diversity of nature was resolved into a dynamic and unified whole: "All the infinite distinctions of bodies one from another are explained by the greater or lesser penetration of these bodies by the rays [of the sun]" (16 March 1872; 48:150).

As Tolstoy's science evolved, so did his understanding of human things. Whereas in *War and Peace* it was useful to conceive of the self as an atom influenced by and influencing outside forces but remaining essentially independent of them, in *Anna Karenina* the self-contained individual is seen as a dangerous immoral fallacy, an "excruciating falsehood" [*muchitel'naia nepravda*]; as Levin sees the image of the human individual as a "bubble-organism" (8.9).[14]

Kantian Epistemology

The whole theory of atoms, Strakhov explained in *The World as a Whole* (400), had evolved because of a critical mistake of philosophical materialism, a mistake that had its origin in the relation of the human mind to the outside world. In developing his argument, Strakhov began with the indubitable existence of matter. The natural sciences concerned themselves with the "external world of nature" (ibid., 405). By the word *external* Strakhov meant everything that was by definition outside the mind, or spirit, which was "the point . . . from which what exists is being examined." What this examination revealed was the *appearance* of things. Materialism as a philosophical system took the appearance of things, along with its two forms, time and space, to be the only reality (ibid., 405–6). Materialists divided the world into form, or time and space, and content, or matter (ibid., 422–23). Instead of regarding form and content as one unity, they then took the content to be what truly exists. In reality, matter separated from its forms was as much an abstraction as time and space. "Atomism" was the form in which it was possible for the materialists to "represent" [*predstavit'*] matter abstracted from time and space.[15] Having performed this operation, the materialists began to dissect the world, "the beautiful harmonic sphere," in search of the essence of matter (ibid., 423). They never asked themselves what besides the appearance of things might exist, even though that something alone could make sense of matter.

Tolstoy singled out Strakhov's discussion of the role of appearance, or "representation" [*predstavlenie*], in materialism for special praise (61:348). It jibed, in the first place, with what he had been reading in Schopenhauer. Schopenhauer believed in the distinction between appearance and "the thing in itself," between the physical and the metaphysical.[16] He wrote that the "physical explanation is always in terms of *cause*, the metaphysical in terms of *will*" (ibid.). As an example he cited the human body, which had both a physical explanation and metaphysically was to be understood as an objectivization of will. While our knowledge of will was subjective, then, Schopenhauer believed that this subjective knowledge was real and, indeed, was the metaphysical basis of reality.[17]

Schopenhauer's reasoning and that of Strakhov and Tolstoy depended on a crucial philosophic principle that they had adopted from Kant. Tolstoy himself claimed in a letter not to have read Kant until 1887, when he discovered the *Critique of Practical Reason*.[18] But in the 1870s he had learned from Schopenhauer about Kant's "introduction of the concepts of space, time, and causality as categories of the mind" from the *Critique of Pure Reason*.[19] In 1870 Tolstoy stated this fact outright. "Kant says that space and time are forms of *our* thought" (48:126). As a self-professed student of Kant, Schopenhauer had begun from this idea, but, like other successors of Kant, he had rebelled against the restrictions that its strict application placed on human knowledge.[20]

The eventual effects of Kant's teaching on Tolstoy's thought are clear if one compares the teaching in chapter 10 of the second epilogue of *War and Peace* with his philosophical tract *On Life*. In *War and Peace*, he had argued that the essence of life, in nature as in mankind, was freedom, which in both realms was given form by necessity, or reason. In *On Life*, on the other hand, he developed the idea of rational consciousness as the essence of human life. Everything else, he argued, took place outside of us, in animal life that in some way was not us. We really know only reason, and therefore we really exist as human beings only if we subordinate our animal existence to its laws (chap. 10). While he was writing *War and Peace*, then, Tolstoy believed that reason and its three forms—time, space, and causality—had an objective, as well as a subjective, existence and was in some way outside of pure life, defined as pure feeling or force. It is time, space, and causality which, in the argument of the second epilogue, place limits on human freedom. Ironically, in passages about freedom and necessity in drafts for the second epilogue, Tolstoy, who had begun reading Schopenhauer for this purpose, cited Kant's argument about the categories of reason as forms of the mind as proof of the metaphysical existence of human freedom (15:251). He still, however, asserted the objective existence of form, or reason (48:111). In *On Life* reason has replaced feeling as the constituent element of human life and the source of real freedom. As long as we live only by feeling, we are no different from plants or animals: as human beings we are not alive because we are not free. To truly live we must subordinate our animal to our rational natures (chap. 14). Thus, reason has moved from outside to inside the human subject and become the basis of human individuality as the later Tolstoy defined and defended it. This change or evolution in Tolstoy's thought, I would suggest, is a result of his adoption of Kant's idea of the concepts of reason as categories of the mind, and therefore essentially subjective. The concepts give form to outside phenomena, allowing us, as Strakhov argued in *The World as a Whole* [*Mir kak celoe*], to "represent" [*predstavit'*] them and are themselves liable to representation. The source of the concepts themselves, reason, is not liable to representation and is thereby freed to become the essence of human life.[21]

Tolstoy in 1887 referred to Schopenhauer's Kant, the Kant of the *Critique of Pure Reason*, as "negative,"[22] by which he meant that the *Critique* placed strict limitations on the possibilities of human knowledge. It was typical of Tolstoy's incorrigible optimism eventually to transform a negative concept into the beginning of a new positive moral understanding. His first reaction to Kant's idea, however—and this too is typical—was to work out its negative implications for his earlier theories. It precipitated a new and self-consciously strict subjectivity in dealing with the external world, and, incidentally, was a chief factor in moving Tolstoy's art closer to that of Fet and Tiutchev. Reason wrongly applied, as he wrote in a long attack on modern science in his diary in 1870, destroys the thing it studies, leaving only forms or categories of the mind (48:116–17). Whereas in 1868, while working on the second epilogue, he had declared that "only form is objective" (48:111), in 1870 he explicitly denied its objectivity: "Motion, space, time, matter, the form of motion—the circle, the ball, the line, points—all are only in us" (48:117).

This sentence is part of a long diary entry that is the high water mark of Tolstoy's new subjectivity. In the 1870s, Kant's subjectivization of the categories of human reason underlay Strakhov's and Tolstoy's vision of life as one organic whole, in which "bodies" interacted freely, and were all made up of differing proportions of matter and sun, which Tolstoy defined as itself a different type of matter (48:130–62 passim).

Thus, Strakhov wrote of the science of atoms in *The World as a Whole* that it "is an ideal view; atoms are the creation of our thought" (376).[23] In reality, as Strakhov envisaged it: "there are no *simple bodies*, no atoms; there are no independent forces distinct from time immemorial, there is nothing unchanging, existing in and of itself. Everything is dependent [on something else] and everything *flows*, as Heraclitus has already said."[24]

Central to Tolstoy's new science was the axiom that "we do not know spaces without matter and cannot imagine them" (48:148). All matter moved and expanded, and it stopped moving only when it encountered an obstacle, that is, another body (48:160–61). "Space" was therefore entirely occupied by "bodies," which all immediately bordered one another (48:92). Putting this together with those phenological nature descriptions that Kupreianova has singled out as new in the 1870s,[25] one can discern a concerted attempt on Tolstoy's part to banish time and space altogether as abstract concepts or "forms" outside of their appearance in phenomena. Tolstoy was determined to get behind appearances, to describe the world and human life bypassing mind and its categories altogether, and he was convinced that only art, not science, could accomplish this (48:118).[26]

The Attack on the Individual

Behind mind was unity. In early 1876 Tolstoy wrote to Strakhov: "I define life as the separation off [*ot'edinenie*] of a part that loves itself from the rest" (62:243). This definition is an addendum, no doubt recognized as such by his correspondent, to the long discussion of the meaning of life contained in Tolstoy's 30 November 1875 letter to Strakhov. Tolstoy had written there that to live means to love oneself and to want to die means to love what is not oneself (62:226). This idea, too, has its beginning in the notebook in 1870 that contains Tolstoy's ruminations on science. There he explicitly linked Kant's designation of rational categories as subjective with individualism: "Kant says that space and time are forms of *our* thought. But besides space and time, there is [another] form of our thought—*individualism*" (48:126) Tolstoy had taken the Rousseauian (and modern) doctrine of self-love as the essence of life a step beyond Rousseau and thereby transformed it. Love of self now appeared as a temporary aberration, a mistaken application to the individual of the idea of love that was coexistent with life in the soul. Self-love gained authority by its grounding in a general idea of love, but the authority of the individual was weakened because it appeared as the false object of love.

Tolstoy made it clear in the 1876 letter to Strakhov that he was correcting an understanding of human nature that was too solipsistic. He continued: "Without this definition of life a circle would inevitably be repeated, according to which man would be God, the center of everything. — Life is the separation of a part from the rest.[27]

The perfection of the individual represented as a circle usurped or even replaced the perfection of God, without whose existence there could be no ultimate synthesis and moral standards. We see here how close Tolstoy came in his own thought, and prior to any acquaintance with Nietzsche to the idea of the Nietzschean superman. To ward off the effects of individualism as later fostered by Nietzsche's philosophy and propounded by such writers as Andrei Belyi,[28] he sacrificed his own earlier belief in the metaphysical reality of the individual.

In this passage Tolstoy may have had in mind the danger of solipsism inherent in his own early Rousseauist solution to the problem of the reconciliation of happiness and goodness. No longer was it possible to say, as Tolstoy had done in 1862, that "man is born perfect." In his essential being the human individual as individual is imperfect, because he loves himself more than he loves the whole of which he is a part.

Tolstoy's battle against a mechanistic worldview undermined his defense of the infinite variety of nature and of the human individual that had been characteristic of his work in the 1850s and 1860s. Then, his opponents had been rationalist social radicals who in the name of rational progress ran roughshod over the irrational particularities of life. In the 1870s these particularities, however much Tolstoy may have stated the contrary, became the enemy. They were the appearance of things that hid a deeper common reality denied by atomistic physics. In *War and Peace* Tolstoy had located himself in the middle ground, between the Charybdis of all-devouring nature, on the one hand, and the Scylla of rampant individualism, on the other. Now he found himself veering toward Charybdis.

The Denigration of the "Personality"

As this story unfolds, it is important to keep in mind that Tolstoy resisted the abandonment of the possibility of individual happiness with might and main, and in *Anna Karenina* he resisted it mostly successfully. *Anna Karenina*, unlike *Master and Man* for instance, contains no unironic example of a person consciously sacrificing himself for another. (Karenin's ultimately unsustainable Christian love for Anna is a significant exception to this.) In both *Anna Karenina* and *War and Peace* characters who seem to live for others are suspect: Sonia and Varenka both lack the vitality to make lives of their own and cannot serve as models for the truly vital characters. These characters, if they are to be fulfilled and happy, must establish contact with the rhythms of nature and live by them. In plain language, this means once again that they must come to terms with the fact that they have bodies and want physical as well as spiritual fulfillment. They must join real with ideal. This holds true for the gentry as well as for peasants, for Dolly as for the peasant mothers with whom she finds she has so much in common.

In both novels people take part in communal efforts that respond to and are supported by natural rhythms. In *War and Peace*, soldiers exert themselves in war. In *Anna Karenina* peasants wrest their livelihood from nature in a struggle for survival through labor that becomes for Tolstoy a more acceptable substitute for war. But within natural rhythms, the successful characters retain their individuality. Levin cannot be a peasant simply because he isn't one: he must follow the gentry ways of his ancestors. And even among peasants, as in the mowing scene, each peasant has his own individual style. This is necessary because the world of nature is still perceived by human beings as made up of individual bodies. It operates through these bodies, and those who, like Koznyshev, Varenka, or Aleksei Karenin, through fear of death deny their bodies are denied access to the natural rhythms that provide individual fulfillment. To the extent, moreover, that the physical world is no longer seen to be interpenetrated by the spiritual according to the Goethean model of living reason, each human body is more particular because it is more a product of mechanical chance. This may explain why, as Leont'ev claims, the descriptions of inner psychic processes in *Anna Karenina* have more organic connection with the past and future of the individual characters than they do in *War and Peace*.[29]

The legitimacy of individual striving in *Anna Karenina* unlike in *War and Peace*, however, depends entirely on individual moral goodness. Here no divine reason excuses mankind's natural and innocent ferocity. An amoral force still exists and remains the essence of life in the individual, but to be humanly acceptable it must be harnessed. So in the mowing scene, the wisest and most experienced peasant while picking mushrooms for his wife is careful not to harm birds who nest in the grass.[30] This old man exemplifies Levin's hopes for himself at the end of the novel. One can both "live"—that is, preserve oneself, have and support a family, and thus participate in the great motion of nature—and still be good. In this wise old peasant the demands of nature—for happiness—and of morality have been reconciled through the intermediary of peasant culture.

Peasant culture teaches that nature must be tamed. This is the meaning of the prescription supplied to Levin by the peasant Fedor. The bad man lives "only for his own need . . . he stuffs his belly"; the good man lives "for his soul" (8.11). Fedor is talking about moral choice: life for the body or for the spirit. In response, Levin feels a crowd of "significant thoughts" released within him. The chapter that follows (12) contains nothing but these thoughts, with Levin's natural surroundings turned into allegory in order to illustrate them. Levin turns inward, not outward, for confirmation of Fedor's idea, because he would not find it in nature.

Without the possibility of perfection for each individual, a chasm between reality and appearance, both in nature and in the human individual, opened up before Tolstoy. As he had before, he continued to believe in the possibility of moral freedom, and he continued to define morality as a willingness to sacrifice one's own interests for those of others. As a psychologist who based his opinions on observation, however, he still saw also that all living creatures acted in their own self-interest. All of them, in other words, acted as if they were defending and nourishing something that really existed. This illusion, which manifested itself most directly in self-love, had to be overcome if human beings were to establish contact with that part of themselves that made them moral and immortal beings. This part Tolstoy no longer saw as natural. It was in tension with the demands of the body, which he now associated with our natural but mistaken sense of our own particularity. Tolstoy invented a science that would jibe with his new found moral philosophy, but he did not, could not, claim that nature as it *appears* to us is anything other than discrete beings each dedicated to preserving and extending himself. As always, he remained faithful to his own experience and to the universal inner feeling of particularity that he knew in himself and found confirmed in his master Rousseau. Rather than deny nature, he turned away from it, to culture and to what he eventually called rational consciousness, as the source of truths inimical to nature. The soul as he understood it was still defined as unity and extent, but both of these natural attributes required taming by supranatural rational consciousness.

Matter exists, Tolstoy wrote in 1876 to Strakhov, and so does the human personality: "there is no more important, simple and indubitable knowledge than the knowledge of one's own personality [*lichnost'*] and of matter" (17–18 May 1876; 62:276). We are unique individuals because we are matter, we have bodies made up of random configurations of matter, and it is no accident that Tolstoy linked the two facts in this passage. While he was writing *War and Peace*, he had imagined a universe in which spirit joined with matter to form human individuals. The individuals thus constituted of both body and soul were seen as "atoms," or as drops of water really existing in and of themselves and interacting until they dissolved and returned to God. In *Anna Karenina*, as in *War and Peace*, Tolstoy affirmed that the life of the individual was real and good, but he redefined what that life was. As a combination of body and soul, it was no longer an "atom," a metaphysically substantiated part of the universe, which was therefore connected to the whole by means of *Verstand*.[31] He now saw the life of the individual as a struggle between body and spirit in which the spirit gives form to the body which would otherwise be shapeless and fluid matter, but can never be fully at home in the body. So in this letter to Strakhov, Tolstoy wrote of *knowledge* [*znanie*] of both the personality [*lichnost'*] and matter [*veshchestvo*]. To know something was to be in some sense outside of that thing, to get a fix on it. While defending the existence of the "personality" and matter, then, Tolstoy was also asserting that the self that knows them was not them. The "personality" was that animal part of us that naturally loves itself, but it was not the knowing or conscious self. Only human beings possessed this knowing self, as a consequence of our reason, and therefore only human beings had the potential and the obligation to choose to moderate the expansive demands of the animal self.

The life of the body in *Anna Karenina* is seen as a continuing process that is defined by the "limits" [*predely*] of birth and death. In two different letters, after his two readings of *Mir kak celoe* in 1872 and in 1876, Tolstoy acknowledged these ideas as having been inspired by Strakhov (61:348; 62:235–38).[32] At the same time he corrected Strakhov's theories. He took Strakhov's explanation of life, understood as a process bounded by life and death, and purged it of what he considered its excessive rationalism. As the metaphysical element that holds living matter together, instead of the Hegelian *dukh*, or spirit, which he criticized in his 1872 letter about *Mir kak celoe*, he substituted love. Love was the metaphysical principle beyond reason and therefore incomprehensible to the human mind which Tolstoy supplied in place of Strakhov's rationalism.[33] The closer one gets to pure love, and, correspondingly, the farther from particularity, the more of a morally free individual one makes of oneself, and the more satisfactorily one navigates along the process of life.

This struggle between animal impulses and the voice of conscience or higher reason is concentrated more than ever in *Anna Karenina* within the individual. In this sense, the individual becomes more important than it was in *War and Peace*. But, I repeat, the individual thus understood transcends nature and overcomes the personality. To the extent possible, the voice of higher reason in the soul sculpts the morally free individual from the raw material of animal "personality" provided by nature.

The Morally Free Individual in
Anna Karenina

The circular shapes, the circle and the ball, that Tolstoy contrasted to the Faustian line in *War and Peace* and that he imagined in that work to be the metaphysical shape of life and the world are relegated in the 1870s, in passages quoted above, to concepts of the human mind. It is all the more striking, therefore, to find these shapes resurrected and put to work in Tolstoy's long philosophical letter to Strakhov of 30 November 1875. Contrasting science with philosophy, Tolstoy wrote that the former depends on logic and the latter on harmony:

> [Philosophy is] the knowledge giving the best possible answers to the question of the meaning of human life and death. . . . In a general sense it is the joining into one single concordant whole of all those bases of human knowledge which could not receive logical explanations. . . . [Every philosophical viewpoint, taken from life,] is a circle or a ball, in which there is no end, middle or beginning, most or least important, but everything is beginning, everything middle, everything equally important or necessary . . . and the persuasiveness and truth depends on its inner concord, harmony. (62:225)

This circle or ball forms instantaneously, when its illogical parts come together (62:224). Just such a harmonious grouping forms in Levin's soul after his conversation with Fedor about Platon Kuzmich. Within the process of life, higher reason, the voice of divine love in the soul, jostles with other voices and on occasion, as when Levin in part 8 contemplates his soul, dominates and creates a harmonious relation among the other voices. "Levin had already ceased thinking and seemed only to be attending to mysterious voices, conversing about something amongst themselves joyfully and intently" (8.13).

At this moment of Levin's deepest contemplation, the realistic circumstances of his situation take on an obtrusively allegoric meaning. The peasant whose creed, idealistic and moderating at the same time, inspires Levin's thoughts is named Platon (Plato) Kuzmich (cosmos).[34] Levin's discoveries occur on a journey that he takes on his own and on foot, but his deepest thoughts, his uncovering of the "sense of life," come when he has lain down in the grass beside the road. The journey is symbolic of Levin's life, and his rest represents a withdrawal from active life into contemplation. It is only during such a rest that he can achieve harmony of soul. Levin sees a little insect [*bukashka*] which represents to him the physical life of all living things, and, in the proper spiritual relation to this other life, even as he thinks, he reaches out in active goodness to help it. But, in an act meant to convey both the independent will of the other and our inability to know that will, the insect spurns his assistance and takes flight.[35] When Levin thinks about the church, a flock of sheep representative of the faithful appears. In this setting the cart that arrives to pick him up functions like the *telega zhizni* [cart of life] of Pushkin's well-known allegorical poem. The horse and the coachman that together convey Levin represent the beast and the peasant who serve the physical needs of the gentry. Once back on the "cart of life," Levin's best resolutions and his harmony of soul melt away. He snaps at the coachman and glowers momentarily at his brother. This is both the final act of the allegory and the transition back to the realistic drama in which it is embedded. Objects shed their symbolic significance as the character through whose eyes the reader sees them returns to the process of life and his struggles to inject moral significance into the process. Levin finds out, however, in a moment alone at the end of chapter 14, that his spiritual lodestone in fact remains intact, and as he makes this discovery, the physical world around him, in this case the apiary, again takes on allegorical overtones.[36]

The voices that Levin overhears within himself converse harmoniously and "intently." At this moment he is fully himself, not only independent of the external world but able to infuse it with allegorical significance. The episode is a reprise of Pierre's musings in the night camp, a reprise, however, with an important difference. Pierre had identified with the moon as the unifying element in the landscape. Levin finds no counterpart either to his own knowing and contemplating self (that which overhears) or to his harmonious voices in nature. It may be that harmony does obtain in nature as it does in his soul, but he has no way of knowing that directly. If it does, then the harmony is imposed on what we call nature from outside and above it, just as the harmony in Levin's soul at this moment depends on principles not inherent in it (organization by the divine love from which it is separated). In any case, the knowing self at this moment of contemplation is *outside* the voices which represent different and usually conflicting impulses.[37]

Levin "had already ceased thinking." With this crucial phrase, Tolstoy located a point of repose within the soul and saved that soul from "all-devouring Nature." Life—nature—continues in Levin's soul in the form of the busy and harmonious conversation buzzing therein, but Levin himself, the knowing and "attending" self, hears this buzzing as background noise as he simply contemplates. This is Tolstoy's new version of the *sentiment de l'existence* that Olenin experienced in the stag's lair. In *The Cossacks*, however, this feeling emanates from the "animal" personality and expresses the living reason within the personality. Unlike Olenin, Levin experiences his existence from the outside and from the point of view of intellect rather than feeling, and so in his essential being as an individual he is alienated from physical life. His *sentiment de l'existence* is spiritual, so alienated from matter that even the object of Levin's contemplation for the moment seems disembodied, a circle of whispering voices.

The knowing self judges and weighs what has happened or is about to happen and the decisions it makes create a moral individual out of the process of life.[38] In *War and Peace*, moral fortitude came to Pierre from nature, in the form of a new feeling of "joy and strength," of "being ready for anything." In *Anna Karenina*, to be good means to be able to resist the impulses of nature, not, as in *War and Peace*, to give in to them. Those who live by impulse alone, though they serve their own self-love, in fact have no inner core, no real individual moral freedom. They are not depicted simply as bestial, like the Kuragins in *War and Peace*, who live entirely for the body. They are seen as determined parts of the continually changing mechanical process to which the body belongs. Thus, even Stiva finds himself behaving dishonorably against his will because circumstances—his need for money, for instance—dictate his behavior.

Nature by itself and so far as we can know it, as I have argued, is submoral in *Anna Karenina*. The divine pageant which we cannot understand but which involves the whole world of *War and Peace* has moved indoors in Tolstoy's second novel, to the "interior struggle" that Levin acknowledges in the symposium in the restaurant. After his acceptance of Kant's epistemology, Tolstoy came to see morality as an entirely internal matter, without, so far as we can know, any objective correlative in nature. Nature is automatically good (and so not moral), but he wrote of evil that it "is not in the world. All evil is in our souls and can be destroyed."[39]

Just as there are two kinds of freedom in *Anna Karenina*, the freedom to flout law and the freedom to be lawful, so there are two kinds of individuality based on the two freedoms. The reward for goodness in *Anna Karenina* seems to be a wholeness and unity of self that is discovered rather than given. *Discovery* is a more appropriate word than *creation* here, because we are not talking about something arbitrary and therefore unique. The key to legitimate selfhood in each individual is the discovery of the good self that all, in fact, have in common. And to obey this good self means voluntarily to moderate what we as "personalities," or bodies, want.

Resting at the side of the road, Levin affirms the faith of simple people as a guide for seekers like himself; in so doing he affirms the legitimacy, a legitimacy conveyed by moral consequences, of subjective but universal perceptions that are not true to objective reality.

Lying on his back, he looked now at the high, cloudless sky. "Don't I know that this is infinite space and that it is not a round vault? But no matter how I squint and how I strain my vision, I cannot see it as not round and not limited, and, despite my knowledge of infinite space, I am indubitably right when I see the firm blue vault, I am more right than when I strain to see beyond it."

Once again, as in *War and Peace*, the shape of metaphysical truth is round: this is still to be distinguished from the linear shape of scientific, analytic truth. Levin admits that what he sees is not objectively real, but he wants to affirm the reality and especially the moral power of subjective insight. Subjective insights are so universal and so powerful in the individual that it would be a lie for anyone, even the most highly trained physicist, to claim that he could actually perceive what he knew through reason to be objective reality. In the same way, Tolstoy reasoned, the religiosity of simple people has authoritative power because of the universal hunger for spiritual meaning. He wanted to show how the simple common sense and even the poetic subjectivity of the peasant is the ground for his moral superiority to modern, Faustian man.

In this scene we have been examining—part of an episode of heightened consciousness in Levin—Levin is injecting not goodness but metaphysical truth into objective reality. He treats nature in a way not possible in *War and Peace*. Prince Andrei does not see the sky as a "firm blue vault." On the contrary, when he first sees the sky he is drawn into and transformed by a vision of infinity, the limitlessness that in *Anna Karenina* Levin is determined to shut out. And when Pierre finds confirmation of the meaning of his individual life, he draws infinity into himself (as Werther does before he meets Charlotte).[40] There is no disjunction between subjective and objective reality, only the penetration by the subject of the hidden, moral meaning of nature. In *Anna Karenina*, Tolstoy seemed to be claiming that consciousness gives nature meaning that it otherwise, so far as we can know, would lack. Without consciousness, life seems the amoral process and Darwinian struggle for existence that Anna on her final journey perceives it to be.[41] Without higher laws, everything appears as tawdry as it does to Anna in her final hours. It is just work, the relentless treadmill ending in death so starkly revealed to Levin in part 8 as he watches a peasant nag turn a grindstone. Human consciousness, then, does not simply illuminate; it transforms human life and nature, so that moral truths can even contradict the realities of nature and still be true.

As in *War and Peace*, then, Tolstoy in *Anna Karenina* affirmed the freedom, and hence the moral responsibility, of the individual. Levin does succeed in constructing a life for himself. The round blue vault of the sky in his revery represents not only his stubborn commitment to his own subjective vision, but also an image, round and hard, of his own hard-won, real, and legitimate individuality. It is built out of the harmony of thoughts that comes to him as he rests by the road. This individuality is fragile; it breaks down continually, but Levin can return to it whenever he has a moment to himself.

At this level, too, in *Anna Karenina* drama prevails over "linkage." Levin's individuality, unlike Pierre's, is supranatural and therefore at odds with the "personality" that manifests itself in the impulses that drive him. Pierre accepts himself, laughing, as both an autonomous and a determined being, whereas Levin sees himself as truly himself only when he can constitute himself, as he does beside the road and in the apiary.

Synthesis and Lyrical Daring Once Again

It would be wrong, however, to end our examination of *Anna Karenina* on this note of drama. In the final analysis it, like *War and Peace*, is built on metaphysical foundations that not only establish the reality of the individual soul, but of objective moral standards that support and nourish that soul. It depends, in other words, on the existence of an overarching synthesis that gives shape and meaning to the details both of the life of the individual and of mankind.

The synthesis underlying *Anna Karenina* takes concrete form in Levin's buzzing circle of voices and in his vision of the heavenly vault. Tolstoy was referring to this synthesis with its characteristic circular shape when he wrote to Strakhov in 1876 about the "linkages" [*scepleniia*] that bind the novel together.

> In everything, almost everything that I have written, I have been guided by a collection of thoughts linked together to express myself; but each thought, expressed separately in words, loses its sense, it is terribly demeaned when you take it from that linkage in which it is found. The linkage itself is not established by thought (I think), but by something else, and to express the basis of this linkage directly in words is in no way possible; but it is possible only indirectly—in words describing images, actions, situations. (62:270)

This image of the structure of *Anna Karenina* is related, on the one hand, to the definition of a philosophical viewpoint as quoted above from the 1875 letter to Strakhov, and, on the other, to a definition of religion penned during the same period (and entitled "A Definition of Religion—Faith" [17:357–58]). It is worth quoting for the light it sheds on what does hold all the individual thoughts in the novel together:

> Religion is the collection into one harmonious whole of all explanations or answers to those inescapable and solely interesting questions in life about life and death, [questions] to which reason gives me a partial answer, [a collection] more harmonious than which I know no other, and in which as a result I believe and consider to be indubitably true and by which I guide myself in every act of life. (17:357)

What establishes the "collection of thoughts" is religion, which, Tolstoy hoped as he was writing *Anna Karenina*, could be expressed in its essence by art. There is really no difference here between religion and what Tolstoy would call true philosophy. In toto and as a philosophic project, *Anna Karenina* represents Tolstoy's attempt in the 1870s through art to get beyond scientific thinking and thereby present a true picture of reality. This picture is avowedly subjective, since we have access to the spiritual, moral realm only through feeling and especially consciousness. Tolstoy's letter about linkages is a response to a 5 March 1876 letter from Strakhov in which he wrote that he had been thinking about Tolstoy's "subjectivism, and about how you [Tolstoy] are searching for a way out of this subjectivism."[42] It is clear that Tolstoy believed, as he was finishing *Anna Karenina*, that he could anchor his subjectivity in a transcendental reality and that he could express that reality through his art. He had succeeded for the second time and through a different path in finding *podmostki* [scaffolding] that allowed him to build an image of metaphysical reality.

The existence of this scaffolding is revealed in Levin's final encounter with the clearing sky in part 8. By making the proper moral decisions and, no less important, by living the right life, Levin has already found meaning in his own soul. He now confidently projects that meaning onto nature.

> It had already grown completely dark, and in the south, where he was looking, there were no storm clouds. The storm clouds loomed from the other direction. From there lightning was flashing and distant thunder could be heard. Levin was listening to drops falling monotonously from the lime trees in the garden and looking at the familiar triangle of stars and at the Milky Way with its branching passing through its midst. At every flash of lightning, not only the Milky Way, but the bright stars as well disappeared, but, as soon as the lightning died out, again, as if thrown by some accurate hand, they reappeared in the same places. (8.19)

This description of nature is a prose poem based on individual, subjective, but universal human perceptions. The Milky Way seems, for instance, to move through the Summer Triangle because the stars of the Milky Way are so much fainter. As he had done in the haystack scene,

Levin goes on to reaffirm more generally the validity of his heartfelt feelings while acknowledging their subjectivity. He argues for the essential importance of subjective perception in science, but he does so mainly in support of his avowedly subjective belief in moral law.

> [Levin believes in] the one evident, indubitable manifestation of Divinity . . . the laws of the good, which were revealed to the world through revelation, and which I feel in myself, and in the recognition of which I not only join but, willy-nilly, am joined with other people into one society of believers, which is called the church.

Taking place in this setting, and connected in Levin's own ruminations with the night sky, his profession of faith stands as a poetic illustration, whether intended or not, of Kant's famous linkage, from the conclusion of the *Critique of Pure Reason*, between the stars above us and the moral law within us.[43]

Eikhenbaum, with the subtlety and intuition characteristic of him, links Levin's gazing at the stars after his failure to communicate his philosophic discoveries to Kitty with a letter Tolstoy received from Fet in 1876.[44] This letter contained both Fet's poem "Sredi zvezdy" [Amongst the Stars], and his complaint about the price of kerosene. This combination of the high poetic—the poem—and the prosaic—the kerosene—struck Tolstoy as the mark of the true poet, and, according to Eikhenbaum, Tolstoy demonstrated the existence and even the connection of the two in this episode at the end of his novel. Fet, as Eikhenbaum goes on to show, returned the compliment in related comments in a letter about the connection in *Anna Karenina* of Nikolai's death and the birth of Mitia: birth and death are "two holes [from the prosaic] into the spiritual world, into Nirvana. These two visible and eternally mysterious windows are birth and death" (ibid., 184).

For Eikhenbaum, Fet's poem exemplifies the "lyrical daring" that Tolstoy so admired in him and borrowed from him. In chapter 6 I have already discussed how Tolstoy's own "lyrical daring" evolved in the 1870s to something closer to that of Fet and Tiutchev. "Amongst the Stars" and Tolstoy's imaginative adaptation of it in his novel illustrate both the shift in Tolstoy's version of lyrical daring from the 1860s to the 1870s and an underlying similarity with the earlier position that makes a form of lyrical daring still possible.

In the 1870s Tolstoy no longer believed in a God who concerned Himself with human affairs as He had seemed to on a grand scale in *War and Peace*. He believed instead, as he wrote Fet in April 1876, in "that God, more undefined, farther away, but higher and more indubitable."[45] This God redeems mankind and nature simply by existing. His worth for mankind is encapsulated in "Amongst the Stars," which Tolstoy praised for its "philosophically poetic character, which I expected of you" (ibid., 327). Tolstoy especially admired "what the stars say. And the last stanza is especially good." In this poem, the poet wants to identify with the stars, but cannot because they are not mortal as he is. The poet cannot, as he did in the spring poem so admired by Tolstoy, "come to you with a message" from Nature. This form of lyrical daring so magnificently employed in *War and Peace* is no longer possible, because man and nature are no longer seen as simply one.

The stars explain:

My zdes' gorim, chtob v sumrak neprogliadnyi
K tebe prosilsia bezzakatnyi den'.

Vot pochemu, kogda dyshat' tak trudno,
Tebe otradno tak podniat' chelo
S lica zemli, gde vse temno i skuchno,
K nam, v nashu glub', gde pyshno i svetlo.

[We are shining here, so that into the impenetrable dusk
Endless day appears before you.

That is why, when it is so hard to breathe,
It is joyful for you to raise your brow
From the face of the earth, where all is dark and dreary,
To us, into our depths, where all is splendid and bright.]

The stars are symbols of Eternity, windows into Nirvana, just as death and birth were for Fet among the events of the workaday world in *Anna Karenina*. Their significance, however, lies in the very fact that despite the best efforts of the poet they remain mysterious, "other." They do not belong to him as they had seemed to belong to Pierre at the bivouac. They promise that something else besides what analytical reason reveals to us exists and relieves the intolerable darkness of merely material life. This is why Levin, as he gazes at the stars, can go beyond the physical mechanics of perception to impute conscious intention to what he sees above him. The stars reappear "as if thrown by some accurate hand." Thus, in a moment of heightened subjectivity, does God make a brief appearance in *Anna Karenina*, and thus, this time strictly confining himself to subjective intuition ("as if"), does Tolstoy again join real and ideal, reaffirming the existence of universal moral law, and the synthesis that alone gives meaning to human life. This synthesis does not contradict the dramatic nature of *Anna Karenina*. On the contrary, as I have argued, without it, and without moral law, there could be no inner drama of good and evil. Without it, *Anna Karenina* would be *Dallas*, a soap opera in which characters without fixed principles strive to maximize personal pleasures.

Conclusion _____

DESPITE the naturalism of his later works, including *Anna Karenina*, in comparison with *War and Peace*, Tolstoy moved in the 1870s toward a greater subjectivism that anticipated the open subjectivism and symbolism of the Silver Age in Russian literature. In tandem with this development, the importance of the individual actually increases in his art. At the same time, however, he placed careful limits on subjectivism at the point where it seemed likely to affect the possibility of morality. Perhaps the best way to recapitulate these developments would be to summarize a contemporary document, a long essay by Strakhov entitled *The Fundamental Concepts of Psychology* [*Ob osnovnykh poniatiiakh psikhologii*] that was published in 1878.

It should be clear from earlier discussions just how intense a friendship existed between Tolstoy and Strakhov in the 1870s. Each borrowed from the other, and each credited the other with contributing to his spiritual and intellectual growth. Strakhov's essay reflected this intimacy. When discussing perceptions of reality, for instance, Strakhov used Tolstoy's example from *Anna Karenina* of the "blue vault" of the sky to establish the significance, if not the objective reality, of this universal human perception.[1] Strakhov wrote Tolstoy that it seemed to him that he wrote for Tolstoy alone;[2] while in praising the essay, Tolstoy wrote his friend: "I must say that two years ago I would have valued your work even more; now what you are proving to me is already too indubitable and simple (as it is for 99.9999 percent of mankind)" (29 May 1878; 62:425).

The general purpose of Strakhov's essay was to deduce all the parts of the soul as well as the existence of the world from Descartes's original formula: I think, therefore I am. By thinking, according to Strakhov, Descartes meant "the whole totality of psychic, subjective phenomena."[3] What Descartes called the mind, in other words, is what Strakhov called the soul (ibid., 1:41). Everything, including the body, whose existence can be doubted, is part of the external world, while everything certain is part of "our inner world." This inner world, as Strakhov defined it, he understood to be Descartes's Archimedean point, from which he could investigate everything else (ibid., 1:42). The material world for Descartes, by definition, becomes a world without life, completely objective and thus open to investigation (ibid., 1:47).

Each of us stands in a peculiar relation to the external world and to other human subjects. The external world could be completely unknown, but any part of it that we do know is knowable to everyone. The subjective world, on the other hand, is indubitably known to us, but to no one else (ibid., 1:43–44). To understand another person, we must experience the same thing as that person does. Since what we directly know—ourselves as subject—we cannot directly communicate, we communicate by objectifying our subjective experience, and anything objective is available to all (ibid., 1:45–46).

However much we may communicate indirectly, however, we remain fundamentally isolated from one another, and this fact is reflected in *Anna Karenina*. In *War and Peace*, Pierre and Natasha are bound body and soul to each other in a marriage sanctified by living reason.[4] In their day-to-day life Natasha knows Pierre's thoughts and expresses them better than he does. In *Anna Karenina*, except in certain extraordinary circumstances, Levin cannot communicate his "holy of holies" even to his wife, and accepts this as a necessary limitation of life. The spiritual isolation expressed here deepened after Tolstoy's conversion and casts a pall over all his later works. It is responsible for Edward Wasiolek's impression that in those later works no one needs anyone else.[5] In *Anna Karenina*, as later, one has to understand this isolation as a product of the necessary intermixing of matter with spirit that creates individual life. If, according to Tolstoyan science of the 1870s, "bodies" occupy all of space and therefore literally press against one another, it is also true that no body can occupy the same space as another (48:92). As long as we are part of the physical world, we, as bodies, can therefore never share our "holy of holies" with another.[6] This would only be possible if we could become all spirit, and this, in fact, became Tolstoy's ideal in his later works.

Strakhov concluded the first part of his essay with the assertion that materialists and spiritualists make the mistake of applying tools appropriate for investigating the objective world to the subjective one, and vice versa.[7] In the second part, he continued his examination of the extent and limits of the science of psychology. To the extent that we can objectify phenomena of the soul, and we all do so except for the most simple people, those objectified phenomena become subject to the same analysis as is appropriate to the outside world.[8] Psychic phenomena can be objectified, and hence become a subject of science, of what Strakhov called empirical psychology (ibid., 2:140). But a psychic phenomenon is a suitable subject for science only if objectified by *Me*, by a subject; so every object must have a subject as well. The "pure subject," which Strakhov earlier defined as "spirit, spiritual being" (ibid., 1:44–45), is unchanging, not susceptible to dissection or any objectification. The mistake of empirical psychology is to subject the *I* to the same treatment as other parts of the soul (ibid., 2:146–47).

Having established the existence of a subjective sphere not amenable to scientific analysis, Strakhov next attempted to establish what he called the "real life of the soul." If the life of the soul was only subjective, he argued, there would be no difference between being drunk and sober. But we make a distinction in relation to some assumed truth. "Our entire inner world, which is immediately, in a completely trustworthy way known [*izvesten*] to us, we acknowledge to be unreal in comparison with something different, fully real" (ibid., 2:156). We require that our subjective life be in accord with this reality and substantiated by it.

> Our thoughts have to comprise real knowledge; our feelings have to relate to our real good, they have to be part of our real happiness; our desires have to be possible to realize, destined for realization and [destined to] be translated into real actions. Under these conditions our inner world takes on the significance of full reality and loses its illusory character; life turns from a dream into real life. (Ibid.)

Thus did Strakhov himself attempt to solve the problem he posed to Tolstoy earlier in the decade about the need for metaphysical standards for truth and morality. Thus did he deal with the Schopenhauerian idea of life as an illusion. While completely accepting Strakhov's conclusions here as elsewhere in his essay, Tolstoy precisely at this point quarreled once again with his methods. Strakhov, Tolstoy complained, once again carried his penchant for rational analysis too far in dividing the soul into thought, feeling, and will. He himself therefore invaded the sacrosanct territory of the pure subject, and hence was not able to argue as clearly as he should have for the real existence of "the true, the good and the free," which, Tolstoy affirmed, underlie, respectively, thought, feeling, and will.

Despite this difference between Tolstoy and Strakhov at a crucial point, Tolstoy did not challenge and therefore surely accepted the thoroughly subjectivist perspective of his friend's essay. And like his friend, he, too, saw the need to establish the existence of "real," that is, objective standards of truth and morality in order to turn life from a dream into something substantial. His subjectivism, therefore, did not preclude the existence of eternal truths necessary for morality. To this extent he remained faithful to the Goethean concept of the "reason behind everything that lives."[9]

This limit to Tolstoyan subjectivism ultimately drove an impassable barrier between him and the post-Nietzschean symbolists who became his enemies in the last decades of his life. Here, too, he was siding in a philosophical-historical struggle with Kant and the Savoyard Vicar against Hegel and Fichte. The latter two, writes Susan Shell, believed the mind to be "fully constitutive of its subject," while Kant presented it as "productive of the object's form alone." This limitation on the mind's power is the basis of Kant's Transcendental Idealism, according to which human knowledge depends on an unknowable reality. Human beings, according to Kant, can know only appearances; the boundaries of objective knowledge are coextensive with those of sensible experiences. We cannot know being or properties—God, freedom, immortality—that transcend them. Thus, in Kant, the ideas necessary for morality remain viable, if not knowable.[10] These ideas also provided, in Tolstoy's understanding as enunciated in the second epigraph to this book, the ideals necessary for great art.

The evolution from nature to culture in Tolstoy's writing in the 1870s can be understood as tactical, as a response to the changing political and social climate in Russia. So Eikhenbaum has argued as a general rule that Tolstoy remained an important figure over many decades because he was able to detect alterations in Russian culture and respond to them.[11] From this perspective, Tolstoy's arguments for the morality of nature in the 1850s and especially in the 1860s can be seen as part of a general trend. Leftist ideology in the 1860s rested on a belief in natural sciences. Nature was understood to be rational, and, as such, a model for a political system. The idea of man as animal discredited the whole tsarist regime, the legitimacy of which depended on religion.[12] The laws of society had to be similar to the laws of nature, which the nihilists took to be rational, and evolutionary theory was commonly associated with natural and social "progress." Pisarev and Zaitsev actually wrote of social evolution in terms of the struggle for existence.[13] In arguing for a spiritual element in nature, Tolstoy agreed with the nihilists about the importance of nature, but disagreed with them about its essence, which he took to be nonrationalist and ideal. The freeing of the serfs and the development of capitalism precipitated changes that made nature less important as a model for society. So, in the 1870s, the populists emerged as the successors to the nihilists. Belief in the omnipotence of science faltered.[14] Natural science had been useful for undermining tsarist society, but proved to be less so in providing a model to take its place.[15] For this it was better to look not to nature but to culture, as Mikhailovsky and P. L. Lavrov, the two leading populists, did. Mikhailovsky followed Strakhov in stating: "There is no morality in Nature; morality is desirable but not inevitable. . . . Man must himself unite Nature and Morality."[16] One can see Tolstoy's turn to culture, and especially to peasant culture, as part of this trend. Lavrov, significantly, based his theories on Kantian epistemology. In his view, we have no knowledge of essences, only of phenomena. Man himself is "the source of nature, the source of history, and the source of individual consciousness."[17] Science should rely on intuitive as well as cognitive knowledge so that "the arts and science could complement one another."[18]

On the psychological and personal level, one may attribute the move from nature to culture to a growing alienation from nature caused by the fact that Tolstoy and his family were growing older and so death, which comes from nature, loomed larger. There were no deaths in Tolstoy's family for the first eleven years of his marriage. In the 1870s he lost two young children, his beloved "Auntie" Tat'iana Ergol'skaia,[19] and an aunt (P. I. Iushkova) whose death affected him deeply because she represented the last of the generation preceding him.

These deaths would have disturbed Tolstoy's belief in the possibility of individual happiness by reminding him forcefuly of his own mortality. As I argued in chapter 2, the fundamental desire of the human individual as Tolstoy understood him was for freedom, that is, for a pristine state of particularity. But human particularity for Tolstoy was grounded in the possession of a body. Tolstoy never forgot this basic fact, and he never underestimated the power of the body over the individual. In her 1865 diary his wife remarked that her husband attributed everything—all human behavior—to physical causes.[20] The body, because it is physical, connects the human being to nature, and the young Tolstoy's love of his body spilled over into a love of nature.

At the same time, attachment to the body as the primary source or expression of one's particularity leads to an obsessive concern, typical of Tolstoy, with the end of that body in death. Real and lasting happiness can only be achieved if death can be banished—and this is what happens in *War and Peace*. In it Tolstoy had not yet drawn sufficiently clearly the line between what he later disparagingly called the personality [*lichnost'*] and the reasonable immortal soul present in each individual but in its essence undifferentiated from its divine source. The drop of water that was Andrei Bolkonsky in life is apparently the same drop that returns to its source after death. So Natasha and Princess Maria do not mourn their lover and brother; instead, they wonder where he has gone. It seems, moreover, that he has actually absented himself before his physical end. When Princess Maria sees him on her arrival at the Rostovs, she understands immediately that her brother is not there—and she dries her tears in the presence of an intimation of immortality.

In the 1870s Tolstoy no longer believed in personal immortality of any sort, and this no doubt influenced the evolution of his thought.[21] He began to try to distance himself from his own body, and as he did so, he began to distance himself from nature as well. The freedom he now looked for became less personal and therefore less likely to make him happy. Whereas before he could have his cake and eat it too, he had now to choose goodness (his immortal soul) over nature. One psychological incentive to do so would be the natural desire to desert the sinking ship of the body.

On a philosophical level, one can point to problems with Tolstoy's first synthesis, problems that became glaring as he became concerned less with happiness and more with morality. The difficulties centered around the legitimacy of the association of conscience with nature, a connection that Tolstoy had found originally in the *Profession of Faith* of the Savoyard Vicar. By suggesting that the Savoyard Vicar and the young Jean-Jacques had disagreed on precisely this point, Rousseau showed that he, too, was uneasy with it. As with the young Tolstoy, the naturalness of conscience was both crucial to the Vicar's teaching and its weakest point. Without it, the unity of body and soul and the unity of man with nature that he preached was impossible. Conscience alone makes natural man potentially capable of higher morality. But as Cassirer observes, the doctrine of conscience in the *Profession of Faith*, the foundation of the Vicar's ethical religion and the only direct bridge between man and God, is not really natural.

> The religion that Rousseau is teaching and proclaiming in the *Profession of Faith* does not arise from absorption in the wonders of nature, although the teleological argument retains for him its full force and he declares that it is just as absurd to assume that the world came into being without an intelligent cause as to assume that a work like the *Aeneid* could originate from throwing letters together by chance. But the real miracle that is central for him is the miracle of human freedom and of conscience as the evidence of this freedom. Here he finds the true mediator between man and God.[22]

Cassirer (who does not distinguish between Rousseau's teaching and that of the Vicar) sees the doctrine of conscience as the closest connection between Kant and Rousseau, "the core of Rousseau's religion, and what links it immediately to Kant." It is an inspiration of "the famous apostrophe to duty in the *Critique of Practical Reason*." Given this philosophical-historical connection, "accepted by all accounts of the Kantian moral philosophy" (ibid., 48), it is no surprise that Tolstoy's own route beyond nature and out of Rousseau (on this point) was eventually through the doctrine of conscience propounded by the Savoyard Vicar. It is also not surprising that the later Tolstoy, when he finally discovered or at least took up the *Critique of Practical Reason* in 1887, recognized Kant as his soul mate (64:102, 104, 105–6). What made nature moral for him and kept him in it was Goethean "living reason," which, furthermore, as Cassirer has argued, bears certain similarities to Kant's understanding.[23] Where Kant and Goethe differ most is in Goethe's insistence on penetrating nature through intuition, whereas Kant applied the forms of the understanding to nature (ibid., 91–92). Goethe "sought far more for unity, while Kant was seeking for difference" (ibid., 84).

So, in the 1870s, Tolstoy found himself following a path similar to that which historically had led from Rousseau and Goethe to Kant, from unity to difference. For him, too, the sticking point became the necessity of freedom *from* nature in order to establish the possibility of morality and the existence of God. His mentor was the philosopher Arthur Schopenhauer, who claimed to be a disciple of Kant but who differed from his master in starting his inquiries from the subjective point of view and thus remaining a metaphysical idealist.[24] Tolstoy, whose intellectual orientation remained individualist and subjectivist, originally turned to Schopenhauer to bolster his argument in *War and Peace* for moral freedom within nature. Soon, however, his acquaintance with Schopenhauer steered him away from the Rousseauist-Goethean emphasis of his early years toward the Christian Kantianism of his old age, and his idealism evolved to keep pace.

To write a novel, Tolstoy had to discover a generality, or "thought" as he called it, to draw everything together. While he was struggling to finish *Anna Karenina*, he told his wife that as the unifying thought behind *War and Peace* had been the "people," so the thought behind this current novel was the family.[25] As the people in the earlier work had come together to eject an enemy from Russia, or in an enigmatic passage, simply to migrate from one place to another, so the family in *Anna Karenina* provides an escape from the cynicism and despair of materialism and radical individualism. At certain moments, when Kitty and her baby wordlessly communicate with each other, or when in the proposal scene Kitty understands Levin's cryptic message, souls come together as they had in *War and Peace*.

In passages subsequently excluded from the novel, the first describing the marriage of Levin and Kitty, and the second from the first draft of part 8, Tolstoy made his intention clear:

> He [Levin] felt that the meaning of this act [his marriage] did not consist in pleasure, in present happiness, or in any kind of personal happiness, but that he and she in their blind love for one another involuntarily and unconsciously comprised a part of this eternal and great mystery of the continuation of the human race, which had begun with Adam and Eve, Isaac and Rebecca, as the words of the prayer said, and that participation in this mystery was outside of human will and in the power of an inexplicable and mysterious force, to which, in the person of God, the Church now had resort. (Second half of 1876; 20:392)

[In the Slavic question, society mistakenly felt that it had the people behind it.] Meanwhile the people [*narod*] continued to live the same quiet life, with the awareness that its historical destiny was being fulfilled as it pleased God, and that to forecast or create this destiny was not given to or required of man. (April 1877; 20:549)

Out there, beyond human cognition, God has a plan for mankind as a whole. In *War and Peace* Tolstoy took the significant step of suggesting that the Napoleonic wars, just because they did occur, were somehow part of that mysterious destiny. In *Anna Karenina* he seems to refrain from such conjectures, even to the point of cutting the passage about the historical destiny of the people from the final text, where the people, represented by the old beekeeper, stay strictly within the limits of knowledge and responsibility that the folk has set for itself.[26] As Levin, who counts himself and his father-in-law among the folk puts it, the people do not know in what the general good consists, but they do know that it can only be achieved through "the law of good which is open to every person" (8:16). In *War and Peace* political actions spontaneously assayed by the people were good, while the folk in *Anna Karenina* seem unwilling to undertake any joint political action.

In place of politics, then, we have family life in all its manifestations as the goal of the folk, as well as its formative principle. We recall, however, that while writing *War and Peace*, Tolstoy had suggested in his notebooks that wars occur because families want to expand to fill the greatest possible space (48:108). If that were true, the "ideas" of family and the folk would be the same. Each serves "an inexplicable and mysterious force," which works through biology or, in the case of Kitty and Levin, "blind love," but is ultimately unknowable. In the first novel, the force operates for good or bad on the battlefield; in the second, in the bedroom and the nursery. And as love and war are connected in *War and Peace*, so are they equated in *Anna Karenina*.[27]

There is a difference, however, in the presentation of the family in the two novels. While in *War and Peace* the family is seen as legitimate because it is natural, in *Anna Karenina* it legitimates the purely natural. The completely positive Uncle in *War and Peace* has a family, for instance, without benefit of clergy: he enjoys the favors of his plump housekeeper just as he enjoys her cooking. By contrast, in *Anna Karenina* the young Parmenovs are married for a long time without consummating the marriage. Marriage is seen in that work as bringing an element of chastity or law to the wildness of sexual passion. Using Blackmur's terminology,[28] in *Anna Karenina* "manners" and "momentum" meet in the family, which thereby straddles and combines nature and convention. The passion of Anna and Vronsky, powerful and genuine, leads to disaster, while the equally "blind love" of Kitty and Levin is legitimate because it serves the perpetuation of the human race. Thus, Levin in his "wholeness" [cel'nost'] has as his ideal the family constituted by his parents, whom he did not know, and, the narrator tells us, he yearns even more for his own family than for the woman who will join him in establishing it (1:27). Like Prince Andrei, he does not hurry to marry Kitty, and, Dolly tells him, his absence and his lack of urgency are the main reasons why Kitty refused him the first time (3:10).[29] In the family, and in the peasant culture that exists to sustain it and to tame passion, living reason is reconstituted once again. This time, however, it is constituted indoors, in the church where Levin and Kitty are married, and ultimately in the hearts of those who make the right choices in the novel. Levin's new-found faith turns even nature into a church—he perceives the heavens as a "vault."[30]

Anna Karenina was Tolstoy's last attempt to argue that his own individual happiness and his moral duty could be compatible. A few years later, in his *Confession*, he was already rejecting the whole gentry way of life on which Levin's happiness depends. This difference between these two works depends, I would suggest, on the different relation in them between the subjective and objective elements of Tolstoy's new synthesis. *Anna Karenina* emphasizes the subjectivity of all human knowing and desiring and therefore again legitimates, however uneasily, what is now, in fact, seen by its author as the subjective elements of human particularity, including culture and class affiliation as well as the possession of a particular body. The novel was created and thereby began its independent life while its author hesitated before attacking Orthodox Christianity. In order to accept Orthodoxy, as he did for a time and Levin does in the novel, he had to carry his subjectivism beyond a point where he could long sustain it. He had to argue, as he did in an unfinished work from 1877 to 1878 entitled "Interlocutors" [*Sobesedniki*], that all knowing, even such "indubitable" knowledge as our perceptions of colors, depends on the general accumulated opinion of mankind—"we can't judge about the essence of this knowledge" (17:377). Relying on Kant's epistemology to strengthen the distinction he had absorbed from the Savoyard Vicar between knowable and unknowable truths, he tried for the time being once again to group together all the needs of the individual for happiness and morality into one whole.

The results of the intense subjectivism of the 1870s were great for literature, but impossible for Tolstoy. His individualism did not allow him to accept things abhorrent to his reason (like the exclusiveness of Orthodoxy) or his feeling (the church's policy on war and punishment) for long. In his *Confession*, where he recounted his rejection of the church for these reasons (chap. 15), Tolstoy marshaled all the forces of subjective knowing in the service of the objective truth in which the subjectivity, if it were going to be more than mere psychology, had to be founded. It is striking, in this regard, that his *Confession* is both more and less subjective than *Anna Karenina* is. It depends for its argument on dreams and tropes that are avowedly allegorical, tipping the balance in Tolstoy's "emblematic realism" toward allegory. The argument itself, however, is intended to reflect the objective truth and to brook no compromise with falsehood.

Tolstoy's thought evolved as part of a lifelong effort to secure dignity for the human individual. This effort certainly superceded his commitment to reason, and therefore to philosophy. Hence Zenkovsky's classification of him as a "mystic of the mind," for whom philosophy was always in the service of moral certainty which it could not itself establish. His central pathos was "to understand reality, to make sense of his life."[31] His primary need for his life to make sense was an important reason why Tolstoy wrote fiction, and also the reason why he ceased to value it as highly when he realized that the main subject of art, the life of the feelings, could not, in and of itself, guarantee the meaning he craved.

After 1880 Tolstoy's life's project took him beyond the unity and fulfillment of body and soul, which had been his crowning achievement in *War and Peace* and which he salvaged in *Anna Karenina*. He rejected the body, and therefore nature, as the source of or even a possible participant in higher human goodness. In 1865, in a letter to his sister-in-law, he had been able to exempt married love from a blanket condemnation of human relations as egotistical (61:73). The body thus was seen to participate in "general laws" that naturally carry human beings beyond egotism. In 1879, studying the Bible and commencing the work that resulted in his *Confession*, he stated categorically: "No one desires the good for another person. It is impossible. . . . No one can wish for the general good. All we want is what we lust for [*pokhot'*] . . . everything physical is worthless" (48:323, 324). The answer to this dilemna is Tolstoy's interpretation of the New Testament: "Be reborn in the spirit . . . *be transformed* [*peremenites'*]" (48:324). You have to give up the desires of the body, and with it what is "merry" [*vesolo*] for what is right ("what must be done" [*chto dolzhno delat'*]). You have to live for yourself alone, but your spiritual, not your carnal self, "so that there would be the life of the spirit" (48:324). After 1880, as in *What is Art?* or the first paragraph of *Resurrection*, nature can be "merry" [*vesolo*], that is, innocent, but not good or truly self-sacrificing. Art that celebrates this innocence as part of "the very simplest human feelings" is truly art, but it must play second fiddle to "universal," or "religious" art—and Tolstoy was not one to settle for second fiddle.

The problem with "religious" art, however—as it is explained in *What is Art?*—is that even it is but a handmaiden to what Tolstoy called "religious consciousness." "Art, along with speech, is one of the tools of social relations [*obshchenie*], and therefore of progress, that is of the movement ahead of mankind toward perfection." Art in and of itself is morally neutral: it is good or bad depending on its relation to the "religious consciousness" of the times (chap. 16). As such, it could not completely absorb Tolstoy as it had done when he believed that it was the most complete expression of truth. This is why the diaries and notebooks of the two decades in which he wrote *War and Peace* and *Anna Karenina* take up only one volume of the Jubilee edition, while those from 1880 on take up ten. Before 1880 he had done his thinking through his art, while afterward his art in his own mind, or at least in his public pronouncements, became but an instrument of his thought.

Notes ——————————————————————————

Introduction

1. See his 1875 essay "Desnica i shuica L'va Tolstogo" [The Right and the Left Hand of Lev Tolstoy]. Eikhenbaum explains how Mikhailovsky found himself in the position of having to praise a man whose politics he despised (*Lev Tolstoi: Semidesiatye gody*, 51–65). As part of an effort to get Tolstoy to publish *Anna Karenina* in *Otechestvennye zapiski* [Notes of the Fatherland], the journal published his article "Progres i opredelenie obrazovaniia" [Progress and the Definition of Education]. As the journal's chief publicist, Mikhailovsky had to defend Tolstoy's theories from attacks from the Left. Marxists, beginning of course with Lenin's famous articles, have taken a similar approach, contrasting Tolstoy's (conservative) thought and his (progressive) art. See, for example, Marxist critics L. Aksel'rod-Ortodoks (*Lev Tolstoi*) in the 1920s and E. N. Kupreianova in the 1960s (*Estetika L'va Tolstogo*).

2. He later, perhaps under external pressure, added a historical political dimension to his work.

3. *Lev Tolstoi*, 1:35, 212, 234–35, 309–11; 2:7. See also Aldanov (*Zagadka Tolstogo*, 120) and Aksel'rod-Ortodoks (*Lev Tolstoi*, 22–23, 49).

4. It is possible that Eikhenbaum himself, although he paid lip service to Marxism-Leninism, thought that Tolstoyan nihilism mirrored true reality.

5. This specific term comes from a letter to Fet written in October 1875 (62:209), referring to the writing of *Anna Karenina*.

6. On this topic see Zenkovskii, "Problema bessmertiia u L. N. Tolstogo"; Bilinkis, *O tvorchestve L. N. Tolstogo: Ocherki*, 23–24, 335, 388, 407–8; Ginzburg, *O psikhologicheskoi proze*, 408–9; and others.

7. Bilinkis, *O tvorchestve L. N. Tolstogo: Ocherki*, 40.

8. While accepting his emphasis on the importance of peasant culture, I disagree with the outstanding and too little known Tolstoy scholar Ia. Bilinkis that Tolstoy moved from belief in individual moral responsibility to belief in the individual as determined by his class and in the collective moral voice of the peasant (ibid., 190, 335–37). I shall argue instead that Tolstoy turned to folk tradition precisely because it preserved individual moral freedom while solving the problem of the relation of the individual to the community.

9. Quoted in Eikhenbaum, *Lev Tolstoi*, 1:281.

10. See P. V. Annenkov, "I. S. Turgenev i gr. L. N. Tolstoi," in *Sovremennik*, January 1855 (*Vospominaniia i kriticheskie ocherki*, 84–108); N. G. Chernyshevskii [Chernyshevsky], "Detstvo i otrochestvo. Soch. gr. L. N. Tolstogo. Spb. 1856. Voennye rasskazy gr. L. N. Tolstogo. Spb. 1856" (PSS, 3:421–31); K. S. Aksakov, "Obozrenie sovremennoi literatury" (1857), 33–35; A. A. Grigor'ev, *Rannie proizvedeniia gr. L. N. Tolstogo* (1862), 37,39.

11. *Kriticheskie stat'i*, 208.

12. *Lev Tolstoi*, 1:34.

13. 5 March 1860; quoted in Zaidenshnur, *"Voina i mir" L. N. Tolstogo*, 9.

14. Mikhailovskii [Mikhailovsky], "Desnica i shuica L'va Tolstogo," 448.

15. The English, whose political culture Tolstoy despised for what he considered its cold individualism, clearly saw these limitations in Tolstoy and criticized them. See Maude, *The Life of Tolstoy*, 2: 46–47, 441–42; Bayley, *Tolstoy and the Novel*, 40–42; and Wilson, *Tolstoy*, 243.

16. Bilinkis, *O tvorchestve L. N. Tolstogo: Ocherki*, 23–24. See also Eikhenbaum (*Lev Tolstoi*, 1:80–81), who writes that *Childhood* was part of a trend toward autobiographical novels in the early 1850s.

17. Zenkovsky, *A History of Russian Philosophy*, 1:322.

18. Bursov, *Lev Tolstoi*, 13. On Herzen's defense of the individual, see also Zenkovsky, *A History of Russian Philosophy*, 1:277 passim.

19. L. N. Morozenko sees an historical connection between the confessional philosophizing of Stankevich and Tolstoy's explorations of his inner self in his diaries and elsewhere ("U istokov novogo etapa v razvitii psikhologizma (Rannie dnevniki Tolstogo i Chernyshevskogo)," 118–19). I discuss Tolstoy and Stankevich in chapter 3.

20. Vucinich, *Science in Russian Culture: 1861–1917*, 13.

21. Quoted in Walicki, *A History of Russian Thought from the Enlightenment to Marxism*, 213. See also Zenkovsky, *A History of Russian Philosophy*, 1:338–40.

22. Zenkovsky, *A History of Russian Literature*, 1:364.

23. On page viii of the introduction, Gershenzon states his general principle that progress takes place through the lives of individuals. Both Pavel Annenkov and Pavel Miliukov seem to take the same view. For Annenkov, see his justification for writing the Stankevich biography and correspondence, *Nikolai Vladimirovich Stankevich*, 7–13 passim; for Miliukov, see "Liubov' u 'idealistov tridcatykh godov.'"

24. Mandelbaum, *History, Man & Reason*, 6.

25. *Hidden in Plain View*, 9–36. In this chapter Morson also discusses Tolstoy's attempts to write "archetypal" or "impersonal" biography. Once again, for Tolstoy, working within the tradition of metaphysical idealism, his own biography could be authoritative in a way not possible today.

26. Gershenzon, *Istoriia Molodoi Rossii*, 84. One of these "chosen ones," N. V. Stankevich, became a particular hero of Tolstoy. (More on this subject in chapter 3.) Tolstoy's metaphysical idealism made him an anachronism among realists of his own time, and eventually forged a bond between him and writers of the Silver Age.

27. Zenkovsky, *A History of Russian Philosophy*, 1:243.

28. Dowler, *Dostoevsky, Grigor'ev, and Native Soil Conservatism*, 49.

29. It is also important to keep in mind that Tolstoy was a proud member of the Russian aristocracy which, under the Romanov dynasty, had been systematically deprived of its political rights. His father was a veteran of 1812 who after returning from Paris lived out his life on his estate rather than compromising his aristocratic freedom as a civil servant. Lev himself was twenty years old in 1848, when revolution in Europe caused Nikolas I to stifle all independent political thought in Russia. His character shaped by these circumstances, Tol-

stoy's attachment to the state was weak, his attitude toward it rivalrous and vengeful, and his aristocratic pride concentrated to an unnatural extent on himself.

30. Zenkovsky, *A History of Russian Philosophy*, 1:6, 398–99.

31. Tolstoy's correspondence while he was writing *Anna Karenina* reveals the difference between the author and his creation as he himself construed it. As he was commencing the novel in October 1875, he wrote to Fet of the need for what he called *podmostki* [scaffolding], in order to give unity and higher meaning to it (62:209). (He also wrote on this subject in his diary in 1873; see 48:67.) A year and a half later, in March 1877, he wrote that his work was going well "and I continue in the delusion that what I am writing is very important, even though I know that in a month I'll be ashamed to remember this" (62:316). At the same time, he was writing to his closest confidants of his religious doubts and inability to believe in God. (See letter to S. S. Urusov, 21 February 1876; 62:249; letter to A. A. Tolstaia, 8–12 March 1876; 62:256, 261; letter to A. A. Tolstaia, 15–17(?) April 1876; 62:266–67; letter to A. A. Tolstaia, 10–11 January 1877; 62:306; letter to A. A. Tolstaia, 5–9 February 1877; 62:310.) *Anna Karenina*, then, is a novel written by a man tormented by religious doubts, but itself built with "scaffolding," that is, ideas, without which it cannot stand or be understood.

32. From the mid-1870s on, Pascal became one of Tolstoy's chief inspirations.

33. *Pensées*, 83.

34. *Ocherki bylogo*, 320–31. On Tolstoy's superstitions, see also Sukhotina-Tolstaia, *Vospominaniia*, 425, and Maude, *Life of Tolstoy*, 2:293.

35. *Tolstoy*, 148.

Chapter One
Analysis and Synthesis

1. Boris Eikhenbaum, for instance, finds in the diary of the forties both a fascination with Hegelian metaphysics and a rejection of that metaphysics for "practical philosophy," that is, science, ethics, and the language of psychological analysis. The fifties, then, becomes for Eikhenbaum the time when Tolstoy exploded romantic canons of art and created an aesthetics based on the implications of his radically new psychology. See *Lev Tolstoi: Semidesiatye gody*, 215.

2. "Obraz Kutuzova i filosofiia istorii v romane L. Tolstogo 'Voina i mir,'" 198. Even Eikhenbaum mentions Chicherin's "Hegelianism," defining it as his penchant for finding the eternal in everything, as the main reason for Tolstoy's attraction to him in 1858 (*Lev Tolstoi*, 2:27). Babaev follows up Skaftymov's lead and discusses Tolstoy's debt to Hegel in establishing the genre of *War and Peace* (*Lev Tolstoi i russkaia zhurnalistika ego epokhi*, 119–21). I would add that it is no accident that Tolstoy's closest friend in the 1870s, N. N. Strakhov, was a self-avowed Hegelian. See Chizhevski, *Gegel' v Rossii*, 165.

3. In an important sense, according to Chizhevski, Hegel was the founder of a specifically Russian philosophy. Since Hegel represented the end of Western philosophy, Russian philosphy would take up where the Western, negative tradition left off. See *Gegel' v Rossii*, 19–21.

4. In his article on Herzen originally published in 1870, Strakhov also stresses the importance of Hegelianism in Russia, and he says that Hegelian method, the dialectic, is more important than particular Hegelian ideas. See "Literaturnaia deiatel'nost' Gercena," 58–59. In *Mir kak celoe*, which, as I shall argue in chapter 6, had a profound effect on *Anna Karenina*, Strakhov in the introduction again stated his fundamental allegiance to Hegelian method (*Mir kak celoe*, vi).

5. Terras, *Belinsky and Russian Literary Criticism*, 4.

6. Bilinkis remarks that in the naturalist school of the 1840s, reality was re-produced by a compilation of details; in the 1850s and 1860s, by contrast, the details were chosen from an artistic concept of reality (*O tvorchestve L. N. Tolstogo: Ocherki*, 109); see also Babaev, *Ocherki estetiki i tvorchestva L. N. Tolstogo*, 192–97. The French critic Eugène-Melchior de Vogüé, in his important book *The Russian Novel* (1886), saw synthesis, and a concomittant tendency to idealism, as the dominant feature of Russian, as opposed to French, realism. See O'Bell, "Vogüé, *The Russian Novel* and Russian Critical Tradition," 305–6, 309–10.

7. Eikhenbaum, *Lev Tolstoi*, 1:196–99.

8. Terras, *Belinsky and Russian Literary Tradition*, 236.

9. Solov'ev, *Esteticheskie vozzreniia Chernyshevskogo*, 7.

10. Fridlender, "Estetika Chernyshevskogo i russkaia literatura," 18.

11. Mandelbaum, *History, Man & Reason*, 22.

12. Fridlender, "Estetika Chernyshevskogo i russkaia literatura," 20.

13. Chernyshevsky followed Feuerbachian materialism which rejected meta-physics to concentrate on "anthropological" philosophy. This philosophy con-cerned itself only with human problems, which were to be solved only through human experience (Mandelbaum, *History, Man & Reason*, 24). (Marx and En-gels, by contrast, developed a materialist metaphysics based on the categories of science which, they claimed, were dialectical [ibid., 24–25].) As the Soviet Marxist aesthetician G. A. Solov'ev explains it, Chernyshevsky accepted but transformed the Hegelian notion of the beautiful as a "unity of idea and form" (*Esteticheskie vozzreniia Chernyshevskogo*, 66–67). All human activity, not just art alone, strives for this unity, which is achieved to the extent that our ideas define matter (nature) and become realized in it. Unlike Marx, Solov'ev says, Cherny-shevsky never found a true synthesis—he remained an "enlightener," an ana-lyzer—only because he did not universalize the "work" or idea by which man transforms himself from an animal into a human being (ibid., 67). On the main point, however, the Marxists and Chernyshevskians agree: they are materialists who dogmatically reject the idea of spirit.

14. PSS, 3:17–19.

15. Dowler, *Dostoevsky, Grigor'ev, and Native Soil Conservatism*, 40.

16. Chizhevski, *Gegel' v Rossii*, 220.

17. Terras, *Belinsky and Russian Literary Tradition*, 221–22.

18. *Strashnaia veshch'*; Gusev, *Lev Nikolaevich Tolstoi: Materialy k biografii s 1855 po 1869 god*, 116.

19. See Fet, *Moi vospominaniia*, 1:105–7; Grigorovich, *Literaturnye vospomi-naniia*, 250; Annenkov, *Vospominaniia*, 643–45. On Tolstoy's relations with his new friends during this period see Eikhenbaum, *Lev Tolstoi*, 1:208–35, and

Gusev, *Lev Nikolaevich Tolstoi: Materialy k biografii s 1855 po 1869 god*, 22–25, 41–46.

20. "Detstvo i otrochestvo. Soch. gr. L. N. Tolstogo. Spb. 1856. Voennye rasskazy gr. L. N. Tolstogo. Spb. 1856," PSS, 3:421–31.

21. Gusev, *Lev Nikolaevich Tolstoi: Materialy k biografii s 1855 po 1869 god*, 128.

22. Grigor'ev, *Rannie proizvedeniia gr. L. N. Tolstogo*, 37.

23. Ibid., 39–40. In a letter from around this time Botkin gives almost exactly the same explanation for Tolstoy's silence at the end of the fifties (Sergeenko, *Tolstoi i ego sovremenniki. Ocherki*, 139–40). For a more complete description of Grigor'ev's argument and Tolstoy's reaction to it, see Emel'ianov, "Geroi Tolstogo v istoriko-literaturnoi koncepcii Apollona Grigor'eva."

24. *The Young Tolstoy*, 66–67.

25. Members of the same generation (both born in 1828), each participated in the scientific revolution which replaced the philosophizing of the forties. Each kept a diary in the early fifties, dissecting his own psyche with a view to understanding himself and others (Morozenko, "U istokov novogo etapa v razvitii psikhologizma [Rannie dnevniki Tolstogo i Chernyshevskogo]," 113). Eikhenbaum also notes the similarity between Tolstoy and Chernyshevsky in this regard and suggests that Chernyshevsky understood the writing style of the young Tolstoy because it was like his own in origin and method (*Lev Tolstoi: Semidesiatye gody*, 246–47). Both participated in the cult of the individual so typical of nineteenth-century philosophy and art. And therefore both had somehow to bridge the resulting gap between the interests of the individual and those of society (Ivanov, *Istoriia russkoi kritiki*, 4:119; Ginzburg, *O psikhologicheskoi proze*, 408–17).

26. Nikolaev, *L. N. Tolstoi i N. G. Chernyshevskii*, 10.

27. Both Chernyshevsky and Tolstoy were moralists in the Russian tradition whose science and philosophy were in the service of ethics (Zenkovsky, *A History of Russian Philosophy*, 1:6,7,95).

28. Chernyshevskii [Chernyshevsky], PSS, 11:201 (pt. 3, chap. 29).

29. Eikhenbaum claims that the play is a parody of the language of the intelligentsia and in particular *What Is to Be Done?* (*Lev Tolstoi*, 2:215–16).

30. Ivanov, *Istoriia russkoi kritiki*, 4:529–33.

31. Eikhenbaum, *Lev Tolstoi*, 2:96. Eikhenbaum himself is also shocked at Tolstoy's radical rejection of education (*Lev Tolstoi: Semidesiatye gody*, 36–39).

32. PSS, 11:228.

33. Ivanov, *Istoriia russkoi kritiki*, 4:519.

34. Mandelbaum, *History, Man & Reason*, 25.

35. Löwith, *From Hegel to Nietzsche*, 97.

36. See above, Introduction.

37. Emphasis mine; PSS, 3:422–23.

38. Emphasis mine; *Vospominaniia i kriticheskie ocherki. Sobranie statei i zametok P. V. Annenkova: 1849–1868*, 2:105.

39. For a general discussion of this form of psychology and its origins in Locke, see Mandelbaum, *History, Man & Reason*, 152. Gustafson's description of Tolstoy's associationalism and its kinship to Chernyshevsky is excellent. See *Leo Tolstoy: Resident and Stranger*, 292–302.

40. *Aesthetics*, 2:960.

41. *Leo Tolstoy: Resident and Stranger*, 293–97.

42. In his very first diary, in 1847, he noted that he was reading *Faust* (46:247–50); and in later life he told V. F. Lazurskii that he had read all of Goethe (quoted in *L. N. Tolstoi v vospominaniiakh sovremennikov*, 2:28). The Soviet critic Chistiakova claims indeed that Tolstoy turned to Goethe during every creative period of his life ("Tolstoi i Gete," 118).

43. Von Gronicka, *The Russian Image of Goethe*, 1:177–79, 184.

44. Chizhevski, *Gegel' v Rossii*, 194. They were still admired in the 1860s by Strakhov as masterpieces of Hegelian thinking (ibid.). See also Strakhov, "Literaturnaia deiatel'nost' Gercena," 56–60; and Vucinich, *Science in Russian Culture: A History to 1860*, 291.

45. Von Gronicka, *The Russian Image of Goethe*, 1:244.

46. *From Hegel to Nietzsche*, 6.

47. "Goethe and Tolstoy," 95 and passim.

48. Melzer, *The Natural Goodness of Man*, 38.

49. *From Hegel to Nietzsche*, 9.

50. Thus, I agree with Ginzburg that in *War and Peace*, at least, Tolstoy accepted the sadness and evil of life, but I do not agree that he affirms life without measuring it according to an ideal marker ("O romane Tolstogo 'Voina i mir,'" 135). On the contrary, only his (Goethean) idealism made it possible for him to embrace nature unreservedly.

51. Cassirer, "Goethe and Kantian Philosophy," 87–89.

52. Magnus, *Goethe as a Scientist*, 227–28.

53. Ibid., 237–38. For a similar argument, see Lewes, *The Life of Goethe*, 290.

54. "Goethe and Kantian Philosophy," 82.

55. Quoted in Price, "Tolstoy and the Forms of Life," 191. Price cites *Marcel Proust on Art and Literature 1896–1916 (Contre Sainte-Beuve)*, trans. Sylvia Townsend Warner (New York: Meridian, 1958), 378–79; and Walter A. Strauss, *Proust and Literature: The Novelist as Critic* (Cambridge, Mass.: Harvard University Press, 1959), 168–71.

56. *Leo Tolstoy: Resident and Stranger*, 202–13. I would suggest, moreover, that Gustafson and Morson (*Hidden in Plain View*), whose work seems so different, meet at this source in Goethe. Gustafson has emphasized the symbolic aspect of Tolstoy's realism, while Morson emphasizes the way meaning for Tolstoy is embedded in specific situations. The two agree that details and generalities, the fox and the hedgehog, do exist in Tolstoy. It is the coexistence of these two elements and their interrelatedness that comes from Goethe, and that is a constant feature of Tolstoy's prose from beginning to end. Two other fine essays that treat this subject are Hardy, "Form and Freedom in *Anna Karenina*," and Price, "Tolstoy and the Forms of Life."

57. Viëtor, *Goethe: The Thinker*, 14.

Chapter Two
The Young Tolstoy's Understanding of the Human Soul

1. *Leo Tolstoy: Resident and Stranger*, 225.

2. Eikhenbaum, *Lev Tolstoi: Semidesiatye gody*, 244.

3. 48:67. In *O psikhologicheskoi proze* (438–39, 440–41), Ginzburg discusses how Tolstoy analyzes both good and bad in the human soul. Babaev remarks of Levin that he knows everything negative, and the search for something positive is what motivates him (*Roman i vremia*, 41). Like his creator, Levin, in Tolstoy's understanding, is a Cartesian. The approach of the young Tolstoy to the creation of a literary style that would reflect and transmit his Cartesianism was similar and related: as Eikhenbaum puts it, he came to literature as if it had never existed before (*Lev Tolstoi*, 1:42).

4. Melzer, *The Natural Goodness of Man*, 31.

5. Gustafson, *Leo Tolstoy: Resident and Stranger*, 217.

6. Melzer, *The Natural Goodness of Man*, 39–40. I am greatly indebted to Melzer's fine book in the interpretation of Rousseau that follows.

7. Ibid., 41. Melzer continues on the next page to draw out the implications of Rousseau's position, which "would seem to be one ground of Rousseau's generally undefended assumption that men are by nature asocial and solitary."

8. Viëtor, *Goethe: The Thinker*, 145.

9. *Emile*, 4:279n. Melzer also draws a connection between this view and Cartesianism (*The Natural Goodness of Man*, 42).

10. "The Expressive Self in *War and Peace*," 519.

11. Gustafson, *Leo Tolstoy: Resident and Stranger*, 218–19.

12. *The Natural Goodness of Man*, 26.

13. Melzer, *The Natural Goodness of Man*, 45. This natural expansiveness is the reason why, as Morson argues in chapter 7 of *Hidden in Plain View*, the self is in practice never whole.

14. Gustafson, *Leo Tolstoy: Resident and Stranger*, 224–25.

15. *The Natural Goodness of Man*, 89–91.

16. *Leo Tolstoy: Resident and Stranger*, 225.

17. On the relation of the individual and the community, see Ginzburg, "O romane Tolstogo 'Voina i mir,'" 126; *O psikhologicheskoi proze*, 408. Ginzburg also discusses the analytic and synthetic sides of Tolstoy's psychology. See *O psikhologicheskoi proze*, 326–27.

18. Zenkovsky, *A History of Russian Philosophy*, 1:338.

19. Gusev, *Lev Nikolaevich Tolstoi: Materialy k biografii s 1855 po 1869 god*, 224.

20. Ostrovskii, *Molodoi Tolstoi v zapisiakh sovremennikov*, 120.

21. Ibid., 92. Imitating Rousseau and thumbing his nose at laws of comme il faut which at other times so captivated him, one summer vacation, while he was at Kazan University, Tolstoy also briefly wore an all-purpose garment, sewn by himself, that served as his bedding at night (ibid., 108–10).

22. Carden, "The Expressive Self in *War and Peace*," 521.

23. Ostrovskii, *Molodoi Tolstoi v zapisiakh sovremennikov*, 92. Quoted from the memoires of Paul Boyer, published in 1901.

24. Kupreianova (*Estetika L. N. Tolstogo*, 80–86), for instance, uses it to ground her contention that the Swiss philosopher Weiss, an epigone of Rousseau, had an influence on Tolstoy's thought.

25. Eikhenbaum, *The Young Tolstoy*, 29–30; Wachtel, *The Battle for Childhood*, 37–38.

26. As the editors of the twenty-volume Soviet edition of Tolstoy point out (*Sobranie sochinenii v dvadcati tomakh*, 1:457).

27. On the replacement in Rousseau of transcendent perfection as the goal of human life by authenticity or sincerity, see Melzer *The Natural Goodness of Man*, 21–22. Silbajoris sees a connection between Rousseauian authenticity and Tolstoy's idea of art as infection, or fundamental, "authentic" communication of emotion. See *Tolstoy's Aesthetics and his Art*, 35.

28. Melzer, *The Natural Goodness of Man*, 42.

29. It is at this point, I would suggest, that Tolstoy parted ways with Dostoevsky, the other great Russian student of Rousseau. Dostoevsky accepted the radical freedom inherent in Rousseauian individualism; indeed, his whole oeuvre can be understood as an elaboration of the consequences of that natural freedom for the individual and society.

30. Eikhenbaum, *The Young Tolstoy*, 42–44.

31. As Eikhenbaum claims in *Lev Tolstoi: Semidesiatye gody*, 215.

32. On the subject of Plato and Tolstoy, see Orwin, "Freedom, Responsibility and the Soul: The Platonic Contribution to Tolstoi's Psychology"; Carden, "The Recuperative Powers of Memory: Tolstoy's *War and Peace*"; and Gutkin, "The Dichotomy Between Flesh and Spirit: Plato's *Symposium* in *Anna Karenina*."

33. End of April–3 May, 60:293–94. It is odd, as Gary Saul Morson has pointed out to me, that Tolstoy would claim not to have found Christian truths in the Gospels. I think that, rather like one of his own soldiers reporting on a battle, he exaggerates for effect. He also probably enjoys scandalizing his pious "auntie."

34. *Emile*, 263–64.

35. Galagan, *L. N. Tolstoi: Khudozhestvenno-eticheskie iskaniia*, 56. Galagan is the only critic I know to comment extensively on Tolstoy's 1852 reading of Rousseau.

36. *Emile*, 294.

37. Galagan's assertion to the contrary (*L. N. Tolstoi: Khudozhestvenno-eticheskie iskaniia*, 55), I cannot find, at least in published texts, proof that Tolstoy concerned himself with the specific notion of conscience before this encounter with the *Profession of Faith*.

38. *Emile*, 289.

39. *Emile*, 286.

40. Galagan shows convincingly how the extended night landscape that precedes this declaration illustrates its truth. See *L. N. Tolstoi: Khudozhestvenno-eticheskie iskaniia*, 42–47.

41. *Emile*, 290.

42. The Vicar's "incontinence" was discovered because out of respect for marriage he slept only with virgins (*Emile*, 267).

43. On the power of suppressed sexuality to make man sociable, see Allan Bloom's introduction to his translation of *Emile* (15–17).

44. See, for instance, 15.9, where the compassion of simple soldiers for the enemy is linked to the stars.

45. *Emile*, 290.

46. Ibid., 286.

47. "The Expressive Self in *War and Peace*," 521.

Chapter Three
The First Synthesis: Nature and the Young Tolstoy

1. See, especially, Kupreianova, *Estetika L. N. Tolstogo*, 138–39.

2. 46:133–34. This passage may explain the suicide in "Notes of a Billiard Player." In that typically Tolstoyan outburst of confession and didactic moralism, written in two weeks in the fall of 1853, the noble young Prince Nekhliudov escapes an inconquerable gambling lust by committing suicide.

3. The strikingly Kantian flavor of this passage is understandable in light of the historical importance of the *Profession of Faith* in the development of Kant's moral philosophy, an importance I briefly discuss in the conclusion to this book. Tolstoy is arguing here, as Kant did, that we cannot disprove the existence of the things necessary for morality (such as the immortality of the soul); but that we cannot prove that the idea of eternity has an existence outside of the human mind that conceives it.

4. *Emile*, 287–88.

5. *L. N. Tolstoi: Perepiska s russkimi pisateliami*, 17.

6. The story "Biriuk," for instance, in *Sportsman's Sketches*, depends on the narrator's mistaken identification of Biriuk with the stormy night.

7. On meeting the young writer in person, Nekrasov wrote to Botkin that Tolstoy was "a dear, energetic, noble youth—a falcon—and perhaps an eagle" (Gusev, *Lev Nikolaevich Tolstoi: Materialy k biografii s 1855 po 1869 god*, 4). In May 1857, writing from Paris, he repeated this compliment to Tolstoy himself, calling him "bright falcon [*iasnyi sokol*]," and adding in parentheses that "I don't know if I've told you this, but in my thoughts I call you nothing else" (*L. N. Tolstoy: Perepiska s russkimi pisateliami*, 42). Turgenev invented a less flattering nickname for his new friend; borrowing from Schiller's *Ode to Joy*, he named him "Troglodit . . . for his wild zeal [*dikuiu revnost'*] and bull-like stubbornness" (9 December 1855; PSS, Letters, 2:328). Nekrasov and Turgenev in different ways both pay tribute to Tolstoy's energy, which makes him, for better or for worse, like a force of nature: hence they look to nature and the primitive state for epithets to describe him.

8. Galagan on "The Raid," *L. N. Tolstoi: Khudozhestvenno-eticheskie iskaniia*, 44.

9. *Emile*, 278.

10. Galagan, *L. N. Tolstoi: Khudozhestvenno-eticheskie iskaniia*, 44. For a general description in English of the different drafts of "The Raid," see White, "An Evolutionary Study of Tolstoy's First Story, 'The Raid.'"

11. *V. P. Botkin i I. S. Turgenev: Neizdannaia perepiska, 1851–1869*, 61–62.

12. Zenkovsky, *History of Russian Philosophy*, 1:328.

13. See chapter 1.

14. *A. A. Fet: Ocherk zhizni i tvorchestva*, 103.

15. On 3 January 1857, see *V. P. Botkin i I. S. Turgenev: Neizdannaia perepiska, 1851–1869*, 110.

16. *Sochineniia*, 378.

17. Vucinich, *Science in Russian Culture: A History to 1860*, 282.

18. Botkin, "A. A. Fet," *Sochineniia*, 371.

19. Bukhshtab, *A. A. Fet: Ocherk zhizni i tvorchestva*, 16.

20. Gusev, *Materialy k biografii s 1855 po 1869 god*, 120.

21. *L. N. Tolstoi: Semidesiatye gody*, 182.

22. See "Dnevnik lishnego cheloveka" [Diary of a Superfluous Man] in Turgenev, PSS, Works, 5:219.

23. Offord, *Portraits of Early Russian Liberals*, 82–89.

24. *Perepiska L. N. Tolstogo s V. P. Botkinym*, 85.

25. 29 November 1856; *V. P. Botkin i I. S. Turgenev: Neizdannaia perepiska, 1851–1869*, 95–96.

26. Offord, *Portraits of Early Russian Liberals*, 82.

27. See, for instance, the letter of 2 December 1856 from E. Ia. Kolbasin to Turgenev in *Turgenev i krug "Sovremennika,"* 299.

28. Gusev, *Materialy k biografii s 1855 po 1869 god*, 120.

29. Sreznevskii, *Perepiska L. N. Tolstogo s V. P. Botkinym*, 4.

30. *P. V. Annenkov i ego druz'ia*, 579.

31. To honor his friend, Tolstoy named Nekhliudov's estate in *Youth* Kuncevo.

32. See his regular diary as well; 47:78–81, 87, 93.

33. Gusev, *Materialy k biografii s 1855 po 1869 god*, 111, 154–55.

34. *Umnica i pylkaia devushka*; 9 January 1857; 47:110.

35. Gusev, *Materialy k biografii s 1855 po 1869 god*, 301–2.

36. Brown, *Stankevich and His Moscow Circle*, 65.

37. Annenkov, *Stankevich*, 2:(Correspondence) 17–24.

38. *A Sentimental Journey*, 94.

39. *Hidden in Plain View*, 202–4. Galagan, however, in her important investigation of Tolstoy and Sterne, points out that in the part of *A Sentimental Journey* that Tolstoy translated, Sterne discusses passions of reason as well as those of the heart. Chief among these is pride (*L. N. Tolstoi: Khudozhestvenno-eticheskie iskaniia*, 24–25). On the idea of "flux of feeling" [*tekuchest' chuvstv*] borrowed from Sterne, see also Bursov, *Lev Tolstoi*, 74.

40. Bursov, *Lev Tolstoi*, 73–74. Eikhenbaum was the first to point researchers in this direction in *The Young Tolstoy* (48–55). On Sterne's influence see also Ruby, "Lev Tolstoj's Apprenticeship to Laurence Sterne."

41. *The Young Tolstoy*, 52.

42. The Jubilee edition of Tolstoy incorrectly assigns these lines to chapter 119 (46:46). Tolstoy obviously read the novel in French translation.

43. *A Sentimental Journey*, 117.

44. Quoted in Gromov, *O stile L'va Tolstogo: Stanovlenie "dialektiki dushi,"* 161.

45. Chizhevski, *Gegel' v Rossii*, 53, 238.

46. *O stile L'va Tolstogo: Stanovlenie "dialektiki dushi,"* 163. See also Mostovskaia, who distinguishes between the aesthetic theories of Tolstoy and his friends in the 1850s on the basis of Tolstoy's concern for "the pursuit of perfection" (*usovershenstvovanie*; "Lichnost' khudozhnika u Gogolia i Tolstogo," 106–7). For a brief discussion of the meaning of *usovershenstvovanie*, see chapter 5.

47. Brown, *Stankevich and His Moscow Circle: 1830–1840*, 101–2.

48. *Gegel' v Rossii*, 34.

49. Annenkov, *Nikolai Vladimirovich Stankevich: Perepiska ego i biografiia*, 24.

50. Edward J. Brown calls Annenkov's biography a hagiography suitable to the ideas of the fifties and tries in his book to reconstruct what the "real" Stankevich might have been like (*Stankevich and his Moscow Circle: 1830–1840*, 45). For our purposes, however, the saint, as he lived on in the memories of Tolstoy's older contemporaries and was thence passed down to younger men like Tolstoy, is more important than the man.

51. PSS, Works, 6:606–7.

52. Reported by memoirists; Gusev, *Letopis' zhizni i tvorchestva L'va Nikolae-vicha Tolstogo*, 117. The first idea for "Kholstomer" [Strider] is recorded in Tolstoy's diary of 31 May 1856 (47:78).

53. PSS, Works, 6:394.

54. P. Sakulin, "Idealizm N. V. Stankevicha," *Vestnik Evropy*, February 1915, 264 (quoted in Brown, 125); Brown, *Stankevich and His Moscow Circle: 1830–1840*, 125; Kupreianova, *Estetika L. N. Tolstogo*, 67.

55. *Estetika L. N. Tolstogo*, 66–78.

56. *Moia metafizika*; Annenkov, *Nikolai Vladimirovich Stankevich: Perepiska ego i biografii*, 19.

57. Miliukov, "Liubov' u 'idealistov tridcatykh godov,'" 76.

58. Annenkov, *Nikolai Vladimirovich Stankevich: Perepiska ego i biografiia*, Correspondence, 172–74.

59. On the essential mysteriousness of nature for Turgenev, see Bilinkis, *O tvorchestve L. N. Tolstogo: Ocherki*, 167.

60. Annenkov, *Nikolai Vladimirovich Stankevich: Perepiska ego i biografiia*, Correspondence, 19.

61. *Polnoe razumenie*; Chizhevski, *Gegel' v Rossii*, 77.

62. See 11–12 June, 46:61–62; 12 June, 46:63–64; 3 July, 46:65; 10 August, 46:80–81. See also the notebooks of March 1847 (46:3–4).

63. "A. A. Fet," *Sochineniia*, 358.

64. *O tvorchestve L. N. Tolstogo: Ocherki*, 188.

65. I partially disagree at this point with Galagan's interesting interpretation of this story and "The Storm" (*metel'*; *Lev Tolstoi: Khudozhestvenno-eticheskie iskaniia*, 60–63). Galagan argues that stasis in human life as it is depicted in these stories comes from obsessive passions of the body; I think it comes from fearfulness and the desire to protect and nurture the self in the face of natural flux. Fear, of course, is also a passion, but not an expansive one. Galagan later makes good use of her idea of stasis in human life in her discussion of the snowstorm in *Anna Karenina* and *Master and Man* (ibid., 139–47).

66. For the connection of these ideas to expressivist theory, see Carden, "The Expressive Self in *War and Peace*."

67. As we know from a letter from Tolstoy responding to her reaction and defending his story (60:264–66).

68. PSS, Letters, 5:216.

69. *Rannie proizvedeniia gr. L. N. Tolstogo*, 51–52. A particularly good article on this period is M. O. Gershenzon's "L. N. Tolstoi v 1856–1862 gg."

70. Tolstoy had his love affair in mind when he was working on this set of

variations on a theme. He called one version, which he wrote in Italy, "Aksinia" (Gusev, *Lev Nikolaevich Tolstoi: Materialy k biografii s 1855 po 1869 god*, 391). Gusev believes that Tolstoy never published his "Idyll" because its main character was Aksinia (ibid., 586).

71. Viëtor, *Goethe: The Thinker*, 69.

72. *Istoriia russkoi kritiki*, 4:423.

73. In his first review of Tolstoy's work in 1854, Annenkov wrote that the place for thought in art is psychological analysis (*Vospominaniia i kriticheskie ocherki*, 99–100), and he said that thought and art marry well in Tolstoy's work in the form of "analysis" (*issledovanie*; ibid., 104–6). Tolstoy probably read and remembered this review, and in any case certainly discussed Annenkov's ideas with him. Annenkov's psychological analysis is the "inquiring poetry" of Tolstoy's 1857 letter to him.

74. Gusev, *Materialy k biografii s 1855 po 1869 god*, 62–63.

75. Bulgakov, *Biblioteka L'va Nikolaevicha Tolstogo v Iasnoi poliane*, pt. 2, 2:148.

76. *Materialy dlia biografii A. S. Pushkina*, 157–58. See also 291. As Shilov points out in his introductory essay to the 1985 republication of Annenkov's biography of Pushkin, Annenkov, in opposition to earlier romantic criticism, portrayed Pushkin as a "poet of thought," as concerned above all with harmony and balance and in this respect resembling Annenkov ("P. V. Annenkov i ego 'Materialy dlia biografii A. S. Pushkina'" [ibid., 49, 51].

77. In a letter to P. D. Golokhvastov, 9–10 April 1873, 62:21–22.

78. *Lev Tolstoi: Semidesiatye gody*, 279–336; see 286–91.

79. Ibid., "Tolstoi na kavkaze," 243–53.

80. Ibid., "Tolstoi v 'Sovremennike,'" 290. Eikenbaum may have chosen not to discuss this subject because it was politically dangerous for him to do so.

81. For more on this subject, see above, chapter 1.

82. This is a leitmotif of *What Is to Be Done?* The "enlightened," that is, the reasonable man will identify himself so fully with mankind that he will ignore his particular self-interest in order to advance the interest of the whole. See, for instance, Kirsanov's reasoning about sacrificing his love for Vera Pavlovna in part 3, chapter 20. For a judicious appreciation of *What Is to Be Done?* in English, see Feuer, "What Is to Be Done about *What Is to Be Done?*"

83. 1:35–37, 151, 235.

84. Kuzminskaia, *Moia zhizn' doma i v Iasnoi Poliane*, 308.

85. *Sochineniia gr. L. N. Tolstogo*, 172.

86. Von Gronicka, *The Russian Image of Goethe*, 2:144.

87. "Goethe and Tolstoy," 116.

88. See above, chapter 1.

89. See the Prologue, line 337 (*Faust*, 88–89).

90. 1, ll. 1336–37, ibid., 158–59.

91. Lewes, *The Life of Goethe*, 93.

92. Viëtor, *Goethe: The Thinker*, 100.

93. "The Recuperative Powers of Memory: *War and Peace*," 91. Another interesting article about good and evil, light and shade, in *Anna Karenina* is Mandelker's "The Woman with a Shadow: Fables of Demon and Psyche in *Anna*

Karenina." Although her emphasis is more on folklore, Mandelker sees the Goethean connection to this theme through *Faust.*

94. Magnus, *Goethe as a Scientist*, 231–33.

95. Von Gronicka, *The Russian Image of Goethe*, 2:18. Note how Goethe ties man and nature together by linking the fundamental rhythms of the universe with the beating of the human heart.

96. Turgenev, PSS, Works, 8:544. V. F. Lazurskii reports that Tolstoy valued three works of Turgenev in which the older writer's usual philosophical uncertainty gives way to insight into truth: these are "Faust," "Enough," and "Hamlet and Don Quixote" (quoted in *L. N. Tolstoi v vospominaniiakh sovremennikov*, 2:48).

97. In the very first drafts of the novel, as Tolstoy created characters, he was already matching opposites, like the prototypes of Andrei and Pierre, or Natasha and Andrei as lovers (for instance, 13:14). The best overall treatment of opposites as a structural principle in *War and Peace* is the essay by Albert Cook, "The Moral Vision: Tolstoy."

98. *Vospominaniia i kriticheskie ocherki*, 287.

99. According to S. L. Tolstoi from his reminiscences of the 1870s, quoted in *L. N. Tolstoi v vospominaniiakh sovremennikov*, 1:174.

100. *Vospominaniia i kriticheskie ocherki*, 295, 297.

101. In this article Tolstoy went so far as to argue that God had created progress in order to separate mankind from its original goodness and thereby to make the struggle for goodness possible (8:321–22). This is actually a variation of his vision, in *Anna Karenina*, of the created universe as a battleground of good and evil.

Chapter Four
Nature and Civilization in *The Cossacks*

1. Turgenev, for instance, even in 1874, after *War and Peace*, considered it Tolstoy's "chef d'oeuvre." See PSS, Letters, 10:207.

2. Tolstoy used this metaphor in his well-known letter of 1858 to A. A. Tolstaia defending "Three Deaths" (60:265).

3. For more on this subject, see above, chapter 3.

4. Ivan Ivanov, a late-nineteenth-century critic sympathetic to the "men of the sixties," points out the irony of such heroes of resistance insisting on the doctrine of submission to circumstance (*Istoriia russkoi kritiki*, 4:440).

5. After Lukashka has shot the Chechen warrior, he stays to watch for other enemies while his companions go for help. Despite the obvious danger, "the fact that he might be killed never entered his head." For emphasis Tolstoy places this significant sentence at the end of chapter 10. Lukashka does not know what death might mean for the man he has killed because it has no meaning for him.

6. See Orwin, "The Unity of Tolstoi's Early Works."

7. Such constructions, in which the verb has no direct subject, are common in Russian.

8. Turgenev, *PSS*, Works, 8:554.

9. Ibid., Letters, 5:113.

10. See above, chapter 3.

11. The idea for Olenin's sentiment came from a dream Tolstoy had on 26 December 1862, which he reported the next day in his diary: "Schiller said to me in a dream: no matter what you may be, dust which will be dust, or a frame in which one part of the Single Divinity is expressed . . . I don't remember further what he said. But really isn't this my final conviction—happiness is the greatest seizing of Divinity in width and depth" (48:83). Happiness is thus seen as the spiritual as well as the material goal of the individual.

12. Emphasis mine. Prince Andrei repeats these sentiments before the battle of Austerlitz (3.12). It should be noted, furthermore, that neither here nor in the passage about the sticky web of love has Olenin really succeeded in loving others rather than wanting them to love him.

13. The final appearance of the "web of love" in Tolstoy's fiction is, of course, as the spider webs that comprise Nikolenka's army and, "ahead of him," glory itself in his vision at the end of the first epilogue. Like his father, he will chase the "mysterious force and glory that even now is above me [Andrei] in this mist" before the Battle of Austerlitz (3.12). Nikolenka is at the beginning of a quest that may lead, as it did for his father, from a natural and expansive love of glory to the search for the God Who makes him want to sacrifice himself for others.

14. Opul'skaia, *Kazaki* ("Tvorcheskaia istoriia 'Kazakov'"), 386.

15. See *O tvorchestve L. N. Tolstogo: Ocherki*, 161. Bilinkis also distinguishes between the naturalness of the cossacks and the fuller naturalness of the self-conscious Olenin (ibid., 188).

16. "Reason engenders vanity and reflection fortifies it; reason turns man back upon himself, it separates him from all that bothers and afflicts him. Philosophy isolates him; because of it he says in secret, at the sight of a suffering man: Perish if you will, I am safe" (Rousseau, *The Second Discourse*, 132). Rousseau went on to claim in this passage that savage man is more compassionate than civilized man. Tolstoy began to write *The Cossacks* with this supposition, but changed his mind after he read Homer.

17. This is how Strakhov understood Platon. See "Literaturnaia deiatel'nost' Gercena," 29–30.

18. So, as the character of the cossack came into focus for Tolstoy during a crucial period in 1857, he wrote that he is "wild, fresh, like a Biblical [Old Testament] legend" (47:146); he is "not modest, but wild" (47:214). The word I have translated as "wild"—*dikii*—is also the Russian term for savage in the phrase "savage man."

19. Lukashka's sidekick Nazarka is a worse cossack than Lukashka because of his squeamishness. He cannot bring himself to dispatch a pheasant he has caught in a trap (7).

20. Opul'skaia, *Kazaki* ("Tvorcheskaia istoriia 'Kazakov'"), 363–67.

21. Letter to Botkin; quoted in ibid., 364.

22. *Kazaki*, 183.

23. Letter to Botkin, quoted in Opul'skaia, *Kazaki* ("Tvorcheskaia istoriia 'Kazakov'"), 364.

Chapter Five
The Unity of Man and Nature in *War and Peace*

1. Kuzminskaia, *Moia zhizn' doma i v Iasnoi Poliane*, 255. Compare this to a letter to Kuzminskaia written in 1886, in which Tolstoy declared: "I live only by the fact that I believe that pie is not eternal, while human reason is" (63:393). In the Tolstoy family circle, pie (*pirog*) was a code word for something that made people happy.

2. "Russkaia bellitristika v 1863 g." in *Vospominaniia i kriticheskie ocherki: Sobranie statei i zametok P. V. Annenkov, 1849–1868*, 2:297.

3. For the distinction between the natural and savage stage of human history, see Orwin, "Nature and the Narrator in *Chadzi-Murat*," 133–35.

4. Kuzminskaia, *Moia zhizn' doma i v Iasnoi Poliane*, 151.

5. Eikhenbaum calls *War and Peace* antihistorical, and says that Tolstoy's contemporaries like Turgenev did not understand this side of the novel (*Lev Tolstoi*, 2:262–63).

6. *Emile*, 280.

7. War, Tolstoy explained in the second epilogue (6), is an extreme example of a "communal activity" [*sovokupnoe deistvie*] organized so that those who do the killing transfer responsibility for it to those who do not. Tolstoy imagined that such an activity was shaped like a cone, with ordinary soldiers forming its base, and the general at its apex.

8. "The Expressive Self in *War and Peace*," 525.

9. *Tvorcheskii put' L. N. Tolstogo*, 238–39. Gusev also discusses this passage and Tolstoy's response to it (*Lev Nikolaevich Tolstoi: Materialy k biografii s 1855 po 1869 god*, 406–8), as does Rzhevsky (*Russian Literature and Ideology*, 122–24).

10. Gusev, *Materialy k biografii L. N. Tolstogo s 1855 po 1869 god*, 406.

11. *Byloe i dumy*, 392.

12. *Tolstoy in Prerevolutionary Russian Criticism*, 27.

13. Lidiia Ginzburg explores this theme in "O romane Tolstogo 'Voina i mir.'" Written during the Second World War and published in a military journal, this remarkable article about patriotism in *War and Peace* shares the immediacy of Olivier's *Henry V*.

14. *Hidden in Plain View*, 92.

15. No doubt Tolstoy owed a debt here to W. H. Riehl, dubbed the "Western Slavophile" by Iu. F. Samarin, and perhaps to Slavophile Konstantin Aksakov as well. Eikhenbaum discusses Tolstoy's involvement with Riehl (*Lev Tolstoi*, 2:52–81), while Andrzej Walicki draws a connection between Riehl and Aksakov on the basis of Aksakov's ideas as expressed in a memorandum sent to the new emperor Alexander II in 1855. In this memorandum, entitled *On the Internal Affairs of Russia*, Aksakov, like Riehl, made a telling distinction between the role of the people, which he called the "land" [*zemlia*], and the state. Absolute monarchy, Aksakov claimed, was the best form of government precisely because it kept the people from soiling itself and its moral truth with politics. The people, as keepers of an inner truth cherished through the generations, handed over the sphere of politics to the state, while the state left all social matters to the people. Ivan Aksakov drew attention to the similarity of his brother's ideas

to those of Riehl, whom he quotes: "Das deutsche Volk ist kein politisches Volk, sondern ein soziales" (The German people are not a political, but rather a social people; see Walicki, *The Slavophile Controversy*, 248–56).

16. Berlin discerns this in "Tolstoy and Enlightenment," passim.

17. The best discussion of this concept is in chapter 2 of Kupreianova's *The Aesthetics of L. N. Tolstoy* [*Estetika L. N. Tolstogo*]. She traces the philosophy of *usovershenstvovanie* back to the Enlightenment, and particularly to Rousseau and Kant, who according to her is indebted to Rousseau for precisely this part of his teaching. Her account, which accurately reflects the Russian perspective, does not consider the possible difference between Rousseau's notion of *perfectibilité*, which is in and of itself morally neutral, and the Russian and specifically Tolstoyan concept which, as she correctly states, implies moral improvement. (Melzer relates *perfectibilité* in Rousseau to the malleabilty of human nature as originally elaborated in Locke [see *The Natural Goodness of Man*, 45, 49–50].) This moral component is added or emphasized in the German idealistic adaptation of Rousseau's idea, in which form the idea was adopted in Russia.

18. Even Herzen in "Robert Owen" does not go so far as to deny that human life is improving: on the contrary, he is optimistic about a future without religious or political myths because "the striving of people toward a more harmonious existence is completely natural, there is no way to stop it, just as there is no way to stop either hunger or thirst" (*Byloe i dumy*, 396).

19. For a detailed comparison of Nekhliudov and Nikolenka, see Orwin, "The Riddle of Prince Nekhliudov."

20. See the end of chapter 1 for a discussion of this crucial concept.

21. Gustafson develops this theme subtly and at length; *Leo Tolstoy: Resident and Stranger*, chapter 7.

22. "'Voina i mir' L. N. Tolstogo," 93. The idea of harmonic or circular reasoning certainly owes something to Plato's *Phaedo*, where Socrates justifies death in this way. "If generation were in a straight line only, and there were no compensation or circle in nature, no turn or return of elements into their opposites, then you know that all things would at last have the same form and pass into the same state, and there would be no more generation of them (*The Dialogues of Plato*, 1:456).

23. "'Voina i mir' L. N. Tolstogo," 87–89.

24. Hamburger, too, notes the "open form" of *War and Peace*, its lack of a closed narrative built around an event with a definite beginning and conclusion. Hamburger attributes this both to the autobiographical basis of all of Tolstoy's art and to its dependence on naturalness and the inner laws of life. See "Tolstoy's Art."

25. Here I disagree with Bocharov, who believes that the idea of finding the truth at one's feet is a criticism of the infinite sky at Austerlitz. The idea of harmony and "neposredstvennaia" [immediate] life epitomized by Platon Karataev is thus, in his opinion, not reconciled in the novel with the conscious, analytical life (ibid., 94). Bocharov claims further that Tolstoy wanted to unify the analytical and immediate in the novel, "but this was not in his power" (ibid., 97). Carden makes a similar argument in "The Expressive Self in *War and Peace*," 532–33.

26. I remind the reader of Belinkis's related point about Tolstoy's cossacks, cited in the previous chapter, that they are "nesoznatel'no razumny" (unconsciously reasonable; *O tvorchestve L. N. Tolstogo: Ocherki*, 161). Bilinkis was referring to the cossacks' unself-conscious adherence to the laws of nature. Similarly, Platon has imbibed a natural and reasonable way of life from peasant tradition.

27. This is in a variant of the soliloquy before Austerlitz (13:528).

28. "'Voina i mir' L. N. Tolstogo," 32–35.

29. In the 1870s, according to his eldest son Sergei, Tolstoy was also reading Goethe and particularly recommended *Herman and Dorothea* to his children (*Ocherki bylogo*, 97).

30. Observe also the connection through Halley's Comet of Pierre's passion for Natasha and the events of 1812 and the comparison of conquered Moscow to a woman raped by Napoleon (11.19). I discuss the first in chapter 2, and Gustafson has discussed the second (*Leo Tolstoy: Resident and Stranger*, 39).

31. Bocharov sees how public and private situations in the novel are connected by themes of freedom and disaster ("'Voina i mir' L. N. Tolstogo," 8–14).

32. See *Emile*, 278. Observe, moreover, that to the extent that Tolstoy elaborates the divine law of war, it is circular or oppositional—West to East, East to West—rather than progressive.

33. This is a particularly interesting example of God's existence in the novel separate from His creation, because in the same chapter nature seems to urge the combatants to stop fighting. In its implicit justification for war, *War and Peace* again resembles *Herman and Dorothea*. In this poem war is seen to bring out the good and noble, the compassionate, in men. War makes men wise.

> The Pastor having heard and marked the man
> Of peace and order, him he thus bespoke:
> In times, grave sir, when men live undisturb'd,
> In self-sufficient ease, sharing the fruits
> Of ev'ry rich returning month and year,
> In these free times, fools deem that they are wise;
> And wisdom walks in open day unseen,
> So imperceptible her interference.
> But let the rough wild day of tempest come,
> When howl the fiends of mischief, and distract
> The vulgar sense, not knowing where to fly,
> Crying for safety, meeting nought but danger,
> Then comes the sage, in all his majesty!
> And, if he speak, the fool is dumb; and, if
> He look, or nod, or point, the fool will fly;
> Most happy then if he could but obey. (91–92)

34. In "O romane Tolstogo 'Voina i mir,'" Lidiia Ginzburg also probes the positive aspects of war for Tolstoy (130).

35. See Orwin, "The Unity of Tolstoi's Early Works."

36. The lesson learned there is not confined, as Bocharov and another excel-

lent Soviet critic, F. M. Fortunatov ("Peizazh v romanakh Tolstogo i Turgeneva") would have it, to the historical realm.

37. See Orwin, "The Unity of Tolstoi's Early Works," 456–58.

38. This explains why, as Bilinkis notices, in a diary passage of 9 July 1854,
Tolstoy associated the Caucasus with two "contradictory" themes: war and
freedom (*O tvorchestve L. N. Tolstogo: Ocherki*, 137).

39. I elsewhere, at the beginning of chapter 7, translate *sopriaganie* as "linkage," the fundamental philosophical principle in *War and Peace*. I should note in
this context that *sopriagat'* comes to Pierre in his dream as a garbled version of
the coachman's utterance to him in reality: *nado zapriagat'*. This phrase may be
translated "It's time to hitch up" or "to yoke up": this is yet another instance of
pairing in the novel.

40. "O romane Tolstogo 'Voina i mir,' " 130.

41. In 1876 Strakhov published one volume of Grigor'ev's works (*Sochineniia
Apollona Grigor'eva*). This was the only volume of Grigor'ev to appear until
Savodnik's fourteen-volume *Sobranie sochinenii* in 1915–1916.

42. "Sochineniia grafa L. N. Tolstogo," in *Kriticheskie stat'i*, 154–55.

43. Significantly, Strakhov does not praise the cossacks as heroic or ideal as
he does the soldiers in the Sevastopol stories. Instead, he defends Olenin as
idealistic (*Kriticheskie stat'i*, 162).

44. Ginzburg makes a similar point about the relation of negative and positive in Tolstoyan analysis. See *O psikhologicheskoi proze*, 448.

45. Kuzminskaia, *Moia zhizn' doma i v Iasnoi Poliane*, 308.

46. See Orwin, "Nature and the Narrator in 'Chadzi-Murat,' " 131–32.

47. See Fortunatov, "Peizazh v romanakh Tolstogo i Turgeneva: Eticheskie
funkcii i khudozhestvennaia struktura."

48. This is Tolstoy's solution to this problem in *War and Peace*. In *Anna Karenina* he conceives of free will as something different.

49. Rubinshtein, "Filosofiia istorii v romane L. N. Tolstogo 'Voina i mir,' " 80.

50. Bayley notes that Dolokhov's face has a greenish tint during the raid and
suggests that he might be afraid (*Tolstoy and the Novel*, 175–76). There is also that
terrible moment at the mill pond (8.18) when Dolokhov, in order to save his
own skin and to clear a path of escape for himself across a dam, lures others
ahead of him and already on the dam to their deaths out onto the thin ice of the
pond.

51. This comparison, of course, links him to the wolf that Nikolai Rostov
hunts while on leave at home.

52. In earlier drafts, Tikhon was called *Shestipalyi*, "Six-fingered," as if he
had paws rather than hands.

53. Eikhenbaum explains that this distinction comes from S. S. Urusov. See
Lev Tolstoi, 2:341–85, esp. 355. Urusov was a close friend of Tolstoy whom he
had met during the Crimean War. He was a mathematician, a chess player with
a European reputation, and a devout Orthodox Christian. Tolstoy wrote in
1906 to Sergeenko that those interested in him personally should read his correspondence with Strakhov and Urusov. Unfortunately, on learning that Tolstoy
had repudiated the church, Urusov destroyed the seventy letters his friend had

written to him in the 1860s and 1870s (S. L. Tolstoy, *Ocherki bylogo*, 338–46). See also Eikhenbaum, *Lev Tolstoi*, 2:282–368, passim.

54. 48:88, 89. See also first epilogue, 1, and the drafts, 15:193.

55. Both in the novel itself (9.1; first epilogue, 1) and in "A Few Words about *War and Peace*," Tolstoy compared the actions that nations take as a whole to life among bees. See also his unsent letter dated 10 January 1867 to Iu. F. Samarin, 61:157–58.

56. "O romane Tolstogo 'Voina i mir,'" 126.

57. *O stile L'va Tolstogo: Dialektika dushi v "Voine i mire,"* 271–79.

58. Ibid., 274. In chapter 5 of *Leo Tolstoy: Resident and Stranger*, Gustafson discusses the difference between knowing something from an outside perspective and what he calls "affective consciousness," knowing it from the inside.

59. Bocharov is commenting on this same characteristic of the Kuragins when he writes of Anatole that he is freer than Pierre because of his, Anatole's, "senselessness" [*bessmyslennost'*] ("'Voina i mir' L. N. Tolstogo," 69). See also, 32–35.

60. Veresaev speculated, in fact, that a defect of *War and Peace* was that it was not realistic enough about human cruelty (ibid., 124).

61. This difference in education and perhaps temperament is reflected in a disagreement between Tolstoy and Veresaev about the meaning of the epigram to *Anna Karenina*. See Eikhenbaum, *Lev Tolstoi: Semidesiatye gody*, 166–67; and Babaev, *Lev Tolstoi i russkaia zhurnalistika ego epokhi*, 208–9. For Veresaev Anna was a tragic Nietzschean heroine who fails because she does not have the courage to throw herself fully into her new life. Tolstoy rejected this interpretation, saying simply that Anna dies because she sins. She neglects conscience and pays the price.

62. Zaidenshnur, *"Voina i mir" L. N. Tolstogo*, 162. That Tolstoy originally gave the Bolkonskys and the Rostovs the surnames of his mother and father reveals his hidden personal interest in the relation of reason and feeling in himself.

63. At the same time, in a natural continuum he turns from love of glory to love of and search for God. Tolstoy signaled this turning by having Andrei at the end of his revery about the sky on the battlefield utter the words "Slava Bogu," [thank God], which translated literally means "Glory to God" (3.16).

64. See Rubinshtein, "Filosofiia istorii v romane L. N. Tolstogo 'Voina i mir,'" 102–3.

65. See also Carden's compelling explanation of the splinters of light that the gravely wounded Andrei balances on his chest in his hallucinations at Mytishchi ("The Recuperative Powers of Memory: Tolstoy's *War and Peace*," 97).

66. Andrei's temperament is also Hegelian in the Russian context, because it is too rational. In a passage that seems to anticipate Andrei's state of mind in *War and Peace*, here is how K. S. Aksakov described Hegelian philosophy in the 1845 poem "Dva priiatelia" [Two Friends]: "I mir mne otkryvalsia novyi, / Gde mysl'iu vse ozareno, / Gde krasok net, gde vse surovo, / Ot pestroty ob-nazheno" [And a new world opened before me, / Where everything was illu-

minated by thought, / Where there were no colors, where all was bleak, /Bared of color and variety]. See Chizhevski, *Gegel' v Rossii*, 180.

67. *Hidden in Plain View*, 268.

68. *L. N. Tolstoi: Perepiska s russkimi pisateliami*, 270.

69. Gusev, *Lev Nikolaevich Tolstoi: Materialy k biografii s 1855 po 1869 g.*, 687.

70. *L. N. Tolstoi: Perepiska s russkimi pisateliami*, 262. Veresaev hints at the connection between Pierre and Goethe by quoting lines from *Faust* about the eternal in life (*Zhivaia zhizn'*, 205).

71. Von Gronicka, *The Russian Image of Goethe*, 2:145. See also 48:33.

72. *O stile L'va Tolstogo: "Dialektika dushi" v "Voine i mire,"* 272–76.

73. In an alternative interpretation, Richard L. Chappie makes the intriguing suggestion that red and blue are the colors of sky and water at the ford ("The Role and Function of Nature in L. N. Tolstoy's *War and Peace*," 88).

74. Kant's distinction between *Verstand* and *Vernunft* underlies the thought of Fichte and Schelling as well, and, according to Zenkovsky, was introduced into Russia by Slavophile thinkers Kireevsky and Khomiakov. For them, *Verstand* gave rise to Western rationalism and Christianity, and *Vernunft* to faith as practiced by the Eastern Orthodox Church (*A History of Russian Philosophy*, 1:192–94). Here, then, was one of those crucial moments in which Russian thinkers used Western thought to create anti-Western Russian philosophy and even theology.

75. I am grateful to professor James C. Morrison of St. Michael's College at the University of Toronto for his explanation, which I have here summarized, of *Vernunft* and *Verstand*.

76. Fink, *Goethe's History of Science*, 106.

77. See Lewes, *The Life of Goethe*, 336–39; for a more sympathetic treatment of Goethe's theories representing an early twentieth-century perspective, see Magnus, *Goethe as a Scientist*, 125–99.

78. Hugh Nisbet, quoted in Fink, *Goethe's History of Science*, 194. See also Weizsäcker, "Goethe and Modern Science," especially 121–22.

79. *Goethe: The Thinker*, 57, 79. Of "objective idealism" Viëtor writes: "The divined, unknown, transcendent thing is experienced in the actual, and in such a way that the individual becomes aware of the connection of things in pure contemplation, calmly beholding. In the universal harmony is revealed the divine essence, whose elucidation is all reality, the particular as well as the general. That we are thus capable of discovering the invisible in the concrete, and of following its paths through actuality, guarantees an inner community of our spirit with the world spirit. The laws which are valid in the universe must also be operative in human cognition" (ibid., 57). The term *emblematic realism* is Gustafson's. See above, chapter 1.

80. There is no evidence that Tolstoy read Kant or knew anything about his philosophy until the late 1860s, when he read about him in Schopenhauer. I will discuss Tolstoy and Kant in chapter 7.

81. See chapter 3.

82. Gusev, *Lev Nikolaevich Tolstoi: Materialy k biografii s 1855 po 1869 god*, 487.

83. Viëtor, *Goethe: The Thinker*, 82–83.

84. *Ist es der Einklang nicht, der aus dem Busen dringt / und in sein Herz die Welt zurücke schlingt?*; verses 140–41. The translation in the text is Kaufmann's.

85. *Tolstoy or Dostoevsky*, 270. See also Carden, "The Expressive Self in *War and Peace*," 530.

86. Could not the letter in which this phrase occurs lurk as a subtext to this scene? In 1862 Botkin wrote to Tolstoy that he had been very ill but that he was keeping his spirits up. "I am living like a snail in its shell, and I feel myself the master of infinite space. You yourself are a master of infinite space, it looks out from your shining deep eyes" (*L. N. Tolstoi: Perepiska s russkimi pisateliami*, 175). Compare this image with Goethe's pronouncement, linking microcosm with macrocosm, that "within us too there is a universe" (quoted in Viëtor, *Goethe: The Thinker*, 69). It is clear that in the arts Goethe was one of the founders and greatest practitioners of metaphysical idealism as defined by Mandelbaum.

87. "The Expressive Self in *War and Peace*," 530.

88. He also wrote in the drafts to the novel that we are freest at our most contemplative, as "scholar, artist, thinker" (14:13).

89. It is suggestive in this context to learn from Babaev that at Anna Pavlovna Sherer's salon the young Pierre follows Rousseau's arguments in rejecting Abbè Morio's scheme for eternal peace, which goes back to Abbè de St.-Pierre at the beginning of the eighteenth century (Babaev, *Lev Tolstoi i russkaia zhurnalistika ego epokhi*, 114).

90. *Emile*, 294.

Chapter Six
From Nature to Culture in the 1870s

1. Second half of April 1876; *Perepiska L. N. Tolstogo s N. N. Strakohvym*, 81.

2. See chapter 5.

3. Although the first edition was not particularly successful, the revised edition, *Novaia Azbuka*, published in 1875, went through twenty-eight editions in Tolstoy's lifetime and sold twenty million copies.

4. Ultimately in his pedagogical theories, "he moved from an original denial of the right to educate children—a pedagogical anachronism—to the opposite extreme: not religious education 'in general,' but an imposing on children of the specific doctrine which he himself professed" (Zenkovsky, *A History of Russian Philosophy*, 1:397).

5. In 1885, in an article in *The European Herald* [*Vestnik Evropy*] entitled "Landscape in the Contemporary Russian Novel" [*Peizazh v sovremennom russkom romane*], K. K. Arsen'ev noticed that from the end of the 1860s, landscape description in Tolstoy's art had become shorter and more "subjective," that is, more tied to the mood of a character and less a subject in its own right (240–41).

6. Bilinkis, *O tvorchestve L. N. Tolstogo: Ocherki*, 357.

7. So in drafts to *The Decembrists*, which Tolstoy took up again in 1877–1878, he described a newborn child as "pure as the first human being straight from the hands of God" (70:282).

8. See two enthusiastic letters to A. A. Tolstaia in early 1876 (62:262, 266) and also a letter to Fet in April 1877, praising the *Pensées* (62:320).

9. *Pensées*, 66–72.

10. *Azbuka*, 463. See also S. L. Tolstoi, quoted in *L. N. Tolstoi v vospominaniiakh sovremennikov*, 1:176.

11. It is interesting that Ben Eklof, an authority on peasant education in the nineteenth century, makes similar claims about the peasant attitude toward education after the emancipation. Eklof makes no reference to Tolstoy, but he argues that schools developed just as Tolstoy said they did, in response to pressure from peasants and through peasant work. He also says that peasants wanted children to acquire literacy but no learning that might destroy or alter their peasant culture. See "Peasants and Schools," 115–32.

12. 62:235–36. Strakhov himself had written something similar in 1872, in *Mir kak celoe* (268) which, as we shall see below, Tolstoy knew well. Tolstoy opposed the peasants acquiring more science than they needed in their daily lives, because he wanted to encourage them to trust their own observations rather than the received thoughts of others. This was especially important for him since moral knowledge came to them from common sense. In his instructions to teachers in his *Azbuka*, Tolstoy cautioned against relating the amazing achievements of science, because knowing such things would teach a student to trust words rather than the student's own thoughts. See *Azbuka*, 187.

13. *O tvorchestve L. N. Tolstogo: Ocherki*, 317–18, 319. Bilinkis is helpful because he tries to understand the peasant as Tolstoy did, as an exemplar of a way of life that Tolstoy came to regard as the only possible moral one. It is important, however, to distinguish labor from the "feeling of moral truth" in the souls of the peasants. For reasons of his own Bilinkis does not do this, and, indeed, as a Marxist, he is too anxious to make a distinction between labor and nature. Both labor and the "feeling of moral truth" are indeed manifestations of God in Tolstoy's opinion, but for Tolstoy the former represented the proper use of the body and the proper way to preserve the body, while the latter represented its proper restraint.

14. Kupreianova, *Estetika L. N. Tolstogo*, 149–50.

15. Therefore, I would have to disagree with Bilinkis that after 1880 Christian morality for Tolstoy in and of itself was "natural" [*estestvennaia*]. See *O tvorchestve L. N. Tolstogo: Ocherki*, 186.

16. As quoted at the beginning of this chapter.

17. McLaughlin, "Some Aspects of Tolstoy's Intellectual Development: Tolstoy and Schopenhauer," 188.

18. Mandelbaum, *History, Man & Reason*, 7.

19. *Lev Tolstoi: Semidesiatye gody*, 95–97.

20. Mandelbaum, *History, Man & Reason*, 323–24.

21. *Essays and Aphorisms*, 52.

22. *Second Discourse*, 117.

23. Here Schopenhauer agrees with Pascal, who speaks of nature as corrupt (Pascal, *Pensées*, 158). By this Pascal means, following standard Christian doctrine, that human beings as a result of the Fall have become selfish (ibid., 153–54). Here, too, his opinion jibes with that of Schopenhauer, though Pascal was

a Christian and Schopenhauer was not. Schopenhauer may have been the matchmaker who brought Tolstoy and Pascal together.

24. *Essays and Aphorisms*, 63.

25. Ibid., 196. The Savoyard Vicar or his creator might respond by asking where Schopenhauer the atheist acquired the idea of sin.

26. McLaughlin, "Some Aspects of Tolstoy's Intellectual Development: Tolstoy and Schopenhauer," 188.

27. *Essays and Aphorisms*, 62–63.

28. Emphasis mine; 183–87.

29. Schopenhauer, *Essays and Aphorisms*, 134.

30. Mandelbaum. *History, Man & Reason*, 314–17.

31. "Some Aspects of Tolstoy's Intellectual Development: Tolstoy and Schopenhauer," 215, 219, 231, 244.

32. *Ocherki bylogo*, 47.

33. McLaughlin, "Some Aspects of Tolstoy's Intellectual Development: Tolstoy and Schopenhauer," 196.

34. "Stiva," 355. Galagan believes that Anna is just such a Schopenhauerian, who awakens from the "sleep of life" and kills herself (*Lev Tolstoi: Khudozhestvenno-eticheskie iskaniia*, 134–38).

35. *Leo Tolstoy: Resident and Stranger*, 226.

36. *Emile*, 267.

37. Gustafson, *Leo Tolstoy: Resident and Stranger*, 220.

38. Quoted in Viëtor, *Goethe: The Thinker*, 13.

39. *Essays and Aphorisms*, 196.

40. Kupreianova, *Estetika L. N. Tolstogo*, 148–49.

41. Tiutchev, *Lirika*, 1:424.

42. *Lev Tolstoi: Semidesiatye gody*, 178 passim.

43. Tolstoy's later position also brought him closer to Chernyshevsky, whose equation of reason and morality he praised in 1910. See Nikolaev, *L. N. Tolstoi i N. G. Chernyshevskii*, 65.

44. It is represented, for instance, by the sphinxes that adorn Madame Rostova's bedposts.

45. Tolstoy's choice of lightning may have been influenced by a passage from an article on Darwin that Strakhov published in 1872 on the occasion of the translation into Russian of Darwin's *Origin of Man and Natural Selection*. Tolstoy read the article and praised it highly in a letter to Strakhov at the time (3 March 1872; 61:274). Materialists, Strakhov wrote, do not appreciate the fact that the replacement of divine judgment by chance as an explanation for catastrophic natural events actually creates more problems for human understanding than it solves. The example he gave was that of a person struck down by lightning. "Darvin (1872–1873)," 260–62. (Strakhov's reasoning in this article may, in turn, have been affected by Tolstoy's discussion of old and new theories of history at the beginning of the second epilogue of *War and Peace*.) The old explanation of such an event "confirms that there is meaning in this death, while the new one proves that it is completely senseless" (ibid., 261). Why does chance rule, killing the greatest genius as easily as anyone else? Looked at this

way, the scientific revolution ceases to be an occasion for rejoicing. Strakhov faulted Darwin and the materialists with whom he associated him for their human superficiality: they were not even aware of the human problems that their scientific explanations left unsolved.

Tolstoy was aware of the debate about Darwin in the 1870s and, like most Russians, he opposed social Darwinism. Strakhov, not coincidentally, was the first Russian to attack this concept (Todes, *Darwin Without Malthus*, 40), and Tolstoy directly attacked the Malthusian side of Darwin in *What Then Should We Do?* (ibid., 43–44). In 1910, on his deathbed, in a letter to his children Sergei and Tatiana, he attacked Darwinism and the idea of the struggle for existence as morally empty concepts. Sergei writes that his father was referring to the son's Darwinism in his student days, that is, the late 1870s when Darwinism was much discussed at Iasnaia Poliana (*Ocherki bylogo*, 268).

46. But also as the Savoyard Vicar would see it.

47. Thus, Citati contrasts the presence of God in *War and Peace* with His absence in *Anna Karenina* (*Tolstoy*, 157–58, 186).

48. We must accept everything as ordained by God. The most astonishing example of this creed was Tolstoy's assimilation of natural necessity to higher morality in *On Life*. There, in chapter 34, he contended that even a human being torn to pieces by wolves had to acknowledge his complicity in his own destruction because "he himself had killed thousands of living beings and devoured them."

49. Kupreianova, *Estetika L. N. Tolstogo*, 151–54.

50. In the same letter to Strakhov in which he wrote of Pushkin, of the new novel (*Anna Karenina*) that he was writing, and of the essential mysteriousness of life, he announced that he was cutting all the asides by the rational narrator (the *rassuzhdeniia*) from the new edition of *War and Peace* that he was preparing (62:24–25).

51. *Perepiska L. N. Tolstogo s N. N. Strakhovym: 1870–1894*, 21.

52. Tolstoy himself later claimed that Darwinism in the 1870s "pushed him in the opposite direction, a spiritual one" (Babaev, *Roman i vremia*, 20).

53. According to Gerstein, Tolstoy also used it in writng his *Azbuka* (*Nikolai Strakhov*, 176).

54. *Mir kak celoe*, xiii.

55. *Leo Tolstoy: Resident and Stranger*, 120.

56. *Perepiska L. N. Tolstogo s N. N. Strakhovym: 1870–1894*, 21.

57. He concurred with Goethe, then, who had said that "we are in Nature research pantheists, in poetry polytheists, morally monotheists (Viëtor, *Goethe: The Thinker*, 82).

58. *Mir kak celoe*, 13, 47.

59. In "Literaturnaia deiatel'nost' Gercena," Strakhov draws a connection between pantheism and Christianity. "Pantheism presupposes a closer bond between God and the world, but then substantively does not change the relation between them. Everything in the world depends on God, everything is moved by Him, the fate of peoples and world history is directed by Divine Will, events have a secret meaning often inaccessible to us. God leads mankind to goals known to Him—these are concepts which are equally characteristic of

ordinary Christian piety and of pantheism" (68). They are also characteristic of history as Tolstoy described it in *War and Peace*. Veresaev picks up on this tendency in *War and Peace* and claims that life and God are one and the same thing there (*Zhivaia zhizn'*, 209). See also Leont'ev ("Analiz, stil' i veianie; O .romanakh gr. L. N. Tolstogo," 57–58), who calls Andrei a "philosophic pantheist," rather than an Orthodox Christian.

60. *Perepiska L. N. Tolstogo s N. N. Strakhovym: 1870–1894*, 29–31.

61. See his unsent letter to Strakhov of 25 March (62:16–17).

62. See above, chapter 3. Babaev points out the connection between the second sentence of the novel "Everything was confused in the Oblonsky household," and the Pushkinean hierarchy that Tolstoy regarded as his artistic goal at the time (*Roman i vremia*, 8–11).

63. "Goethe and Tolstoy," 116.

64. 15 February 1870. From the diary of Tolstoy's wife, quoted in *L. N. Tolstoi v vospominaniiakh sovremennikov*, 1:145.

65. *Perepiska L. N. Tolstogo s N. N. Strakhovym: 1870–1894*, 32–3.

66. Not coincidentally, he was also returning to the underlying premise of the individualism which he espoused from his earliest years, the particularity and therefore freedom of the individual. On this subject, see chapter 2.

Chapter Seven
Drama in *Anna Karenina*

1. Babaev points out that Dostoevsky, in his "Diary of a Writer" said of the 1870s that everyone was looking for something on which it would be possible to depend morally. See *Roman i vremia*, 12.

2. For the connection of *sopriaganie* to *mir*, see Bilinkis, *O tvorchestve L. N. Tolstogo: Ocherki*, 268–73 passim.

3. This was Dostoevsky's understanding of the novel as articulated in the "Diary of a Writer." See Babaev, *Lev Tolstoi i russkaia zhurnalistika ego epokhi*, 197–204.

4. For another examination of the symposium and its significance for the novel, see Gutkin, "The Dichotomy Between Flesh and Spirit: Plato's *Symposium* in *Anna Karenina*."

5. I remind the reader of the relationship between "cel'nyi" and "cel'" discussed in the previous chapter.

6. As Blackmur calls it in his well known article, "The Dialectic of Incarnation: Tolstoy's *Anna Karenina*."

7. The reference to Plato is obvious. Kuzma became a popular Russian name as the Russian form of Cosmas, for St. Cosmas, whose name comes from the Greek word *cosmos*. Tolstoy no doubt discovered this when he was studying Greek in the early 1870s.

8. *Roman i vremia*, 166–75.

9. May 1856; 46:178. See Katarskii, "Dikkens v literaturnoi zhizni Rossii," 16–17.

10. *Roman i vremia*, 172.

11. For an exposition of the distinction between vulgar and philosophic ep-

icureanism and their relation to one another, see Nichols, *Epicurean Political Philosophy*, 192.

12. "Stiva," 349.

13. Todes, *Darwin Without Malthus*, 119.

14. Vucinich, *Science in Russian Culture: 1861–1917*, 129.

15. "But the thing was that Prince Mishuta [Stiva] did not recognize meaning in life as a whole and could never arrange things in such a way so as to be serious, just and good in life, and he had thrown up his hands at this a long time before, but then in the course of this life, in the dream of life, he was as he had come from his mother: a tender, good and sweet person" (20:107). As is typical for him, Tolstoy chose eventually to illustrate Stiva's character, rather than explain it directly as the narrator does in this passage from the draft.

16. Nichols, *Epicurean Political Philosophy*, 20–21.

17. See Babaev, *Lev Tolstoi i russkaia zhurnalistika ego epokhi*, 194–97.

18. "Chto sluchilos' po smerti Anny Kareninoi v *Russkom Vestnike*," 237.

19. Babaev gives the history of Fet's article and discusses it (*Lev Tolstoi i russkaia zhurnalistika ego epokhi*, 204–11).

20. Blackmur puts it best: "What separates both Anna and Levin from the ruck of rebels is that they make their rebellions, and construct their idylls, through a direct confrontation and apprehension of immediate experience. There is nothing arbitrary about their intentions, their decisions; there is nothing exclusive or obsessed about their perceptions, only their actions" ("The Dialectic of Incarnation: Tolstoy's *Anna Karenina*," 128). On the moral hierarchy in the novel, see Eikhenbaum, *Lev Tolstoi: Semidesiatye gody*, 173; and Ginzburg, *O psikhologicheskoi proze*, 440–41.

21. Quoted in *L. N. Tolstoi v vospominaniiakh sovremennikov*, 2:98–99.

22. It is clear from my exposition that I must disagree with Babaev's characterization of the novel as "determined," and therefore "epic" (*Lev Tolstoi i russkaia zhurnalistika ego epokhi*, 209).

23. *A History of Russian Literature*, 250.

24. By contrast and following Tolstoy's own designation in 1865 of *War and Peace* as a "poema," Eikhenbaum has called it a "philosophical poem" ([*filosoficheskaia poema*] *Lev Tolstoi*, 2:262–63). It is a dramatization of the basic process of life eventually encapsulated in the title with its Goethean polarity.

25. See Bilinkis, *O tvorchestve L. N. Tolstogo: Ocherki*, 195–279; Zaidenshnur, "'Voina i mir' L. N. Tolstogo," 66–70; Bocharov, "'Voina i mir' L. N. Tolstogo," passim; Galagan, *L. N. Tolstoi: Khudozhestvenno-eticheskie iskaniia*, 93–99.

26. *Lev Tolstoi i russkaia zhurnalistika ego epokhi*, 133. In fact, in the first complete redaction of the novel, in the so-called fifth variant, people gossiping about Ana [sic] remark that you have to speak ill of people, "otherwise, there'd be nothing to say, since happy peoples have no history" (*Anna Karenina*, 719). Morson also discusses this aphorism, which has important implications for his theory of prosaics. See "Prosaics and *Anna Karenina*," 5.

27. Babaev, *Lev Tolstoi i russkaia zhurnalistika ego epokhi*, 133.

28. *O tvorchestve L. N. Tolstogo: Ocherki*, 385–86.

29. For another explanation of Tolstoy's decision to begin the novel with the aphorism about unhappy families, see Babaev, *Lev Tolstoi i russkaia zhurnalistika ego epokhi*, 134.

30. "The Dialectic of Incarnation: Tolstoy's *Anna Karenina*," 141.

31. Morson goes farther to argue that Nikolai is the real hero of *War and Peace* (*Hidden in Plain View*, 243–47), and Dolly—the hero of *Anna Karenina* ("Prosaics and *Anna Karenina*," 4–5).

32. In a letter responding to the interpretation put forth by V. V. Veresaev, see Babaev, *Lev Tolstoi i russkaia zhurnalistika ego epokhi*, 208–9.

33. Feuer points to the crucial importance in the novel of the hunger for definition, which appears with Stiva in the opening scene ("Stiva," 353–54).

34. *Vozvdizhenskoe* is an adjectival form referring either to a Christian holiday, *Vozdvizhenie*, the Exaltation of the Cross, or to a church named after the holiday. The verbal root, *dvig*, means "move" (Townsend, *Russian Word Formation*, 246.) The name *Pokrovskoe* has the same relationship to another Christian holiday, *Pokrov*, the festival of the protection of the Virgin, but in the nineteenth century the word *pokrov* was also used to mean shelter or protection.

35. *Perepiska L. N. Tolstogo s N. N. Strakhovym: 1870–1894*, 81.

36. Jackson, "Chance and Design in *Anna Karenina*," 317.

37. At one point in the creation of his novel, Tolstoy explicitly acknowledged the relation of Anna to Pushkin's heroines by giving the Karenins the surname Pushkin (*Anna Karenina*, 719). His sister-in-law Tat'iana Kuzminskaia claimed that he took Anna's physical appearance from Pushkin's daughter, M. A. Gartung (*Moia zhizn' doma i v Iasnoi Poliane*, 418). On the literary influence of Pushkin on *Anna Karenina*, see Babaev, *Roman i vremia*, 217–31. An excellent article in English on Pushkin's influence on *Anna Karenina* is Sloane, "Pushkin's Legacy in *Anna Karenina*."

38. "Chance and Design in *Anna Karenina*," 321–22.

39. See, for instance, Gustafson, *Leo Tolstoy: Resident and Stranger*, 118–32; and Morson, "Prosaics and *Anna Karenina*," 8.

40. *Lev Tolstoi: Semidesiatye gody*, 160–73.

41. "And at the same moment she was horrified at what she was doing. 'Where am I? What am I doing? What for?' She wanted to rise, to lean back; but something enormous and implacable . . . "

Chapter Eight
Science, Philosophy, and Synthesis in the 1870s

1. "The rapid growth of Russian scientific thought during the 1860s was stimulated by news from abroad. The late 1850s and the 1860s were one of the most exciting periods in the history of modern science. These were the years that witnessed the triumph of spectral analysis, structural chemistry, transformist biology, non-Euclidean geometry, experimental physiology, and many other theories and experimental complexes. There was also an extensive reorganization of social sciences on the model of the natural sciences. Above all else, this was a period of uncompromising attacks on metaphysics and the con-

current growth of new philosophical systems. French positivism, English utilitarianism, and German materialism and neo-Kantianism had perhaps only one thing in common—an avowed compatibility with scientific thought" (Vucinich, *Science in Russian Culture: 1861–1917*, 6–7).

2. At Kazan University Tolstoy studied for a while in the Faculty of Mathematics and, although he was a poor student, he retained a lifelong interest in mathematics and related subjects. By contrast, there is no evidence that he actually studied the physical and biological sciences until the 1870s, when he took them up in order to write the *Azbuka*.

3. Harman, *Energy, Force and Matter*, 37–40.

4. "The concepts of the balance of natural powers and the unity and interconversion of natural phenomena had a continued and significant influence on the development of physics in the nineteenth century, although these ideas were ultimately divorced from the imponderable fluids theory. Faraday and Joule developed the concept of the balance of powers into the theory of the convertibility and indestructibility of natural powers or "forces," one of the conceptual strands that, transformed, became explicated around 1850 as the conservation of energy" (Harman, *Energy, Force and Matter*, 20–21).

5. Daltonian atomism, "the theory held by most leading scientists during the first nine decades of the nineteenth century," was "based on the assumption that atoms were both indivisible and immutable." Only at the end of the century did Ernest Rutherford introduce the concept of "'the electronic constitution of the atom'" (Vucinich, *Science in Russian Culture: 1861–1917*, 149).

6. *Mir kak celoe*, 378–79.

7. Rubinshtein draws the connection between Urusov's theories and positivism because, he points out, those theories depend on a separation between laws that can be known and essences that cannot. See "Filosofiia istorii v romane L. N. Tolstogo 'Voina i mir,'" 94, 98–99.

8. This something is different from the spark of "freedom" (*volia*) that in *War and Peace* allows human beings to join in *obshchaia zhizn'* [the common life] even at the risk of losing their lives.

9. It would not be much of an exaggeration to say that the entire metaphysics of *War and Peace* grew directly and indirectly from the pages in the *Profession of Faith* that follow the lines about human vanity that Tolstoy had copied into his notebook in 1852. The Vicar has three articles of faith "from which you will easily deduce all the others without my counting them out" (*Emile*, 281). He believes that (1) "a will moves the universe and animates nature" (ibid., 273), that (2) "if matter moved shows me a will, matter moved according to certain laws shows me an intelligence" (ibid., 275), and that (3) "man is . . . free in his actions and as such is animated by an immaterial substance" (ibid., 281). These three maxims encompass both the beliefs of the writer of *War and Peace* and the chief problem that the novel addresses, that of the relation of determinism and freedom. See Eikhenbaum for another possible source of this theme in the ideas of M. P. Pogodin (*Lev Tolstoi*, 2:334 passim). The two hypotheses do not contradict each other, because Tolstoy's acquaintance with the ideas of the Vicar would have made him more receptive to Pogodin.

10. Melzer, *The Natural Goodness of Man*, 41. See above, chapter 2.

11. *The Sorrows of Young Werther*, 3.

12. Hamburger, using the garden scene in *Youth* as her example, writes eloquently about this property of Tolstoyan narrative. See "Tolstoy's Art," 77.

13. While he was finishing *Youth* in 1856, Tolstoy actually read *Werther* and pronounced it "enchanting" [*voskhititel'no*] (47:93). On 8 July Tolstoy recorded in his diary that "For *Youth*: I read Heloise" (47:214). Von Gronicka remarks that *Werther* appeared in Russia just after *La Nouvelle Heloise* and was interpreted in the light of Rousseau's novel (*The Russian Image of Goethe*, 1:11). Karamzin, moreover, emphasized the dependence of *Werther* on *La Nouvelle Heloise* (ibid., 14). If Tolstoy, in the Russian tradition, gave *Werther* a sentimental, Rousseauist interpretation, he, too, must have sensed the connection between the two works and his own. For another example of the direct influence of *Werther*'s hymn to nature, see the so-called "Fragment of the 1857 Diary" [*Otryvok dnevnika 1857*], 5:202–3. There Tolstoy confessed in Wertherian dithyrambs that he disliked grand vistas, preferring instead those landscapes that reveal the variety of nature as well as its infinity. The main theme of his confession, significantly enough, is that for any landscape to captivate him he must feel himself to be present in it and ultimately to be "part of all this infinite and beautiful whole." In other words, the "chief pleasure" of such a landscape is the legitimization of the individual self.

14. This image may have been inspired by Strakhov's comparison, in *The World as a Whole* [*Mir kak celoe*], of materialist science's equation of an organism to a bubble in a waterfall (39–40). Another possible source would be Schopenhauer, who wrote of two kinds of self-knowledge—that gained from without, through empirical perception, according to which man appears as a mere bubble, as opposed to that from within, in which the self is "all-in-all" (*Essays and Aphorisms*, 141).

15. In the words of Linda Gerstein, Strakhov's "stress on metamorphosis rather than atomism . . . would put him comfortably in the company of those rebels against the physics of being in the name of the metaphysics of becoming which we associate with pre-Darwinian biology. Once life has been defined as the aspiration to perfection, one can see how closely Strakhov the scientist and Strakhov the philosopher are joined in the same quest. Those scholars who compartmentalize Strakhov into 'scientist,' 'philosopher,' and even 'literary critic,' present a misleading case; these roles were in fact identical, they illustrate the same battle against materialism on different fronts" (*Nikolai Strakhov*, 27–28). On "idealistic" science in Russia, see Vucinich, *Science in Russian Culture: A History to 1860*, 283–85. Schellingian scientists like the physicist M. G. Pavlov in the 1830s taught that experimental science could enrich our understanding of nature, but that, because it did not proceed from general principles, it could not penetrate the innermost depths of nature (ibid., 283).

16. *Essays and Aphorisms*, 56.

17. Tolstoy also would have found Strakhov's discussion helpful in establishing not only the real unity of what Strakhov called "external nature," but also the real existence of those things that cannot be represented. Strakhov wrote that we think without "predstavlenie," that passions, feelings, desires, and the whole inner life (*dushevnoe*) existed only in time, not in space, and so

were only partly susceptible to "predstavlenie" (*Mir kak celoe*, 412). Materialism was wrongheaded at its core because it separates the perceiver (the mind, or spirit) from the perceived (nature).

18. 62:102, 104, 105–6. Both Kupreianova (*Estetika L. N. Tolstogo*, 106) and Jahn ("Tolstoi and Kant," 61–62) take Tolstoy at his word in 1887 that he had not read Kant before this time. It is interesting to note, therefore, that in his ecstatic letter to Fet in 1869 about his discovery of Schopenhauer, Tolstoy claimed also to have been reading Kant (61:219). On 22 December 1877, moreover, Fet wrote Tolstoy that he had bought and would bring him the *Critique of Pure Reason*, to which Tolstoy responded that he already had it, and wanted the *Critique of Practical Reason* (*L. N. Tolstoi: Perepiska s russkimi pisateliami*, 349, 350). S. L. Tolstoy also claims that his father often thought about Kant, as well as Schopenhauer, in the late 1870s (*Ocherki bylogo*, 103). The truth may be, therefore, that Tolstoy's claim to have discovered the *Critique of Practical Reason* only in 1887 was an exaggeration reflecting his enthusiasm for Kant at the time.

19. Jahn, "Tolstoi and Kant," 61–62.

20. See Mandelbaum, *History, Man & Reason*, 275, 314–15. For Schopenhauer's own tribute to Kant as the discoverer of the "ideality" of time and space, see *Essays and Aphorisms*, 51. This, he wrote, "is the key to all true metaphysics, because it makes room for a quite different order of things than that of nature."

21. In connection with this change, note Rubinshtein's observation that in the later philosophical tracts *O novom zhizneponimanii* [On the New Life-Understanding] and *O zhizni* [On Life] Tolstoy no longer attacked the idea of reason as the mover in history or saw history as a mysterious action of God. Instead, reversing himself on this point, he portrayed history as the revelation of the laws of reason ("Filosofiia istorii v romane L. N. Tolstogo 'Voina i mir,'" 102–3). Aksel'rod-Ortodoks also sees the connection between Tolstoy's later theory of rational consciousness and Kant (*Lev Tolstoi*, 93–96).

22. In a letter to Strakhov, 64:105. He wrote that twenty-five years earlier Schopenhauer had taught him that "his [Kant's] center of gravity is negation." Tolstoy went on to say that, in fact, the negative *Critique of Pure Reason* is the "cleared-out place" on which Kant erected the "temple" of his positive teaching in the *Critique of Practical Reason* (64:106).

23. Strakhov goes on to argue that Descartes had founded the theory of atoms by dividing matter from spirit and then positing that each point of matter existed in its own space, or extent (ibid., 378).

24. Ibid., vii.

25. See, for instance, 48:179–86. Kupreianova, *Estetika L. N. Tolstogo*, 149–50.

26. It is interesting to note in this connection the different uses of time in *War and Peace* and *Anna Karenina*. In the earlier novel, important events occur within the same time period and are thereby contrasted as illustrations of the metaphysics of opposites. Important examples of this are Natasha's birthday party and the deathbed scene at the beginning, and especially the death of Petia and the rescue of Pierre toward the end. There are similar comparisons in *Anna Karenina*—the death of Nikolai and the discovery of Kitty's pregnancy occur at the same time, for instance. Elsewhere in the novel, as Jahn has observed, time

is manipulated by the narrator to bring together and contrast characters. So, for instance, in part 1 appearances of Anna and Levin alternate with one another although the two are rarely in Moscow at the same time. See "A Note on the Organization of Part I of *Anna Karenina*," 83.

27. 62:244. In 1890 Tolstoy reported in his diary that he had dreamed that human life was "not a circle or a ball with a center, but a part of an infinite curve from which that which I see and understand has the appearance of a ball" (51:15).

28. See, for instance, Belyi's article entitled "Tolstoy and Culture" [*Tolstoi i kultura*] in which he defends irreducible individualism as the source of creativity (154), and presents Tolstoy as one of those great individuals who effect culture. It is also interesting in this regard to note that at least once Tolstoy himself admitted that he found Nietzsche fascinating. Maude quotes him as saying even as he decried his amorality: "He [Nietzsche] was a real madman, but what a talent! I was absolutely charmed by his language when I first read him. What vigour and what beauty! I was so carried away that I forgot myself. Then I came to and began to digest it all. Great God, what savagery! It is terrible to drag down Christianity like this!" (*Life of Tolstoy*, 2:438).

29. "Analiz, stil' i veianie; O romanakh gr. L. N. Tolstogo," 64–66.

30. Compare him to Lukashka in *The Cossacks*, who correctly perceives Nazarka's inability to throttle a snared pheasant as a sign of weakness (7). See above, chapter 4, note 19.

31. This concept is discussed extensively in chapter 5.

32. In *Mir kak celoe*, Strakhov had described life as a process rather than a "body." The example he used was that of a candle flame, whose parts change continuously, but which nonetheless has a defined form (68–69). It is possible that Tolstoy borrowed the metaphor of life as a candle from this passage in Strakhov. Death forms the "limits" between which this process takes place, limits that help define the process (120).

33. In Strakhov's opinion, expressed in 1876, Tolstoy was also a pantheist (ibid., 87).

34. See the previous chapter, note 7.

35. This *bukashka* may be related to another insect, a *koziavka* [gnat], which makes two appearances in Tolstoy's diary of 1870 (48:126, 128). Of the gnat Tolstoy wrote that to him it seemed like an individual, but that it was impossible to know what it was to itself.

36. The passage under discussion is an excellent example of Gustafson's "emblematic realism" (in *Leo Tolstoy: Resident and Stranger*; see above, chaps. 1 and 5). I have found Gustafson's term and his discussion of it very useful, and my discussion of nature in *Anna Karenina* is in part a response to it. I do not entirely agree with Gustafson that Anna has no contact with nature, or that "the experience of nature is [always] an experience of grace" (ibid., 213). I have chosen instead to emphasize the tension between matter and spirit or between naturalism and allegory which plays itself out in the lives of Anna and Levin.

37. The idea of the soul as made up of different voices goes back to Tolstoy's first unpublished and unfinished work, entitled "A History of Yesterday."

38. The knowing self is in action when Levin returns to his estate after Kitty

has rejected him. "He felt himself to be himself and wanted to be no one else" (1.26). "He felt that in the depths of his soul something was forming, measuring and settling" (1.27).

39. Quoted in Bialyi, "'Vlast' t'my' v tvorchestve L. N. Tolstogo," 95. Therefore, Bialyi concludes, social reform must proceed through the reform of each individual.

40. *The Sorrows of Young Werther*, 3.

41. Darwinism, Strakhov claimed in the 1872 article that Tolstoy read and praised highly, derives from a belief in "the *absence of laws*, in the reduction of phenomena to the play of circumstances" ("Darvin (1872–1873)," 276).

42. *Perepiska L. N. Tolstogo s N. N. Strakhovym: 1870–1894*, 79. It was probably comments like this one that prompted Zenkovsky to write that Strakhov was attracted to Tolstoy as someone whose "search for a religious foundation and interpretation of culture" could save man from being dissolved in nature (*A History of Russian Literature*, 1:410).

43. Kupreianova, *Estetika L. N. Tolstogo*, 106–10.

44. *Lev Tolstoi: Semidesiatye gody*, 183.

45. *L. N. Tolstoi: Perepiska s russkimi pisateliami*, 317.

Conclusion

1. *Ob osnovnykh poniatiiakh psikhologii*, pt. 1, 38.

2. *Perepiska L. N. Tolstogo s N. N. Strakhovym*, 177.

3. *Ob osnovnykh poniatiiakh psikhologii*, 1:39.

4. Veresaev discusses the love of Natasha and Pierre as a true intermingling in a chapter of *Zhivaia-zhizn'* entitled "Love-Unity" (138–45).

5. *Tolstoy's Major Fiction*, 199. On this subject, see also Babaev, *Ocherki estetiki i tvorchestva L. N. Tolstogo*, 166–67. Babaev also sees the change from unity to isolation of characters in Tolstoy's fiction from *War and Peace* to *Resurrection*, but he explains this change historically.

6. In the fall of 1871 Tolstoy met Tiutchev by chance on a train and talked to him for four hours. He wrote of his meeting with this "great, majestic and child-like old man" [*genial'nyi, velichavyi i ditia starik*] in a letter to Strakhov. His conversation with Tiutchev led him to reflect how on the highest spiritual levels each human being goes his own way, even if he holds the same view of life as his interlocutor (61:261–62). It is possible that this very fact of the spiritual isolation of each human being was a topic of conversation between the two men, and that Tolstoy was influenced in his reflections after their meeting by Tiutchev's belief that "a word once spoken is a lie" [*slovo izrechennoe est' lozh'*]. Eikhenbaum discusses this meeting at some length. See *Lev Tolstoi': Semidesiatye gody*, 176–78 passim.

7. Ob osnovnykh poniatiiakh psikhologii, 1:49. David Joravsky documents the general tendency of Russian psychology in the nineteenth century to make a distinction between psychic and physiological phenomena, and he mentions Tolstoy as a prominent member of that movement. See *Russian Psychology: A Critical History*, 116–19.

8. *Ob osnovnykh poniatiiakh psikhologii*, 2:138.

9. Thus, if the art of poetry, as of teaching, is, as Silbajoris puts it, "the art of learning how to communicate . . . the essence of one's personality," then, as Silbajoris states elsewhere, the sincere must have an objective reality. See *Tolstoy's Aesthetics and His Art*, 66, 84. Silbajoris's whole illuminating explanation of how the facts of Tolstoy's narration are all connected by their relation to their creator's personality (ibid., 18, 61, 76, 109, 164–66) must be understood within the equally important fact of Tolstoy's "realism," his insistence, rightly emphasized by Silbajoris, that art is imitation, not creation (ibid., 14).

10. This summary of Kant's position I have taken from Shell, *The Rights of Reason*, 40–42.

11. *Lev Tolstoi*, 1:234–35, 365; 2:13.

12. See Vucinich, *Science in Russian Culture: 1861–1917*, 15; Joravsky, *Russian Psychology: A Critical History*, 56; Todes, *Darwin Without Malthus*, 29.

13. Todes, *Darwin Without Malthus*, 29–31.

14. Vucinich, *Science in Russian Culture: 1861–1917*, 21.

15. Todes, *Darwin Without Malthus*, 35. For the connection of *Anna Karenina* to the populist movement, see also Bilinkis, *O tvorchestve L. N. Tolstogo: Ocherki*, 290–91.

16. From an article published in 1869, quoted in Gerstein, *Nikolai Strakhov*, 157.

17. Quoted in Vucinich, *Science in Russian Culture: 1861–1917*, 23.

18. Ibid., 24. By contrast, "Pisarev and Antonovich had proclaimed that the arts should be subservient to science, that their primary function must be to popularize scientific knowledge" (ibid.). Zenkovsky also discusses Lavrov's Kantianism (*A History of Russian Philosophy*, 1:361).

19. Actually a distant relative who had raised him after the death of his parents.

20. S. A. Tolstaia, *Dnevniki*, 1:76.

21. Gorky thought that the old man Tolstoy whom he observed sometimes hoped, his reason to the contrary, that he might be granted physical immortality (*Reminiscences*, 44). Both this hope and a sneaking belief that it might be fulfilled no doubt stemmed from Tolstoy's enormous vitality and his feeling that something so alive could not utterly vanish.

A curious proof of Tolstoy's changing attitude toward his body and the natural necessity to which it is subjected is to be deduced from a fact mentioned in Kathleen Parthé's article "Tolstoy and the Geometry of Fear." Parthé points out that the square as a symbol appears first in Tolstoy's fiction in Natasha's image of Pierre as " 'blue, dark-blue and red and he is square,' " and then in the red, white and square room in "Notes of a Madman," with its origins in Tolstoy's experience at Arzamas in 1869 (86). In both cases, I would suggest, squareness represents physical reality, but while Pierre's earthiness is positive, the room's mere materiality is horrifying.

22. "Kant and Rousseau," 53–54.

23. See "Goethe and Kantian Philosophy," 61–98.

24. Mandelbaum, *History, Man & Reason*, 314.

25. From the diaries of S. A. Tolstaia, quoted in *L. N. Tolstoi v vospominaniiakh sovremennikov*, 1:149.

26. It is no accident here that the beekeeper is a figure from an idyll, the genre that excludes politics and public life.

27. Kitty feels "like a youth before battle" as she prepares for the evening at which both Vronsky and Levin will be present (1:13). She rises to the challenge of nursing the dying Nikolai like a soldier in battle (5:19). Anna, fearing suicide, feels "the evil spirit of battle" between herself and Vronsky (8:12).

28. In "The Dialectic of Incarnation: Tolstoy's *Anna Karenina*."

29. In the drafts Tolstoy went farther—too far—saying that Levin's feeling for Kitty was "so far from sensuality that he often feared that he would not have children" (20:183).

30. In *War and Peace* there were churches in the landscapes seen by Nikolai as he looks out from the desperation of battle, and by Pierre the morning after his meeting with Platon; in each of these cases the churches are indications that the landscape is itself sacred.

31. "Problema bessmertiia u L. N. Tolstogo," 29. Roman Rolland similarly called Tolstoy a "mystic of Reason" (*Tolstoy*, 146).

Works Cited

Aksakov, K. S. "Obozrenie sovremennoi literatury." *Russkaia beseda* 5 (1857): (*Obozrenie*) 1–39.

Aksel'rod-Ortodoks, L. *Lev Tolstoi.* 2d exp. ed. Moscow: Gosudarstvennaia akademiia khudozhestvennykh nauk, 1928.

Annenkov, P. V. *Materialy dlia biografii A. S. Pushkina* with second volume *Kommentarii k materialam dlia biografii Pushkina,* ed. K. V. Shilov. Moscow: Izdatel'stvo "Kniga," 1985.

———. *Literaturnye vospominaniia.* Leningrad: Academia, 1928.

———. *Nikolai Vladimirovich Stankevich: Perepiska ego i Biografiia.* 2 vols. Moscow: V vipografii Katkova i Ko., 1857.

———. *P. V. Annenkov i ego druz'ia.* St. Petersburg: Izdanie Suvorina, 1892.

———. *Vospominaniia i kriticheskie ocherki: Sobranie statei i zametok P. V. Annenkov, 1849–1868.* Vol. 2. St. Petersburg: Tipografiia M. Stasiulevicha, 1879.

Ardens, N. N. [N. Apostolov]. *Tvorcheskii put' L. N. Tolstogo.* Moscow: Izdatel'stvo akademii nauk SSSR, 1962.

Arsen'ev, K. K. "Peizazh v sovremennom russkom romane." *Vestnik Evropy* 3 (1885): 222–61.

Babaev, E. G. *Lev Tolstoi i russkaia zhurnalistika ego epokhi.* Moscow: Izdatel'stvo Moskovskogo universiteta, 1978.

———. *Ocherki estetiki i tvorchestva L. N. Tolstogo.* Moscow: Izdatel'stvo Moskovskogo universiteta, 1981.

———. *Roman i vremia: "Anna Karenina" L'va Nikolaevicha Tolstogo.* Tula: Priokskoe knizhnoe izdatel'stvo, 1975.

Bayley, John. *Tolstoy and the Novel.* New York: The Viking Press, 1966.

Belyi, Andrei. "Tolstoi i kultura." In *O religii L'va Tolstogo: Sbornik statei,* 144–71. 1912. Reprint. Paris: YMCA Press, 1978.

Berlin, Isaiah. *The Hedgehog and the Fox: An Essay on Tolstoy's View of History.* 1953. New York: Simon and Schuster, 1970.

———. "Tolstoi and Enlightenment." In *Tolstoy: A Collection of Critical Essays,* ed. Ralph Matlaw, 28–55. Englewood Cliffs, N.J.: Prentice-Hall, 1967.

Bialyi, G. Ia. " 'Vlast' t'my v tvorchestve L. N. Tolstogo." In Bialyi, *Russkii realism konca XIX veka,* 68–95. Leningrad: Izdatel'stvo Leningradskovo universiteta, 1973.

Bilinkis, Ia. *O tvorchestve L. N. Tolstogo: Ocherki.* Leningrad: Sovetskii pisatel', 1959.

Blackmur, R. P. "The Dialectic of Incarnation: Tolstoy's *Anna Karenina.*" In *Tolstoy: A Collection of Critical Essays,* ed. Ralph Matlaw, 127–45. Englewood Cliffs, N.J.: Prentice-Hall, 1967.

Bocharov, S. " 'Voina i mir' L. N. Tolstogo." In *Tri shedevry russkoi klassiki,* 7–103. Moscow: Izdatel'stvo "Khudozhestvennaia literatura," 1971.

Botkin, V. P. *Sochineniia. Stat'i po literature i iskusstve. Pis'ma.* Vol. 2. St. Petersburg, 1891.

Brown, Edward J. *Stankevich and His Moscow Circle: 1830–1840.* Stanford: Stanford University Press, 1966.

Bukhshtab, B. Ia. *A. A. Fet: Ocherk zhizni i tvorchestva.* Leningrad: Izdatel'stvo "Nauka," 1974.

Bulgakov, V. F., ed. *Biblioteka L'va Nikolaevicha Tolstogo v Iasnoi poliane.* Vol. 1, pt. 2. Moscow: Izdatel'stvo "Kniga," 1975.

Bursov, B. I. *Lev Tolstoi: Ideinye iskaniia i tvorcheskii metod, 1847–1862.* Moscow: Gosudarstvennoe izdatel'stvo khudozhestvennoi literatury, 1960.

Carden, Patricia. "Career in *War and Peace.*" *Ulbandus Review* 2, no. 2 (Fall 1982): 23–37.

———. "The Expressive Self in *War and Peace.*" *Canadian-American Slavic Studies* 12, no. 4 (Winter 1978): 519–34.

———. "The Recuperative Powers of Memory: Tolstoy's *War and Peace.*" In *The Russian Novel from Pushkin to Pasternak,* ed. John Garrard, 81–102. New Haven: Yale University Press, 1983.

Cassirer, Ernst. "Goethe and Kantian Philosophy." In Cassirer, *Rousseau, Kant and Goethe,* 61–98. New York: Harper and Row, 1963.

———. "Kant and Rousseau." In Cassirer, *Rousseau, Kant and Goethe,* 1–60. New York: Harper and Row, 1963.

Chappie, Richard L. "The Role and Function of Nature in L. N. Tolstoy's *War and Peace.*" *New Zealand Slavonic Journal* 11 (Winter 1973): 86–101.

Chernyshevskii, N. G. [Chernyshevsky]. *Polnoe sobranie sochinenii v piatnadcati tomakh* [PSS]. Moscow: Goslitizdat, 1939–1953.

Chistiakova, M. "Tolstoi i Gete." *Zven'ia. (Sbornik materialov i dokumentov po istorii russkoi literature)* 2 (1933): 118–29.

Chizhevski, D. I. *Gegel' v Rossii.* Paris: YMCA Press, 1938.

Citati, Pietro. *Tolstoy.* Trans. from Italian by Raymond Rosenthal. New York: Schocken Books, 1986.

Cook, Albert. "The Moral Vision: Tolstoy." In *Tolstoy: A Collection of Critical Essays,* ed. Ralph Matlaw, 111–26. Englewood Cliffs, N.J.: Prentice-Hall, 1967.

Dowler, Wayne. *Dostoevsky, Grigor'ev, and Native Soil Conservatism.* Toronto: University of Toronto Press, 1972.

Eikhenbaum, Boris. *Lev Tolstoi.* 2 vols. 1928/31. Reprint (2 vols. in 1). Munich: Wilhelm Fink Verlag, 1968.

———. *Lev Tolstoi: Semidesiatye gody.* Leningrad: Izdatel'stvo "Khudozhestvennaia literatura," Leningradskoe otdelenie, 1974.

———. *The Young Tolstoy.* 1922. Trans. and ed. Gary Kern. Ann Arbor: Ardis, 1972.

Eklof, Ben. "Peasants and Schools." In *The World of the Russian Peasant: Post-Emancipation Culture and Society,* ed. Ben Eklof and Stephen P. Frank, 115–32. Boston: Unwin Hyman, 1990.

Emel'ianov, L. I. "Geroi Tolstogo v istoriko-literaturnoi koncepcii Apollona Grigor'eva." In *L. N. Tolstoi i russkaia literaturno-obshchestvennaia mysl',* ed.

G. Ia. Galagan and N. I. Pruckova, 158–72. Leningrad: Izdatel'stvo "Nauka," 1979.

Fet, A. A. "Chto sluchilos' po smerti Anny Kareninoi v *Russkom Vestnike.*" In *Lev Tolstoi* 2:231–48. Literaturnoe nasledstvo, 37–38. Moscow: Izdatel'stvo akademii nauk SSSR, 1939.

———. *Moi vospominaniia 1849–1889.* Part 1. Moscow: Tipografiia A. I. Mamontova, 1890.

Feuer, Kathryn B. "Stiva." In *Russian Literature and American Critics: In Honor of Deming B. Brown,* ed. Kenneth Brostrom, 347–57. Ann Arbor: University of Michigan Press, 1984.

———. "What Is to Be Done about *What Is to Be Done?.*" In Chernyshevsky, *What Is to Be Done?*, vii–xxxviii. Ann Arbor: Ardis, 1986.

Fink, Karl J. *Goethe's History of Science.* Cambridge: Cambridge University Press, 1991.

Fortunatov, F. M. "Peizazh v romanakh Tolstogo i Turgeneva." *L. N. Tolstoi: Stat'i i materialy. Uchenye zapiski Gor'kogo universiteta,* 77 (1966): 25–56. (Rpt. and rev. in Fortunatov, *Puti iskaniia: O masterstve pisatelia.* Moscow: Sovetskii pisatel', 8–83.)

Fridlender, G. M. "Estetika Chernyshevskogo i russkaia literatura." In *N. G. Chernyshevskii: Estetika, literatura, kritika,* ed. A. N. Iesuitov, 17–51. Leningrad: Izdatel'stvo "Nauka," 1979.

Galagan, G. Ia. *L. N. Tolstoi: Khudozhestvenno-eticheskie iskaniia.* Leningrad: Izdatel'stvo "Nauka," Leningradskoe otdelenie, 1981.

Gershenzon, M. *Istoriia molodoi Rossii.* Moscow: Tipografiia Tovarishchestva I. D. Sytina, 1908.

———. "L. N. Tolstoi v 1856–1862 gg." In Gershenzon, *Mechta i mysl' I. S. Turgeneva,* 131–69. 1919. Reprint, with foreword by Donald Fanger. Providence, R.I.: Brown University Press, 1970.

Gerstein, Linda. *Nikolai Strakhov.* Cambridge, Mass.: Harvard University Press, 1971.

Ginzburg, Lidiia. *O psikhologicheskoi proze.* Leningrad: Izdatel'stvo "Sovetskii Pisatel'," Leningradskoe otdelenie, 1971.

———. "O romane Tolstogo 'Voina i mir.'" *Zvezda* 1 (1944): 125–38.

Goethe, Johann Wolfgang. *Faust.* Trans. and introduction by Walter Kaufman. New York: Anchor Books, 1961.

———. *Herman and Dorothea. A Poem.* Trans. Thomas Holcroft. London: T. N. Longman and O. Reis, 1801.

———. *The Sorrows of Young Werther. The New Melusina. Novella.* Trans. and introduction by Victor Lange. 10th printing. New York: Holt, Rinehart and Winston, 1967.

Gorky, Maxim. *Reminiscences of Leo Nikolaevich Tolstoy.* Trans. S. S. Koteliansky and Leonard Woolf. New York: B. W. Huebsch, 1921.

Grigor'ev, Apollon. *Rannie proizvedeniia gr. L. N. Tolstogo.* Vol. 12, *Sobranie sochinenii Apollona Grigor'eva.* Ed. V. F. Savodnik. Moscow, 1916.

Grigorovich, D. V. *Literaturnye vospominaniia.* Leningrad, 1928.

Gromov, Pavel. *O stile L'va Tolstogo: Stanovlenie "dialektiki dushi."* Leningrad:

Izdatel'stvo "Khudozhestvennaia literatura," Leningradskoe otdelenie, 1971.

Gromov, Pavel. *O stile L'va Tolstogo: "Dialektika dushi" v "Voine i mire."* Leningrad: Izdatel'stvo "Khudozhestvennaia literatura," 1977.

Gusev, N. N. *Lev Nikolaevich Tolstoi: Materialy k biografii s 1855 po 1869 god.* Moscow: Izdatel'stvo Akademii nauk SSSR, 1957.

———. *Letopis' zhizni i tvorchestva L'va Nikolaevicha Tolstogo: 1828–1890.* Moscow: Goslitizdat, 1955.

Gustafson, Richard F. *Leo Tolstoy: Resident and Stranger; A Study in Fiction and Theology.* Princeton: Princeton University Press, 1986.

Gutkin, Irina. "The Dichotomy between Flesh and Spirit: Plato's *Symposium* in *Anna Karenina.*" In *In the Shadow of the Giant: Essays on Tolstoy,* ed. Hugh McLean, 84–99. Vol. 13, California Slavic Studies. Berkeley: University of California Press, 1989.

Hamburger, Käte. "Tolstoy's Art." In *Tolstoy: A Collection of Critical Essays,* ed. Ralph Matlaw, 65–77. Englewood Cliffs, N.J.: Prentice-Hall, 1967.

Hardy, Barbara. "Form and Freedom in *Anna Karenina.*" In Tolstoy, *Anna Karenina,* ed. George Gibian, 877–99. New York: W. W. Norton, 1970.

Harman, P. M. *Energy, Force, and Matter: The Conceptual Development of Nineteenth-Century Physics.* Cambridge: Cambridge University Press, 1982.

Hegel, G. W. F. *Aesthetics. Lectures on Fine Art.* Trans. T. M. Knox. Vol. 2. Oxford: Clarendon Press, 1975.

Herzen, A. I. *Byloe i dumy.* Parts 5–8. Moscow: Gosudarstvennoe izdatel'stvo khudozhestvennoi literatury, 1962.

Ivanov, Ivan. *Istoriia russkoi kritiki.* Parts 3–4. St. Petersburg: Izdanie zhurnala "Mir bozhii," 1900.

Jackson, Robert Louis. "Chance and Design in *Anna Karenina.*" In *The Disciplines of Criticism: Essays in Literary Theory, Interpretation and History,* ed. Peter Demetz, Thomas Greene, and Lowry Nelson, Jr., 315–29. New Haven: Yale University Press, 1968.

Jahn, Gary R. "Tolstoi and Kant." In *New Perspectives on Nineteenth Century Russian Prose,* ed. George Gutsche, 60–70. Columbus, Ohio: Slavica Publishers, 1982.

Joravsky, David. *Russian Psychology: A Critical History.* Oxford: Basil Blackwell, 1989.

Katarskii, I. M. "Dikkens v literaturnoi zhizni Rossii." Introduction to *Charl's Dikkens: Bibliografiia russkikh perevodov i kriticheskoi literatury na russkom iazyke, 1838–1960,* 6–24. Ed. Iu. V. Fridlender and I. M. Katarskii. Moscow: Izdatel'stvo vsesoiuznoi knizhnoi palaty, 1962.

Kupreianova, E. N. *Estetika L. N. Tolstogo.* Moscow-Leningrad: Izdatel'stvo "Nauka," 1966.

Kuzminskaia, T. A. *Moia zhizn' doma i v Iasnoi Poliane. Vospominaniia.* Kiev: Izdatel'stvo "Mistectvo," 1987.

Leont'ev, K. "Analiz, stil', i veianie: O romanakh gr. L. N. Tolstogo." Reprint, with foreword by Donald Fanger. Providence, R.I.: Brown University Press, 1965.

Lewes, George Henry. *The Life of Goethe.* New York: Frederick Ungar, 1965.

L. N. Tolstoi v vospominaniiakh sovremennikov v dvukh tomakh. Moscow: Goslitizdat, 1955.

Löwith, Karl. *From Hegel to Nietzsche: The Revolution in Nineteenth-Century Thought.* Trans. from German by David E. Grene. New York: Garland Publishing, 1984.

Magnus, Rudolf. *Goethe as a Scientist.* New York: Henry Schuman, 1949.

Mandelbaum, Maurice. *History, Man & Reason. A Study in Nineteenth-Century Thought.* Baltimore: The Johns Hopkins Press, 1971.

Mandelker, Amy. "The Woman with a Shadow: Fables of Demon and Psyche in *Anna Karenina*." *Novel* (Fall 1990): 48–68.

Mann, Thomas. "Goethe and Tolstoy." In *Thomas Mann: Essays of Three Decades*, trans. H. T. Lowe-Porter, 93–175. New York: Alfred A. Knopf, 1947.

Maude, Aylmer. *The Life of Tolstoy.* 2 vols. in 1. Oxford [Oxfordshire]: Oxford University Press, 1987.

McLaughlin, Sigrid. "Some Aspects of Tolstoy's Intellectual Development: Tolstoy and Schopenhauer." *California Slavic Studies* 5 (1970): 187–245.

Melzer, Arthur M. *The Natural Goodness of Man: On the System of Rousseau's Thought.* Chicago: The University of Chicago Press, 1990.

Merezhkovsky, D. S. *Tolstoi as Man and Artist. With An Essay on Dostoevski.* London: Archibald Constable, 1902.

Mikhailovskii, N. K. [Mikhailovsky]. "Desnica i shuica L'va Tolstogo." In *Sochineniia N. K. Mikhailovskogo*, 3:424–59, 484–551. St. Petersburg: Izdanie redakcii zhurnala "Russkoe Bogatstvo," 1897.

Miliukov, P. "Liubov' u 'idealistov tridcatykh godov.'" In Miliukov, *Iz istorii russkoi intelligencii*, 73–168. 2d ed. St. Petersburg: Izdanie tovarishchestva "Znanie," 1903.

Mirsky, Prince D. S. *A History of Russian Literature.* New York: Alfred A. Knopf, 1949.

Morozenko, L. N. "U istokov novogo etapa v razvitii psikhologizma (Rannie dnevniki Tolstogo i Chernyshevskogo)." In *L. N. Tolstoi i russkaia literaturno-obshchestvennaia mysl'*, ed. G. Ia. Galagan and N. I. Pruckova, 112–32. Leningrad: Izdatel'stvo "Nauka," 1979.

Morson, Gary Saul. *Hidden in Plain View: Narrative and Creative Potentials in 'War and Peace.'* Stanford: Stanford University Press, 1987.

———. "Prosaics in *Anna Karenina*." *Tolstoy Studies Journal* 1 (1988): 1–12.

Mostovskaia, N. N. "Lichnost' khudozhnika u Gogolia i Tolstogo ('Portret' i 'Al'bert')." In *L. N. Tolstoi i russkaia literaturno-obshchestvennaia mysl'*, ed. G. Ia. Galagan and N. I. Pruckova, 99–111. Leningrad: Izdatel'stvo "Nauka," 1979.

Nichols, James H., Jr. *Epicurean Political Philosophy: The De rerum natura of Lucretius.* Ithaca, N.Y.: Cornell University Press, 1972.

Nikolaev, M. P. *L. N. Tolstoi i N. G. Chernyshevskii.* Tula: Priokskoe knizhnoe izdatel'stvo, 1978.

O'Bell, Leslie. "Vogüé, *The Russian Novel* and Russian Critical Tradition." In *American Contributions to the Tenth International Congress of Slavists: Sofia, September 1988*, ed. Jane Gary Harris. Columbus, Ohio: Slavica, 1988.

Offord, Derek. *Portraits of Early Russian Liberals: A Study of the Thought of T. N.*

Granovsky, V. P. Botkin, P. V. Annenkov, A. V. Druzhinin and K. D. Kavelin. Cambridge: Cambridge University Press, 1985.

O religii L'va Tolstogo: Sbornik statei. 1912. Reprint. Paris: YMCA Press, 1978.

Orwin, Donna. "The Unity of Tolstoi's Early Works." *Canadian-American Slavic Studies* 12, 4 (Winter): 449–63.

————. "Freedom, Responsibility and the Soul: The Platonic Contribution to Tolstoi's Psychology," *Canadian Slavonic Papers* 25, 4 (December 1983): 501–17.

————. "Nature and the Narrator in 'Chadzi-Murat.'" *Russian Literature* 28 (1990): 125–44.

————. "The Riddle of Prince Nekhliudov," *Slavic and East European Journal* 30, 4 (Winter 1986): 473–86.

Ostrovskii, A., ed. *Molodoi Tolstoi v zapisiakh sovremennikov.* Leningrad: Izdatel'stvo pisatelei v Leningrade, 1929.

Parthé, Kathleen. "Tolstoy and the Geometry of Fear." *Modern Language Studies* 15, 4 (Fall 1985): 80–94.

Pascal, Blaise. *Pensées.* Trans. by A. J. Krailsheimer. London: Penguin Books, 1966.

Perepiska L. N. Tolstogo s gr. A. A. Tolstoi: 1857–1903. Vol. 1, *Tolstovskii Muzei.* St. Peterburg: Izdanie obshchestva tolstovskogo muzeia, 1911.

Perepiska L. N. Tolstogo s N. N. Strakhovym: 1870–1894. Vol. 2, *Tolstovskii muzei.* St. Petersburg: Izdanie obshchestva tolstovskovo muzeia, 1914.

Plato. *The Dialogues of Plato.* Trans. Benjamin Jowett. Vol. 1. New York: Random House, 1937.

Price, Martin. "Tolstoy and the Forms of Life." In Price, *The Forms of Life: Character and Moral Imagination in the Novel,* 176–203. New Haven: Yale University Press, 1983.

Rolland, Roman. *Tolstoy.* Trans. Bernard Miall. New York: E. P. Dutton, 1911.

Rosanova, S., ed. *L. N. Tolstoi: Perepiska s russkimi pisateliami.* Moscow: Gosudarstvennoe izdatel'stvo khudozhestvennoi literatury, 1962.

Rousseau, Jean-Jacques. *Emile or On Education.* Introduction, translation, and notes by Allan Bloom. New York: Basic Books, 1979.

————. *The First and Second Discourses.* Trans. Roger D. and Judith R. Masters. Ed. Roger D. Masters. New York: St. Martin's Press, 1964.

Rubinshtein, M. "Filosofiia istorii v romane L. N. Tolstogo 'Voina i mir.'" *Russkaia mysl'* (July 1911), pt. 2, 78–103.

Ruby, Peter. "Lev Tolstoj's Apprenticeship to Laurence Sterne." *The Slavic and East European Journal* 25, 1 (1971): 1–21.

Rzhevsky, Nicolas. *Russian Literature and Ideology: Herzen, Dostoevsky, Leontiev, Tolstoy, Fadeyev.* Urbana: University of Illinois Press, 1983.

Schopenhauer, Arthur. *Essays and Aphorisms.* Trans. and ed. R. J. Hollingdale. London: Penguin Books, 1970.

————. *On the Basis of Morality.* Trans. E. F. J. Payne. Indianapolis: Bobbs-Merrill Educational Publishing (The Library of Liberal Arts), 1965.

Sergeenko, P. *Tolstoi i ego sovremenniki. Ocherki.* Moscow: Izdanie V. M. Sablina, 1911.

Shell, Susan Meld. *The Rights of Reason: A Study of Kant's Philosophy and Politics.* Toronto: University of Toronto Press, 1980.

Silbajoris, Rimvydas. *Tolstoy's Aesthetics and His Art.* Columbus, Ohio: Slavica Publishers, 1990, 1991.

Skaftymov, A. "Obraz Kutuzova i filosofiia istorii v romane L. Tolstogo 'Voina i mir.'" In Skaftymov, *Nravstvennye iskaniia russkikh pisatelei: Stat'i i issledovaniia o russkikh klassikakh,* 182–217. Moscow: Izdatel'stvo "Khudozhestvennaia literatura," 1972.

Sloane, David. "Pushkin's Legacy in *Anna Karenina.*" *Tolstoy Studies Journal* 4 (1991): 1–23.

Solov'ev, G. A. *Esteticheskie vozzreniia Chernyshevskogo.* Moscow: Izdatel'stvo "Khudozhestvennaia literatura," 1978.

Sorokin, Boris. *Tolstoy in Prerevolutionary Russian Criticism.* Miami, Ohio: Ohio State University Press, 1979.

Sreznevskii, V., ed. *Perepiska L. N. Tolstogo s V. P. Botkinym. Pamiatniki tvorchestva i zhizni.* Vol. 4, 3–88. Moscow, 1923.

Steiner, George. *Tolstoy or Dostoevsky: An Essay in the Old Criticism.* New York: Vintage Books, 1961.

Sterne, Laurence. *A Sentimental Journey Through France and Italy.* London: Oxford University Press, 1968.

―――. *The Life and Opinions of Tristram Shandy, Gentleman.* Ed. Howard Anderson. 1st ed. New York: Norton, 1970.

Strakhov, N. N. "Darvin (1872–1873)" [originally published as "Perevorot v nauke" and "Posledovateli i protivniki"]. In Strakhov, *Bor'ba s zapadom v nashei literature: Istoricheskie i kriticheskie ocherki.* Bk. 2, 250–80. 3d ed. 1897. Reprint. The Hague, Paris: Mouton, 1969.

―――. *Kriticheskie stat'i ob I. S. Turgeneve i L. N. Tolstom (1862–1885).* Vol 1, 145–78. 4th ed. 1901. Reprint. The Hague, Paris: Mouton, 1968.

―――. "Literaturnaia deiatel'nost' Gercena." In Strakhov, *Bor'ba s zapadom v nashei literature: Istoricheskie i kriticheskie ocherki,* 1–137. 1870. Reprint. St. Petersburg, 1882.

―――. *Mir kak celoe: Cherty iz nauki o prirode.* 2d ed. 1892.

―――. "Ob osnovnykh poniatiiakh psikhologii." Parts 1, 2. *Zhurnal ministerstva narodnogo prosveshcheniia* 197, 5, 6 (May, June 1878): part 2, 29–51; part 2, 133–64.

―――. *Sochineniia gr. L. N. Tolstogo.* In Strakhov, *Kriticheskie stat'i ob I. S. Turgeneve i L. N. Tolstom (1862–1885).* Vol. 1, 145–78. 4th ed. 1901. Reprint. The Hague, Paris: Mouton, 1968.

Sukhotina-Tolstaia, T. L. *Vospominaniia.* Moscow: Izdatel'stvo "Khudozhestvennaia literatura," 1981.

Terras, Victor. *Belinsky and Russian Literary Criticism: The Heritage of Organic Aesthetics.* Madison, Wis.: The University of Wisconsin Press, 1974.

Tiutchev, F. I. *Lirika.* 2 vols. Moscow: Izdatel'stvo "Nauka," 1966.

Todes, Daniel P. *Darwin Without Malthus: The Struggle for Existence in Russian Evolutionary Thought.* New York: Oxford University Press, 1989.

Tolstaia, S. A. *Dnevniki.* 2 vols. Moscow: Izdatel'stvo "Khudozhestvennaia literatura," 1978.

Tolstoi, L. N. *Polnoe sobranie sochinenii*. 90 vols. Moscow: Gosudarstvennoe iz-datel'stvo "Khudozhestvennaia literatura," 1928–1958.

————. *Anna Karenina: roman v vos'mi chastiakh*. Ed. V. A. Zhdanov and E. E. Zaidenshnur. Moscow: Izdatel'stvo "Nauka," 1977.

————. *Azbuka. Novaia azbuka*. Moscow: Izdatel'stvo "Prosveshchenie," 1987.

————. *Kazaki: Kavkazkaia povest'*. Ed. L. D. Opul'skaia. Moscow: Izdatel'stvo Akademii Nauk SSSR, 1863.

————. *Sobranie sochinenii v dvadcati tomakh*. Moscow: Gosudarstvennoe iz-datel'stvo khudozhestvennoi literatury, 1960–1965.

Tolstoi, S. L. *Ocherki bylogo*. Tula: Priokskoe knizhnoe izdatel'stvo, 1965.

Townsend, Charles E. *Russian Word Formation*. New York: McGraw-Hill, 1968.

Turgenev i krug "Sovremennika." Neizdannye materialy, 1847–1861. Academia, 1930.

Turgenev, I. S. *Polnoe sobranie sochinenii i pisem v dvadcati vos'mi tomakh* [PSS]. Moscow-Leningrad: Izdatel'stvo Akademii Nauk SSSR, 1960–1968.

V. P. Botkin i I. S. Turgenev: Neizdannaia perepiska, 1851–1869. Moscow-Lenin-grad: "Academia," 1930.

Veresaev, V. *Zhivaia zhizn': o Dostoevskom i Tolstom*. 1909–1910. 4th ed. Moscow: Izdatel'stvo "Nedra," 1928.

Viëtor, Karl. *Goethe: The Thinker*. Cambridge, Mass.: Harvard University Press, 1950.

Vogüè, E. M. de. *The Russian Novelists*. 1887. Reprint. New York: Haskell House, 1974.

Von Gronicka, André. *The Russian Image of Goethe: Goethe in Russian Literature of the First Half of the Nineteenth Century*. Vol. 1. Philadelphia: University of Pennsylvania Press, 1968.

————. *The Russian Image of Goethe: Goethe in Russian Literature of the Second Half of the Nineteenth Century*. Vol. 2. Philadelphia: University of Pennsylvania Press, 1985.

Vucinich, Alexander. *Science in Russian Culture: 1861–1917*. Stanford: Stanford University Press, 1970.

————. *Science in Russian Culture: A History to 1860*. Stanford: Stanford University Press, 1963.

Wachtel, Andrew Baruch. *The Battle for Childhood: Creation of a Russian Myth*. Stanford: Stanford University Press, 1990.

Walicki, Andrzej. *A History of Russian Thought from the Enlightenment to Marx-ism*. Stanford: Stanford University Press, 1979.

————. *The Slavophile Controversy: History of a Conservative Utopia in Nineteenth-Century Russian Thought*. Trans. Hilda Andrews-Rusiecka. Notre Dame, Ind.: University of Notre Dame Press, 1987.

Wasiolek, Edward. *Tolstoy's Major Fiction*. Chicago: University of Chicago Press, 1978.

Weizsäcker, Carl Friedrich Von. "Goethe and Modern Science." In *Goethe and the Sciences: A Reappraisal*, ed. Frederick Amrine, Francis J. Zucker, and Har-vey Wheeler, 115–32. Vol. 97, Boston Studies in the Philosophy of Science. Dordrecht, Holland: D. Reidel, 1987.

White, Duffield. "An Evolutionary Study of Tolstoy's First Story, 'The Raid.'"
 Tolstoy Studies Journal 4 (1991): 43–72.

Wilson, A. N. *Tolstoy*. New York: W. W. Norton, 1988.

Zaidenshnur, E. E. *"Voina i mir" L. N. Tolstogo: Sozdanie velikoi knigi*. Moscow:
 Izdatel'stvo "Kniga," 1966.

Zenkovskii, V. V. [Zenkovsky]. "Problema bessmertiia u L. N. Tolstogo." In *O
 religii L'va Tolstogo: Sbornik statei*, 27–58. 1912. Reprint. Paris: YMCA Press,
 1978.

Zenkovsky, V. V. *A History of Russian Philosophy*. 2 vols. New York: Columbia
 University Press, 1953.

Index